American Leviathan

American Leviathan

Empire, Nation, and Revolutionary Frontier

———◆◆———

PATRICK GRIFFIN

🖑 *Hill and Wang*

A division of Farrar, Straus and Giroux

New York

Hill and Wang
A division of Farrar, Straus and Giroux
18 West 18th Street, New York 10011

Photo credits: p. 2, Tom Quick memorial monument, courtesy of Pike County Historical Society; p. 272, George Rogers Clark monument, c. 1920s, no. RG-30/1/3.913, Special Collections, University of Virginia Library

The Library of Congress has cataloged the hardcover edition as follows:
Griffin, Patrick, 1965–
    American leviathan : empire, nation, and revolutionary frontier / Patrick Griffin. —
1st ed.
        p. cm.
    Includes bibliographical references and index.

    1. Frontier and pioneer life—Ohio River Valley.   2. Ohio River Valley—History—
Revolution, 1775–1783.   3. Frontier and pioneer life—West (U.S.)   4. West (U.S.)—
History—To 1848.   5. United States—Territorial expansion.   6. United States—
History—Revolution, 1775–1783.   7. United States—History—Revolution,
1775–1783—Influence.   I. Title.

F517.G79 2007
977.1'02—dc22   2006033786

Paperback ISBN-13: 978-0-8090-2491-9
Paperback ISBN-10: 0-8090-2491-8

Designed by Jonathan D. Lippincott
Map designed by Jeffrey L. Ward

www.fsgbooks.com

For the Griffins

It is true, I had forgot that . . . I mean the common people, who easily believe themselves oppressed, but never oppressive . . . Democratical gentlemen had received them into their counsels for the design of changing the government from monarchical to popular, which they called liberty.

I have seen in this revolution a circular motion of the sovereign power through two usurpers, from the late King to this his son . . . It moved from King Charles I to the Long Parliament; from thence to the Rump; from the Rump to Oliver Cromwell; and then back again from Richard Cromwell to the Rump; thence to the Long Parliament; and thence to King Charles II, where long may it remain.

A. Amen.

> —Thomas Hobbes, *Behemoth*, dialogues 1 and 4

Contents

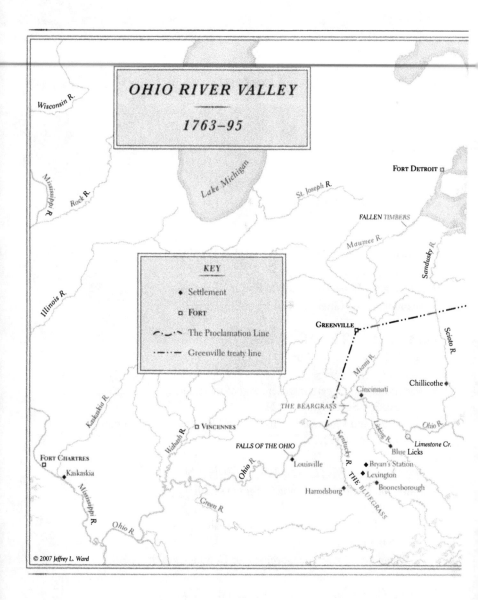

OHIO RIVER VALLEY
1763–95

Wisconsin R.

Lake Michigan

Mississippi R.

Rock R.

St. Joseph R.

FORT DETROIT □

FALLEN TIMBERS

Maumee R.

Sandusky R.

KEY

◆ Settlement

□ FORT

⌐·—· The Proclamation Line

—·—·— Greenville treaty line

Illinois R.

GREENVILLE □

Scioto R.

Miami R.

Cincinnati

Chillicothe ◆

THE BEARGRASS

Kaskaskia R.

□ VINCENNES

Wabash R.

FALLS OF THE OHIO

Louisville

Kentucky R.

Licking R.

Ohio R.

Limestone Cr.

Blue Licks

FORT CHARTRES
□

◆ Kaskaskia

Ohio R.

◆ Bryan's Station

◆ Lexington

THE BLUEGRASS

Harrodsburg ◆

◆ Boonesborough

Green R.

Mississippi R.

Ohio R.

© 2007 Jeffrey L. Ward

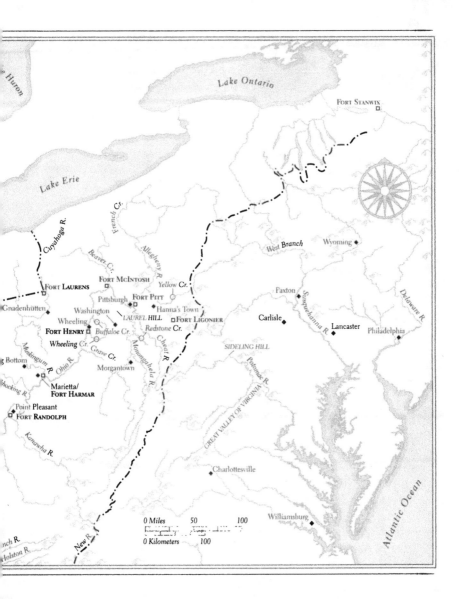

Lake Huron

Lake Ontario

FORT STANWIX

Lake Erie

Cuyahoga R.

French Cr.

Beaver Cr.

Allegheny R.

West Branch

Wyoming

FORT LAURENS

FORT MCINTOSH

Yellow Cr.

Paxton

Susquehanna R.

Delaware R.

Gnadenhütten

Pittsburgh

FORT PITT

Hanna's Town

Carlisle

Lancaster

Philadelphia

Washington

LAUREL HILL

FORT LIGONIER

Wheeling

Redstone Cr.

FORT HENRY

Buffaloe Cr.

Wheeling Cr.

Grave Cr.

SIDELING HILL

g Bottom

Monongahela R.

Cheat R.

Muskingum R.

Ohio R.

Morgantown

Potomac R.

Marietta/
FORT HARMAR

Point Pleasant

FORT RANDOLPH

Kanawha R.

GREAT VALLEY OF VIRGINIA

hocking R.

Charlottesville

Williamsburg

Atlantic Ocean

0 Miles   50   100

0 Kilometers   100

nch R.

New R.

Holston R.

American Leviathan

Tom Quick's Monument

From the Seven Years' War through the American Revolution and until the Whiskey Rebellion, a frontiersman haunted the American imagination. Growing up on the Pennsylvania frontier as the eldest of ten, Tom Quick was one of those faceless, poorer men squatting or holding small tracts and struggling to achieve competency. Something, however, set him apart from his neighbors: Tom Quick had pledged to exterminate every Indian he came across. Before 1763, he did not seem destined to become an Indian slayer. Like many young boys on the frontier, he hunted, fished, and played with young Delawares in the woods around the cabin his father had built, counting them among his closest friends. That is until the end of the French and Indian War, when a young Delaware shot and scalped his father, stripping him of his silver cuff links and shoe buckles. His father's murder transformed Tom Quick. "The blood of the whole Indian race," he reputedly declared, "is not sufficient to atone for the blood of my father." Tom Quick then promised to kill a hundred Delawares before he died.[1]

Quick killed Indians hunting, sleeping, eating, and drinking. He shot, tomahawked, stabbed, and bludgeoned Indians. He pushed Indians off of cliffs. He slaughtered them when sober and when drunk. He butchered men, women, and children, as well as whole families. As he put it after he had "dashed out the brains" of an infant, "Nits make lice." He preyed on some close to his home, including the Delaware who had scalped his father, and ambushed others far away. During the American Revolution, he roamed frontier regions like the Ohio River valley in search of Indians but not as a patriot. Quick refused to join any militia. He would not support the British, either. Disaffected from any cause, he used the chaos of the period as a license to kill. Quick's reign of terror continued after the United States gained its independence as westerners still struggled with violence. Although proclaimed a monster by officials in these years, in the estimation of common settlers he seemed to stand alone against the indifference of government. In a world of all against all, in which civil society had ceased to exist, only he and his ilk could impose some sort of order. In particular, his unapologetic individualism appeared the only solution to incessant Indian raids. When authorities captured Quick, no jail could hold him because other frontier folks who had lost friends and relatives on the "dark and bloody ground" that the frontier had become came to his rescue.

Quick's spree ended in 1795. As legend had it, he had slaughtered ninety-nine Delawares when he fell ill with—ironically—smallpox. As he lay dying, he pleaded with his family to drag one last Indian before the foot of his bed within rifle range. By 1795, however, few Indians lived on the Pennsylvania frontier. When Quick made his final request, some sense of order had come to the West as the violence and uncertainty that had gripped the region for decades had ended. So, too, had the presence of Indians in places like the Ohio valley. Quick died one Indian short of his grisly goal.

After Quick's death, his legend grew as westerners embellished stories of his vow, his guile, and the many Indians he had killed. The tale began to take even more extraordinary twists. One story that circulated transformed Quick into a deus ex machina, rescuing families under attack from Indians in the nick of time. In one such telling, he arrived breathless to confront and kill a few Indians besieging a house just as the father inside, low on ammunition, was preparing to sacrifice his own children and take his own life rather than see them suffer at the hands of "savages." Another tale that made the rounds after he had died went something like this: After Quick was buried, a starving Indian came across the grave, dug up the body, and ate the liver. He then died of smallpox, a fitting end for the hundredth victim. Similar legends had whole villages wiped out by the diseased liver. In tales such as these, Quick achieved in death and a time of peace what he could not in life and a period of war.

By the early nineteenth century, easterners were reading romanticized accounts of stories like the Quick myth as books and pamphlets appeared cataloging the exploits of frontiersmen. In these years, the ideas of "frontier" and "revolution" enthralled Americans. In many ways, together they epitomized who Americans were, capturing invented notions of collective self carved from memory, shared experience, and circumstance.[2] Less than a generation after the Revolution, writers extolled the virtues of the frontier and the critical role of the American Revolution—as well as the violence that was their hallmark—in creating the democratic and civilized man. Writers like James Eldridge Quinlan, who published a popular tract on the Quick myth, conceived of places like the Ohio valley at the time of revolution as American crucibles, regions where broader national dynamics writ small could be observed.[3] The Ohio valley continued to fascinate nineteenth-century Americans much as it had less than a generation before when Thomas Jefferson, George Washington, and Benjamin Franklin invested in its land, believing like most of their fellow citizens that America's future lay there. With its promise of land and independence, it still attracted the most mobile men and women from the margins of society in the East, as well as speculators and financiers. Now peaceful, it had been contested country. The Ohio valley had once been home to other immigrants, most notably Delawares, Shawnees, and Mingoes, and it witnessed appalling violence before, during, and after the American Revolution. As Americans as a whole understood, the region and its varied peoples featured in the rise and fall of British empire in America before the war and in the fortunes of the American nation after the war. By the early nineteenth century, in other words, the history of what had been one of Tom Quick's hunting grounds for many defined the character of American character.

With time, Americans elevated the likes of Tom Quick to sacrosanct status. By the end of the nineteenth century, the Quick tall tale had been rediscovered and had become the subject of popular books and even a play titled *Tom Quick, the Avenger; or, One Hundred for One*. Its author claimed Quick took his vow to defend the defenseless and out of regard for the memory of a father savagely executed:

> *By the point of the knife in my right,*
> *and the deadly bullet in my left;*

By heaven and all there is in it,
by earth and all there is on it;
By the love I bore my father,
here on his grave I swear eternal vengeance
against the whole Indian race.
I swear to kill all, to spare none;
The old man with the silver hair,
The lisping babe without teeth,
the mother quick with child, and
the maid in the bloom of youth shall die.
A voice from my father's grave cries
Revenge! Eternal revenge![4]

According to another account, Quick was "the very ideal of strength," tall, powerful, agile, and bright, an individual untethered from society. He was "rather a rough-looking representative of the early settlers" of the frontier. Standing against the malice of the wealthy, the indifference of government, and savagery, he defined the virtues of the common man. In 1889, Pennsylvanians gathered in his hometown to erect a monument topped with a nine-foot-tall Passaic zinc obelisk dedicated to "the memory of Tom Quick, the Indian slayer, the Avenger of the Delaware." The unveiling ceremony, which *The New York Times* covered the following day under the headline "In Honor of Tom Quick," took place amid fanfare after the erection of a liberty pole and speeches by prominent locals.[5] The monument, of course, memorialized a myth, not a man. Yet the men and women gathered to celebrate Tom Quick saw in him all that the American Revolution still meant. Quick epitomized the triumph of civilization and democratic values over savagery. Although he had sacrificed innocents, he did so in the service of a broader white civilization. He was its leading edge, society's unrefined precursor and necessary evil.

Late-nineteenth-century Pennsylvanians were not alone in finding meaning in men like Quick. The historians and cultural icons George Bancroft and Frederick Jackson Turner, who were writing as frontier legend captured the attention of Americans, also believed that the American Revolution fulfilled a destiny and that the frontier created a distinctive people, uncontaminated by the trappings of hereditary power, relentless class conflict, and vexing ethnic questions that dogged the Old World. If the Revolution signaled the arrival of a distinctively conceived nation, the frontier provided the requisite labor. As Turner explained, on this unforgiving line between savagery and civility, men and women developed those traits most closely associated with Americanness. They did so by taming a place and conquering the savage peoples who inhabited it. Better considered a process than a place, the frontier taught settlers the lessons of democracy. Here, out of necessity, they discovered the virtues of self-reliance and freedom from the dictates of government. Fighting Indians and scrambling to survive, in other words, created the conditions for the triumph of popular political participation. The Revolution as event and the frontier as process therefore confirmed America as the exceptional nation that many a century ago—then flush with hope about the place of the United States in the wider world but wary of growing tensions at home—assumed that it was.

The legends of men like Quick became the stuff of American myth. By taming a frontier, settlers like him had transformed the way society functioned in the West and, as Turner suggested, in the larger nation as well. "No one can read their petitions," Turner wrote, "denouncing the control exercised by the wealthy landholders of the coast, appealing to the record of their conquest of the wilderness, and demanding the possession of the lands for which they have fought the Indians, and which they had reduced by their ax to civilization, without recognizing in these frontier communities the cradle of a belligerent democracy." Here men and women had "turned their backs upon the Atlantic Ocean" and created a "society free from the dominance of ancient forms." In regions like the Ohio valley, "the struggle for democratic development first revealed itself, and in that area the essential ideas of American democracy had already appeared."[6] Violence on a "fighting frontier" straddling a line separating "civilization and savagery" shaped the culture of the West and by implication the larger nation, and competition molded the character of a people now schooled in "self-sufficiency" and "individualism."[7]

Since that time, Tom Quick's image has suffered some crippling blows. His role as "Indian slayer" now supplants his place as precursor of democracy. In the 1970s, his vow and misdeeds became the subject of a folk song by one of the founding members of Peter, Paul and Mary, characterizing him as the harbinger of a racist dark age. "I feel the old world dying, spread-eagled on the wall," the lyrics went, as Quick "killed and killed avenging wrong for right."[8] In 1997, after decades of protests, unknown assailants destroyed the monument with sledgehammers, thereby declaring that the fallen Quick now stood for many ills that plagued America. Just as the monument came tumbling down, so, too, did old certainties about the nature of American society. Since Turner's time, scholars have developed increasingly sophisticated interpretive tools and models of change. Years of professionalization, the insights of new schools of thought, exhaustive investigations of what had been overlooked peoples and areas of inquiry, a renewed appreciation of the power of ideas, and frankly more enlightened attitudes about the darker aspects of the American experience have led to fundamental reconsiderations of revolution and frontier.

As a result, Quick now only haunts the margins of memory. On one level, the reasons why reflect the conflicting ways we now view frontier, revolution, and the nature of American society. More to the point, the fate of Quick is bound up in the ways we have assumed that American exceptionalism is an American taboo, an issue to be ignored, rejected, or condemned, but not explained or dissected. Some argue that, far from central to the American narrative, the American Revolution's revolutionary character proved limited, not as radical and as far-reaching as the quaint work of earlier scholars had led us to believe. The Revolution settlement may have transformed the fortunes of wealthier white men. Elites ensured, however, that women and blacks saw no change in their servile status. Poorer folks still clung to the edges of society. And Indians entered an even more troubling new period that would consign them to oblivion.[9] In many ways, the American Revolution may have amounted to a "failed" revolution.[10] Similarly, the "frontier," that line that historians once regarded as a crucible of American virtues, now looms in our history as an American curse. Around the same time historians began questioning the nature of revolution, they began to recognize the racist implications of viewing American experience as a contest between civility and savagery and in the process lost confidence in frontier as a useful interpretive tool. Those who reluctantly clung to frontier insisted that we view it from the perspective of Indians by facing east from it, not west at it.[11] This generation of historians, who have sought to recover the experiences of marginalized peoples, took issue with frontier and the revolutionary nature of the Revolution, in part, to challenge the nation's mythic exceptionalism, an idea that an earlier generation of scholars had hoisted on the shoulders of infamous characters like Quick. To their eyes, notions of American distinctiveness appeared as flawed explanations of the past or justifications for the inequalities of the present.[12] The memory of Quick's exploits mattered insofar as they defined the pernicious and embarrassing aspects of American history and culture.

Or Quick had become irrelevant. Those historians who have recovered the ideas that animated the American Revolution suggest that settlers like him have little to tell us of the meaning of the American Revolution. These scholars, as a rule, do not bridle at the label of exceptionalism. Whether or how America differs from other nations does not capture their attention, and if it does, it occasions little concern. They do not see the American Revolution as a failure; rather, they suggest it succeeded on its own terms. The outcomes of revolution, as well as its radical character, reflected the measured sensibilities of the founders, men who paved the way for democracy and who developed the liberating principles that would one day extend freedom to those excluded at the time of the Revolution. These men of virtue set the terms of debate, and common people emulated them, even to the point perhaps of corrupting the Revolution settlement. The frontier does not figure into this understanding of the American Revolution. In fact, if frontier settlers appear at all, they do so almost as anti-founders, living antitheses of all the founders espoused. If the Revolution failed to live up to its enlightened promise, these types of people—grasping, egalitarian, vice-ridden—not the founders, were to blame.[13]

Tom Quick's fortunes, therefore, reflect predominant understandings of frontier and revolution. In the late nineteenth century, as Americans were coming to grips with the effects of industrialization, justifying white conquest of the West, and groping to make sense of America's role in the world, historians crafted a story of the triumph of white civilization and democratic values. That ground has since shifted, and as it has, we have been engaged in an extended referendum over the founders and their republican experiment, a debate in which the frontier does not feature, or, if it does, only as the epitome of the flawed nature of American society. Tom Quick proved indispensable to one generation, worthy of a monument, and eminently dispensable to another, better condemned and destroyed, or ignored. Almost fittingly, given the assumptions of historians of all stripes today, the demolished monument to Tom Quick's memory remains in a storage shed, unlikely to be reerected.

Quick's removal from the story of the American Revolution tells us something more. The master narratives we have of the American Revolution fail to contain Tom Quick because they cannot contain him. For one group, frontier settlers matter insofar as they remain victims of elites, resist new class-based forms of domination, contest the market economy, or embody radical principles in the face of conservative backlash. But race hatred places them outside the bounds of the story. Or settlers serve as embarrassing counterexamples to the enlightened principles of the founding and illustrate how little the frontier—and perhaps by extension, common men and women—had to do with revolution. Viewing the settlers' world in all its complexity, however, would threaten to expose the limitations of master narratives that preclude common people from either playing meaningful roles or playing two distinct roles at once, one of the virtuous settler manipulated by sinister forces, the other of the race-addled Indian slayer.

This book argues that to understand the American Revolution as more than a tale that speaks to contemporary concerns, of either the nineteenth- or the twentieth-century variety, means recovering Tom Quick's world. Doing so entails exploring the nature of the empire people like him helped topple, the nature of the nation they helped construct, and the nature of the difficult transition that marked the shift from one to the other. Re-creating the totality of experience of men and women who, much like Quick, inhabited the edges of American society and who exist on the margins of its memory, in fact, gives us new purchase on the meaning of the Revolution. But not in comforting ways. The Revolution, of course, created a liberating and troubling legacy. One aspect, however, cannot be disentangled from the other. The experience of frontier settlers in places like the Ohio valley reveals the ways in which ambivalence defined the process of revolution in America. On the frontier, common men and women helped construct new notions of sovereignty, and in the process gained unprecedented political rights. They contended with speculators and eastern financiers who sought to deny them traditional rights to land,

and in the process lost unfettered access to land. They negotiated these trade-offs in the violent crucible of revolution, and in the process came to see Indians as inherently inferior and to base the assumptions upon which society would be reconstituted on this idea. Understanding the relationship between these dynamics of sovereignty, human difference, land, and society—or entering Tom Quick's world—means seeing beyond condemnation and celebration as we explore revolution, frontier, and the nature of American society.

Between 1763 and 1795, the years Quick trolled the woods for victims, westerners not only participated in a war of independence but engaged in a revolution that ushered in fundamental changes in social relations, political allegiances, and assumptions about the relationship between individuals and society. In the West, uncovering the process of revolution, rather than focusing on its ideological content, be it radical notions of equality, race hatred, or republican virtue, provides the ideal vantage point to witness the transformation of society. On the frontier, that process was stripped down to its essence. In places like the Ohio valley, settlers struggled with the very stuff of revolution: violence, uncertainty, competition, disorder, and the frenzied and contradictory attempts to reestablish order. In so doing, of course, western settlers were transformed from subjects to citizens as British empire gave way to American nation. But something more fundamental was at work. The contest to re-create society after it had disintegrated—as well as the competition, manipulation, and negotiation that went hand in hand with this struggle—defined the period. As westerners contended with one another in a Hobbesian world, they had to define who they were and what type of world they inhabited, and it was from this process that emerged stories and beliefs that we would later associate with the stuff of American exceptionalism.[14]

These unlikely founders were often faceless and always elusive. They moved down rivers, through passes, and on roads built by armies during the Seven Years' War to the Ohio valley in search of land and competency. Although most came from or through Pennsylvania or Virginia, settlers traveled from many regions on the Eastern Seaboard. With large numbers of men and women arriving in America in the wake of the Seven Years' War, some came directly from ports abroad. Yet no single ethnic group predominated. To this region ventured a motley mix of peoples, including Scots like Hugh Henry Brackenridge; Irish like the Widow Mahon,

George Croghan, and William Preston; German speakers and their children like Lewis Wetzel and Frederick Stump; descendants of English men and women like Michael Cresap and Daniel Boone; and settlers of Dutch descent like Tom Quick. Blacks, too, most of them in bondage, also peopled the Ohio valley, including a ferryman known to us only as "Bob."[15] These people listed here proved exceptional. Some, like Croghan and Brackenridge, we know a fair amount about. Others, like the Widow Mahon or Bob, we can only catch the briefest glimpses of in the historical record. Most settlers come down to us as people with no names, mobile men and women disparaged as "banditti" by their better-documented and wealthier neighbors or simply referred to by officials as settlers. Ironically, it would be these elusive people, misunderstood and misused by elites, who would objectify and mischaracterize Indians.

Given the shadowy nature of the common men and women who peopled the Ohio valley, as well as the difficulty of re-creating the worlds through which they moved, we could be forgiven for believing that their experiences did not usher in the revolutionary transformations that defined the region and the period. Maybe we should privilege what we can call structural issues, such as the shifting balance of power among imperial regimes on the frontier and what such shifts entailed for Indian-white relations. It seems reasonable, for instance, to suggest that the western world crossed some critical threshold when the French left North America in 1763, when the Americans gained their independence from Britain, or when the British-American contest for the Midwest ended in 1815. As Indians lost the ability to play one empire off of another, possibilities for meaningful cultural understanding vanished.[16] Looking to the colonial past, we could make the point that expansion seemed almost inevitable, or at least inexorable. Perhaps the blame lay with an all-encompassing racist impulse—one unleashed, revealed, or refashioned at the moment of revolution. From these perspectives, however, either revolution proves incidental to change or people prove subordinate to forces beyond their control. The ways in which men and women tried to come to grips with revolutionary process on the frontier point in other directions, illustrating that revolution fundamentally transformed American society and that people stood at the center of this dynamic.

It would also seem wiser to explore how elites gave birth to the defining features of the West, bound up in that contradictory phrase "empire of liberty." We could argue that the American empire arose from or was created by ideological imperatives. It is far more edifying to view the conquest of western lands as part of, say, Washington's vision, Jefferson's concept of republicanism, or the unintended consequences of elite-brokered ideas, be these rooted in race or rights, than to admit that common people in constrained circumstances served as midwives to the birth of a troubling western world. How the founders viewed the frontier, of course, mattered a great deal, as did the ideas they espoused. But once we examine in detail the world of common people, as well as their interactions with Indians, officials, and easterners, a different, more complex—and perhaps less edifying—narrative emerges, one in which negotiations over property, the fate of Indians, and notions of sovereignty between the faceless many and the renowned few informed and were informed by the revolutionary process.

Of course, debates about the status of race or human difference, deference or popular sovereignty, and land took place long before the Revolution. Indeed, on earlier American frontiers, especially in the years 1675 and 1676, when settlers slaughtered Indians in New England and the Chesapeake region, Puritans and adventurers had employed the language of racial subordination and refused to exhibit deferential attitudes toward their betters. In other words, this twinned dynamic of the demonization of others and the valorization of the "people" epitomized relations on frontiers from time to time during periods of profound tension and violence. Similarly, at these junctures, debates about the nature of landownership or access to land divided the wealthy and well-connected from the poorer sort. The Revolution heralded a break with these patterns, not in the sense of forging something new, but in codifying and solidifying these fluid pasts. What had been peripheral and murky ways of understanding human difference became unambiguous and central to American concepts of society and inclusion and exclusion. What had been ephemeral ideas about the participation of common people in society became the bedrock of the American nation. And what had been unresolved arrangements about rights to land would find resolution. The Revolution did more than canonize change, nor was it an uneventful piece of a broader pattern of colonial continuities; it made the ephemeral permanent, the marginal fundamental, the ambiguous clear, and the fluid definitive.

Easterners also measured the success and failure of their revolution by the trade-offs with which westerners grappled. They, too, struggled with race, status, and the meaning of opportunity and rights. They also crafted new notions of sovereignty. In eastern towns and cities, the wealthy gained greater leverage over the poor. And as order was restored, a final Revolution settlement emerged through a process of negotiation. Through their revolution, westerners created covenants that drew a number of conclusions that other Americans were also embracing: that race, not class, should represent the most salient marker of identity; that contempt for Indians and those of other "inferior" races could be valorized; that individual rights to life, liberty, and security should have sacrosanct status for white men, but only the wealthy could enjoy unfettered ownership of property.

But what is exceptional about the West is the clarity with which we can view the process of revolution, and appreciate the formative role common people played in epic events while acknowledging the uncomfortable truth that victim could be victimizer and that our evolving sense of "who we are" reflects these realities. On the edges of frontier, the ways in which men and women, speculator and squatter, managed the contradictions inherent in the process that ever threatened to revive chaos emerge as the central story. In this place at this time, new American myths allowed westerners to make sense of the liberating and troubling ambiguities of the Revolution settlement. Reconciling the disjunctions between the vision of human equality enshrined in popular sovereignty and the racist impulses that defined Indians as inherently inferior, as well as the image that the West offered opportunity for all whites with the reality that wealthy speculators enjoyed state-sponsored access to the choicest lands, entailed remembering and forgetting. Americans would remember the Revolutionary frontiersman as a romanticized individual, an expert Indian fighter, and an almost migratory and unselfish storm trooper for a broader white "civilization" while forgetting struggles waged by the poorer sort against speculators and government officials. Through the crucible of a violent revolution on the frontier, this durable myth, emerging during the nation's defining period, would help shape the cultural parameters of post-Revolutionary American society as it would come with time to epitomize the mythic exceptionalism of the United States.

What Americans also ultimately forgot, and what these fables obscured, was perhaps the greatest myth of all: the role of the state in securing this contradictory Revolution settlement. Settlers may have entertained their own ideas about sovereignty, land, and race. They may have threatened authorities with the specter of unending chaos to achieve this frontier vision. But only the state could restore order and security—or better, create a "commonwealth"—in the West, caught in the grips of revolutionary chaos and violence. The American state both emerged from and brought to an end the revolutionary process. In doing so, it laid out the cultural imperatives of a new nation quite different from those of the empire it eclipsed. The American Leviathan would destroy Indians and protect settlers as it would guard the rights of common white men to access to the political process. Although benignly construed as an "empire of liberty," it would also consign settlers to marginal lives on the edges of society as it ensured elite access to land. Just as the state would deliver the frontier from its state of war, so it would defend the new commonwealth taking shape in the West.

The American Revolution, therefore, was America's frontier. In the Revolutionary crucible, as an old imperial order collapsed and a new national order emerged, notions of human difference, sovereignty, and society shifted in fundamental ways. And with the birth of a nation through a period of intense and profound struggle, as well as the contradictions inherent in the process, westerners and Americans in general re-created "who they were" as well. It's not surprising, therefore, that the myth of America's frontier took shape because of revolution and that frontier experience shaped the myth of the American Revolution. Less event than process, revolution represented the consummation of a violent struggle to reconstitute sovereignity and to secure new sustaining myths out of the disorder and uncertainty of a society that had ceased to be. More than a line, zone, borderland, or process, frontier was a place in time on the edge of intersecting broader worlds defined by competing notions of sovereignty, human difference, land, and society. At the intersection of the two, distinctive conceptions of landownership, the relationship between individual and society, and ways of conceiving other groups converged and clashed but were ultimately transformed, redefined, and resolved. Flux and uncertainty therefore marked both, which only the state could remedy and myth obscure. Ironically, it was this intersection, this juncture of these dynamics—both transnational in character—that made America American.

On one level, what follows is a narrative of a revolution—a story of the rise and fall of an empire, the crisis of sovereignty and competition that ensued, and the negotiations that went into constructing a nation. On another level, this is a tale of how elusive people on the frontier, like Tom Quick—people who were written about but who did little writing—made sense of and participated in this process and, in so doing, came to be. This, then, is a study of perceptions, misperceptions, and changing realities, a story of how reactive subjects manipulated by their betters and subject to the narrative of events became active citizens through the revolutionary process as they began to animate the narrative of events. This transition would have dramatic implications for Indians, the American nation-state, and American culture. For the frontier revolution reveals a final liberating, yet troubling, truth. The shift from empire to nation and the transition to modern conceptions of sovereignty, land, and race were not only imposed from above, at the center, but also achieved from below, on the margins. On the one hand, we would like to believe that common people, not the founders, steered the course of revolution, that they determined their own destinies. On the other hand, it is difficult to acknowledge that these unlikely founders won their rights, however limited they turned out to be, at the expense of other peoples. After all, the pressures that inspired Indian hating did not descend from the top down, but arose from the bottom up. To see this irony as part and parcel of a "populist" impulse misses the point.[17] In fact, that a Janus-faced people created a contradictory settlement goes to the heart of the meaning of the American Revolution and is as American as any frontier myth.

PART I

State of Nature

The obligation of subjects to the sovereign, is understood to last as long, and no longer, than the power lasteth, by which he is able to protect them. For the right men have by nature to protect themselves, when none else can protect them, can by no covenant be relinquished. The sovereignty is the soul of the commonwealth; which once departed from the body, the members do not receive their motion from it.

—Thomas Hobbes, *Leviathan*, chapter 21

ONE

Drawing the Line:
The Ideology of British Empire
in the American West

In 1773, a hard-drinking fur trader and frontier diplomat by the name of George Croghan received an extraordinary letter from "a Person intirely unknown" to him. "The celebrated Dr. Robertson of Edinburgh," Scotland's historiographer royal and principal of its preeminent university, was "engaged in writing a History of America" and contacted Croghan to discover his views of Native Americans.[1] William Robertson had asked prominent theorists in Britain and on the Continent for their understandings of Indian culture, inquiring how and why it differed from European social norms. He did so by designing and sending out questionnaires to test competing theories on human development. One theory held that over time societies either progressed toward civility or degenerated into barbarity and savagery of their own accord; the second argued that climate, nature, or some combination of the two determined the shape of a culture and its people.[2] In his previous work on Scotland's past, Robertson had favored the former, arguing that Scots possessed capabilities every bit as estimable as their English neighbors to the south. Scots had appeared more primitive in the past, he claimed, because Scottish culture had languished for centuries at a lower stage of development. Now he wished to see if this hypothesis applied to the New World.

And so he turned to Croghan. Robertson could not have picked a more unlikely person with whom to discuss these points than this prototypical frontiersman. After all, Robertson enjoyed universal renown as a best-selling author of a pathbreaking history of Scotland. He towered as a figure at the heart of Scotland's rise to intellectual preeminence during the eighteenth century, and counted among his friends such luminaries as David Hume and Adam Smith.[3] Croghan did not move in such lofty circles. He had no formal education, spent much of his time in the company of besotted traders, and knew little if anything of prevailing cultural theory. What Croghan had was a great deal of knowledge about Indians.

Robertson's questions hinged on how Indians differed from Europeans. "Is the bodily Constitution of the Indians as vigorous and Robust as that of the Inhabitants of the Ancient Continent," his questionnaire began. He wondered if the "beardless countenance" was "natural to all Indians," if "the appetite of the Indians for food [was] greater or less than the Europeans," and if their "period of human life [was] longer or shorter." As well as probing Croghan for his understanding of essential differences, Robertson peppered him with questions about Indian behavior. He asked about the "Industry and Ingenuity in their Works of Art," their notions of religion, and their views on property. His queries led to one of two conclusions: either Indians differed innately from Europeans and thus were essentially and irredeemably inferior; or difference stemmed from culture and they had a capacity for improvement and shared a common human nature.

Croghan gave Robertson unambiguous answers to these loaded questions. Croghan argued that Indians indeed differed from Europeans. Their views of property did not jibe with European norms, they bore hardships with greater fortitude, they lived shorter lives, and "they are Nott Industres Nor are they frugal." They died from diseases, especially smallpox, at greater rates than Europeans did. Indians, Croghan argued, had a "Savige Dispsion." Yet Croghan believed that culture, not nature, explained human difference. "The want of Hair on thire bodys," he argued, arose as "they acustome themselves to pluck itt out when young." They died earlier because of the pernicious influence of European settlers, "as they have mostly Larnd from us all our vises, purticklerly a predominant pasion for Spereoutes Liquers." But, according to Croghan, they embraced the same fundamental moral assumptions that Europeans did. "Thire Naturall morels," Croghan wrote, "is Ginerally a Disposision to honesty hospitality and fair Daling." Croghan did not deny that Indians lived in an inferior state. But affirming Robertson's suspicions and earlier beliefs, he claimed they would do so "Till they become Civilised." And civility, he concluded, "no doubt might be Cultivated."

This transatlantic dialogue between the center and the fringe of the Atlantic world on the nature of Indians, and the assumptions that gave these discussions meaning, lay at the heart of the British Empire in America in the years after 1763. With the victory over France in the Seven Years' War that won Britain a region stretching from the Atlantic seaboard to the Mississippi River, officials had to figure out how to control one of the greatest territorial empires the world had ever seen and how to govern the diverse peoples who inhabited a wilderness an ocean away from the British Isles. These pressing concerns captured the talents and imaginations of prominent men at the center like Robertson and obscure men on the margins like Croghan. And their shared sensibilities about culture would provide the answers to these questions.

Although the empire had taken physical shape with the signing of the Treaty of Paris in 1763, the empire's cultural contours and the ideology that gave direction to imperial governance emerged from fundamental questions about the meaning of human difference. As Britain's empire in the New World shifted from one defined by maritime commerce and settlement to one based on territorial control, Britons had to confront the meanings of different cultural traditions in new ways. To do so, they would use older cultural blueprints that were rooted in myth, culture, and history and that had been applied in places like Ireland and Scotland. They also had at their disposal newer ideas that were emerging to systematize and legitimate these older sensibilities at the very moment they had to figure out how to govern diverse peoples. In the years after 1763, Britons on both sides of the Atlantic employed these older and newer concepts in a dialogue, very similar to the one engaged in by Croghan and Robertson, over how best to view peoples with alien ways and different physical characteristics.

This dialogue centered on a thin line on a map. The Proclamation Line, so called because it arose from a royal proclamation of 1763, divided the continent of North America along the spine of the Appalachians into two distinct worlds. East of the line, men and women would be governed like and conceived of as members of the British nation. They would enjoy the status of subjects. The West, a region off-limits to subjects and defined as *terra nullius*—literally, a no-man's-land—would be rationalized by the ideas that Robertson and Croghan debated.[4] No one argued that inhabitants west of the line would enjoy a status similar to that of colonists in the

East. Rather, questions focused on whether or how Indians could ever become subjects. Ultimately, officials agreed with Croghan and Robertson: Indians in the West could become subjects, but because their culture languished in a savage state and the civilizing process would take time, those officials would consider the West as in a "state of nature," applying a theoretical concept of time to a place. In such a primitive place locked in a savage stage of development, the status of subjecthood had no meaning. And this belief defined the cultural and territorial boundaries of British empire in America.[5]

The Crown wasted little time trying to bring order to the immense holdings it gained from the Seven Years' War. On October 7, 1763, the government issued a royal proclamation, laying out the broad principles of its plan for the West. To govern the "extensive and valuable Acquisitions in America, secured . . . by the late Definitive Treaty of Peace," the Crown established new governments for Quebec, East Florida, West Florida, and the Caribbean island of Grenada. Officials hoped that men and women would people these new colonies where old inhabitants and new migrants would "confide in our Royal Protection for the Enjoyment of the Benefit of the Laws of our Realm of England" and live securely in their "liberties and Properties."[6]

Although the proclamation suggested the ways in which the British would treat subjects in America, it had to tackle the problem of America's vastness. Indeed, when Britons tried to wrap their minds around this new "*American* Empire," most seized on the idea that size mattered. One writer at the time gushed that "this vast acquisition [was] above four times larger than all the lands of *Britain* and *Ireland*."[7] West of the Proclamation Line, distances proved daunting whether by land or by water. A return trip on foot from Philadelphia to the Mississippi could take six or seven months.[8] In this world intersected by rivers, from the headwaters of the Ohio one had to travel more than 150 miles to get to the Muskingum, an additional 200 to the Scioto, 484 to meet the Great Miami, nearly 560 to arrive at the Kentucky, and more than 800 miles to reach the Mississippi.[9]

In figuring out how to govern peoples, therefore, officials first had to make sense of space. The line served as a means to do so by prohibiting subjects in older colonies and the newly proposed colonies along the Atlantic seaboard, who enjoyed all the privileges of British subjects, from settling in the West. Because the Crown deemed it "just and reasonable, and essential to our interest, and the Security of our Colonies," Indians west of the line would live "under our Sovereignty, Protection, and Dominion on lands reserved to them."[10] The plan stipulated that "no private person, society, corporation or colony be capable of acquiring any property in Lands belonging to the Indians either by purchase of or Grant or Conveyance."[11] The dividing line between the East and the West fell "beyond the Heads or sources of any of the Rivers which fall into the Atlantic Ocean from the West and North West." The region west of the Atlantic watershed "to the Mississippi was intended to be a Desert for the Indians to hunt and to inhabit."[12] If subjects from the East attempted to move west, they would do so "on Pain of our Displeasure," the proclamation read.[13] If deference alone failed to restrain subjects, troops were to be stationed beyond the line "for the Security of North America, and the Establishment of Commerce with the Indians."[14]

The royal proclamation stood for a great many things to a great many people. For a start, it emerged from the experience of the Seven Years' War. The war had started when Indians, the French, and colonists came to blows over settlement of trans-Appalachian lands. For six years after hostilities commenced in 1754, settlers and Native Americans from the Ohio Country transformed the frontiers of the colonies into killing fields. Fighting what became a world war almost broke the British treasury, as the government had to send thousands of British troops across the ocean once it became clear that colonial forces and leaders could not manage such an enormous task. Unfettered competition for the West, often sponsored by maverick eastern colonial governments, had touched off the conflict, convincing the Crown that the future management of Indian land could not be left in the hands of local officials.[15]

The Lords Commissioners of Trade and Plantations—or more simply, the Board of Trade—which had authority for managing the American colonies and imperial trade in general, took it upon themselves to direct American affairs with greater energy and scrutiny than they had before the war. These Lords of Trade drew up the Proclamation Line to ensure that tensions along the American frontiers would remain at manageable levels in the wake of such a costly war. The course of the line reflected the principles and boundaries laid out in 1758 when British and colonial officials met with eastern and western Indians at Easton. The Treaty of Easton stipulated that white settlement should not extend beyond the Appalachian Mountains. For this guarantee, western Delawares ended their raids on frontier settlements. But although Indians played a central role in these treaty negotiations, they had no say in drawing up the royal proclamation. Simple in design but not sustained by any grand vision — save an impulse to centralization — the line amounted to the most expedient course and rational response available to British officials, given American realities.[16]

Another group conceived the Proclamation Line as part of an older mercantilist vision for America. According to this way of thinking, America formed an integral part of a British maritime empire based on commerce, one that had begun to take shape a century earlier. As trade with America had grown to remarkable levels over the course of the eighteenth century, it made good financial sense to think of the new empire in older terms. As the Irish-born member of Parliament Edmund Burke put it, neither force nor control but bonds of affection and commerce "light as air" should hold the empire together.[17] The Proclamation Line played an important role in such a system. New American holdings represented "new fields" for commerce, in particular the newly proposed colonies. If men and women would settle along the littoral — "with the universal empire of that extended coast," as one member of the Board of Trade put it — then Britain would continue to prosper from American trade.[18] The Lords of Trade believed that by precluding settlement in the American West, they had fastened on "the most frugal and reasonable method of settling the new colonies with useful and industrious inhabitants."[19] The land to the west had little use at the present for British trade. "As the North American productions are weighty and of great bulk," one planning proposal read, "water Carriage is extremely necessary to convey them to the Sea Side for exportation." The country west of the line could have "little or no communication with the Mother Country, or be of much utility to it."[20]

Whatever its theoretical utility, the Proclamation Line left a great deal up in the air. Plans for the new empire mandated that "every part of the British Dominions however circumscribed should be under some Jurisdiction or other," but inexplicably excluded the West from such consideration. And what of subjects who traveled west of the line in regions where no jurisdiction prevailed? Would they be under military jurisdiction, "the

Civil Power of the Neighboring Provinces," or no authority at all?[21] And what about former French subjects who lived west of the Proclamation Line, in the Illinois Country, for example? How were they to be governed? Finally, the Proclamation Line's intended purpose seemed to shift as ministries in Britain came and went. While some viewed it as a short-term measure, others regarded it as a more permanent fixture.[22] Indeed, one leading official in England went so far as to call the proclamation "a very silly" document, one that amounted to a series of undigested impulses.[23]

To add to the confusion, an inadequate numbers of troops with few resources would guard the line. The former French settlement of Detroit would serve as headquarters for seven companies of seventy-five men garrisoning posts and forts in the West. Officials dispatched two additional companies to the confluence of the Ohio and Mississippi rivers.[24] But these meager numbers could never control the vast region west of the mountains. Therefore, the Lords of Trade had little choice but to rely on the deference of subjects to make the plan work. In a word, the royal proclamation seemed to provide for an empire on the cheap, revealing from the outset a British failure of will to make good on what was promulgated on paper.[25]

Finally, some saw the Proclamation Line as a way of dealing with a problem of race. A small number of British officials in America viewed Indians as a breed apart, animal-like, and inherently inferior. No sooner had hostilities ended in North America than they flared up again. After defeating the French at the famous battle on the Plains of Abraham in Quebec, the military commander of North America, Sir Jeffrey Amherst, initiated shortsighted policies that let Indians know in no uncertain terms that the conquered region now belonged to Britain. Under Amherst's rule, the British installed an aggressive garrison government in the West by reining in trade and ignoring Native American diplomatic protocol. Incensed at these restrictive and ironfisted policies in the years before the government put the royal proclamation in place, Indians in the West from the Ohio valley to the upper Great Lakes region launched a daring rebellion against British authority all throughout the region. Under the leadership of an Ottawa war chief named Pontiac and the spiritual charisma of the Delaware prophet Neolin, these groups laid siege to nearly every major British fort and outpost.[26]

As the "rebellion" against established authority unfolded, some argued that only stern measures could "reduce the Savages to Reason."[27] Amherst called for the most pernicious means to do so. Infamously, he proposed that "Blankets and an Handkerchief" infected with smallpox be sent as a "present" to Indians besieging a British fort, proclaiming, "I hope it will have the desired effect."[28] In short, he advocated any means "to Extirpate this Execrable Race," including genocide.[29] Encouraging his subordinates to take measures that could "put a most effectual stop to their *very being*," Amherst considered the human dignity of Indians to be a fiction created by "our treatment of them." They could, he intoned, "never be considered by us as a people to whom we owe rewards; and it would be madness, to the highest degree, ever to bestow favors on a race who have so treacherously, and without any provocation on our side, attacked our Posts, and butchered our Garrisons."[30] For Amherst, the Proclamation Line served as a barrier keeping savages in their place. It separated two distinct and unbridgeable worlds—one Indian, the other white—and therefore symbolized these hardened realities.[31]

But to conclude that the Proclamation Line emerged from or confirmed racist thought overlooks some crucial points. For starters, many contended that the Proclamation Line represented a refutation of Amherst's flawed policies and racist attitudes. Shortsighted measures, one official suggested, had guaranteed that "our most Valuable Frontiers were Depopulated, our outposts with most of their Garrisons destroyed, and the Trade ruined."[32] "Ignorance" of the way that things worked in America led Amherst to pursue his explosive path. "Our former negligence and disregard gave first rise to all the cruelties committed," wrote a British official in America, adding, "Our misconduct since has continued their aversion to us."[33] Members of the Board of Trade also laid the troubles at Amherst's feet, noting that his racist policies had only emboldened Indians. "The measures you have taken for putting an end to the Indian war," a member of the board informed Amherst, "have not yet produced the desired effects; but to the contrary the Insurrections of the Indians are considerably increased and almost become general."[34] In some respects, therefore, the Lords of Trade drew up the Proclamation Line as an enlightened measure to clean up Amherst's mess and to reestablish some common ground with Indians. And for his failure, the board recalled him on the aptly named "Weazel Sloop of War" on November 18, 1763.[35]

The issue of race and the Proclamation Line also begs the question of whether the British could consistently conceive of Indians as inherently inferior. In other words, looking at the Proclamation Line as the central feature of a racist approach to empire in America means the British must have harbored what we would call "modern" conceptions of racial difference, that physical characteristics denoted and determined capabilities and capacities. But most did not or could not think along these lines. To begin with, Britons did not have a great deal of substantive experience with "exotic" peoples before 1763. Yes, they had a small number of slaving factories on the West African coast and a few trading posts in India. Moreover, colonists from England had settled in America in the seventeenth century. And British troops had gained firsthand knowledge of Native American warfare during the Seven Years' War. Yet the British had never tried to exert control over a great number of indigenous people far from home in a sustained manner. Therefore, we can only catch glimpses of British conceptions of human difference at work where the stakes mattered, and that involved peoples much closer to home. No doubt, when we explore English expansion into the "Celtic fringe" of the British Isles, what we see is not for the squeamish. The English had an appalling track record with the Irish and Scots on their borders. The rationale for subjugation or what even some would consider genocide, however, stemmed from notions of culture, not race.[36]

During the period just before Britons were trying to devise a plan for governing Indians in America, the English, some Irish, and some Scots were finally figuring out—in theory at least—how to make sense of one another. In a word, they were coming to terms with what it meant to be British. Throughout the sixteenth and seventeenth centuries, as English power extended to the marchlands of Britain and Ireland, and into the eighteenth century, when the early modern process of state formation reached its apogee, men and women throughout the Atlantic archipelago created new notions of national belonging by devising some measure to decide who was "in" and, just as significant, who was "out." Prescriptive markers of identity emerged to determine who belonged to the nation, positing that if one followed basic English ideas of subjecthood, one could become British. These markers revolved around a voluntary set of criteria, including loyalty to the Crown in Parliament, the celebration of "British" freedoms, such as consent of the governed, allegiance to the ancient constitution that underscored these liberties, and affiliation with the Reformed

Protestant tradition. Protestantism, liberty, and loyalty marked Britons off from their Continental enemies such as the French while allowing peoples of varied ethnic backgrounds throughout the three kingdoms to become — on paper at least — one.[37]

The "barbarous" and "savage" peoples on the British marchlands proved nagging exceptions to this rule, but exceptions that proved the rule. Officials considered Catholics in Ireland subjects, but subjects in need of reformation before being able to enjoy the rights and privileges of citizens. Even the so-called Old or Gaelic Irish, those whose ancestors had inhabited the land before the first sustained waves of settlement in the late Middle Ages, could become "British." But doing so meant undermining the Catholic faith and destroying the rude culture of a "savage" people. Similarly, in Scotland, the Risings of 1715 and 1745 against established British rule underscored in popular imagination the enduring barbarity of Highland culture, which was based on the clan system, Gaelic language, and a pastoral economy. For Highland Scots, the civilizing mission entailed abandoning old traditions in favor of more polite ways. In the years following the 1745 Rising, therefore, the Highland system of landownership rooted in the clan underwent a thoroughgoing — and brutal — makeover. But the promise of Britishness lay open to Highlanders as well, once they rejected their cultural traditions. Even in these extreme cases when violence or coercion was applied to help a recalcitrant society "develop," a people's culture — not race or ethnicity — mattered.[38]

To adapt this sensibility of human difference to a wider world, as well as the notion of "civility" that animated it, scholars were systematizing and further developing these ideas that had allowed the English to comprehend the Scottish and Irish "other." In the process, notions of basic human equality gained new intellectual sophistication. Indeed, at the very moment the British confronted in a meaningful and sustained way the diverse peoples of the American West, a new science of human difference was emerging. While Continental thinkers tended to dwell on the differences between peoples and societies, arguing, for example, that human diversity emerged from differing climates, theorists in Scotland were positing very different views that judged all people as essentially similar.[39]

The originator of this Scottish, and later generally British, understanding of humanity was the Irish-born Francis Hutcheson. Hutcheson set out to refute the pessimistic vision of human nature championed by thinkers such as Bernard Mandeville and Thomas Hobbes. A Hobbesian impulse to self-preservation did not drive men to create society. No, contra Hobbes—and contra John Locke—Hutcheson argued that the pursuit of benevolence, an innate "moral sense" every bit as real as the more physical senses, encouraged virtue and made man a social creature, pressing him to join others in the common good. Rights did not grow from the ability of individuals to amass things for themselves and did not stem from reasoning capabilities. Rather, equality had its origins in benevolence.[40]

This simple observation would have revolutionary implications for understanding those with alien ways. If reason made men equal—as Locke had supposed—then those who appeared irrational could be deemed inferior. If a Hobbesian obsession with self-love and the impulse to protect the self by hoarding property defined men as men, then those who had no notions of property were something less than human. But according to Hutcheson, the social contract stemmed not from self-interest or reason but from a moral sense all peoples possessed. Environment could heighten or dull the innate moral sense that made all equal, but environmental possibilities or constraints never put those sentiments there in the first place.

This "moral sense" understanding of humanity lay at the heart of emerging British understandings of human diversity. Animated by a Hutchesonian belief in innate benevolence, Scottish thinkers were explaining perceptible human difference not through essential, unchangeable traits, such as skin pigmentation, but by an emerging system of thought called stadial theory. At its most basic, the theory posited that societies moved through discrete and observable stages of development, hence the term "stadial." Each society began at a hunter-gatherer stage, proceeded over time to become pastoral and then agricultural, and finally evolved into a commercial stage. As a society progressed through each level, the manners and morals of the people shifted to reflect the appropriate stage, from the savage to the barbarian to the sophisticated. Man's innate sensibility to a moral capacity drove stadial development as well as moral refinement. The theory, therefore, could survey all societies through space and time, plotting each along a different stage of the developmental path. A number of prominent Scottish scholars, including Adam Ferguson, Adam Smith, David Hume, and William Robertson—one of the first historians to adapt the method to historical narrative—subscribed to this developmental model and Hutcheson's notion that innate human sociability sustained it. As Robertson put it, "Nations, as well as men, arrive at maturity by degrees."[41]

Because the intellectual rationale for stadial ideas grew out of the cultural ferment of national integration—when English, Irish, and Scots had to rationalize one another's traditions—it offered a means to make sense of the alien ways of indigenous peoples. At one extreme, lionizing the development of "British" polite culture and commercial society and focusing on cultural traits such as barbarity and sophistication—but not ethnicity—allowed Scots to assert their Britishness and full participation in the nation. For Scots such as Robertson, portraying Scotland as developed and polite validated the Scottish people as full-fledged British subjects. With the Union of 1707, which yoked Scotland and England through the institution of a British parliament into one nation, Robertson believed that the Scots were reaching the highest levels of cultural evolution. Once "adopted into a constitution, whose genius and laws were more liberal than their own," he wrote, the Scots "have extended their commerce, refined their manners, made improvements in the elegancies of life, and cultivated the arts and sciences."[42] At the other extreme, the theory offered a way to comprehend the most "savage" people. The theory therefore had applications far beyond Scotland.

The Irishman Edmund Burke, who was able to rise from obscurity to the heights of British influence because his father had abandoned the Catholic faith, believed that Scots such as Robertson had "unrolled" the "Great Map of Mankind." "There is no state or Gradation of barbarism, and no mode of refinement," he declared, "which we have not at the same instant under our View."[43] All could discern the dynamics that animated the most primitive societies now and in the past, as well as the most polite in the present and, presumably, in the future. Lowland Scots had achieved parity with the English by making their way to the highest stage of social development. Highlanders still languished a rung below, yet one above most of the "barbarous" Irish. "Savage" Indians—still in a rude state of nature—found none beneath. But they still clung to the ladder of humanity and could expect over time to make an ascent.

Of course, this history and the stadial theory that emerged from it proved ethnocentric. After all, a decidedly English model of "civility" determined who belonged in the nation and who did not.[44] Moreover, the model worked better in theory than in practice. Irish converts to Protestantism or Highlanders who turned their back on Gaelic tradition did not enjoy the same opportunities as well-heeled Englishmen. Finally, these ideas rationalized underdevelopment and discrimination just as they justified appalling brutality. But they also repudiated essentialist visions of human difference, that a person's worth hinged on innate or unchangeable characteristics. In understanding the origins and meaning of human difference, one could disregard a person's history, race, or ethnicity.[45] Cultural genocide, the kind resorted to with the Irish to "make them British" or the type envisioned to "reduce Indians to civility," could be contemplated and employed. But racist genocide lay beyond the pale—in theory at least—for Britons.[46]

The well-worn model of civility and the new sophisticated theories that were emerging offered powerful blueprints for understanding Native Americans and the West. Indians, of course, lay at the bottom end of the stadial ladder, a "savage" people living in a "state of nature," a place and time untouched by history. And this is the way most travelers conceived of the region west of the line. In 1766, for example, as Capt. Harry Gordon, the British chief engineer for North America, made his way down the Ohio, he envisioned a newfound Garden of Eden. The river from the Muskingum to the Scioto, he recounted, "is most beautiful [with] a number of islands . . . of different sizes, but all covered with the tallest of Timber." God's hand lay everywhere. The Falls of the Ohio "only runs rapid over a ledge of a flat Limestone Rock, which the author of Nature has put there, to keep up the waters of the Ohio; and to be the cause of that beautifull stillness." The banks along the Ohio had a mysterious, primeval quality. Along it, "we discovered laying about many large bones, some of which the exact Pattern of Elephant Tusks."[47]

Writers extolled the "fruitfulness of these fresh virgin lands" that made the region west of the line "a terrestrial paradise."[48] The "charming" nature of the region even stunned the most jaded veterans of the frontier, such as George Croghan. He noted that "Buffaloes, Bears, and all sorts of wild Game, are extremely Plenty here" and that "a good Hunter might supply an hundred Men with meat, and that without much fatigue to himself." It was by his lights "one of the finest countries in the known world."[49] As one writer put it, the whole region west of the mountains was "the healthiest . . . most pleasant, and most Commodious Spot of the earth known to European People—Supposing a State of Nature."[50]

As visitors west of the line relied on ideas that loomed large in European myth to comprehend this land before time, theory and experience with others on Britain's cultural marchlands offered powerful lenses to understand and govern America's "savages." One of the chief architects of the Proclamation Line and head of the Board of Trade, William Petty, the Earl of Shelburne, made the connections between Britain's past in Ireland and its present in America. Born in Ireland, Shelburne was a protégé of Lord Bute's and a friend and patron of Scottish thinkers, including Adam Smith.[51] Shelburne also was the namesake of his great-grandfather, a man who played a prominent and infamous role in the plantation and subjugation of Ireland by the English a century earlier. Shelburne subscribed to his ancestor's views of the "savage" Irish he grew up around. Raised in Kerry, Shelburne believed he had a solid grasp on the Irish character. He found the country "quite uncivilized, peopled by Catholicks, [and] reduced by frequent rebellions." He chafed at "the uncultivated, undisciplined manners and that vulgarity which make all Irish society so justly odious all over Europe." Shelburne did not demonize the Irish "race." His critique centered on culture. A savage people required a firm hand; indeed, he fondly recalled his English ancestors who had "kept that barbarous country in strict subordination."[52] Such ideas had legitimated the conquest of Ireland, but they also had a way of making men like Shelburne, born in that savage country, British.[53]

Enduring and newly invigorated notions of civility were at the heart of Shelburne's ideas of what the royal proclamation meant for America, the empire, and Indians. Lands in America not peopled by British subjects, including the territories out West, he argued, "are not, nor will they for some time, be in a capacity to receive the full impression of this free constitution to its full extent, for either they are not inhabited at all, or by such as are under a legal disability of being admitted efficient members of the community so as to act in any judicial or legislative capacity."[54] In a paper addressed to the king, Shelburne argued that the region beyond the line should not be placed under a government like Quebec, Nova Scotia, or Grenada, regions presumably peopled by individuals further along the developmental path. "Their nature and situation in general" and "the present temper and disposition of the Indians" made moot the point of government in the West. At the present, Indians "would consequently pay no obedience or yield any subjection to laws or constitution to them unknown and founded on principles the most adverse to their nature and consciences that can be imagined."[55] New colonies existed only where people eligible for the full benefits of subjecthood lived. Indians need not apply.

So prevalent were these notions of human difference that Shelburne claimed "it would be both endless and unnecessary to enter into arguments to support the principles upon which this policy is founded."[56] One official who embraced these principles and who played a critical role in developing a working plan for the Proclamation Line was Sir William Johnson. An immigrant from Ireland who had converted from Catholicism to Anglicanism, Johnson managed some estates in the Mohawk River valley in the colony of New York while earning renown as a fur trader. During the Seven Years' War, he served as a military commander, for which he received a baronetcy, and as a diplomat to the Six Nations of Iroquois, with whom he enjoyed close relations. Befitting his station, Johnson amassed a fortune, took Mohawk mistresses, and built a baronial estate in which he employed Irish harpists and dwarfs as jesters for entertainment.[57] After the Board of Trade considered enacting the royal proclamation for North America, its members contacted Johnson for his views and help in dealing with the Indians west of the line. The board, hoping to use Johnson's expertise, charged him to use his "judgement" to help develop "a proper plan for the future management and direction of these important interests, to the satisfaction of the Indians, the benefit of free trade, and the security and interests of His majesty's dominions."[58]

Johnson wasted little time in informing the board that he was the right man for the job. "I have during 25 years experience," he responded to the board's request, "acquired some knowledge of the power and abilities of the Indians, and the principles on which they Act."[59] Johnson did not underestimate his abilities. "I was called to the management of these People," he recounted, "as my situation, and opinion that it might become one day of service to the Public, had induced me to cultivate a particular intimacy with those People, to accommodate myself to their manners, and even to dress on many occasions."[60] His expertise established, he cautioned that Indian sensibilities had to be taken into account in managing the western empire. The Indians, he told the board, "will never be content with our possessing the Frontiers, unless we settle limits with them, and make it worth their while."[61] He therefore agreed in principle with a Proclamation Line.

Blaming Jeffery Amherst's racist policies for the problems on the frontier, Johnson argued that any plan for management of the West must reject such ideas.[62] A new, more enlightened approach was necessary, one that required British officials to "cultivate a proper understanding with the Indians."[63] While Johnson usually argued that Indians could not enjoy the privileges of subjecthood, he rejected Amherst's essentialist logic in coming to this conclusion. "Many people in America," Johnson told the board, "have been too apt to despise Indian strength, till fatal necessity has convinced them of their abilities." Such people "entertain[ed] a contempt for them merely, because they are not civilized, and that they never experienced what a few Indians . . . are able to accomplish." Quite to the contrary, "the Indians, I do assure your Lordships, are no wise inferior to us in sagacity and stratagem, qualities most essentially necessary in this Country." Though not essentially inferior, Indians could not be subjects. "I know," Johnson argued, "that many mistakes arise here from erroneous accounts formerly made of Indians; they have been represented as calling themselves subjects, altho, the very word would have startled them, had it ever been pronounced by any Interpreter." Instead, they "desire to be considered as Allies and Friends."[64]

To become subjects, Indians had a few difficult hurdles to clear. First, Johnson argued, they had to concede British sovereignty over their lands. And for the time being, this they would not do. Indians beyond the line "called themselves a free people who had independent Lands, which were their ancient possessions." In their minds, "the Country was still theirs."[65] What Johnson called the "Western Indians," groups including the Delawares, Shawnees, and Mingoes of the Ohio Country and the peoples of the upper Great Lakes, have "never been conquered, Either by the English or the French, nor subject to the Laws," and "consider themselves as a free people."[66]

Second, to become subjects, Indians had to become civilized. Johnson knew of one such group that had nearly made the leap to civility, in this case Indians who lived under colonial governments east of the line. Indians living in the East, Johnson argued, had rejected the lifestyle of Indians living in the West.[67] What Johnson called "the small domesticated Tribes" provided a ready example.[68] In a letter to Shelburne, Johnson discussed the position of one such group within the imperial scheme, the Wappinger and Stockbridge Indians of New England. These he considered "upon a very different footing from the rest." Through "length of time"

and "now surrounded by the White Inhabitants," they had "become Domesticated." They had "laid aside Hunting," the "industrious amongst them
employ themselves in fishing, labouring or other work," and "the majority
have submitted to the Laws." In other words, they acted as subjects.[69]

Johnson argued that for the imperial system to work, the British would
have to pave the way for subjecthood. Johnson reduced his administrative
plan "to two heads." It involved, "first, the satisfying the Indians on the subject of their uneasiness, particularly concerning their lands." Second, it required "regulating the Department of Indian Affairs in such a manner, as
shall best tend to the security of peace, and the promoting His Majesty's
interest amongst the Indians." To accomplish these formidable tasks,
Johnson argued that the Indians had to be secure in their holdings "until
such time as they thought proper to dispose thereof."[70] The Proclamation
Line, he believed, served this purpose, preventing "future unfair dealings
with the Indians" while addressing "past grievances."[71] With "their apprehensions removed," he promised, "their attachment to us would acquire a
solidity not to be shaken." Civility would then follow. He concluded that
"time, intercourse with us and instruction in Religion and learning, would
create such a change in their manners and sentiments as the present generation might live to see, together with an end to the expences and attention which are as yet indispensably necessary to attain these great purposes
and to promote the safety, extend the settlements and encrease the commerce of this Country."[72] Although for the moment Indians were "an
uncivilized people," these methods would "discover the true means of
managing their affairs so as in time to render them peaceable, and useful
members of Society." Although in a state of nature, they, too, had a capacity to join the social compact.[73]

Trade, Johnson claimed, would induce Indians to embrace civilizing
influences. Advocating trade, of course, did not represent a new departure.
From the earliest days of settlement, settlers had traded European goods
for animal pelts with Indians up and down the Atlantic seaboard, but with
often tragic results. Over time, Indians grew dependent on European
manufactures and alcohol, native skills eroded as they adopted European
technology, and as Indians fell into debt, they forfeited the most precious
commodity they possessed, land. Indians, unsurprisingly, regarded traders
as a sordid lot. Any new scheme, therefore, had to regulate trade and pro-
hibit fraudulent traders from dealing with Indians.[74]

Johnson therefore advocated "the establishment of Trade on principles of strictest equity." Traders were "the only British subjects, with whom the Indians are acquainted," and as such "the Traders then become in great measure the only people by whom they can form a judgement of the English, and indeed the only white People seen by the Nations most distant." If the civilizing mission required Indians to form a "conception of our abilities and integrity," traders played an important role in the system, "capable of giving them, favourable, or disadvantageous impressions of the whole Nation." If "men of strict probity or worth" could not be found for the job, then "they should be kept within such bounds, and under such regulations as will prevent them at least from prejudicing us, in the eyes of these people at the very commencement of our intercourse with them."[75] On this issue, the peace of the empire rested. After all, in Johnson's estimation, Indians were "capable of being dangerous enemies to the growth and Trade of the Colonies, or of becoming strong friends and great promoters of both, and useful members of society."[76]

If trade enticed Indians, religion civilized. Johnson supported the cause of Anglican missionaries with the zeal of a convert. In fact, the Society for the Propagation of the Gospel, a group based in London and charged with proselytizing the Indians in colonial America, made Johnson one of its members. Johnson envisioned an important role for this group in the new imperial scheme. "The appointment of good Missionaries," he declared, "is highly requisite" for the board's "Plan for the future management of Indian Affairs."[77] As one writer put it, "in their present Pagan state," Indians exhibited "cruel revengeful tempers." To "endeavour civilizing them" meant "instill[ing] into them the principles of the true Religion: Which we have hitherto neglected, equally to our shame and loss."[78] Although a promoter of Protestantism, he advocated an old Catholic model of conversion, one developed by French Jesuits a century earlier. Instead of making Indians British to make them Christian, Johnson made a case for Christianizing Indians to turn them into civil subjects. Only the "Venerable Society for propagating the Gospel (of which I have the honor of being a Member)," Johnson declared, possessed the means and "Men of spirit" to accomplish this difficult task.[79]

The SPG was well suited to the civilizing mission before it. In 1750, a minister associated with the group had declared that Christianity "forms [people] for Society. It civilizes Mankind. It tames the fierceness of their Passions, and wears off the Barbarity of their Manners."[80] William Smith, who was born in Aberdeenshire, Scotland, served as provost for the College of Philadelphia, and became a chief advocate of the SPG's civilizing mission, had seen this dynamic at work before. While a university student in Scotland, Smith had witnessed the ravages and brutal repression of the 1745 Jacobite Rising, as well as the ways the British state tried to shatter "barbarous" Highland cultural ways. In the wake of the Seven Years' War, Smith agreed with Johnson on the central role conversion had to play in the new imperial scheme.[81] In his plan for "Civilizing and Christianizing the numerous Tribes of Indians in the West," Smith considered the Indians "savages" and "heathens." But like Johnson he believed that they could be redeemed. While Smith disagreed with Johnson about the specific means of civilizing Indians, the stadial assumptions that saw Indians as human were the same for both.[82]

Even missionaries living on the frontier saw Indians in these terms. Thomas Barton, an Anglican minister on the Pennsylvania frontier, had also emigrated from a cultural periphery, in this case Ireland. His work, he believed, encouraged "many barbarous nations who are immersed in the grossest Idolatry without even the knowledge of the God that made them, to become subjects of Great Britain."[83] Echoing Smith, he believed Indians "were susceptible of good impressions . . . [and] could be prevailed upon to exchange their savage barbarity for the pure and peaceable religion of Jesus."[84] True religion therefore had a critical role to play in the imperial civilizing scheme. Officials debated the details and the approaches to be used, but they never questioned the merits of doing so either for order in the West or for making "savages" into "subjects."

The task of convincing officials in London that this civilizing vision should animate any scheme for the West fell to Johnson's chief lieutenant, George Croghan. Croghan must have cut a strange figure in front of the Lords of Trade. Barely lettered, born a Catholic in Ireland, and shaped by life on the American frontier, he would seem a poor choice to champion Johnson's plan for imperial management in London. But then again, maybe he was the perfect choice to advocate the centrality of the civilizing mission for empire. After all, he had risen from obscurity to become a man of substance in America. He had rejected the superstitions of the Church of Rome for the sophisticated established church. And like Johnson, he had evolved from a faceless immigrant and lowly trader among the Indians into an official of the Crown in America. If he could be redeemed, then surely Indians could as well.[85]

Croghan arrived in London on February 11, 1764, and wasted little time in attending to Johnson's scheme. Two days later he hand-delivered a letter detailing Johnson's vision on how the West should be administered. But the board members concerned themselves with other matters. Croghan sat around London for nearly four months waiting for an audience.[86] America appeared an afterthought in London.[87] Finally, on June 7, Croghan had a meeting with the Lords of Trade, during which they discussed Johnson's plans and probed Croghan for his thoughts on the West.[88]

Once before the board, Croghan pressed for Johnson's scheme. He did so, though, using an unconventional approach, arguing that the West demanded immediate attention because of the pernicious influence of the French. He recommended that the board consider establishing a government in the region, asking "whether it would be good policy at this time" to "plant a respectable colony, in order to secure our frontiers, and prevent the French from any attempt to Rival us."[89] Croghan and the board understood the potential challenge that the French presented. But Croghan pointed to a more immediate concern. "The French and the Indians," he warned, "have been bread up together, like children, in that Country, and the French has always adopted the Indian Customs and manners, trated them civilly and suppl'd their Necessitys . . . by which mains they gain'd the Hearts of the Indians."[90]

According to this view, the French corrupted the Indians as the Indians corrupted the French. A British traveler to the village of Kaskaskia along the Mississippi saw a town with "a number of houses, some Large, but meanly built, with good Lotts behind them for Gardens." The plots went to waste, however, because the settlers "make little use of them . . . in general being very indolent." The post next to the town, Fort Chartres, was nearly toppling into the river. Another town nearby, Prairie du Rocher, he also found in a "ruinous" condition.[91] Croghan considered the people there "an Idle lazey people, a parcel of Renegadoes from Canada and much worse than the Indians."[92] Similarly, Thomas Gage, who had taken over as military commander of North America after Amherst's departure, declared that they "lived a lazy kind of Indian life."[93] Such was the consequence of mutual corruption. French traders plied Indians with alcohol and supplied them with guns, while the more primitive habits of the Indians rubbed off on the French. "Several of them," another officer wrote, "have remained so many Years with them that they are become Savages."[94] If men and women could ascend the ladder from savagery to civility, they could just as easily descend it.

For this reason, the board had to establish government in the region. A pamphleteer argued that "of all *North America*, the place of most importance to *Britain*, and where a new Colony is most requisite, is at the *Forks of the Mississippi*." The writer prophesied that like colonists east of the line "the greater security of their whole rights and properties, under the mild equitable *British* Government, than under the arbitrary power of *France*," would induce them to embrace Britishness. "These new subjects," he concluded, "under the cherishing wings of *British* protection and liberty, will, before many years, by civil usage and prudent management, entirely incorporate with their fellow-subjects, without distinction of nation, language, or Religion, as was the case of the *Dutch* in *New York*."[95]

Indians, corrupted by the French, posed the gravest challenge to the region, for it was only with French influence that Indians could threaten the entire imperial scheme. With their stadial lenses in place, officials could not even conceive that the Indians were capable of a concerted, complex military undertaking, the type prosecuted during Pontiac's War. Gage considered the Illinois French, ever anxious to corrupt Indians, "the Sole Cause" of the war.[96] Hitting on a powerful bogey to the British, one commentator claimed that Pontiac's War was "no question excited by French Jesuits and Priests," and the Indians were "wheedled over and depraved by the contagion of their pernicious influence." Through "shameful low practices, they provoke the Indians, who if discreetly used, would keep treaties as strictly as we do; but when exasperated by such glaring injustice, are of all men the most revengeful and cruel."[97]

In discussing the prospects of government on the Mississippi, therefore, officials revealed most clearly their conviction about the plasticity of the human condition and the notion that "savage" behavior was not innate.[98] Men like Croghan and Johnson likened Indians to blank slates or empty vessels.[99] The board agreed. Reiterating their distaste for the manner in which Amherst had dealt with the Indians, the board's members approved the substance of "all the meshers" Johnson recommended. Croghan went on to report to Johnson that the board "att last Consented to Make a boundry between the Indians and us and has made itt an

Artickle of thire plan and Refer'd itt to your Honour to Setle."[100] And members of the board asserted that racist ideology would not define the empire.[101]

Thus, far from merely incoherent, expedient, or race-based, the rationale for the royal proclamation and the imperial "system" that emerged from it reflected prevailing notions of human difference. However ethnocentric, the plan for the West stemmed from assumptions about human redeemability that had emerged in Britain in the early modern period and were being systematized as stadial theory.[102] After consulting officials in America, the board developed a "plan for imperial control of Indian affairs" that closely resembled the ideas aired by the Irish expatriates Johnson and Croghan. The plan, which called for the centralization of administration west of the Proclamation Line, mandated that colonies in the East repeal laws affecting the West. The board then broadened the powers of its two chief Indian superintendents, William Johnson in the northern district west of the line and John Stuart, a Scot, in the South. Each now had the power to call councils with Indians "to hear any appeals and redress all complaints of the Indians," and to serve as or appoint justices of the peace for their regions. In short, each superintendent—and not military commanders—would act as "guardian for the Indians and Protector of their Rights."[103]

The board also endorsed Johnson's two-point plan of civilization. The plan "recommended to the Society for the Propagation of the Gospel in foreign parts, to appoint four missionaries in each District," who were to report to the superintendent. Moreover, the board allowed settlers from the East to trade with Indians in the West so long as they "take out Licences" and did not deal in rum or weapons. The Lords of Trade instructed superintendents to regulate trade, empowering officials such as Stuart to "prevent vagrants and men of bad character being employed."[104] Finally, to free Indians from corrupting influences and to keep the peace for the time being, the plan confirmed the importance of the Proclamation Line. Traders might travel beyond it, troops might be garrisoned on the western side of it, and missionaries might proselytize over it, but the West belonged to Indians.[105]

This is not to say that Indians held the land as sovereign. After all, the whole system, premised on notions of Indians' cultural inferiority and dependence, rested on paternalistic assumptions that went hand in hand with the civilizing mission. The board drew up the line not to confirm Indian sovereignty but to "favor and protect" Indians.[106] For the time being, Indians would be subject to British authority, but not subjects. Time and civilizing influences would see to that. Here's how one writer put it, revealing the assumptions that made the new system consistent with British thought at the time: "By the light of the Gospel planted among these poor Heathens, would the ferocity of their tempers be removed; their Lives and Manners polished; and the Souls of many saved." Over time, Indians in the West "would be fond to imitate us in polite fashions and civilized manners." They "would use apparel; build and live in towns and villages; cultivate lands; and thro' time, study Arts and Sciences." Finally, he added, "instead of being idle wanderers, they would make a great addition of very useful Subjects to the *British* Empire." Indeed, these members of "the human species" would help "bring us to the Era of the highest Glory and Felicity that Britain ever enjoyed."[107] As Johnson put it, "If we conquer their prejudices by our generosity they will lay aside their Jealousys, and we may rest in security. This is much cheaper than any other plan, and more certain of success."[108]

In the months after the royal proclamation took effect, officials also dealt with exceptions to these western rules. The French living in the Illinois Country would be subjects in a non-subject world. "His Majesty," a proclamation issued in 1764 read, "grants to the inhabitants of the Illinois the liberty of the Catholic religion, as it has already been granted to his subjects in Canada." If inhabitants took an oath of fidelity and obedience to the British monarch "and become subjects of His Majesty," they would "enjoy the same rights and privileges, the same security for their persons and effects, and the liberty of trade, as the old subjects of the King." The British would, in short, regard their settlements as islands of eastern subjects in a western world.[109]

Cultural go-betweens made this system work.[110] Because the plan for management of the West relied not on force or limitless resources but on the deference of eastern colonists and the trust of Indians, only men who bought into Johnson's civilizing ideals could fulfill these duties. The Board of Trade allowed each superintendent to appoint three such men— "deputies," as they were called—to ensure the system worked as envisioned.[111] Deputies had to "remove disgusts" between colonists, the British, and Indians, doing all in their power to sustain a middle ground between the cultures while reassuring the Indians that the British were not "coming with a numerous Army, to cut them off, and by Violence, to retain their Country."[112] Almost immediately after the board enacted the plan for the West, George Croghan, now Johnson's chief deputy, headed beyond the line to inform Indians of the new system.[113] This required a delicate touch, entailing the deputy to work on Indian diplomatic terms and remain sensitive to Indian claims of the land while confirming British sovereignty. Indians had to acknowledge "the King of great Britain to be their Father, and to have the Sovereignty of their Country." In return, go-betweens promised that "due care will be taken, by their new Father the King of great britain and his Subjects," so they "might enjoy the blessings of Peace."[114] As Croghan put it, to deal with the Indians would "require some time, and a very even conduct." He understood that "they don't look on them selves under any obligation to us, but rather think we are oblig'd to them, for letting us reside in their Country."[115]

The system also established pockets of civility or areas peopled by subjects beyond the pale in the West. To sustain the fiction that the land "belonged" to Indians, as the royal proclamation stated, they had to "relinquish their claims to the Forts and Posts the English now have in their Country" and accept the right of the British to erect other forts and trading posts so that "the Peace may last for ever."[116] Officials suggested that the Illinois Country should be one such pocket.[117] The area around the confluence of the Ohio, Allegheny, and Monongahela rivers—the headwaters of the Ohio—would serve as another. There, on the site of a burned-down wooden French fort, the British were constructing the mammoth Fort Pitt.[118] Built of brick and stone, Fort Pitt, as a contemporary claimed, was "a most formidable fortification; such a one as will, to latest posterity, secure the British Empire on the Ohio."[119] The system demanded that a "considerable Tract round Fort-Pitt" be set aside for a "military settlement," and one commander envisioned three or more townships placed in the area.[120] In 1765, therefore, William Johnson forged an agreement with Delawares in the region to allow a small settlement within a cannon-shot distance from the fort. Soon enough, a small number of civilians in more than two hundred "houses" and "hutts" lived around it.[121] In sites of civility such as Fort Pitt, deputies negotiated with arriving Indians, missionaries and traders came and went, troops were stationed, and British claims to sovereignty were made manifest.

For immovable structures, forts had a dynamic role to play in the system. While ensuring that colonists stayed east of the line, the system of forts, posts, and civilized pockets also created "a Barrier impenetrable to savages."[122] Forts, in other words, enforced the line in two directions. They also served as nerve centers, tying together trade routes and through them connecting subject regions. Finally, they maintained order and the integrity of the line while keeping recalcitrant Indians at bay until the civilizing mission proved successful.

Although officials designed the system to keep the peace, they expected tensions from time to time. Indians, after all, still lived in a savage state, and civility would only emerge after considerable time and effort. Deference, after all, was the duty of subjects, not savages. From the start, parties of Indians fired shots over the river and skulked "about the Fort."[123] At times, tensions exploded. On February 22, 1764, for example, within cannon shot of Fort Pitt, six Indians waylaid a group of seven soldiers variously warming themselves by a fire or loading wood on a wagon. One soldier managed to yell, "Stand to Your Arms my Lads there's Indians," before the attack. Another soldier was shot dead, and the Indians "sclp'd, rip't open his body, and took out his heart." The body, "ripped up from the private parts to the throat," was then "carried off by the Savages." Yet another, hit with an arrow in the chest, managed to escape to the fort. And a fourth, providing cover fire for his fleeing comrades, ran from tree to tree and discovered, once safe again, that they had "shot through his clothes in 3 different places."[124]

More troubling still was word that even as Pontiac's War was fizzling out, "Friendly Tribes on the Susquehanna," well east of the Proclamation Line, were planning to continue raiding the frontiers of the colonies and were rounding up reinforcements.[125] Rumors swirled in the months after the royal proclamation took effect of "some Mischief having been done at a place, I think they call, Wyoloosing" on the upper Susquehanna.[126] Troublingly for the maintenance of the system, officials tended to interpret such events through stadial lenses, refusing to entertain the possibility that Indian actions exposed the patronizing logic upon which the myth of the West had been constructed.

If the system required Indians to accept its foundational myths, it also needed colonists to act in a deferential manner and accept the strictures of the royal proclamation. For the plan for the West to work, colonies—and by implication their speculating elite—had to forgo claims to the West. By the reckoning of some, Pennsylvania's charter extended west to the Ohio River and included the region around Fort Pitt, an area well west of the line. Virginia had an even more ambitious charter. It took in "all unculti-vated Lands to the Westward, and therefore may go to the South Sea." The king, therefore, under the proclamation, halted their borders east of the line by fiat.[127] Where deference failed, force would succeed. Far from def-erential subjects, some colonists appeared as "Licentious Ruffians," who proved as difficult to restrain "as it is to prevent robberys on the high-way in England."[128] One of the roles of garrisons, of course, was to stop those who refused to be hemmed in by the law. Commanders at forts and posts therefore dispatched troops from time to time to remove squatters and to destroy the cabins they had built.[129]

When they headed west, illegal settlers entered a no-man's-land, a re-gion that except for a few pockets could not by definition contain subjects. Subjects entering such lands surrendered their rights. Officials came up with a number of strategies, ranging from tearing down cabins to threaten-ing "the Penalty of Death," to punish those who ignored the royal procla-mation.[130] But ultimately squatters had to fend for themselves. Since they entered a region with no government, they were regressing to the state of nature. Shelburne ordered military commanders to warn settlers west of the line that they were "out of the Protection of any Province."[131]

Thomas Gage had his doubts about the feasibility of the civilizing mis-sion. The Indians' "Education and the whole Business of their Lives is War and Hunting." Nonetheless, he knew that the system must prevail. The British, he believed, had "to turn this Rage for war from Ourselves, and di-rect it to other Objects."[132] This meant that anyone foolhardy enough to ig-nore warnings would suffer at the hands of Indians. And the British would do nothing about it. Gage worried that if settlers moved west, "the Indians will break out, and that they will fall upon the Settlements," making "a General War of it." "Should it be impossible to divert this Storm," he warned, "we must use our endeavours to point out to them the proper Ob-jects of their Resentment, and to guide them . . . where this lawless and abandoned Crew reside."[133]

He also admitted the new system's premises. The blueprint for empire in the West, of course, emerged to tackle practical problems in the wake of one bloody war and in the midst of another. But its ideology stemmed from an enduring myth embellished with new intellectual polish. This ideology served a number of purposes. It offered a way to make sense of peoples with alien cultural ways. It also provided a means for managing the West while rationalizing the marginalization of Indians. Finally, it provided a conceptual fig leaf for peace, allowing the British to believe they were doing all in their power to maintain order in the West despite the meager resources and troops they applied to the task. In the minds of officials, to hold the system together would not—and must not—require overwhelming force, but deference from subjects and encouragement for subjects in the making. In this way, imperial ideology reflected the constraints of the possible.

Despite the tensions evident on the frontier in the months after the royal proclamation went into effect, the region west of the line appeared to be calming down. In early 1765, William Johnson reported to the Board of Trade that the Shawnees, Delawares, and Mingoes of the Ohio Country had either signed treaties with his deputies or were suing for peace.[134] "The country," Gage triumphantly reported to the board, perhaps in a fit of wishful thinkng, "is restored to its former Tranquility."[135] But for the moment of tranquillity to last, others would have to accept the new system and its sustaining myths with the same zeal as its architects did. And signs were pointing in other directions.

TWO

Crossing the Line:
The Limits of Empire in the West

No sooner had Gen. Thomas Gage declared the frontier "tranquil" than the West awakened. The first signs appeared in late 1763 as the place that he had called "Wyoloosing" exploded into violence. As Johnson had warned the board—and as friendly tribes on the Susquehanna had reported—western Indians were indeed launching raids. For a long time, Indians and speculators and settlers from Pennsylvania and Connecticut had competed for control of this area on the upper Susquehanna valley, known as Wyoming. By the time western Indian war parties were descending on Wyoming, Connecticut settlers had moved into the disputed region once more. This time, however, Delawares slaughtered the "Yankees."[1]

When word reached the Pennsylvania settlement closest to Wyoming, settlers feared the worst. For years, these men and women from Paxtang, or simply Paxton, had pleaded with Quaker officials to send troops to protect their vulnerable settlements. No help had come. After news of the massacre reached them, and convinced they "were likely to get no assistance from the Government, some Volunteers went out at our own Expence determined to drive our Enemies from our Borders."[2] When these "Paxtang Rangers" reached Wyoming, they could not believe their eyes. They found the remains of settlers tortured in horrific ways. Rather than wait for such an attack on their own settlement, they opted for a preemptive strike.[3] And soon they heard a rumor that allowed them to act.

On lands belonging to the Penn family just south of Paxton, called

Conestoga Manor, lived a small group of domesticated Indians known as the Conestogoes. Unlike the more numerous Delawares and Shawnees, who had headed over the mountains to the Ohio Country as German and Irish immigrants overran the region in the 1730s, the peaceful Conestogoes remained. Now it was rumored that Will Sock, one of these "domesticated" Indians, was providing intelligence to belligerent Delawares from the West. The rangers meant to remove this threat to their neighbors and put an end to this treachery in their midst.[4] Instead, they put an end to all the Conestogoes they encountered.

On the morning of December 14, 1763—less than two months after a royal proclamation set forth the idea that Indians were redeemable as humans—these frontiersmen butchered all the Indians they found on Conestoga Manor. When they got word that a number of surviving Conestogoes had holed up in the workhouse at Lancaster for safety, the rangers, now known as the Paxton Boys, rode off to the county seat, stormed the workhouse, and slaughtered the remaining Conestogoes they found there. In all, they murdered twenty men, women, and children. When they learned that the Quaker government in Philadelphia had rounded up other vulnerable Indians in the region to protect them, the Paxton Boys set off for Philadelphia to put an end to these "Quaker Indians" as well. If hunting these Indians down meant toppling the provincial government, then so be it.[5]

The Paxton Boys and their supporters seemed a crazed and deluded mob that could not tell the difference between peaceful and hostile Indians. Paranoid, they were convinced that a conspiracy was afoot. Despite the denials of British and Pennsylvania officials, as well as the Conestogoe Indians themselves, the frontier settlers had "long been convinced . . . that the Indians that lived as Independent Commonwealths among us or near our Borders were our most dangerous Enemies, both in the last and present War, altho they still pretended to be our Friends."[6]

The massacres at Conestoga Manor and Lancaster, as well as the march of the Paxton Boys to Philadelphia, loom large in our understanding of the American frontier, a narrative that goes something like this: Made up of the poorer elements of colonial society, these down-and-outs with few opportunities and trapped between two worlds—one white, the other Indian—lashed out at the most vulnerable. And this act of projection represented an awful watershed for America, a critical aspect of a broader process of "ethnic cleansing" on the frontier. With these race-addled shock troops, Indians from this point forward could expect no quarter when they encountered whites.[7]

Benjamin Franklin thought as much. By his lights, the Paxton Boys—"Christian White Savages," as he called them—had killed the innocent Indians because of their "reddish brown Skin, and black Hair." In moving down the stadial ladder to the savage state of Indians west of the mountains, they had descended to the level of racists. Franklin would also claim his intervention prevented even more widespread savagery.[8] Back from an extended stay in England, to which he would return in a few months, Franklin led a small delegation to meet with these vigilantes on the edge of Philadelphia, listened to their many grievances, told them officials would take their case under consideration, and sent them on their way back to the frontier. Thanks to Franklin, the trouble had ended—for the moment.[9]

Like much of Franklin's life, however, this story is shrouded in myth. True, Franklin had met the Paxton Boys on the road to Philadelphia. But the threat of British military intervention sent them packing home. The "horrid Murders committed by some People of Pennsylvania on the domesticated Indians" had appalled British officials in America and London, and when Pennsylvania's government proved "too feeble" to apprehend the butchers, the governor applied to General Gage "for a Military Force to support the Civil Authority in the execution of the Law." Gage responded by sending three companies toward Philadelphia. "Without the Interposition of the King's Troops," Gage averred, "there is reason to believe, that much Blood would have spilt in that City."[10] Sovereign British power, in short, ensured that the crisis did not overwhelm the colony's political institutions and that violence would not become more widespread.

Franklin's version of events can no more be taken at face value than his contention that frontier settlers had crossed some racist Rubicon. In fact, his observation oversimplifies how men and women in communities like Paxton conceived Indians. While we can never know for certain why the Paxton Boys butchered the Conestogoes or if their actions resonated with all or even most settlers, we know this much: their supporters devised subtle justifications as to why most on the frontier condoned Paxton-like violence that were lost on Franklin. No doubt, the vast majority of frontier men and women hated Indians. For most, though, race—the color of Indian skin and the sheen of Indian hair—was not the issue per se. Apologists, in fact, articulated the same assumptions about human difference to rationalize the slaughter of innocents that officials had used in drawing up the Proclamation Line. True, they made the startling claim that "savage" Indians west of the line and those "vagabonds," as they put it, living in the East did not differ at all. In so doing, however, they suggested that settlers in regions near the line did not have the luxury of waiting for the civilizing mission to take hold. In other words, they shared the same ideals about the nature of Indians that officials like Johnson and Shelburne espoused. But they came to different—and troubling—conclusions about the implications of such ideas.

The actions of the Paxton Boys and arguments supporting them, therefore, presented a grave challenge to imperial ideology and the new plan put in place for the West. Once it became clear that British troops would protect the Indians, common settlers throughout the West grew enraged. And now the British had to contend with the "Fury of the Country People."[11] One commander declared that the troops "were intended to make the People see, that they are under [British] Protection, which will prevent any Violence."[12] But settlers did not see things this way. The commanding officer of the British post near Philadelphia where the Indians were held heard the people were marching "on different roads to this place" and readied for an attack, preparing "grape shott fearing a Crowd of People Braking in." They never did, but milled around the makeshift fort and buzzed about the taverns of the city, threatening violence.[13] They let authorities know in no uncertain terms that deference had its limits. After all, they declared, they "had hitherto done Nothing inconsistent with our Duty to the best of Kings, with our Privileges as British subjects, the Dignity of Government, or the Character of good Subjects."[14]

These events east of the line signaled something amiss with the new system for the region west of the line.[15] As a Pennsylvania official argued, the "high Insult" to government and "the Cruelty of the Action" would have "fatal Consequences" for "Indian affairs."[16] As pressures mounted on the frontier, officials in America and London clung to the well-worn and comfortable assumptions that underscored the whole system. But retreating to the prevailing cultural blueprint of civility ensured that officials could not see the full extent of the challenge before them. On paper, the system looked consistent, taking shape around prevailing understandings of subjecthood and human difference. In practice, it created a host of problems. A plan devised to close the West off from eastern settlers ironically opened the West to more settlement. A system designed to ease hatreds between groups heightened them. A vision of empire intended to bring greater management to empire by dividing America between subject and non-subject regions, in fact, unleashed forces that could not be managed. And in such circumstances, deference and good faith, the keystones of sovereignty for the new system, stood little chance of defining the ways in which settlers and Indians would gauge British intent and engage empire. In short, the imperial plan was flawed.

In the months after the massacre, officials scrambled to address "a World of Complaints" west of the line.[17] Although officials had hoped that the region—after nearly ten years of warfare—was calming down, they feared a return to hostilities and fretted over the viability of the system they had created. Most alarmingly, as Johnson put it in late 1765, "there is little reason to expect that our People in general will ever treat the Indians with . . . kindness and civility."[18]

Tensions in the area were rising. Even after peace treaties were signed, Delawares and Shawnees continued their raids east of the mountains. The summer of 1764 proved particularly bloody.[19] Although the British could not expect savages to act like subjects, the scale of the attacks astonished officials. On May 26, 1764, for example, Indians fell on a party of settlers working near a fort in Augusta County, Virginia. They laid siege to the fort for six hours, killing and wounding fifteen and taking sixteen prisoner. About the same time, they took a slave driving a wagon, along with the man, woman, and child accompanying him.[20] And in one particularly grisly episode, six Indians attacked a pregnant Pennsylvania woman, whom they did "rip up" and scalp.[21]

To add to the confusion, the letter and the spirit of the royal proclamation were being ignored. Speculators were vying for lands west of the mountains, forming companies and dispatching surveyors, as if the Proclamation Line did not exist. These people had "reassumed their old conduct with regard to Lands. Sundry grants were projected and applied for in places most alarming to, and tenderly affecting the Indian's Rights."[22] Trade seemed out of control. Although officials recognized the importance of trade for civilizing Indians and for the benefit of the empire, they feared traders were working against these goals. Johnson argued they "excite troubles and disputes with the Indians to answer their private views" and use "every artifice to trade where they please without being restricted to the Posts." These men evaded inspection and traded what, when, and with whom they wanted.[23]

This free-for-all atmosphere compromised British strategy. Officials had gone to great lengths to ease tensions on the frontier. To quiet the mayhem in the West, commanders threatened Indians with chastisement, going so far as to organize an expedition into the Ohio Country to deal with renegades. At the same time, they dispatched subordinates to treat with Indians to bring peace to the region.[24] They also required that Indians return all the prisoners taken during the two previous wars, taking Indian hostages to ensure good faith. Throughout the summer of 1764 and into the spring of the following year, Delawares, Shawnees, and Mingoes came into Fort Pitt and other posts with the men, women, and children they had captured on raids over the previous decade and had adopted as their own. Many were women and young girls, some of whom had vanished when less than ten years of age.[25]

But even though captured family and friends were being handed over during this delicate time, settlers were killing Indians with abandon. Johnson found the "frontier inhabitants of Pennsylvania, Maryland, [and] Virginia" in a "spirit of Frenzy." "Under pretext of revenge for past injuries, tho' in manifest violation of British faith and the strength of the late Treaties," he declared, they "attacked, robbed and murdered sundry Indians of good character and still continue to do so, vowing vengeance against all that come in their way."[26]

Such attitudes puzzled officials. Why would settlers "grossly misuse all Indians they could find" when the British had made the peace "at a considerable loss and expence"? Johnson wondered.[27] It defied reason. Johnson cited a frightening example of what he meant. On August 20, 1766, a man who was to be executed "for an unparalleled murder committed on two squaws" bellowed at the gallows that "he thought it a meritorious act to kill Heathens, wherever they were found." Johnson ominously concluded that "this seems to be the opinion of all the common people."[28]

Officials informed settlers that Indians would kill them if they ventured over the line, yet men and women continued to go west. As well as "unprovoked violences and Murthers" committed on "Indians under the Protection of His Majesty," settlers were moving "on the Back of the Provinces, without proper authority and beyond the Limits prescribed by

His majesty's Royal Proclamation of 1763," a furious Shelburne intoned.[29] Johnson struggled to make sense of this galling lack of deference. He hoped "delinquents" would face justice, but by 1766 he had come to doubt it could happen. "The increasing licentiousness of the People of late leave me no reason to expect it, for they now bid defiance to Authority and think of settleing where they please . . . beyond the Bounds of any Province," he complained. "But what is worse" was that "they have murdered no less than 15 Indians within these few months past, in the back parts" of Pennsylvania and Virginia. Because of the general tenor of the population, he concluded, "Delinquents cannot be apprehended and some of them have been rescued and Gaols broken open to free them."[30] In short, as John Stuart put it, "these back settlers, pay little or no regard to Law or government."[31]

Such "back settlers," who refused to respect authority, moved over the line, and killed Indians without hesitation or condoned such behavior, posed the chief threat to the whole imperial system. Their actions inflamed Indians, inducing the "savages" to strike back in terrible ways. The bloody summer of 1764 proved that.[32] Johnson admitted that "there are faults on both sides; the Inhabitants will be imprudent, the Indians impertinent." Yet he placed the lion's share of the blame at the feet of settlers. They had, he declared, "a confirmed hatred for all Indians" and had "given many Instances of their Disregard to the Peace and Contempt of the Governments they live under."[33]

To understand this behavior was no mean task. Yet Johnson and almost all Crown and provincial authorities agreed on the reasons why settlers acted the way they did. They did so because of their distance from government. As they moved west, farther from the civilizing influences of society, men and women began devolving, becoming like "savages" themselves, unable to use their reason. Gage argued that the "lawless and Licentious Proceedings of the Frontier Inhabitants" could only be reversed if they were "kept within their Boundary's, and forced into a Subjection to the Laws."[34] Johnson agreed. "The weaknesses of the powers of Government" were to blame.[35] Conditions in the West transformed subjects into "low specimens of British abilities, honor and honesty."[36]

British and provincial officials saw things in the same light. Lord Hillsborough, who took over as head of the Board of Trade in late 1763, argued that "the lawless Disposition . . . too generally prevails in Settlements so far removed from the Check and Controul of Government."[37] Settlers west of the line had become like the Indians around them. Gage described thirty or forty people who had settled on the banks of the Ohio and had tumbled down the stadial ladder as "half naked, chiefly covered with loose, coarse, linnen Frocks, such as the Frontier People Manufacture for themselves, and paint, or colour with Bark." He explained that "they differ little from Indians in their Manner of Life. They have no means to purchase Clothing but by skins, and that induces them to hunt, and consequently to intrude on Indian hunting grounds." Unsettled, uncivilized, unrecognizable as subjects, they were, he said, "strollers."[38] Like the lazy French settlers corrupted by Indians in the Illinois Country, these people seemed to inhabit a strange position in a broader Atlantic world. Trapped somewhere between the civilizing influences they had encountered in the East or in Europe before migrating, they had now devolved as they moved farther and farther from the center; having moved into a region where subjects could not exist, they had ceased to act as subjects.[39]

For the imperial plan to function, officials had to come to terms with this side of the stadial equation. Unless degeneration could be checked, the whole system was imperiled. John Stuart put it this way: Because "such People" were "likely to involve the provinces in perpetual Disputes with the Indians," he wished the frontier was "possessed by industrious People from Brittain and Ireland or the German Protectorates." Even these would prove more civilized than the devolved settlers now in the West.[40] Subjects living in non-subject worlds appeared to men like Stuart as a perversion of the right order of things. Only those uncontaminated by distance from government, those who had not degenerated, could salvage order in the West.[41]

Arguments such as these should not strike us as surprising. After all, if notions of savagery, civility, and subjecthood underscored the imperial system in America, these concepts also offered a means to explain the stresses and strains to that system. But while theories of civility provided ready explanations for the causes, they did not necessarily offer the best explanations. In fact, their inability to remove their stadial lenses left officials unable to see the extent of the problems they were confronting.

Far from impeding access to the West, the royal proclamation had opened the floodgates to the region. The imperial plan, of course, did not stipulate that a government be formed in the Illinois Country. But in coming up with a workable scheme for the West, officials were at pains to draw a distinction between this region along the Mississippi and the rest of the area beyond the line. To ensure that the French would be in no position to corrupt the Indians and to redeem or make good subjects of the settlers there, officials could not consider the Illinois Country a non-subject region like the rest of the West. If settlers, as Gage had declared, were to enjoy rights, then government had to exist to guarantee those rights. This logic was not lost on eastern subjects.[42] Given the debates that went into drawing up a plan for the West, and because these debates hinged on the concept of subjecthood, they opened a gaping loophole that traders and speculators looked to exploit.

George Croghan, who had made a strong pitch before the board for exempting the Illinois Country from the rest of the West, led the charge in pressing for the settlement of the region. No sooner had he returned from London than he set out to take advantage of Illinois's exempt status. In the spring of 1765, Croghan left Fort Pitt with soldiers and neighboring Indians to "obtain possession of the Illinois." Croghan sought to accomplish a number of things. He was heading beyond the line as a go-between to inform western Indians of the new imperial arrangements. He also went as a Crown official, working with the military to secure abandoned French forts and posts to shore up the region. Finally, he left Fort Pitt as a trader and speculator, seeking profits in this area deemed a subject region by the board.[43] He did not make mention of any conflict of interest in pursuing these three objectives.

Nor did others. Indeed, with the promulgation of the royal proclamation, many men moved into the region as if it were business as usual. The imperial plan, of course, enshrined trade as a central feature of the civilizing mission. Enticing Indians to adopt the more civilized ways of subjects meant ensuring that a steady flow of European goods reached the West. Traders saw the main chance and took it. Less than a year after the new plan was put in place, Croghan was sending enormous amounts of goods down the Ohio River to the Illinois Country, including saddles, clothing, kettles, gunpowder, rifles, and rum.[44] In theory, each superintendent had a responsibility to ensure that only reputable men received licenses to trade. In practice, this proved impossible. No sooner had the imperial plan been put in motion than the number of traders began overwhelming Johnson and Stuart.[45] Johnson, for one, saw chaos. With the royal proclamation, he observed, "traders from all quarters now began to push to the

outposts with goods, the majority of whom . . . were as great strangers to
the Indians, as they were to the nature of the Trade."[46] In Johnson's estimation, they abused the system. "These people," he argued, "sell at their own
extravagant rates, blinding the Indians with one Article at a small price,
whilst they take what they please on another." Worse, he had no ability to
stop them. "As they are Subject to no Inspection, neither is there any Law
can be expected here to suppress them," he found.[47]

But old hands at the trade caused concerns as well. More seasoned
traders understood that success required stability, which in turn required
settlement. George Morgan, a principal of the leading Philadelphia trading firm Baynton, Wharton, and Morgan, pleaded with his partners out
east to press for the establishment of a civil government in the region. He
feared that unless a stable society could be created, he would have to send
his trade goods down the river to French-dominated New Orleans.[48] Both
the trade and British mercantile interests, therefore, depended on settlement in the region.[49]

Men like Morgan and Croghan understood that here lay real profits.
Before the wars and before the Proclamation Line was put in place, most
speculators hoped to seize land in the Ohio River valley. In the wake of the
royal proclamation, many shifted their gaze toward Illinois. Traders such
as Croghan hoped to use their knowledge of the Illinois Country and the
imperial system, as well as their experience with Indians, to speculate on
land. For his part, Croghan claimed that the losses by traders sustained
during the French and Indian War and Pontiac's War entitled them to
land in the West. These "suffering traders" banded together under
Croghan's leadership to form a land venture, initially focused on more
than a million acres in the Illinois Country. And such schemes, as Johnson put it, were "daily increasing."[50] American veterans of the Seven Years'
War petitioned for land along the Mississippi. Virginians and Marylanders, who previously had hoped to secure land in the Ohio Country, created their own ventures, the most famous of which was named the
Mississippi Company, which sought more than two million acres between
the Mississippi and the Wabash. Pennsylvania's Assembly made its own
bid for "possession of the Country of the Illinois." These companies relied
on the expertise and business sense of men such as Croghan—who was re-
cruited by a number of wealthy men and firms in Philadelphia and
Williamsburg to work for and join their companies—and Johnson.[51]

Speculators realized that for any scheme to work they had to cultivate influential friends. Croghan and Johnson tried to get Gage involved in their plans, but he would have nothing to do with them. Nonetheless, they found others who would, including Benjamin Franklin; Franklin's son, the governor of New Jersey, William Franklin; and wealthy Virginians such as George Washington, a member of the Mississippi Company and an advocate for veterans' claims to the Illinois Country.[52] These companies tended to be large concerns, outstripping their antecedents in scope and ambition. While most earlier speculative ventures measured land in thousands and tens of thousands of acres, newer western syndicates spoke in terms of hundreds of thousands and millions of acres.[53]

The new scale reflected the sheer amount of land available in the West. It also engendered the new imperial context that now defined the West. Companies tended to be transatlantic in composition. Patronage hierarchies stretched across the ocean in an effort to outflank the intent of the new secretary of state for the colonies, the Earl of Hillsborough, to leave the West untouched. Drawing on the connections of men such as Franklin, the new companies established offices in London, where they could lobby for settlement and try to get influential Britons involved in their schemes. Croghan had delicately felt the board out for such prospects when he had traveled to London to push for Johnson's western vision. After 1766, he and others pushed this agenda with abandon. Benjamin Franklin worked in London as an agent for a number of speculative concerns, as did Samuel Wharton of Philadelphia.[54] Virginians also hired a London agent.[55] For their part, Johnson and wealthy Virginians worked their connections with the Board of Trade.[56]

Agents and members of the companies used the most powerful arguments they could muster to press for settlement of the Illinois Country in the face of stubborn opposition from Hillsborough. They hammered on the theme of "the good of empire," touching on such issues as the mercantile interest and security in the region from French incursion and influence.[57] But the most prevalent rationale employed focused on the issue of subjecthood and redeemability. Croghan pointed out that the British should establish a settlement in "the Center of a prodigious, fine, and large, fertile Country," cultivating good relations with the Indians in the area and treating the settlers as valued subjects. "If civil government is immediately established there," he declared, "and the King's subjects are permitted to settle and mix there, with his new French Ones," the venture would flourish.[58] Success, in short, meant "reducing a wilderness country to a state of cultivation."[59]

In the civilizing scheme, such a plan would "preserve an uninterrupted Harmony and good Faith, between [the Indians] and the Inhabitants of the New Colony." Settlers would "live in Friendship and Brotherly Love" with Native Americans "in the same manner, that their Forefathers and William Penn, and the first Quakers, happily lived together, in Pennsylvania."[60] Good government could, they argued, "regain the Confidence of the natives which is allmost Lost for Some years past by a Shameful Neglect." Negotiating with the Indians for title to the land demonstrated respect for Indians as "an Independent People."[61] If the French could incite Indians to attack the frontiers, British influence could pacify them.[62]

Of course, the whole sordid enterprise based on patronage to lay claim to the Illinois Country smacked of greed, double-dealing, and corruption. But in the early modern British Atlantic system, such arrangements did not raise eyebrows. In fact, patronage networks made this world go round. The man most responsible for obstructing settlement earned his position in such a way. A trimmer if there ever was one, Hillsborough had arisen from the relative obscurity of a County Down landowner to earn Irish and British peerages. Marrying well and amassing vast estates, he had carefully cultivated connections with ins and outs in the British political establishment, and especially with the king, to wend his way up to his position on the board and in the ministry. Indeed, a dedicated pursuit of position made him who and what he was. And as Benjamin Franklin would charge, Hillsborough opposed expansion not out of principle but because he feared the lure of western land would empty his estates in the north of Ireland of tenants.[63]

When Croghan informed Johnson that "to a man" the Board of Trade "Seem'd of opinion that No Indian Agent Should Make any Contracks with Indians fer Lands or be Concern'd in Trade," Johnson dismissed such reasoning.[64] After all, "one half of England" was "Land mad and Every body there has thire Eys fixt on this Cuntry."[65] And in the minds of men like Johnson and Croghan, settling the Illinois Country served Indian and imperial interests and, crucially, jibed with the ideological program of the new plan of empire.[66] In the eyes of those involved, two systems of thought—one rooted in patronage, the other animating empire—did not conflict.

The renewed push for grabbing land west of the line in the face of the restrictions posed by the royal proclamation would have liberating yet dire implications for common settlers. The frenzy for speculation heralded a sea change for what had been a broadly accepted process of frontier development. Predominant patterns of landholding that had given shape to older frontier regions in Pennsylvania and Virginia did not emerge as part of a grand settlement strategy or through a formalized system; rather, in both regions, strategies were contingent on the timing of migration, political and legal concerns, and availability of land. That said, in both places wealthy and poor understood how to get ahead and acted on it. In southeast Pennsylvania during the first great waves of eighteenth-century settlement, settlers, or at times squatters, moved onto unoccupied land. Speculators then laid claim to these and contiguous areas, allowing the earliest settlers to claim land through improvement while pushing off recent arrivals. Land could then be sold to new settlers, and speculators could expect to make tidy profits. The system functioned because even if squatters were warned off and even as prices escalated in more developed areas, there was always more land to settle. The process would then grip these new regions, and in the meantime wildernesses, as contemporaries styled them, would be transformed into settled societies.[67]

The model that prevailed in the Valley of Virginia, though differing from the Pennsylvania pattern in fundamental ways, also allowed poorer people to settle land easily. As soon as prices began rising in places like Lancaster County, Pennsylvania, in the 1740s, young men and women and newly arrived migrants looked south on the eastern edge of the Appalachians for available land. Officials in Virginia encouraged settlement in the "Great Valley"—or Shenandoah—hoping that new homesteads peopled by white Protestant farmers would create a deterrent hedge against potential incursions of western Indians allied with the French. Successive governors granted tracts, measured in tens of thousands of acres, to influential men who hoped to make profits provided they enticed new settlers to the region. The stipulations of their grants, however, ensured that although land would not be free, it would be cheap. Squatters came, yet speculators welcomed them so long as they agreed to legalize and purchase their holdings once they had improved the land or after they had worked it as tenants. If settlers acted in a deferential manner, as they usually did, the system functioned for the benefit of all.[68]

The process that grew out of the two patterns kept social friction at a minimum. The availability of land farther south of Pennsylvania ensured that poorer men and women had somewhere to turn and that perhaps some of them, with luck, could speculate as well. As long as individuals looking for cheap land could travel down the Great Wagon Road on the eastern side of the Appalachians, social unrest did not compromise the way things worked. And here settlers had found stable, well-integrated communities. Throughout most of the eighteenth century, the process worked without many glitches. Many settlement regions east of the mountains, such as the Shenandoah Valley, contained relatively few Indians. Where Indians did live in some numbers, they did not prove hostile, agreed to land cessions, or moved west over the Appalachian Mountains. Indeed, throughout the first half of the eighteenth century, when large numbers of migrants were looking for land, settlers enjoyed a long and unprecedented period of peace on the Pennsylvania and Virginia frontiers.[69] And during periods when migration from overseas surged, especially in the late 1720s, early '40s, and early '50s, land remained available. If Indians did prove hostile, government officials, who had a stake in a functioning system, had good reason to provide some sort of rudimentary defense arrangements for inhabitants.

After 1763, however, frontier America faced a crisis. After the Treaty of Paris was signed, the number of immigrants arriving in New Castle and Philadelphia, as well as Charleston and Baltimore, reached unprecedented levels. Moreover, many of the poorest could no longer afford to settle land in the East. Land prices in southeast Pennsylvania had soared. The Shenandoah Valley had become a settled, populous society by the end of the Seven Years' War with few opportunities for the poorer sort.[70] Settlers could look farther south in the backcountries of the Carolinas as officials in both colonies scrambled to divide their frontiers into counties and to regulate settlement. Many who traveled here in the 1760s, however, encountered a quickly growing, competitive, and tense world that had just witnessed a destructive war against Cherokees and that easterners and local elites were vying to dominate.[71]

Or settlers could look to cross the line. Here, of course, they would face the justifiable wrath of large numbers of "hostile" Indians who had spent the previous ten years in combat with the British and their subjects. And they would be competing with speculating conglomerates that hoped to make a killing. After all, wealthy speculators using powerful connections vied for millions of acres west of the line in an attempt to formalize this informal process of development and to beat squatters to the region. But while the risks were great for common men and women, so, too, were the opportunities. In proscribing speculation and the establishment of government in the West, the royal proclamation, ironically, also provided an umbrella of protection for settlers. The West, now connected to the East by Braddock's Road and Forbes's Road, was a realm beyond law. There were no courts to evict, no laws to protect the interests of the wealthy, no speculative grants to safeguard. In short, the world beyond the line lay beyond regulation. In making the region a "no-man's-land," the proclamation created a land of possibilities for the desperate. If the poor could rely on the older frontier formula of making improvements, they could preempt those speculators who sought to preempt the older land settlement process. For those facing constrained circumstances, the West seemed to offer some hope.[72]

To some extent, officials recognized this push-pull dilemma. The Lords of Trade, for instance, understood the lure of the West. "Exposed to few hardships and struggling with few Difficulties," settlers could expect "with little labour [to] earn an Abundance for their own wants." But since members of the board would not reconsider their position on the West, and since such settlements would not benefit the British economy, the West would lay fallow.[73] Moreover, they expected that prospective settlers looking for land would head to the newly acquired provinces of Nova Scotia and the Floridas. Here, after all, they would find governments and could serve the larger imperial and commercial goals of the British. But officials provided no transportation or incentive to move to these regions. Migrants could walk over the mountains; they could not walk to Nova Scotia.

The constraints prospective settlers faced created unprecedented opportunities for large-scale speculators. More potential settlers meant more money to be made while offering little incentive to provide them safeguards. Under these conditions, members of the great companies were "excited by the near prospect of immediate and considerable Profit." Speculators realized that "a large Body of Land in that [the western] Country will soon be worth money" because "the people are so desirous for settling it," as a well-connected Virginian put it.[74] It behooved them, therefore, to press harder for their schemes.[75]

Under such pressures, the older process of frontier development could

not work. In its place a new, perverted process emerged. A generation before, on earlier frontiers, either settlers or speculators took the initiative in
settling the land. Out West, it would be neither or both. Instead of allowing settlers to "improve" land before moving in, speculators from large
companies kept land "in Reserve waiting for the extinction of the Indians,
or the encrease in value of Lands to the prejudice of all those who want to
occupy . . . small Tracts." Because the Indians in the West showed no signs
of "extinction," they chose the latter course, in the process giving "the utmost discontent to the Indians."[76] The creation of transatlantic networks of
patronage and speculation further eroded the informal nature of frontier
settlement, involving more and more officials far removed from the realities of frontier life and indifferent to the constraints common people faced
or the violence they would confront. Yet because no institutions as by law
established could exist, squatting was widespread in the region.[77]

The perversion of the process spawned a new type of creature who epitomized the changing nature of the frontier: the land jobber. Part squatter,
part entrepreneur, these men went west to scout out the best sites for the
companies. In the bargain, they gained fair-sized holdings for themselves.
As Johnson explained it, once these "Land Jobbers" heard of an available
tract, "they immediately set about engaging two or three Indians to set
their Mark to a Deed which a little liquor and a small present soon affected," leading to further "Jealousy and Defection" among Indians.[78]
Johnson should not have been one to talk. The scheme he and Croghan
had concocted relied on such "low" men. They enlisted the services of
other traders and petty speculators, such as Alexander McKee and Thomas
Cresap.[79] While Cresap's son, Michael, served as an "agent" for George
Washington in the West, other frontier notables, such as Simon Girty and
Michael Stoner, worked for Morgan.[80] These men went to great lengths
to "seduce" Indians, offering even guns as concessions for land.[81]

The land jobbers would work the Indians while the well-connected
lobbied the ministry.[82] Speculating elites refused to raise men for defense,
while at the same time they had little regard for "how much they may irritate the Indians by their unfair purchases or claims."[83] If the poorer sort
wished to move west of the line, this is the world they would enter. If they
expected to stay one step ahead of speculators and land jobbers, they
would do so without protection and against the wishes of the British government. In effect, they faced a choice between their competency and the

rights of "savages." In the years after the Proclamation Line was put in place, the choice would not prove difficult.

Although settlers crossing the line were heading into land that "belonged" to Indians, few had moral reservations about doing so. In fact, many harbored or condoned a violent hatred of Indians. Officials viewed this troubling phenomenon through stadial lenses, claiming that frontier men and women had become as savage as Indians. But the explanation for Indian hating, at this point anyway, was much simpler and more troubling. Frontier people condoned Indian slaughter because of what Indians had done. Settlers conceded that they were "partly demented by their own surmises"—that is, their perceptions of reality in a brutal world—but asserted that Indian hatred stemmed from "their late sufferings under Savage Cruelty."[84] Settlers moving west of the line, in the words of Thomas Cresap, despaired of "being Massicread by a Barberous and Inhuman Enemy" and being "Butchered without Immediate Relief and Assistance."[85] If settlers struggled with inner conflicts or doubts, they did not revolve around self-perception at this point, but had more to do with the ways they understood Indians in the midst of continuing conflict and violence. In the minds of people like Cresap, Indians, not settlers, inhabited a space somewhere between "savagery" and nonhuman status. In the development of these ideas, what Indians did, not what they represented, mattered.

In effect, the British had developed a system based on the redeemability of Indians at a time when few on the frontier could entertain such ideas. Beginning in 1754, men and women on America's frontier endured all the horrors of a brutal war. Certainly, large numbers were killed or captured. But statistics alone obscure the nature of frontier violence. People did not just die or children simply vanish; rather, they did so in appalling ways. In May 1763, for example, as men and women from the region struggled to reach the safety of Fort Pitt, a raiding party led by a Delaware named Wolfe killed a number of women "in such a brutal manner that Decency forbids the Mentioning."[86] Thomas Cresap witnessed an Indian raider stabbing his neighbor in the back before tearing "his Ribs from the Backbone."[87] In 1763 near Fort Pitt alone, thirty-one people had been killed by Indians in less than two months. Among that number were two boys named Collins and Sullivan, who were "killed and scalped"; a man beheaded; a family, including mother, father, grandfather, five sons, and one daughter, "killed"; and the two Delong sisters, who were scalped but not killed. During the same period, even more people died in Cumberland County "Eastward of the Allegheny Mountains." In all, 170 settlers perished in the frontier region near Fort Pitt during that time.[88] Other areas west of the line experienced much the same. In June 1764, for example, Indians killed or took twenty-eight people in one region south of the Ohio River.[89]

Raiders did not spare cultural go-betweens. In the area to the west of the fort, nearly twenty traders—including Lazarus Lowry, who had been working on the frontier with Indians for more than twenty years—and eighty-eight of their servants were killed or taken.[90] An immigrant from Ireland like Croghan, Lowry was killed along with John Quigley by a Shawnee named Wapthamy. Others murdered included men much like Croghan, named Patrick Moran, John Farrell, Patrick Guin, William Lunehehan, Patrick Neal, Patrick Dunn, Matthew McCrea, and William McGuire—traders and indentured servants all—at the hands of Delawares and Shawnees.[91]

Areas as far east as the Susquehanna River experienced prolonged suffering. A migrant to Pennsylvania's frontier, James McCullough, cataloged the fortunes of men and women in the area around Paxton during the 1750s. In July 1756, Indians captured his sons John and James. A month later he recorded "a verey great Slaughter . . . by the indins Wherin 39 persons killed and taken Captives." In November, John Woods, his wife, mother-in-law, and John Archer's wife—McCullough's friends and neighbors—were killed, along with eight or nine other men. Four children were also "Carried off." The carnage continued for years. More killings, more scalpings, more captives, including "11 persons killed at paxton by the indins" in May 1757 and "a very great Slaughter" near Opequon in the Shenandoah in which there were "60 odd killed and taken captive."[92]

For ten years, therefore, men and women from regions such as Paxton and Opequon, where new settlers west of the line would come from or through, had confronted direct threats to their lives, liberty, and property on a regular basis. To be sure, they returned such behavior in kind. When Thomas Cresap's friend, for instance, suffered at the hands of the enemy, his youngest son shot and scalped the Indian.[93] But in the eyes of most men and women on the frontier, only settlers had legitimate grievances. During the wars, William Johnson noted, inhabitants "were murdered, their families ruined, several fine settlements totally destroyed, many of the people carried into captivity among distant Nations, [and] a still greater number killed." Of the "old" traders, such as Lowry, "few had survived." Those who survived, he concluded, "were discouraged."[94]

The "discouraged" could not even entertain the possibility of Indian redeemability. Certainly, apologists for the Paxton Boys' butchery could not. Before the era of violence, they argued, "Pennsylvania was flourishing in Prosperity and Plenty," until, that is, "their Savage Neighbours" attacked. The West then "became wretched and deplorable beyond Description." They claimed that "Great Numbers of the back Settlers were murdered, scalped and butchered, in the most shocking Manner, and their dead Bodies inhumanly mangled." They recounted—and no doubt exaggerated—myriad horrors in detail, including skulls smashed, ribs ripped out, and children "spitted alive and roasted." Indians, they claimed, had captured and tortured hundreds "in every Method of Cruelty which Indian Barbarity can suggest." And tragically, Indian barbarity forced them to "live even worse than the Savages themselves."[95]

But in the apologists' minds, they had not become savages amid savagery. Justifications for the murderous rampage of the Paxton Boys were written, in part, to discredit the Pennsylvania government that did not aid the "bleeding frontier." For these writers, only frontier men and women retained a higher moral vision. Ironically, the polite and pacifist Quakers of Philadelphia had lost touch with the "common Feelings of Humanity," which Indians lacked and which defined civility. Neither group could be "Friends to Liberty." If the Quakers had not become barbarians, settlers wondered, how could they "be so liberal to Savages, and at the same Time not contribute a single Farthing as a Society to help our Distresses"?[96]

At issue, therefore, was civility. Although the peaceful Conestogoes lived east of the line, where civilizing sensibilities should have taken root, they had become "rum debauched and Trader corrupted Thieves and vagabonds," a people "indisputably unfaithful and perfidious." In fact, these Indians acted almost like an independent "little commonwealth" out of step with subjects in the area, aiding and abetting their allies to the west, who lived under no government. Echoing the sensibilities of officials who drew up the imperial plan—but twisting their logic—settlers suggested that a "savage" *imperium* could not exist within a "civilized" *imperio*.[97]

Using such reasoning, they could not stomach the types of arguments that officials used to defend the Indians. In particular, they bridled at the ways Pennsylvanians were "able to extenuate these horrid Barbarities, under the charitable Plea of its being their Custom of making War." Custom meant culture. If Indians killed in horrific ways, Quakers seemed to suggest, they did so because their culture languished in a savage stage of development. Settlers accepted this reasoning, but they did not accept the implications. Living in Philadelphia, Quakers had the luxury of explaining away the reasons for Indian savagery. Frontier settlers did not. And though settlers claimed that officials were "maliciously painting" them "in the most odious and detestable Colours," they did not demonize Indians as "reddish," as Benjamin Franklin suggested. While they referred to themselves as "White People," they accepted the same cultural assumptions that led Quakers to defend Indian "custom." For example, they agreed that the French had "instigated the Indians," suggesting that they, too, saw Indians as empty vessels. Moreover, they did not view all Indians as inhuman enemies. For instance, they regarded the Iroquois as a group that had "ever retained some reputation for Honour and Fidelity" as allies. Although the Quakers had called into question their own civility by refusing to defend the frontiers, even these savages, the apologists argued, had the good sense to make war on the Delawares in the West and had "shook them by the Hair of the Head, as they express it."[98]

Although the Paxton Boys killed with a genocidal mania, most who condoned the murders did not embrace what we could call an essentialist or modern notion of difference. But they employed its language, creating an often muddled and not fully consistent idea of what Indians were and their relationship to society. While they claimed to talk as "white people," they did not view Indians as an alien race and did not refer to Indians by their physical features. They did not, in other words, reject cultural models of understanding difference. Like officials, they considered Indians a "savage" people; unlike officials, they refused to wait for the day when civility would transform Indian culture. Therefore, the templates they used for making sense of human difference remained cultural, but at times the idiom or language that informed those templates was premised on physical characteristics. Frontier settlers during periods of tension inhabited a murky world of meaning in which the cultural mingled often uncomfortably with the essential. Supporters of the Paxton Boys declared the Indians "Wolf-like," but conceded that savagely callous, yet white, Quakers and Indians "were the same." Even though "they are all Perfidious," they still could be "reduced to reason."[99] In short, while the official ideology of the West and the ideological frameworks of settlers were based on a premodern formula that stipulated that Indians were fully human, realities on the ground were pushing in other directions.[100]

During this period of dire stress, even enthusiastic supporters of Indian redeemability dropped such linear thinking. In doing so, they revealed another side of stadial theory. The "sudden, treacherous and unprovoked attack, made by the Indians upon the frontiers of Pennsylvania, Maryland, and Virginia, soon after the publication of the general Peace," made William Smith reconsider the whole civility project. Instead of the civilizing influences of religion flourishing in the West, he beheld "savage enemies afresh on our frontiers, ravaging and murdering with their usual barbarity."[101] He did not doubt that religion in theory could civilize. The issue was one of time.

If Indians lived in the West unmolested, then they would have the time and space necessary to develop. But if whites crossed the line—as they were doing—time was no longer on the side of Indians. In other words, if white and Indian worlds kept colliding, Indians would remain in a savage state and continue to kill, capture, and torture whites. In such circumstances, stadial time literally stood still, and cultural development stalled, dooming any civilizing mission to failure and allowing the insertion of an idiom of race into the premodern framework. Note what Thomas Barton, who like Smith championed the civility project, had to say about Indians during periods of tension. Unlike Smith, Barton lived on the frontier, in Cumberland County, Pennsylvania. When Indians attacked in 1764, he did not attempt to make sense of such behavior. He summed Indians up as "faithless wretches."[102] And he had no scruples about defending their murder. In that year, he wrote his own apology for the Paxton Boys, calling the Indians "perfidious Villains," "heathens," "idle vagabonds," "Cruel Monsters," and "barbarians," mixing the cultural with the essential.[103] The Paxton Boys had the right to take the lives of the Conestogoes. After all, in turning "free born subjects of Britain" and the "brave and Industrious Sons of Pennsylvania" into a people "naked and defenceless," Indians had robbed settlers of their tokens of civility and their mantle of subjecthood. The Conestogoes had not embraced civility, and for that they received their just deserts. These "treacherous Savages . . . by their perfidy, had forfeited their Lives."[104]

Barton revealed a much darker aspect of the stadial vision. And he had done so once before in clearer terms. If pliable Indians who cooperated with the civilizers could be redeemed, recalcitrant ones who refused to allow whites to civilize them had to be chastised. At the height of the Seven Years' War, when Indian raiding parties from the Ohio Country headed east to decimate white settlements on the frontier, Barton wrote an infamous pamphlet titled *Unanimity and Public Spirit*. In it, he called for "Support of our common protestant cause . . . in this time of Public Danger." The Indians in this piece come off as savages engaged in an "inhuman" enterprise inflicting "the Horrors of a Savage War" on "our pure Protestant Faith, our equitable Laws, and our sacred Liberties." Their "resentments" he found "implacable," and their cause "unrighteous." To complicate matters, the French had whipped Indians into this frenzy. "Romish artifice and Knavery" lay behind "savagery." The French Catholic "Sons of Violence" had corrupted the "Savages" beyond the point of redemption. Such a combination promised to do the same to Protestant settlers in America, turning them into "Brutes" and rendering "reason useless." Unless Protestants united to defeat the common foe, they, too, could degenerate like the Indians around them.[105]

Barton's pamphlet portrayed Indians an awful lot like rebellious Irish Papists and Scottish Highlanders, and it reads as if it could have been published during any moment of Catholic-Protestant tension in Britain. In fact, it was. Barton had plagiarized his sermon from one published in London, Dublin, and Belfast during the 1745 Jacobite invasion. By likening Indians to savage, plotting Papists or barbarous clans, he was equating them with bogeys easily identifiable to his contemporaries. By viewing Indians like these groups beyond the pale, Barton was tapping into a deep well of myth and collective memory from whence the stadial notions that he subscribed to had sprung. And as the English had treated such recalcitrant groups in the past, so men and women in the present were justified in treating Indians.[106]

The most pressing and frightening problem the British faced in making their plan work in the West was that these views were shared not only by butchers like the Paxton Boys and missionaries but by nearly all men and women on the frontier. Johnson wrote in despair, "I am so well convinced of the Utter aversion our People have for them in General, and of the imprudence with which they constantly express it."[107] A local official south of the Ohio River complained that the "disposition" of men and women there was "as bad as the Savages."[108] Settlers refused to allow their neighbors to stand trial if they killed Indians. Gage argued that "the Difficulty of bringing those lawless Ruffians to punishment encourages them to every Excess . . . If by chance apprehended, they are rescued, and it is said that bringing them to tryal signifies little, as No Jury wou'd condemn them for murdering or ill treating an Indian."[109]

As they transgressed the line, therefore, settlers also contested the assumptions upon which the line was drawn. Yet even as they used arguments that betokened stadial assumptions, they were articulating something more troubling. They saw themselves as "white," after all. And they refused to believe that Indians in the West differed from Indians in the East. They both were uncivilized. The question was, Were they civilizable? Unwilling to wait for civility to take hold, settlers refused even to entertain such questions. What had emerged on the frontier was a frightening spectrum of opinion ranging from the genocidal impulses of the few to the darker interpretation of the stadial vision of the many, the merger of the premodern and the modern. Frontier settlers did not challenge the bases of British notions of civility—they agreed with them—but in the midst of violence they contested the implications of the civilizing scheme.[110]

As settlers crossed the Proclamation Line, therefore, they entered "a savage unexplor'd country; without roads; without posts," as William Smith put it.[111] They confronted provincial officials "void of compassion," who left them to fend for themselves if they dared cross the line. Land jobbers thwarted their chances of settling the best lands, and traders sold weapons to their enemies. The French, who had "excite[d] and assist[ed] the Indians," might be gone, but now other whites played such a role. Speculators, "bent upon enriching themselves," did not care about their concerns. And of course, they had to face a "savage enemy." If something was not done to put an end to such a conspiracy, "disagreeable disorders among the people" would continue.[112] In other words, the system designed to run on deference, based on a vision of Indian redeemability, and premised on a separation of subject and non-subject lands would confront a people who had little choice but to cross the line, who questioned the redeemability of the savages, and who showed little inclination for acting in a deferential manner.[113]

The imperial plan also required Indians to act in good faith. For the system to function, they had to accept the fine distinction between Indian ownership of the land west of the line and British sovereignty over it. And of course, they had to buy into the civilizing mission. But the flaws inherent in the system that led to landgrabs and unrestrained trade, as well as the movement of Indian-hating whites into the region, ensured that Indians, too, would question the system. They feared that they, too, were the subject of a conspiracy. The disorders in the West "have made us look less in the Indian eyes than ever," argued William Johnson. "They are," he continued, "greatly disgusted at the Ill treatment of their own People, alarmed at the specious Words of Subjection and Dominion, and astonished at the granting of Lands within their Rights."[114] In short, they rejected the paternalistic logic of a system they had no hand in drawing up and the civilizing mission it entailed.

Indians had good reason to be alarmed. "The Western Indians," Johnson claimed, "have heard of the grants of land in that Country, and the Assertion that they acknowledged themselves to be subjects." Such a claim ensured that "their jealousy will be inflamed."[115] They also rejected the way the trade was regulated. Instead of honest traders plying the stuff they desired, unworthy men peddled things they did not need.[116] Daily "insults and indignities" led them to doubt British motives. Most alarming, frontier settlers "began under the spacious pretence of Revenge, but in violation of the British faith, to murder, Robb and otherwise grossly misuse all Indians they could find."[117] Looking east from Indian country, one did not have to make a great imaginative leap to believe that the British intended "to plant colonies in the heart of their country."[118]

In such circumstances, Indians had little choice but to defend their lives, liberty, and property. In particular, younger men who saw their hunting grounds taken over, their relations slaughtered, and posts and settlements arising in their lands would not be restrained. They attacked traders, killed what they called "Virginians"—the catch-all term for land-hungry whites entering the country that "belonged" to them—who made their way down the Ohio River, and savaged white hunters.[119]

The ideological blinders that officials donned did not allow them to understand the scope of Indian resistance or, just as crucial, the forms that it took. Stadial lenses tended to lump all Indians together without regard to the decentralized nature of Indian communities. Although officials broke down Native Americans into distinctive groups, such as Delawares and

Shawnees, their reliance on civilizing rhetoric downplayed the ways in which even these communities were not sovereign entities that could "control" their wayward and young members, but rather cultural amalgams of peoples tied together by kin and place. Certainly, men such as Johnson and Croghan understood the complex nature of Indian polities. But the ideology they espoused foreclosed the possibility of dealing with Indians on their own terms, as groups of peoples divided and energized by generational and regional differences. By failing to see diverse Indian communities for what they were, officials ironically cultivated a concerted Indian resistance that they could not comprehend.[120] In other words, because Indians refused to be defined by the ethnocentric myth that supported the whole British imperial system for the West, they proved a threat in ways that officials in Britain could not literally conceive. The good faith necessary to make the imperial plan work, therefore, was foundering between officials who had to defend a system that Indians were finding odious and Indians who sensed an official conspiracy to rob them of their lands.[121]

While officials were trying to make sense of the mess they confronted, a fresh outrage occurred, one that would have grave implications for the imperial plan for the West and reveal how the flaws in the system were widening into cracks in the empire. In December 1764, as the West was descending once more into violence, Col. Henry Bouquet reported, "I have heard by Chance that some of the Maryland Volunteers"—county militias who had taken part in his abortive march to Shawnee settlements in the Ohio Country—"have murdered an Indian at Pittsburgh." Not only did they kill an Indian in the settlement arising around Fort Pitt, but they also "had the Impudence to bring the Scalp to the settlements, and to produce it publickly with Circumstances too odious to be repeated." The volunteers, in other words, were parading their grisly trophy and whipping up the Indian-hating rabble. To make matters worse, "another gang of Similar Villains are actually in the Woods, with the Same Perfidious Intentions." Behind the line and beyond the line, these vigilantes were roaming.[122]

More troublingly, Bouquet found out that of all people, a "Mr. John Wolgomat," who commanded a company of Maryland militia, "produced publickly" the scalp that belonged not to a faceless Indian but to a "Deputy of the Shawnee" who was being held at Fort Pitt to guarantee the safe return of captives. It especially galled Bouquet that a man who held a position of authority would do such a thing no sooner than the ink had dried on "the Treaty I have made with them" and after he had ordered that "those Nations were for the future to be treated as friends." Although volunteers were under pain of death not to harm Indians, Wolgomat would not arrest a man named James Bow, who had killed and scalped the Shawnee official. On the contrary, Wolgomat had the audacity to display the scalp to a number of justices of the peace in frontier regions.[123] And they did nothing. As a Maryland official lamented, Bow or Wolgomat "could not be convicted of Murder in any Court in this Province."[124] Bouquet worried. "The Licentiousness of the Frontier Inhabitants," he wrote, "in general is carried to a high degree, and unless Severe Measures are taken to restrain them within proper Bounds . . . it will be impossible to preserve Peace with the Indians."[125] As they had learned from the Paxton affair, violent subjects who did not defer to officials could only be reined in by authority. Otherwise such sentiments, if further unrestrained and permitted to become politicized, could threaten any political arrangement.

Bouquet was right to worry about "bounds" geographic and metaphorical, as well as what one official called "the Instability of the present system."[126] No sooner had the new system been put in place than officials like William Johnson realized that something was amiss. At its heart, a plan so consistent on paper unleashed and enabled forces and tensions that officials could not fully comprehend. Without the deference of subjects, without the good faith of Indians in the West, with hatreds between the two groups escalating, and with pressures mounting from traders and speculators, officials now confronted a crisis of empire. To salvage this empire, they had to see beyond the assumptions that sustained it. But this they seemed unable to do.[127]

THREE

Abandoning the Line:
The Failure of Empire in the West

The British, of course, had a ready remedy for buttressing a weakened empire. They could vanquish the Indians. In 1766, William Johnson considered this option. "There are but two methods in our power," he intoned. "We must destroy them all, or make them all satisfied and easy." Johnson still placed his faith in the second proposition, which he did not judge as "so difficult a Task as the prejudiced may pretend, and consists only in dealing justly with them in redressing their grievances."[1] We should not, however, dismiss the first option out of hand.

Just as the civilizing mission could protect Indians in a sanctuary in the West, it also could justify their destruction. After all, such a dynamic had worked with brutal efficiency in the past. The Irish and Scottish blueprints that officials had used to make sense of Indians had also underwritten the slaughter and dispossession of the native Irish and the destruction of Highland culture under the veil of "civility" as English officials either sponsored conquest or turned a blind eye as planters did so in their name. Enlightenment rationality that underscored the stadial approach to understanding indigenous peoples also contained a darker side that could rationalize the destruction of native peoples. These formulas for making sense of others had paved the way for English dominance in the marches in the seventeenth and eighteenth centuries and British mastery of the subcontinent of India in the nineteenth. By 1766, officials such as Johnson were contending with enormous pressures to adapt this approach to the American West as white settlers clamored for the British to support them against Indians.[2]

Perhaps, therefore, instead of asking whether or why the British failed to protect Indians from marauding whites in the West, we should ask why the British did not decimate them. The reason was not that the British had become enlightened by the mid-eighteenth century. Put simply, the British could not afford to follow the formula for conquest. In dealing with crises in the western empire, officials faced the same financial constraints they confronted in trying to include the eastern colonies in a British national system of rights and responsibilities. The need to raise money in the East to ease the burden of debt from the Seven Years' War meant keeping costs down in the West. Conquering Indians would require men and money, both in short supply. Indeed, conquest or even aggressive chastisement would embroil Britain in another enormously expensive war, one that the British feared would bring the French back into the fray.

With the imperial system faltering and the West on the brink of chaos, officials had little choice but to follow Johnson's second proposal. But by doing so, they allowed white settlers, who saw each measure to protect Indians as an attempt to appease an implacable enemy, to set the agenda for imperial governance. The imperial plan as it stood—tethered to an all too permeable Proclamation Line—had no chance of success if settlers did not act in a deferential manner. And given the constraints they faced, this they would not do. In other words, officials lost control of the debate over the West.

In the face of withering challenges to the system, the British began abandoning the imperial plan. The end began as authorities debated the merits of firming up the line or bending it in the face of growing tensions and pressures. Either the West needed government and law to make the line impregnable, or regions west of the line where tensions were greatest should be ceded to subjects from the East. Although officials believed that each approach entailed extending a more rigorous model of sovereignty to the West, they were in fact weakening imperial authority. For a start, shifting the terms of debate over sovereignty from subjecthood to law and institutions removed the possibility that the West would be unmolested. More to the point, either solution undermined the ideology that sustained the imperial plan because both posited that the West had to become a subject region. Therefore, with the debate over the direction of the imperial system, the ideological rationale for keeping the West free from settlement vanished. Although both approaches aimed at restraining white hunger for Indian land, each ensured that speculators and settlers could stake claims where they liked without justification.[3]

The imperial system may have made the West difficult to manage; its abandonment would make the region impossible to manage. By the early 1770s, officials on both sides of the ocean realized as much. "While we are complaining of Injurys and patching up Quarrells in one part," an exasperated Gage explained, "we draw complaints against ourselves in others, by the Misconduct of the Vagabonds who steal into the Deserts."[4] So long as the British refused to sanction force to restrain whites or to vanquish Indians, they could please neither. The empire was cracking apart along the fault lines of its inherent flaws. With violence spreading, speculation rampant, and settlement unchecked, sustaining a plan based on deference and good faith proved delusional. Authorities therefore decided to cede the West to the chaos engulfing it. Maintaining nominal sovereignty over the region, but marching out troops, redirecting resources, and dismantling forts, they abandoned the West a few years after they began abandoning their imperial ideology.

The beginning of the end for British empire in America occurred not in Boston or Philadelphia but on the Pennsylvania frontier near the Proclamation Line. On March 6, 1765, less than seventy-two hours after Britain's prime minister, George Grenville, convened Parliament to discuss America's duties to the British state and to propose the passage of a stamp act, two hundred "Brave Fellows" or "Black Boys," so called for their blackened faces, gathered at a place in the Appalachian Mountains called Sideling Hill to stop a wagon train heading from Philadelphia to Fort Pitt with goods for Indians. Henry Bouquet, now commanding at Fort Pitt, had ordered presents to seal a peace with Indians from the Ohio Country who had been attacking frontier settlements and British posts and to help "cover the death" of the Shawnee deputy murdered and scalped by the Maryland militia.[5] The goods, including wampum and European manufactured items, would, Bouquet hoped, show the good faith of British negotiators and help ease the growing tensions in the region.[6] The goods therefore had significance far beyond their monetary value. They represented nothing less than the stuff of British empire in America.

George Croghan assembled the goods in Philadelphia in February 1765 before heading to Fort Pitt to make ready for the conference between the British and the Indians. Croghan agreed that the goods should be distributed to alleviate Shawnee mourning and to demonstrate British resolve to hold the line against settlers. But he also saw the mission as a means to establish trade in the Illinois Country and to pave the way for settlement of the region. As an accomplished trader, speculator, and frontier diplomat, he was, after all, only doing what the system allowed. Croghan made arrangements with his business partners in the firm Baynton, Wharton, and Morgan to prepare to ship the goods to Fort Pitt. After he arrived at the fort, he instructed the troops to dole out goods from their stores to Indians arriving early because snow had delayed the shipment from Philadelphia.[7]

After a break in the weather, drivers finally starting hauling the goods west via Carlisle. Elias Davison, one of these men, packed forty-nine horse loads for what he could expect to be an arduous and bitterly cold trip west over the mountains. But on nearing the continental divide in central Pennsylvania on the morning of March 5, he ran into a different sort of trouble. Near William Maxwell's place, a group of Black Boys stopped his train, warning him against proceeding over the mountains. Nonetheless, he continued west. A few miles farther on, fifty armed men accosted him, informing Davison all his goods would be destroyed.[8] Another driver, Robert Allison, received more pointed warnings. If he did not turn his train with thirty-two horse loads around, "they would blow his brains out."[9] Davison, conscious of the great cost of his goods, asked if he "could return back with the goods Rather they should be destroyed." The frontiersmen from Pennsylvania replied that if they or their neighbors did not destroy the goods, "the Virginians would stop him at the foot of Sidling Hill," one of the great wavelike ridges of the Appalachians.[10]

The train progressed westward, but the words of the Pennsylvanians proved prophetic. At one in the afternoon of the next day, the Black Boys were running about Sideling Hill "hollowing and shooting." They shot one of the horses and informed the drivers in no uncertain terms that "if they did not leave the Goods and go off the Ground with the Horses in 15 Minutes they would shoot [the rest of] the Horses." The drivers did as they were bid, leaving most of their eighty-one loads. As they peered over their shoulders heading east, the last thing they saw was their goods aflame.[11] All in all, the rioters burned sixty-three loads of goods and killed four horses. They spared a few kegs of rum, afraid they were filled with powder.[12] But they stole nothing, leaving behind what they did not destroy.

On hearing of the incident, the British, who manned a frontier post a few miles east of Sideling Hill, dispatched troops. They caught up with a few Black Boys and dragged them back to Fort Loudoun. The commander at the small outpost, Charles Grant, reported that "the Country People is raising in Arms" and were "determined to Rescue them if possible." Two hundred men descended on the fort, threatening to set it aflame. Grant ordered his men under arms, but—no fool—he turned the suspects over to the local civil authorities, who judiciously released the men on bail.[13]

The Black Boys would never be recaptured. Authorities made some noise—muted at best—about getting to the bottom of the affair, but to no consequence. The proprietor of Pennsylvania, John Penn, and his attorney general headed to Carlisle to lead an investigation, but only after they had the promise of protection "of the king's Troops."[14] Their fear was justified. The men who attacked the trains were, according to one report, "Irish, English, Dutch and Welsh" and hailed from Pennsylvania, Virginia, and Maryland. Moreover, they seemed to have the backing of the "leading people" of the region. Because of this broad base of support, "the vulgar and common people all along the Frontier declare according to report that none of the Trespassers shou'd suffer Death."[15]

At first, officials tried to pin the blame on Croghan, complaining that by playing two games he was inflaming tensions.[16] What galled officials was the belief that men such as Croghan were "opening a Clandestine Trade with the Savages, under the Cover of Presents," a trade that would give him first claim to choice lands.[17] "If you had only minded the Business you were employed in, followed your instructions . . . without takeing upon you to encourage traders," Gage lectured Croghan, "you would not have been involved in any difficultys."[18]

Croghan defended his conduct. He did not hide the fact that a portion of the goods "I had bought for the Crown's use and part belonged to Gentlemen in Philadelphia." Now he pleaded with the British for restitution. Without "my presents," he wrote his partner Benjamin Franklin, he had little hope of securing another critical imperial goal "to open a trade with several Tribes."[19] William Johnson supported Croghan's activities, and eventually the board dismissed the charges against Croghan as arising "thro' the malice of some Persons." Moreover, as Johnson claimed, Shawnees, Mingoes, and Delawares supported Croghan's undertaking in the Illinois Country.[20]

Officials, traders, and even petty speculators laid the blame with disaffected settlers, castigating the Black Boys as "Highwaymen," "Jacobites," "Paxtonians," and "Paxtoneers."[21] Like the defenders of the Catholic King James, who had lost his throne to the Protestant William of Orange during the Glorious Revolution, the Black Boys were treacherously challenging the Crown's authority. Like the disbanded Jacobites of old, they were terrorizing the countryside and attacking subjects on the highway. Just like the Paxton Boys, the Black Boys contested the assumptions upon which the American empire was established and by implication imperial sovereignty. Such "Lawless Inhabitants," after all, posed a clear threat to "all order and Government."[22]

These men and their supporters rejected the new constraints they faced in the West. In their eyes, the land jobbers and traders represented a galling reminder of the difficult bind in which settlers found themselves. According to one settler in the region, most people believed "that these goods were not the present of the Crown, but private property sent out for the advantage of particulars." They especially bridled at the thought that "the goods particularly the Ammunition" would soon be directed at them and their loved ones.[23] Not only did they confront Indians in their efforts to gain competency in the West; they also feared greedy speculators and jobbers who would not hesitate to enrich themselves by arming Indians. The use of trade goods to appease Indians was for the common settler merely the first step in a landgrab by wealthy speculators from the East. With this in mind, they not only destroyed Croghan's goods but for a period threatened any driver going west with Indian goods they could get their hands on.[24]

In the eyes of frontier settlers, the British management of empire looked like a policy of appeasement toward Indians and hostility toward "have-nots" in favor of "haves." For the system to work, of course, officials had suggested that settlers could expect no mercy if they went west of the line or massacred Indians. However, to frontier folk, who had seen their relations, friends, and neighbors killed or captured by Indians, official policy seemed foolish and negligent and Croghan's agenda rapacious and criminal. After 1763, as frontier violence continued, "brave hardy woods men, who were greatly irritated against the savages," one settler argued, "seem to desire nothing more than an opportunity to chastise them for the many cruel Butcheries committed."[25] Settlers in Cumberland County pleaded with officials to recognize their plight. They were gripped by "alarming apprehensions" of £30,000 worth of goods and ammunition—and "powder, lead and scalping knives"—going to a "savage, faithless and unrelenting enemy." The prospect of this happening revived "horrible images" of "murdered families, captivated brethren and friends." The fact that British and provincial authorities—"void of compassion" for settlers, yet "profuse and liberal" to Indians—seemed to care more for the life, liberty, and property of Indians than they did for subjects, albeit subjects beyond the pale, proved too much to swallow.[26]

With their actions the rioters were saying something more. They refused to believe that as they went west, they forfeited their rights as subjects. They would not stand for an informal British policy that would afford them no protection as constraints seemed to squeeze them into the west. The system, as they saw it, conspired to privilege the rights of nonsubject Indians over the rights of white subjects. In other words, they rejected the British ideological formula that deemed them non-subjects once they moved onto lands beyond the line. This criticism went to the heart of a failing empire. Men like Croghan were not resorting to hyperbole when they declared that the actions and the arguments of the Black Boys represented "an End to Civil and Military Power."[27]

The events on Sideling Hill, a prelude of violence to follow, therefore spoke volumes about imperial tensions. In that fateful year of 1765, as subjects in the East demonstrated against the Stamp Act and as subjects in the West contested the meaning of empire in America, a "Spirit of Libertinism and Independence," in the words of William Johnson, prevailed. In Johnson's eyes, both Sons of Liberty in the East and Black Boys in the West were "Enemies to the British Constitution."[28] Johnson despaired. "I cannot see, how it is possible to remedy the foregoing Evils, or effectually prevent the seeds of Discontent from growing into a Rupture," he conceded.[29] He was right. The goods burning on a mountain road stood at the intersection between a British imperial formula and the demands of white settlers who rejected that formula.

As officials predicted, the events at Sideling Hill, as well as the murders along the frontier then being committed, had a poisonous effect on Indian sensibilities.[30] In 1766 and 1767, news came from the Ohio Country, the Illinois Country, and regions to the south of an increasing number of attacks by Indians. George Morgan, who was scouting out trading and speculative opportunities in the Illinois Country, reported that he feared a general war. With rumors swirling of impending attacks, he dared not send peltry back to Fort Pitt. Instead, goods had to go via New Orleans. One of his land jobbers, Simon Girty, informed Morgan that thirty Indians had attacked a small party he was leading. None, save Girty, made it back. The same groups of Indians attacked six Virginians working west of the line.[31] Johnson prophesied an "approaching storm" arising from "fresh discontent amongst most of the Indian nations throughout the Northern parts of this continent."[32]

In the South, John Stuart also struggled to keep the peace. In 1766, he complained that after Virginians had murdered nine Cherokees in Augusta County, the butchers could not be brought to justice, nor could the dead "be covered up."[33] The Cherokees had their revenge. Seven traders of Virginia, crossing the mountains into Cherokee settlements, were "murdered but none of the goods taken away except the Paint." The traders had believed that "a large Party" of friendly Cherokees would be "sent to escort them" to the settlements. Instead, as one of Stuart's deputies noted, "Young Men," unrestrained by their elders, met and murdered them. A stunned Stuart informed Cherokee leaders that these young men had attacked "ten innocent persons who never injured" Indians, as well as traders "who were employ'd in supplying your wants in carrying goods amongst you."[34]

Officials strained to make their overlords in London see the gravity of the situation. Resentment grew as Indians "see themselves attacked, threatened, and their property invaded by a Sett of Ignorant misled Rioters, who defy Government itself," Johnson informed the board.[35] The Lords of Trade got the point. As more bateaux "loaded with goods for the Indians trade" were "stopped and plundered on the Ohio," it now appeared "from authentic intelligence, coming through different channels, that something of moment is in agitation."[36]

The events of the West presented authorities, both metropolitan and provincial, with vexing issues that would lead to fundamentally different understandings of empire. With the system they had drawn up and implemented straining, men such as Johnson, Stuart, and Gage began to believe that the problem was one of what Johnson called "slender authority."[37] Johnson argued that while frontier inhabitants incited violence, the real problem lay with "the powers of Government," which were "really too weak for any material exertion of authority here."[38]

In the summer of 1766, while Indian raiding parties roamed the frontier and settlers were murdering innocent Indians, Croghan argued that the legal structure of the West was not up to the task. In regions along the line, "the Magistrates on the Frontiers, who ought to preserve the peace rather encourage the Killing of [Indians]."[39] More problems surfaced if a crime was committed in regions west of the line, "which are not within the limits of jurisdictions of any civil government." In the wake of the Black Boys disturbances, officials even considered plans to ship these types of miscreants to far-off courts.[40]

But colonial governments did not provide an answer. Crazed whites intimidated them. And in many cases, officials from these governments were sponsoring speculative schemes or making money from the fur trade. Any attempts to use colonial governments to limit settlement, rein in disreputable traders, or prosecute those who would threaten or kill Indians tended to meet "with universal opposition."[41] As Johnson explained, "The Authority of the Commissaries is nothing, and both, the Commanding Officers of Garrisons, and they, are liable to a Civil prosecution for detaining a Trader on any pretence, and should their crime be sent to the next capital, there is no law to punish them."[42] A headman from the Lower Creek Nation named Sallichie got to the heart of the matter. He informed Stuart that "whereas the Virginia people . . . are told by our people that they are over the Line and if they don't keep in the Bounds they will Burn their houses," the whites often responded that "they will burn the Governors House over his Head." He asked, "If the Governor cannot keep these Virginia people under, how can we keep our people under."[43] So colonial authorities stood by as the West descended into violence.[44]

Halting the cycle of violence meant buttressing the line. Because he sensed "a Dissolution of all legal Authority, that Subordination is entirely destroyed, and that all coercive Powers in Government are annihilated," Gage doubted that "either the Law or the Proclamation will have any weight with that Baniditti." He therefore pressed the ministry for "a strong Military Power, to remove them forceably," as he expected "Little assistance in these matters" from the governments of Virginia or Pennsylvania.[45] Johnson similarly pleaded with a secretary of state that "the weaknesses of the powers of Government here, the Disorders amongst the People . . . render it absolutely necessary that I should apply to you Sir that I may be properly supported."[46] Gage wanted more troops to hold the line; Johnson needed more money to keep peace west of the line.

Although on paper an imperial plan based on concepts of subjecthood and non-subjecthood and the redeemability of Indians could work without great numbers of troops or resources, by 1767 officials began to realize that an empire could not exist without laws, government, power, money, or subjects. In other words, they argued that some of the key tenets that went into drawing the line had to be abandoned in order to maintain the line. The West, too, would have to be a subject region.[47]

Johnson saw the disturbances on either side of the line as part of the same problem. "Riotous People" were to blame.[48] In the East, rioters burned officials in effigy and torched houses to signal their disapproval of hated taxes. In frontier regions, settlers murdered Indians, broke into jails, and contested authority.[49] In both places, the "executive Powers of Government are so weakened, and the Populace grown so confident," that stern measures were called for. Like easterners, westerners had to be subject to "powers vested in proper disinterested hands, and confirmed by Act of Parliament." Parliamentary supremacy therefore, the glue that held the British nation together and the bogey of the East, had to be applied to the West as well.[50]

Johnson asked for the impossible. At the very moment he was calling for more troops, Gage had to send a large portion of his scanty force east to deal with disturbances there. In September 1765, Gage agreed to dispatch a hundred troops from Fort Pitt to Annapolis to deal with Stamp Act rioters in Maryland, "tho'," he conceded, "that Fort and it's Communication, will be extreamly weak."[51] One hundred more troops from a regiment of Royal Highlanders left the fort for Lancaster in December.[52] While Johnson called for more resources to treat with Indians, to cover murders, and to keep Indians within the veil of empire, authorities in London were trying to come up with schemes to extract more money from America. When Johnson asked for more funding to settle disputes, Hillsborough preached "œconomy."[53] Cost-cutting measures and disturbances out east, therefore, took their toll on troop levels at the very moment officials were demanding more of them. Gage went so far as to staff smaller posts west of the line with half-pay officers.[54]

By 1768, the West had reached a critical impasse. After troops from Fort Pitt had evicted squatters on the Monongahela River, Gage reported that "Intruders are not only returned upon the Encroachments, but . . . they have been joined by some hundreds more." Eastern speculators—"some principal people"— encouraged such resistance. The military was "somewhat censured" because of "the Lands where People have settled, being claimed within the civil jurisdictions of Pennsylvania and Virginia, tho' evidently beyond the Limits prescribed by the King's Proclamation." Speculators, land jobbers, and squatters therefore acted as if no authority could or should contain them, raising thorny questions about the nature of sovereignty in the West. Indians, of course, retaliated. What officials faced was the "total dissolution of Law and Justice."[55] Croghan informed Benjamin Franklin that the disorder and failure to address it created a "very alarming and Critical Situation of Indian Affairs." Administrators did not have the resources to keep the likes of the Black Boys and Indian killers in check, and when they tried, settlers accused the British of placating their sworn enemies. Without the mandates of money and troops, Croghan feared that "we shall soon be involved in the most general and distressing War with them [the Indians] that America has ever felt."[56]

The breaking point came in 1768 as the British realized the enormity of the problems before them. Early that year, two German settlers, Frederick Stump and his servant John Ironcutter, were selling rum to a group of six Indians in Stump's house on the Pennsylvania frontier when their guests became "much disgusted and troublesome." Stump "took the occasion to murder them all." The next day Stump and Ironcutter rode fourteen miles, murdering four more Indians, and "afterwards throwing their bodies on a heap he set fire to the house and burned them."[57] To add insult to injury, Stump had killed and scalped women and children, a provocative act that added to the calculated nature of the butchery.[58] None could deny that the murders were "barbarous and unprovoked."[59]

Authorities, who issued a £200 reward for their capture, arrested both Stump and Ironcutter after a British officer handed them over to the sheriff at Carlisle for trial in Philadelphia. Authorities knew that no jury in Carlisle would find them guilty. But no sooner were they in custody than they "were forcibly carried off by some of the Riotous Frontier Inhabitants." Settlers scurried inland in fear of Indian retribution for the murders and for the failure of officials to bring the pair to justice.[60]

Another series of murders, another conference. Governor Penn of Pennsylvania requisitioned £2,500 to condole members of the Delawares, Shawnees, and the Six Nations at Fort Pitt. He argued that "there are bad and foolish People of all Nations." He asserted that "the strictest Justice shall be done you, and I make no doubt but you will be satisfied with my conduct." Penn then issued a proclamation to retake the pair, offering £500 for their recapture.[61] Johnson instructed Croghan to meet with the Ohio Indians at Fort Pitt as well. Croghan was to display the presents for covering the dead in public, participate in a condolence ceremony, and "take the Hatchet out of their Heads and bury it deep under a Large Pine Tree so as it shall be no more found." Because "several nations were already but too much exasperated against us," Johnson hoped "that the Indians will consider it as the Rash Act of an Individual . . . without the knowledge or Connivance of the Publick" and that Croghan would assert that the guilty would be apprehended and executed.[62]

But from the beginning, the efforts proved futile. As Croghan went out west to "Condole" the Indians, frontier settlers stopped and checked each load of goods going to Fort Pitt.[63] "The Black Boys," as a settler declared, rode again. They "have come to a Resolution and entered into an agreement absolutely to prevent any supplies whatever going to the Indians." They also "threatened violence" against any British officer who escorted the packhorses. More troublingly, "anonymous Letters are dispersed among us to the following Effect—Governor Penn has turned against us and takes part with the Indians. The Army is coming up among us." The directive ended with a chilling message: "clean up our guns."[64] The Indians, for their part, Croghan noted, had been "called upon by different Nations, to strike, and revenge the Murders committed upon their People by the Inhabitants."[65]

As Indians and settlers abandoned the system, officials realized that to save the empire in the West they would have to abandon it as well. In 1768, in the wake of the chaos of 1766 and 1767, authorities advocated another approach for dealing with the frontier, an older one that had worked in the past and that had given Indians a position of parity in negotiation. Throughout much of the eighteenth century, before the imperial plan was promulgated, colonial governors relied on the Iroquois to police the frontier. To rationalize frontier policy amid myriad competing interests, officials privileged the position of the most powerful group of Indians in the Northeast at the expense of their weaker neighbors. The "covenant chain," the agreement binding many of the colonies to the Six Nations, had proven an effective means of acquiring land, keeping the peace, and simplifying colonial-Indian diplomacy. The paternalistic thrust of the imperial plan, drawn up without the input of the Iroquois, whose influence and strength had waned since the Seven Years' War, had effectively broken the chain. Now men like Johnson grasped the chain anew, hoping to repair and brighten it to bring order to chaos.[66]

A conference with the Six Nations began in grand style on October 24, 1768, at Fort Stanwix in the heart of Iroquoia. Commissioners from Virginia, the governor of Pennsylvania, and the governor of New York—the colonies that had signed on to the covenant chain long ago—attended. Also present was William Franklin, the governor of New Jersey and an influential member of western speculating schemes, as were Croghan and Andrew Montour, one of Morgan's employees in the Illinois Country and a man widely respected by Ohio Indians, who served as an interpreter. Invitations went out to representatives from many nations, including the Shawnees, Delawares, Mingoes, and Senecas from the Ohio Country. On paper, this turned out to be an inclusive affair.[67]

But if the treaty negotiations adopted a middle ground approach as they followed the prescriptions of Native American diplomatic protocol, they also illustrated the truncated form the middle ground was taking by 1768. After the initial rituals, the participants got down to brass tacks. Shawnee representatives explained why few of their leaders attended. A number of their people, they reported, were readying to attack the "English." But officials asserted that their absence did not hinder proceedings. Gage admitted that their "Chiefs went some months ago, amongst the Mississippi Indians," adding that Johnson "does not see any particular necessity of their being present, as the Six nations are the undoubted owners of the lands, and considered as such by the rest." He concluded that they would "pay due submission to whatever the Six nations should agree upon." Following the old logic of the covenant chain, the Iroquois did the talking "in behalf of all the Six nations, Shawnese, Delawares and all other friendly allies and dependents."[68] In truth, the real negotiating took place with the Six Nations before the formal conference got under way.[69]

While Johnson discussed the line with the Six Nations, John Stuart was meeting with Cherokee representatives at Hard Labor, South Carolina, where Stuart emerged with a cession of land from the Cherokees. For gifts and promises to leave the over-the-hill region west of the mountains unmolested, they agreed to cede much of the western reaches of Virginia south and east of the Ohio River to white settlement. Stuart assuaged any sense of guilt with the knowledge that many whites had already settled along places like the Cheat River, and securing this area would lessen tensions in the upper Ohio valley. Moreover, he knew that the ministry and Board of Trade sanctioned a transfer of this size in this region.[70]

Johnson won much more. In his discussions, the Iroquois agreed to hand over the region called Kentucky to white settlement, as well as areas claimed by the colonies of Pennsylvania, Virginia, and New York. This land, perched between the Ohio River to the north and the Tennessee River to the west, pointed like a dagger into the heart of Indian country, pushing the line hundreds of miles west into the hunting grounds of the Shawnees and the Cherokees. Johnson was able to justify this grab on two counts. First, the Iroquois claimed a fictive supremacy over the groups who used the region, asserting the country belonged to them by conquest. Second, through his "suffering traders" enterprise, Croghan had been able to extract promises from Delawares and Shawnees, who "often expressed their sensibility and sorrow for" killing and robbing traders during the two wars, to make reparation by giving the concern land on the Ohio River near Fort Pitt deemed to be useless as hunting grounds for their losses. The Iroquois formally ceded this area as well. Although the proposed region for the cession lay along the eastern side of the river, the principle of reparations offered a powerful inducement to go ahead with the radical readjustment.[71]

Johnson and Stuart could also claim one other victory. They tended to rationalize the massive cessions of land on the grounds that the new regions would provide a safety valve for the pressures gripping the West. Certain that they could do nothing to stem the flow of illicit settlement west of the line, to ease the pressure from speculators and land jobbers backed by eastern colonial officials—especially Virginians, who saw the region as theirs by right and charter—or to dull the hatreds between young whites and young Indians, they believed that securing these regions made good sense.[72] The changes would also benefit a cash-strapped Crown. "Adventurers in Land who used to purchase Tracts of the Savages"—land jobbers, in other words—"might now purchase of the Crown; and be a means to indemnify the Crown for the Expence of this Treaty."[73]

In other words, with few resources or troops forthcoming, Johnson and Stuart resolved to bend the line, further extending subject regions and confiscating Indian lands, to save the western empire. By using the covenant chain to do so—itself the product of the myth of Iroquois supremacy over Indians in the West—Johnson was unwittingly undermining the foundational myths of a system premised on subjecthood and boundaries that he purported to be saving. Indeed, at this critical juncture, when it appeared that settlers could not be restrained, Johnson began to imagine a future without Indians. In a letter to a secretary of state, he argued, "We should not lose our attention to the Frontier Inhabitants." These people were crucial to empire, having the ability to buy far more British manufactured goods than traders ever sold to Indians. In short, settlers represented the empire's financial future, the Indians its past. The trade with Indians, Johnson conceded, "has Limits beyond which it cannot go but must decline in proportion to the decrease of the Indians."[74]

Why Johnson envisioned his brave new world, we'll never know with any certainty. To be sure, it helped pave the way for general acceptance of land cessions west of the line, a move that violated both the letter of the royal proclamation and the spirit of its ideology but enriched officials who played at two games in the West. In this vein, Johnson could make himself and his partners in the "suffering traders" scheme wealthy men—especially those from Pennsylvania—while placating Virginians, who laid claim to the same area, with the promise of Kentucky lands.[75] It also enabled Stuart and Johnson to draw distinctions between useful Indians like the Iroquois and to a lesser extent the Cherokees, on the one hand, and those who were expendable, on the other. Doling out £10,000 worth of trade goods to the Iroquois for the cessions no doubt strengthened Johnson's hand in determining western policy so long as he held fast to the covenant chain. But his conversion began as the system he helped build was falling apart and as his change of heart promised peace. At least that's how he sold it to his English overlords. His mission, he claimed, was "to treat of Peace" with the Six Nations and the Cherokees. For a "handsome recompence," they had agreed to new boundaries and agreed to maintain the peace on the frontiers.[76]

It did not work. Settlers poured into the ceded areas as if, as some newcomers west of Virginia put it, the ministry had removed "those Restrictions which we labour[ed] under in consequence of the Royal Proclamation."[77] As the treaty negotiations were getting under way, men and women were already projecting that the Ohio River "will be the boundary (with regard to [a] New Coloney) Between us and the Indians." These movements, one young migrant named Thomas Lewis argued, "have thrown that place in so much confusion almost as much as the Stamp Act."[78] "This Cuntry setels very fast," as a Virginian named George Rogers Clark put it, creating new opportunities for jobbers. Settlement, however, was not restricted to Kentucky. Men and women streamed into regions throughout the Ohio Country, including areas north of the river.[79] Jobbers raced to strike private deals with Indians for land, bribed deputies to wring concessions from Indians, and surveyed choice plots on both sides of the river because, as one put it, "it will be doing nothing more, than every body else seems to be doing."[80]

Speculators also reoriented their attention to the region. Interest in Illinois gave way to a renewed mania for Ohio, an area more accessible from the East. Croghan refocused his "suffering traders" scheme on the region by claiming concessions from Delawares and Shawnees in the area.[81] As negotiations for the treaties were getting under way, he used some land grants he had acquired in New York as leverage to finance the group's acquisition in the West, what he would call the "Indiana Grant." Other members of Croghan's company sponsored a rival concern in the region, hoping to found a colony of their own. In late 1769, Benjamin Franklin proposed a merger of the companies, chairing a meeting of expatriate Americans and land agents of "inland colonies" in London at the Crown and Anchor tavern. He included some of Britain's leading politicians in the company, such as Thomas and Richard Walpole, as well as Samuel Wharton, a principal of the company that had hitherto focused its resources on Illinois. These "Walpole Associates" created a new company, called, appropriately, the Grand Ohio Company, destined to unite most American interests in colonization of the Ohio Country.[82]

With the line in place and its ideology intact, Illinois lay open. With the line breached and its ideology discredited, the whole West lay open. In 1770, under the leadership of George Washington, Virginians launched their own Ohio Company, ostensibly to grant land to Virginia's veterans of the Seven Years' War. Unlike the Grand Ohio Company's plans to create a new colony, Washington hoped to lay claim to the area for Virginia.[83] Influential Virginians also began lobbying the Privy Council in earnest for their rights to Kentucky and the area around Fort Pitt, which the "suffering traders" regarded as theirs but which Virginians claimed by charter right. Thomas Jefferson entered the western fray in the wake of the Fort Stanwix Treaty by trying to obtain government patents for seven thousand acres west of the mountains. By 1771, a number of these Virginians would also join the Walpole Associates in a joint effort to create an inland colony of twenty million acres to be called Vandalia, in honor of the queen's putative Vandal ancestry.[84]

When the line was first drawn on paper, officials in America did not see any conflict with their private plans for speculation and the viability of the imperial system. And from 1764, they could focus on areas like the Illinois Country because the system deemed it a subject region in a non-subject world. But once Johnson abandoned the civilizing mission for the covenant chain because of the chaos engulfing the region, what had been a system that through its logic and ambiguity allowed Indians and settlers some dominion in the West had now become a zero-sum game. Speculators would become wealthy, and Indians in the Ohio Country would lose their land. Squatters, of course, could head west, but they would be the ones confronting the Ohio Indians. Although men like Croghan, who had a responsibility as an official and hoped to enrich himself in the bargain, expressed hope that by the new arrangement "a Long and Lasting friendship may be kept up between them [the Indians] and his Majesty's subjects," by the time he was writing, the words were ringing hollow.[85]

The ministry rejected the whole sordid arrangement. Hillsborough, a man who more than almost any other defined the corrupt nature of the eighteenth-century British political system, refused to countenance the things he had done for his own private interest being done on his watch. And by 1768, his hand had been strengthened. He now headed a new American department within the ministry that oversaw affairs relating to the colonies and the West. He also served as First Lord of Trade, effectively running that body as well. His growing power did not bode well for the new land rush.[86] Hillsborough upbraided Johnson for his attempt to make policy unilaterally and for exceeding the limits of his instructions.[87] He threatened Stuart that if Virginians did not pay to remake the boundary with the Cherokees, he would let the earlier line stand. The Lords of Trade agreed. They wanted Virginia to assume the cost of the Treaty of Hard Labor, and they questioned "the indiscretion of Sir William Johnson's having admitted the claims of Mr. Croghan, and the Indian Traders, to be introduced into the Negotiations with the six nations touching the Boundary Line."[88]

But speculators refused to be hemmed in by Hillsborough. Emboldened by the recent turn of events, speculators did not have to argue that their plans jibed with the civilizing mission, as they had done for the Illinois Country. Johnson had seen to that. Instead, they could challenge the notion that the Crown had any claim to sovereignty in the Ohio Country and hammered at the restrictions posed by the royal proclamation. If the Iroquois could cede land they had claimed through "conquest," the Crown had no dominion. The Six Nations "had equal Right to grant to us," and "Our Title is certainly good against the King, the Indians Themselves and all the King's other Subjects."[89] If the covenant chain could be used to pry land from Ohio Indians by ignoring the line, it could also serve as a means to clear the way for speculators to claim title to the Ohio Country without having to bother with the logic of the Proclamation Line.

If the line ceased to have practical meaning, then rights had meaning. And as agents suggested, speculators in the West had rights as subjects that neither king nor Parliament could ignore. "The Lands cannot belong to the Realm; But is in the Country of independent Allies, who have never conveyed them to the King; But to you and to us," an agent asserted.[90] With the ideology of the imperial plan compromised, the line had no legal basis. The members of the Grand Ohio Company went ahead with their plans of purchasing land from the Six Nations, proposing a new government for the Ohio Country, and enticing settlers to their claims without apology.[91]

For all the giddy expectations of peace in their time, officials had ignored a critical element of any new plan: the Indians over the line. The covenant chain might have worked in the early eighteenth century, but by 1768 it proved a fiction of the past. Cherokees never acknowledged themselves conquered by the Six Nations.[92] Settlers who may have believed they had free rein in the ceded region were sadly mistaken. Within a year or two of the negotiations at Fort Stanwix, settlers on the New River were reporting that "our County has been depopulated and numbers of the Inhabitants killed and carried into Captivity."[93]

Indians who lived north of the Ohio River rejected the Fort Stanwix Treaty as well. Although Delawares and Shawnees had offered a grudging acceptance of Iroquois claims to the Ohio Country earlier in the eighteenth century, far fewer did so by 1768.[94] Indeed, while the conference at Easton in 1758 recognized Iroquois supremacy in Ohio, it also conceded that Delawares could negotiate directly with eastern officials from that point forward.[95] Yet instead of attending the proceedings at Fort Stanwix, younger Delawares and Shawnees held conferences of their own, trying to create a Pan-Indian confederacy without the blessing of the Iroquois to contest the conspiracy they faced. Belts of wampum circulated in the Ohio Country and farther west, asking the nations to band together.[96] More troubling still, by early 1770, Delawares and Shawnees were traveling to Cherokee towns to firm up peace between the groups and to create an alliance against white encroachment, which officials called the "Scioto Confederacy."[97] With the nations stretching from the Ohio Country to the Mississippi "unanimously agreed to make peace with the Cherokees," little stood in the way of war.[98]

And so the cycle of violence continued. Indians killed whites. Whites slaughtered Indians. Commanders reported more insults to authority.[99] Vigilantes attacked more traders carrying goods to Indians or threw obstructions along the way if British troops escorted pack trains. While rumors impelled some to scurry from the frontier, others arrived. Speculators lobbied in London, preaching about their rights to land, and land jobbers continued their sordid business even as violence engulfed the region. War parties fanned out along the length of the Ohio, attacking boats going down the river. Indians met in secret and the open, planning to kill whites, creating a frenzy among traders. In these circumstances, as rumors flew, "Pannick spread with amazing rapidity" among both white and Indian communities.[100]

The recourse to the outdated and mythic covenant chain during such a volatile time, therefore, did not allow tensions to ease, but heightened them, making any sort of cultural accommodation between whites and Indians impossible. Both parties not only prepared for war; they acted as if they already were at war. The Ohio Indians, Johnson argued, "have for some time discovered that a War is probably at hand, many of them think that it has already commenced."[101] Young Indians north and south "set up the Death Song."[102] What John Stuart's deputy called "the Rogue Man Killer" murdered eight people in one raid. Alexander Cameron described him as "a Blood Thirsty Dog," and he feared "if such Enormous and Repeated Acts are suffered with Impunity they will soon become as habitual as Killing of a Deer."[103] Whites proved no more redeemable. A trader with a "disagreeable temper" called Ramsey "in liquor" killed three men, a woman, and an infant, scalping each of them. He had the audacity to take his trophies to a British fort, where he hoped to collect a scalp bounty. Ramsey claimed he did so because he believed that "War had been actu-

ally commenced between the English and Indians." Officials arrested him
but assumed no jury would find him guilty.[104]

The middle ground had collapsed. In early 1772, the métis Andrew
Montour, an interpreter and go-between who for many years had successfully straddled two worlds, died at the hands of a Seneca. Many Indians
mourned his passing as he was buried near Fort Pitt. The mourners requested rum, which the Crown paid for, and the Indians "drown[ed] their
Sorrows for the Loss of their Friend." It turned out to be quite a wake, as
the assembled consumed more than £7 worth of liquor.[105] These men and
women, of course, were remembering more than a man. They were paying homage to a moment now passed on the frontier and to a process of
cultural accommodation that underscored the viability of the imperial
plan.[106]

They were right to mourn the passing. Indians west of the line now believed "that as the White People have advanced from the Coast, the original Natives have been destroyed, and of the numerous Nations which
formerly inhabited the Country possessed of the English, not one is now
existing." Each day they sensed the whites "drawing closer and closer to
them, and they see it must soon be their turn to be exterminated."[107]

The imperial experiment had also died, and Croghan composed its
epitaph in word and deed. Because of the "repeated Insults" of the "Frontier People almost in every Colony . . . it can not even be supposed that
any Authority . . . will be paid any Regard to by those Unruly Settlers at
this distance, when that Authority can not command Respect at One hundred and fifty Miles Nearer the Seats of Government." As he wrote, no
fewer than five thousand "of his majesty's Subjects have seated themselves
down in an ungovernable manner" in the Ohio Country. As Croghan's influence over events waned with the collapse of authority west of the line,
he resigned his post as deputy, hoping to make as much money as he
could before his world dissolved. By 1771, he and his jobber, Michael
Cresap, had settled down near Fort Pitt, competing with Virginians such
as George Washington to sell title to land to all comers without the authorization of officials in London.[108]

The British Empire in the West came to an end not with a bang or a
whimper but with resignation. In late 1772, word reached London that
the Mississippi River was wearing away the foundations of Fort Chartres.
Unless commanders took quick and costly measures, the river would re-

claim the fort. This place had served as a focal point of the civilizing mission in the Illinois Country, a site where subjecthood prevailed in a larger western non-subject world. But now it had no role. Hillsborough did not instruct Gage to shore up the sagging foundation; rather, he directed him to make plans for abandoning the fort.[109]

After Fort Chartres, British authority in the West came tumbling down like a house of cards. Since Fort Pitt served as an entrepôt to Illinois, it was also expendable.[110] With the imperial system in place, the fort played a critical role in the West. Now it served as a symbol of all that had gone wrong with the imperial scheme. "There are few Posts," Gage argued, "more costly, none more difficult, critical, or dangerous to support in case of a Quarrell with the savages." No fort was "more likely to involve Great Britain in a war with them . . . for it is with the Indians in the District of Fort Pitt, that the Colonies of Pennsylvania, Maryland, and Virginia are so frequently on the Eve of Rupture."[111] In February 1772, Gage ordered "all works going on at Fort Pitt . . . to be stopped directly, and nothing more to be undertaken," and directed that all troops evacuate to Philadelphia.[112] With the abandonment of the forts, officials in London requested that the colonies provide commissioners, smiths, militia, and interpreters to the West. Colonial governments would also supervise the trade. British officials held out no great hopes for this plan of devolution to bring peace to the region. Never before, after all, had colonial governments taken any responsibility for the frontier.[113]

The decision to abandon the West proved to be Hillsborough's last act. A group led in part by some of the prominent investors in the Grand Ohio Company, most notably Benjamin Franklin, who detested the man, successfully pushed for Hillsborough's dismissal. His reluctance to open the West to speculators and clear the way for their title to the Ohio Country did him in.[114] With his resignation, a delighted Samuel Wharton declared, the king and Privy Council, as well as the new secretary of state, Lord Dartmouth, decreed "in favour of a Grant, to the Honourable Mr. Walpole and his Associates; and that a New province shall be established thereon."[115] The man who had risen to the top of the British political establishment through patronage but had decried "private interest" as stymieing imperial interests in the West had fallen just as quickly through patronage. Nonetheless, even he understood the reasons for the failures of the past, as well as the peril of the future. In one of his last letters as secretary of state, Hillsborough wrote, "Every day discovers more and more the fatal policy of departing from the line prescribed by the Proclamation of 1763." The new, rudderless course the British were embarking on in the West was "now likely to have no other consequences than that of giving a greater scope to distant settlements, which I conceive to be inconsistent with every true Principle of Policy." This "will most probably have the effect to produce a general Indian War, the Expence whereof will fall upon this Kingdom."[116]

But officials hoped, nonetheless, that Indians would applaud the abandonment of the West. "Much pains," Gage asserted, "have been taken to keep the Western Tribes well affected to ourselves, and I find they received the News of the Demolition of Fort Pitt as the strongest proof of our Friendship and good Intentions towards them." An Indian agent, Alexander McKee, gushed, "They appeared exceedingly well pleased with the demolition of the works here." If "all the sharp edg'd Tools [were] taken away, it would be the strongest proof of Friendship that cou'd be given them."[117] Nothing of the sort transpired. Regardless of what officials hoped, plans for a grand Indian confederacy went ahead without pause. Stuart informed Dartmouth that the leaders of the "Western Confederacy, at the Head of which are the Shawnese and Delawares," were working to get Creeks and Choctaws involved in an attempt to defend Indian land.[118] Johnson had learned that the largest belt of wampum on record was making its rounds from village to village in the West, inviting Indians from the Ohio to the Mississippi to fight "the English."[119]

After the British had gone, the line still stood. But now it had no ideological rationale or practical meaning. And so the press for the West continued apace. Traders worked without restriction, selling anything they wished to Indians, as there was "little prospect . . . of any such Regulations being made in the colonies." Settlers flooded west "without any title whatsoever," and most of them "have a hatred for, ill treat, rob, and frequently murder the Indians . . . They are in general, a Lawless sett of People, as fond of Independency as" Indians. In 1763, few lived west of the line. By 1774, perhaps as many as fifty thousand did. Like the rioters in the East, they paid no regard to government, "owing to Ignorance, prejudice, Democratical Principles, and their remote Situation." Johnson found that little had changed with the abandonment of empire. "The landed Men," he lamented, "protect them or a rabble rescue them from the hands of

Justice."[120] In the absence of the British, Gage hoped, settlers would finally have to live with the implications of the world they had brought into being. "Let them feel the consequences," he declared, of abusing Indians, for "we shall be out of the Scrape."[121]

The British had learned through hard experience there was no pleasing all parties in the West, nor could they afford to "quell" dissidents as "a Dublin mob."[122] If all the various groups in the West did not buy into the system, accept its premises, and act in a deferential manner or with good faith, there was no saving the empire without force. This is the world the British were leaving behind as they marched east of the Proclamation Line, which had all but vanished under the pressures upon it. For once, the threat of "an Indian war," mentioned at nearly every difficult juncture, now would prove prophetic. While a military commander informed Dartmouth of events in the East, most notably that "some opposition will be made to the importation of Tea, reported to be sent by the East India Company," he also laid out the future of the West. "I am informed from Fort Pitt," now little more than a ruin, "that there is a constant emigration of families going to settle on the banks of the Ohio." The Indians would kill a great deal of them. Yet the boats would continue coming. "Such settlements as these," he concluded, "so far from all influence of the Laws, will soon be the Azilum of the lawless, and the repair of the most licentious inhabitants of His majesty's already most extensive Colonies in America."[123]

When travelers first encountered the West in 1763, they had imagined an idyllic place, a land of unfettered opportunity and beauty. Digging deep into European myth, they described it in rapturous terms as a "state of nature." European culture, of course, had another vision of the state of nature, one in which life was "nasty, brutish, and short." By the late 1760s, travelers were beginning to see the West in these Hobbesian terms.[124]

PART II

State of War

Out of civil states, there is always war of every one against every one. Hereby it is manifest, that during the time men live without a common power to keep them all in awe, they are in that condition which is called war ... In such condition, there is ... no society; and which is worst of all, continual fear, and danger of violent death; and the life of man, solitary, poor, nasty, brutish, and short.

—Thomas Hobbes, *Leviathan*, chapter 13

FOUR

Revolution and Chaos: Lord Dunmore's War and the Search for Order

A s he made his way into a postimperial West in 1773, a visitor from the East chronicled attacks on Indians, the killing of settlers, and a general aura of violence and fear gripping the region. He saw more. Passing by the area around the abandoned Fort Pitt, he saw "the Bones yet in Sight" of Indians, colonists, and British regulars killed during an early engagement of the Seven Years' War. The dead had not buried the dead, nor had the living.[1]

With the British withdrawal, the West not only conjured the ghosts of the past but had become—as one put it—a place "not made to be inhabited by men."[2] With authority absent, chaos prevailed. A Moravian missionary named John Heckewelder, who visited the Ohio Country in 1773, encountered a frightening world. Men formed themselves into gangs to "rove through the country in search of land, either to settle on or for speculation." Others "destitute of both honour and humanity" became a "rabble." These believed "that to kill an Indian, was the same as killing a bear or a buffalo, and would fire on Indians that came across them by the way."[3]

Some thrived on disorder. As William Trent, a veteran of the region, argued, in such a "State of Nature Every one might possess himself of and retain" any "Vacant" land.[4] Unsettledness invited adventurers. One such "young gentleman from Virginia" was George Rogers Clark. He "with several others inclined to make a Tour in this new world" to stake a claim and make a name for themselves less than a year after the British had left.[5] The

West belonged to such as these. "Without a king," as a western Virginian whose neighbor's children had been "captivated" by Indians explained, "Every doeth according to freedom of his own Will."[6] Without sovereign power, while most relied on their guile to survive, some had the ambition to try to remake the West as they saw fit. In the years after the failure of the British imperial plan, many struggled to impose their imprint on the region and fill the imperial void, to remake the fabric of society with the limited materials of the day.

One more than most. John Murray, the royal governor of Virginia and fourth Earl of Dunmore, attempted to manage the disorder and fear westerners confronted. In the process, he tried to reestablish authority in the West. A Scottish peer whose family had been allied with the Jacobite cause, Lord Dunmore asserted Virginia's sovereignty to the area west of the mountains, contesting the claims of Pennsylvania and Vandalia through violence, manipulation, bluff, bluster, and shrewd management. Far from decrying chaos, he and his agents learned to use it for their purposes and for the benefit of Virginia's speculating elite. Dunmore did so by playing upon the hunger for land of "young gentlemen" such as George Rogers Clark and established planters like George Washington.

This course alone would not win the West. Prevailing entailed gaining the support of squatters and poorer settlers. Wealthy Virginians pandered to common men and women, demonizing Indians and promising to accomplish what the British could not have contemplated. Virginians would vanquish the natives. They exploited divisions between and among Native American groups, made use of the fear and hatred of Indians espoused by ordinary men and women, and engineered a war. With good reason, a Pan-Indian confederation had frightened the British, who feared another general war. Dunmore and his followers invited the prospect of warfare, realizing that fear and Indian hatred strengthened their hand.

Dunmore's push for reconstituting authority, however, placed common settlers in a bind. By 1773, of course, most men and women applauded Dunmore's aggressive approach to Indians. Yet they also looked to the West for land. British strategy had stymied both. In its aftermath, they hoped for a new form of authority that would end once and for all what they regarded as an Indian menace and allow them to settle where they pleased. Dunmore and his followers had other plans. They would attempt to rid much of the Kentucky country of Indians, using the manpower of settlers to do so. But the land would not be inherited by the poor. Before the conflict, common settlers had some leverage, as Dunmore needed them to claim the Ohio Country. After they had been manipulated, they had none. The notion that the lower sort had any real power— at this juncture, anyway—was a myth. Neither common settlers nor Indians compelled Dunmore to take this path; rather, in the midst of disorder he and local officials regarded and treated both as pawns to be moved about the West for his benefit and in the interests of Virginia's elites.[7]

If one surveyed this "new world" beyond the mountains in 1774, it appeared that the wealthy had won the West at the expense of Indians and poorer whites. Dunmore had reasserted authority by using settlers, conquering Indians, and managing disorder. He had done so by reconstituting sovereignty, which took its shape in the West through the creation of new boundaries for Virginia and through the conquest of lands claimed by Indians. Now he would attempt to force both settler and Indian to acknowledge the new status quo, one based on the idea that sovereignty defined by lines and war was located in the hands of elites acting for themselves and Virginia as much as for the Crown. Or so it seemed less than two years after the region had descended into chaos.[8] The event commonly known as Lord Dunmore's War, therefore, represented the first concerted attempt to transform a Hobbesian state of nature into a state of society. This competitive and violent process to re-create a fallen world where the unburied dead still haunted the present—and the struggles that followed for the next ten years—would define the West in the wake of British abandonment.

"I was sorry for your misfortune in loosing your Negroe Boy," wrote James Robertson to his friend William Preston in 1774. Born in Ireland, Preston had settled in Virginia, where he cultivated influential friends and became a man of some social standing and wealth. After the Seven Years' War, he had moved to western Virginia and continued to live there even after the British had abandoned the West. Robertson sent his letter of condolence for the loss of one of Preston's slaves to Indian raiders. But he also encouraged Preston to count his blessings. Other men, some wealthier than he, most not, had suffered a great deal more. Be thankful, his friend counseled. "It is lucky it did not happen to be your wife or one of your children," Robertson concluded.[9] In a region west of the mountains stretching from Fort Pitt to Kentucky claimed by colonists through the Treaty of Fort Stanwix, Indians from north and south of the Ohio River demonstrated their resolve to hold on to their land by striking isolated settlements with brutality and efficiency. Reports came in to British officials of raiding parties breaking into houses, killing or capturing women and children, servants and slaves, and of skirmishes breaking out along the frontier.[10]

Without the restraints of legitimate authority, the West lay in a state of undeclared but very real war. The innocent, of course, suffered the most. John Stuart lamented how "unprovoked and atrocious" violence defined the tenor of life in the region. He cited one such example. In the summer of 1773, two unarmed Cherokees—one nineteen, the other twenty—who were traveling along the Broad River "went to a house in sight to begg a Little Milk." The woman who answered the door announced that her husband and her son were away. Nonetheless, she "gave them some milk and set some victuals before them." As they were eating, the son returned home. Without a word, he took "his Riffle gun in his hand [and] levelled it with an Intention to kill both." He shot one. The other "he felled with a blow of his Gun, which was given with such violence on the Poll of the neck, as broke the gun in pieces." While the young Cherokee gasped and struggled, "he finished his bloody work with an ax." When the father entered and saw the carnage, "he helped his son to sink the Bodies in the River," where they lay undiscovered for nine days. The son was arrested. But later he escaped.[11]

Indians were not blameless. A few weeks later, a Cherokee murdered a trader without "malevolence or premeditated Intention."[12] It seems the two were holding an impromptu marksmen competition one morning. Joking afterward with their unloaded guns, they "snap[ped] them empty at each other. They having Loaded themselves Pretty well with Rum." Later and without explanation, the Cherokee "presented his gun, said that he would kill a White Man, drew the Triger, and was good to his Word."[13] The numbers killed in such senseless incidents were not great—one report cited eighteen killed in the space of a few months in 1773—but the effects were. After such incidents, traders balked at going over the mountains to deal with Indians. They argued that they would find "nothing there among the white People but War and Rumors of War."[14] Perhaps most troubling, many of these murders took place in an intimate world where settler knew Indian. The moral was clear. In the summer of 1774, the known and the unknown served as legitimate targets.[15]

An "alarming Spirit" gripped the region.[16] Yet opportunists saw the chaos as a chance to claim land. Patrick Henry bought over three thousand acres of land on the Holston and Clinch rivers about this time.[17] To be sure, speculators such as Henry could not expect to make a windfall in a short period of time. As one settler put it, "I think money is scarcer here (if possible) than Grace."[18] Nonetheless, they understood that despite the violence, people still came. Indeed, if past was prologue, it was only a matter of time before those able to pay would make their way over the mountains. George Washington, for example, spent much of 1774 trying to secure groups of migrants from the palatinate to people his extensive claims on the south bank of the Ohio River near the mouth of the Scioto.[19] He also sought to secure land in the area for veterans of the Seven Years' War and to enrich himself. Now even "Officers of the independent ranging companies," who had not fought with the formal blessing of Virginia's leaders, tried to get their fair share as well.[20]

Defunct smaller ventures, such as the Loyal Company and the Greenbrier Company, rose once more to press older claims. George Mason even championed the rights of the newly resurrected Ohio Company, a scheme created in the 1740s.[21] Some jobbers and strollers with no claims to land tried any means fair and foul to get their hands on land. Some claimed it by right of improvement, others by purchasing lots from Indians for liquor and goods. In this state of uncertainty, no one knew for sure who held legitimate title. Some conceded that only Indians had any clear title to the land. Others did not. Most believed that the Crown had no right above individuals. Officials of eastern governments might claim the West, but none had made good on their words. Companies held overlapping claims, some recent, others from long ago. And the varied rhetorical strategies that claimants used to lobby for land—whether in Ohio, Kentucky, or Illinois—only muddied the waters.[22]

No power restrained either the murderous or the greedy. After troops were marched out and Hillsborough stepped down, the British had become little more than observers in a region over which they still held nominal sovereignty. Sir William Johnson continued to admonish his superiors to address the chaos and problems of the West even after troops had marched out.[23] Yet he had no authority to restrain settler or Indian.[24] As a Virginian complained, "When any of our People is robbed or murdered by the Indians there is but little ado about it by the Superintendent." He informed a deputy, "You have borne some part of the Blame for this inattentive conduct, indeed some has gone so far as to assert that your written orders have been found incouraging the Indians to use acts of violence."[25]

In 1774, Parliament passed the Quebec Act, a measure intended to bring some degree of civil authority to the province of Quebec, as well as areas north and west of the Ohio River as far as the Mississippi. The act did so by enlarging Quebec to encompass the subject regions of the Illinois Country and the settlements around places like Detroit and by giving the enlarged area its own civil government. But the act made no provision for the region south and east of Fort Pitt—in other words, much of the upper Ohio valley—or the Kentucky Country, the areas into which settlers were streaming and speculators and jobbers had set their sights. The Quebec Act, in other words, did not affect the areas ceded on paper by the Treaty of Fort Stanwix.

While the British did not make good on claims of sovereignty, others did. Beginning in 1773, three colonies attempted to secure the region. Two of these, Pennsylvania and Virginia, already existed in fact. The third, Vandalia, existed only on paper. Thomas Wharton, a principal of the Vandalia scheme, wrote his brother that "the country is thickly settled for 150 Miles below Fort Pitt," even after the British had left. Settlers had "erected two good Grist Mills, and have large Quantities of Winter Grain in the Ground."[26] By George Croghan's reckoning, "at least 60,000 souls" had already settled on Vandalia lands that he had originally claimed through his "suffering traders" scheme. He overestimated. Nonetheless, large numbers of men and women, who were also taking advantage of the vacuum of sovereign power to settle the West, needed some form of government.[27] But no sooner had the Board of Trade and the ministry confirmed the Vandalia grant than lawyers for the Crown held it up over a number of technicalities, imperiling plans for "the Country We expect to possess."[28]

While Samuel Wharton worked in London to disentangle these matters, his brother in Philadelphia devised new arguments to buttress their claims. Both tried their best to use the violence and competition for land as a means to bring their plans for the inland colony to fruition. Only order—the type provided by government—could end chaos, the very existence of which made evident the "absolute Necessity of a Civil Establishment."[29] Disorder therefore served as leverage for the Vandalia supporters, who hoped to use practical problems to overcome legal obstacles. And, as Thomas Wharton knew, time was of the essence.[30]

He was right to worry. Officials in Pennsylvania also attempted to claim the region. Although the Crown had not ratified Pennsylvania's authority over the area, officials argued that Fort Pitt and the area north of the line recently laid out by Mason and Dixon and east of the Ohio River lay within its bounds. Charter claims, they argued, superseded the pretensions of Vandalia. The wedge of land between the Monongahela and the Allegheny rivers where the fort had stood, therefore, was Pennsylvania's western outpost, its toehold in the West. In making this claim, though, they relied on more than arguments. Pennsylvanians understood that sovereignty entailed institutions and clear boundaries. They therefore created courts and new counties. With the British withdrawal from Fort Pitt, the Pennsylvania Assembly established the County of Westmoreland. Its jurisdiction encompassed the growing town of Pittsburgh and areas to the south and east of the settlement. The governor of Pennsylvania also issued proclamations for the region, even offering rewards for the capture of known criminals and Indian killers who defied "the authority of government."[31]

Pennsylvanians contested all other claimants to the region. They admonished settlers to acknowledge Pennsylvania's authority and jurisdiction, obey its laws, and respect its courts and surveys.[32] They even brought suit against George Croghan, who, as principal and booster of the Vandalia scheme, refused to recognize Pennsylvania's authority over the lands on which he lived. He would not pay taxes on the lots he acquired after the British left, as well as on barracks, an orchard, and a garden in the shadow of the ruined fort.[33] An agent for the Penn family in the area and large property owner, Arthur St. Clair, asked a local magistrate put there by Pennsylvania officials to order up "powder and ball" for Westmoreland County. Defraying the expenses of frontier settlers, promising some sort of protection, and taking a vocal role in the management of the region, St. Clair hoped, would bind the people to Pennsylvania and overcome their fear—justified in the past—of the negligence of Quaker pacifist rule.[34]

While Vandalians tried to lobby for their land and Pennsylvanians built institutions, Virginians did more, declaring through their actions that authority, not jurisdiction, mattered. As soon as he arrived in Virginia in the fall of 1771, Dunmore approached the Crown for a large grant of land in the West. His request was denied. He then tried to take in the name of the Crown for Virginia what was denied by the Crown to Virginia. Doing so, as one traveler to the West put it, "set the whole country in a blaze."[35]

In August 1773, Lord Dunmore traveled to the ruins of Fort Pitt, which he declared within Virginia's bounds. The ten thousand who he estimated lived near Pittsburgh, he argued, had "neither magistrates to preserve rule and order among themselves nor militia for their defence," adding, "The people flocked about me and beseeched me . . . to appoint magistrates and officers of the militia."[36] Less than a year later, Dunmore issued a proclamation of his own. The rapid growth of population in the region ceded by the Treaty of Fort Stanwix, a development he called "an Object of real Concern to His Majesty's Interest," required him to bring order to the area. In his proclamation, he chastised Pennsylvanians for creating an "imaginary Authority" in the West and abusing "laudable Adventurers" from Virginia who had settled west of the mountains. Because of "Pre-occupancy" and Virginia's ancient charter rights, Dunmore demanded that all west of Laurel Hill — an area that encompassed the Vandalia colony and Westmoreland County — shift their allegiances to Virginia.[37] The massive region stretched from Laurel Hill — more than fifty miles east of Fort Pitt — to as far west as the Mississippi south of the Ohio River.

Staking this claim no doubt made good political sense. Almost from his arrival, Dunmore, who had little patience for popular assemblies, tried to rule Virginia in an autocratic way. In fact, he intended to make the most of his time in the New World. He lived in a palatial setting in the rather dingy provincial capital of Williamsburg; although by all accounts married to a beautiful woman, he was, according to one contemporary, "a consummate rake," and like many other royal colonial governors of the eighteenth century, Dunmore hoped to amass wealth and power in America.[38] As an unpopular colonial governor, Dunmore could use the West to cultivate the support of the wealthiest and most influential inhabitants, who had a great interest in frontier speculation, people such as Patrick Henry and George Washington, as he enriched himself. He understood that it was these who stood to lose a great deal if Pennsylvania or Vandalia prevailed in the competition to claim the West.[39]

Dunmore therefore approached the West with a heightened sense of urgency. He and his followers accused Pennsylvanians of colluding with Indians and encouraged Virginians to resist Pennsylvania's authority in word and deed. In one such incident, Westmoreland County authorities had arrested three men for "throwing down a man's house" who supported the Pennsylvania interest. Soon afterward, fifteen armed men, claiming that "they had authority," broke down the prison door. Maj. William Crawford, a Virginia official, friend and confidant of Washington's, and speculator in the region, had drafted them to do so, they alleged, adding that they "had a warrant from a Magistrate in Virginia." One of the raiders, David Vance, purported to have "positive Orders that if any Pennsylvania officers would offer to take him or any of them with precepts under the Government of Pennsylvania to shoot them and that he would do it." One Pennsylvania justice of the peace coolly replied, "Boys you are early up to buy a Rope to hang yourselves," before calling for silence and reading the Riot Act "so that every Spectator might hear." The raiders paid no heed. They handed out pistols to all the prisoners, telling them "now to clear their own way."[40]

Jailbreaks were nothing new on the frontier and were a common expression of discontent with government, but government-sponsored jailbreaks were new. Dunmore's agents went further. They intimidated Pennsylvanians, especially those serving in the West in an official capacity—for example, arresting the trader and Pennsylvania supporter Richard Butler on trumped-up charges.[41] About the same time, twelve "armed men" surrounded the house of a justice of the peace for Westmoreland County and "throwed Stones and attempted to break open his Doors and Windows to the great Terror of his Family." While doing so, they shouted "that they would show him what Virginia Boys could do." They kept it up from 9:00 p.m. until midnight.[42] Armed gangs roamed the streets of Pittsburgh after Dunmore asserted his claim. The place became what one visitor called an "infamous nest of cutthroat[s] . . . ruffians and plunderers."[43]

By April 1774, Dunmore was instructing some Virginians in the region "to Survey Lands in the uninhabited parts" of the areas ceded by the Treaty of Fort Stanwix. Since the surveys would form the basis of subsequent allotments, it was critical that the surveyors finish their jobs. Of course, they were moving into dangerous territory, hunting lands claimed by the Shawnees and Cherokees. Dunmore therefore dispatched Michael

Stoner and Daniel Boone, men with a great deal of backwoods experience, to see if the surveyors had carried off their task in Kentucky. The two set off "across the Country to the Falls of Ohio" and would return by the Cumberland River. If they came across the surveyors, they would bring them and, just as important, their vital field notes.[44] Capt. Thomas Bullitt worked the area around the Falls of the Ohio. Some went even farther west.[45]

With the surveying teams moving about the country, Dunmore encouraged wealthy Virginians to press for entries.[46] He allowed officers from Virginia who had served in the Seven Years' War—now some of the leading lights of Virginia society—to "take out Patents for their lands of one thousand Acres in each Survey," large sections of land far beyond the means of common men and women. They could then "subdivide it into as many patents as they please."[47] It was understood that after the lands were laid out "in one general Survey," they would be subdivided into lots "not to be less than 6d per acre, and to be liable to pay 4/2 per hundred quit rents."[48] In short, Dunmore styled himself a patron of the speculating elite, some of whom supported rival companies. While the companies could guarantee nothing, Dunmore promised good title on bounty patents if speculators moved on his orders.[49]

Once made public, Dunmore's surveying plans set off a frenzy in the East for western lands, and wealthy Virginians now pressed for specific lots.[50] But Dunmore's strategy also lured common men and women, many of whom had settled on lands claimed by Vandalia. Virginians, as one Vandalia principal complained, issued "prohibiting orders" forbidding the sale of Vandalia's "Ohio lands." More people, therefore, deserted the sinking enterprise.[51] Sir William Johnson declared that a flood of people hoping to preempt the claims of speculators by staking out lots were deluging Kentucky, "the old claims of Virginia conspiring to encourage them."[52]

Needless to say, the renewed activity alarmed the Shawnees, on whose lands most of the surveyors worked. Alexander McKee, a deputy of Johnson's living along the Ohio, reported that the Shawnees saw settlers "overspreading the Hunting grounds of our Young men." Shawnee leaders "have had many disagreeable Dreams this Winter about the matter." They feared for their young men, who might prove "foolish enough to make Reprisals without waiting to apply to the great men."[53] Shawnee representatives appealed to Johnson for help, claiming that Virginians were settling as far down the Ohio as the Big Bones and, most troubling, that the Cherokees and Six Nations seemed to approve, citing the Treaty of Fort Stanwix as authority.[54] But Johnson could do nothing.

Virginians backed their provocative acts with military might. No sooner had Dunmore sent out surveying teams than officials of the new Virginia region named West Augusta called for a muster of all eligible men to enroll them in the local militia.[55] In early 1774, he ordered troops marched into the decrepit Fort Pitt. The measure had symbolic significance. It announced to all of Virginia's rivals that authority and troops trumped claims.[56]

Dunmore chose a man as calculating as himself to spearhead his efforts in the West. John Connolly had been born in southeastern Pennsylvania and trained as a physician in Philadelphia, an occupation he gave up for a military career. He married a woman as ambitious as himself: Susanna, known as Sukey. She had a violent temper and was having an affair—or at least it was rumored—with the trader and interpreter Simon Girty. Connolly was also recognized as one of the most avid speculators in the Pittsburgh region.[57] Dunmore appointed him one of seven magistrates for Pittsburgh, a militia captain for the area, and commander of Fort Pitt. Connolly took command of Fort Pitt in January 1774, manned it with what one visitor called "people of the most infamous and abandoned characters," and, as an honor to his patron's pretensions, renamed it Fort Dunmore.[58] So hated had Connolly become to the Pennsylvanians in Pittsburgh that Arthur St. Clair had him arrested, leading to howls of protest from Dunmore and Virginia's Council and threats of rescuing him by force.[59]

Dunmore and Connolly staged this show of authority, in part, to impress settlers and squatters. Amid rival claims, the support of common men and women was crucial to Dunmore's plans. But winning over the men and women who had settled in the Ohio valley would be no mean feat. Indeed, courting wealthy speculators with the lure of land invited popular rebellion. Settlers who claimed rights by improvement swore "Vengeance against any person that will pretend to lay on their warrants and it appears to me their will be more Blood shed this Insuing year, if the people persist in laying on what they call their rights."[60] Dunmore therefore had to work at cross-purposes. He needed the support of settlers to reconstitute authority; he needed to restore order to see to the interests of speculators.

Dunmore discovered that if the people had leverage over him, he had some of his own over them. Indeed, fear was on his side. As one of his surveyors put it, settlers "are much more fearful of the Indians than I expected to find them." Some fled on reports of Indian raids "in such haste that they left all their stock, and greatest part of their Household Furniture."[61] Surveyors alarmed Indians. Indians, in turn, threatened common settlers with vengeance. And for his part, Dunmore could offer both settlers protection and speculators secure claims. In this way, insecurity served his purposes.

In 1773 and 1774, Dunmore used the chaos and violence of the region to his own advantage. And in these years, the West offered ample opportunities for cultivating terror. In late 1773, Capt. William Russell, a Fincastle County justice of the peace, and Daniel Boone, along with thirty men, women, and children from Virginia, "set out with an Intention to Reconoitre the Country towards the Ohio and settle in the Limits of the expected new government." After they had left for Kentucky, the large party separated into three groups. In the first were most of the women and children, the cattle, and the baggage. Behind them followed five white men, two slaves, and Captain Russell's young son. Russell brought up the rear. One evening while they slept, the middle party came under attack. One of the slaves, four of the white men, and Russell's young son perished. In the morning, Russell came across the mangled corpses. A "dart and arrows" had pieced his boy's body, and beside him lay a "war club." A spear found in one of the other bodies was thought to be Cherokee. The raiders also tortured and killed one of Boone's sons. The raiding party, the survivors believed, had targeted and tracked the group throughout the preceding day.[62]

Dunmore declared that the murderers would suffer "the Certain Vengeance of the Virginians."[63] He was right, but in ways he scarcely hoped to imagine. The only survivor from the sleeping party, a fellow by the name of Crabtree, decided to take matters into his own hands.[64] In the spring of 1774, it was reported that he was on the hunt for Indians. When he heard of "37 Warriors" in the vicinity, he set off to find "two or three, defenceless wretches." He came across one such Cherokee named Billy at a horse race at Watauga. Although Billy had nothing to do with the murders, Crabtree killed him.[65] Fear swept the settlements. Few dared venture down the Ohio River or through the Cumberland Gap.[66] A surveyor and land agent declared that the "sober minded" detested men such as Crabtree, lamenting that because of the murderous disposition of squatters like him, "perhaps the profligate part of the nation is both our Judges and executioners."[67]

But even if Crabtree confounded officials by making the trip to the West more dangerous, his murder of Billy served a purpose. Common people rallied around the murderer, and Crabtree could not be dismissed as a senseless Indian killer. While Dunmore's agents feared the "consequences" of his provocative actions, they conceded that "it would be easier to find 100 men to screen him from the Law, than ten to bring him to Justice." Moreover, the killing increased tensions in the West, allowing Dunmore to portray himself as a defender of frontier folk even while he undermined their claims. Crabtree's killing and the Russell murders, after all, were "in every ones mouth." The people, it seemed, teetered between hostility and vengeance, on the one hand, and fear and trepidation, on the other.[68]

In the wake of the tit-for-tat killings, the violence escalated. In the spring of 1774, as Thomas Wharton explained, "one Black and others . . . about 170 Miles below Fort pit saw some Indians on the opposite side of the River. They gave them an invitation to come over to the House which the Indians did." The men killed each of the Indians. The following day two Indians visited the house of Michael Cresap, the son of Thomas Cresap, who had served Lord Baltimore in the earlier border dispute with the Penn family. Throughout much of 1773 and 1774, Michael Cresap had been a man of so many loyalties that at the time it was hard to know if he was working for the government of Vandalia or Virginia.[69] When they arrived at Cresap's place, the Indians "told him that there was War" and tried to rob him. Cresap "pulled pistols out of his pocket," shooting them. He then took his canoe to an Indian settlement, where he and a band of his neighbors "killed a Number of Men, Women, and Children." Wharton had heard that Cresap's murderous spree took the lives of forty-nine.[70]

Cresap's actions plunged the West into chaos. It was reported that at a place called Yellow Creek he had killed the family of the Mingo war leader Logan, who then went on a vengeful tear, slaughtering settlers in the region along Redstone Creek where Cresap and his henchmen lived. On one of his raids, Logan killed and scalped a settler named William Speir, his wife, and four children, leaving an ax sticking in Speir's chest.[71] Although the British had no power in the region, Sir William Johnson scurried to put together a conference with the Six Nations over Cresap's actions. While meeting with the Iroquois to discuss a way out of what looked to be a hopeless situation, Johnson was "seized with a Suffocation of which he expired in less than two hours."[72]

In fact, Cresap had not murdered forty-nine Indians. True, he had ambushed a small party only partially made up of Indians, killing a Shawnee and a Delaware. And according to one witness, Cresap had sworn that "he wou'd put every Indian he met with on the River to death, and that if he could raise men sufficient to cross the River, he wou'd attack a small village of Indians living on Yellow Creek."[73] True to his word, he and his party attacked a group of Shawnees who came across his plantation.[74]

But Cresap did not kill Logan's family at Yellow Creek. A party led by Daniel Greathouse did.[75] One of Johnson's agents, Alexander McKee, dispatched a report, relaying the details of the massacre as they were told to him by William Crawford. Crawford, who was working for Dunmore's agents, ran into Greathouse on his way to Pittsburgh. Greathouse "presented several Indian scalps" to Crawford and told him this tale: He and his men had lured four Indians, two men and two women, to drink with them on Yellow Creek. "Finding them intoxicated," he killed and scalped the four. He did the same to two others who ventured from their nearby camp to see what the commotion was. He then prepared an ambush for six other Indians in a canoe, shooting four. Two fell into the river, two slumped into the canoe. One, gravely wounded, escaped. But after he made his way to the Indian camp nearby, the killers "heard the women and children at the camp raise a very melancholly cry." One of the men then shot a woman in the forehead who had a child on her back. "After some Altercation between those Murderers whether they should put the child to death," Crawford reported, one argued that they should "dash" its "brains out." Eventually, however, "they agreed to take it along with them." The father, it turned out, was a trader. They would send the child to him. Although Crawford considered this "a barbarous murder," worse was to follow. Greathouse's gang captured Logan's kin. They would later be slaughtered as well, including Logan's pregnant sister. According to one account, her unborn child was ripped from her body and "stuck on a pole."[76]

Regardless of who had committed the atrocities, the man who took over as superintendent after William Johnson's death—his nephew—

noted a change in behavior after the Cresap incident and the murder of the Russell boy and James Boone. Large parties of Virginians, Guy Johnson argued, had penetrated into Indian country, exacting vengeance and building forts.[77] Dunmore had more than vengeance on the mind. After all, Russell and Boone's party was heading to the lands between the Ohio and the "Waters of the Cherokee River," a region "the settling of which is now encouraged by Government." Dunmore had to act to keep both approaches to the Kentucky Country open, the Ohio River route and the Cumberland Gap. If he did not clear the way, speculators and prospective settlers would abandon the West.[78] After the incidents, Connolly mobilized the militia and reported that it appeared Indians in the Ohio Country were preparing for war.[79]

While Cherokee leaders pleaded with younger men to practice forbearance, many would not. These people were, in a word, "formidable."[80] "The hour that I so much dreaded (as to the peace of the country)," a fearful official wrote, "is now I am apprehending near at hand. The Cherokees has at length commenced hostilities."[81] The specter of a war with the Cherokees threw the West into "an uproar." The settlers of William Preston's own Fincastle County, he lamented, were "flying in Crowds, leaving their Farms in Ruin and Desolation." The West "is now almost a Frontier." Those who stayed began building small community forts into which those from the surrounding countryside could flee in times of alarm. Preston found this "an uncomfortable way of living; but any thing is better than Running." Settlers, he argued, fled "withal not a Drop of Blood spilled or an Indian seen."[82]

Hostility the likes of Dunmore and Connolly welcomed. But panic was another matter. If settlers fled, they served no one's interests. Dunmore's agents therefore pressed the people to stay. Dunmore raised the idea of constructing a large fort along one of the trouble spots, the mouth of the New River, a place where troops could patrol the Ohio and the interior tributaries. Two other outposts were constructed at the mouths of Wheeling Creek and the Hockhocking River.[83] When William Christian met Dunmore in Williamsburg, he was advised "to use his best endeavours to prevent the flight of the inhabitants." Christian was also "to give assurance to the people that the War should be carried into the enemies country." Dunmore feared above all that the "great part of the county would be evacuated." Christian, William Preston, and Arthur Campbell spent the next three months attending to this task, encouraging others, as one put it, "to make a stand."[84] Within two months, Christian learned that settlers had erected four forts on the Clinch manned with 115 men.[85]

Vigilance was required to keep the people from running.[86] Constant flashes of violence required local justices of the peace and militia commanders to hope that rising fears would "draw out" militias from neighboring counties and give the people the courage they needed to hold fast.[87] After all, even if inhabitants heeded such advice, the people in the newly erected forts would largely be women and children. The men would need to range for the enemy. This is the dilemma Michael Woods faced. He followed Preston's advice, building a small blockhouse on Rich Creek in Fincastle County that he christened Fort Dunmore. He counted 140 in the fort, mainly women and children. He begged for more ammunition. Without it, the people might flee.[88]

Although Preston admonished others "to stand our ground and to buld forts for our defence," inhabitants complained that "our scatered situation maks it very deficualt."[89] In these circumstances, few had any alternative but flight.[90] Militia commanders reported difficulties getting men to muster at all. To leave family and kin during such a volatile period invited tragedy.[91]

Under these circumstances, when the success or failure of Dunmore's plans rested on the shoulders of settlers, local officials did all in their power to accede to popular demands. Dunmore ordered the raising of militias in alarmed counties, but as officials called out the men on Moccasin Creek to muster, they allowed them to take the "unprecedented step" of selecting their own captains, determining where they would range, and dispatching their own scouts. Settlers wanted to set up defenses on their own terms. Because they feared the people were "about to desert their plantations," officials listened to their demands.[92] To ensure men turned out, Preston and the others tried to pick popular officers, such as Daniel Boone, to lead companies. Officials also pandered to Indian hatreds. Because "the men seem resolute for a sculp or two," one militia leader "offered £5 for the first Indian hand that will be brought into the fort."[93]

Officials, no doubt, groped to discover which group of Indians in fact had been responsible for murders—both real and imagined. Nonetheless, they understood that the Cherokees would serve neither their purposes nor Dunmore's. And by July 1774, officials began changing their story about Cherokee hostility.[94] Although "the young men were for immediate revenge," the "chiefs" were "very much for peace," they suggested. The Cherokees were not planning to rise with the Shawnees against the Virginians; indeed, an official reported that a Cherokee had tracked down and killed a Shawnee who reputedly had killed a white woman. These Indians "were friendly and kind and expressing the greatest regard for the white people."[95]

Virginia officials now claimed the whole campaign against the Cherokees had been sustained by "false reports." In June, Christian declared that "the news of the peoples being killed at Copper creek proved false."[96] On July 4, he received word that "some people were killed at muddy creek last week." By this time, however, he declared, "I never depend on reports unless well attested there being so many false ones."[97] Rumors such as these emerged from the kind of atmosphere they engendered. They provoked the sort of crisis Dunmore and his agents were beginning to hope for; but they also produced panic.[98] In such an atmosphere, in which one false report could set off an exodus, the Cherokees proved too formidable an enemy for Dunmore's plans for the West to work.[99]

Dunmore therefore moved to neutralize the Cherokees diplomatically. In that tense summer, he dispatched William Preston to meet with the Cherokees to defuse the situation. Preston chided them for the murder of the Russell party. But instead of demonizing the Cherokees in general, he blamed "Hot headed young men" for the attack, supporting the contention of Cherokee leaders. Preston sought to create common ground with leaders who did not want to become engaged in a bloody war with the Virginians. Acts of violence, Preston declared, were not sanctioned by Dunmore or any officials of Virginia. They were perpetrated by "a very few of the most worthless abandoned of white People who acted from the basest and most unmanly Principles." Specifically, he acknowledged the "unmanly and barbarous" murder committed by Crabtree. He promised justice and hoped that Cherokees would not attack the innocent.[100] For their part, the Cherokees eventually executed one of their own involved in the murder of Russell's son.[101]

The British, of course, had confronted a similar dilemma. Pleasing settlers, Indians, and speculators had proved impossible for them. Keeping these groups apart seemed the only way to maintain a semblance of order and avoid all-out war. Dunmore and local officials figured a different way out of this dilemma. Or better, they were presented with a solution. As they began to believe that the Cherokees were not—nor for their purposes could be—behind most of the bloodshed on the frontier, they fastened on a new and, as it turned out, more useful enemy, one sure to enrage but not terrify the settlers, the Shawnees. For a start, because settlers and speculators were competing for Shawnee lands and raiding parties attacked settlements from time to time, both groups hated them. Moreover, the British had isolated the Shawnees diplomatically to win the blessing or at least acquiescence of other Indian groups for the Fort Stanwix Treaty. Finally, because they could not put a large number of men in the field, they did not pose nearly the same threat as the Cherokees. In 1774, the Shawnees appeared weakened, alone, and divided.[102]

As Preston worked to make peace with the Cherokees, Christian was preparing scouting parties to engage the Shawnees.[103] In late June, the Pittsburgh militia indeed attacked Shawnees who had arrived at the settlement with traders. By July, bands of frontier militia were launching small raids into Shawnee country, and in August they attacked and burned an abandoned Shawnee settlement and five smaller villages on the Muskingum.[104]

Near the end of the summer of 1774, men and women were on knife edge, standing fast on the frontiers to protect the homes they had built but anxious to get at the Shawnees.[105] By this point, Dunmore had declared that "hopes of a pacification can be no longer entertained, and that these People [Shawnees] will by no means be diverted from their design of falling upon the back parts." The Assembly in Virginia, "though they were sufficiently apprised of it," would not act. So Dunmore would. He ordered militias to prepare for defensive or offensive operations and the construction of small forts "in such places as would serve best to protect the adjacent settlers."[106] Already fresh reports were arriving of Shawnee belligerence, including a rumor that a raider had taken "five or six small scalps," presumably belonging to children.[107] The greatest task Dunmore and his agents now faced was "endeavouring to divert them [settlers] from believing it is the Cherokees" who attacked settlements—even if this was the case—"which seems to be their greatest terror."[108]

The governor of North Carolina informed British officials that the Earl of Dunmore "really believes that colony [Virginia] is engaged in a most serious War with the Indians."[109] To Virginia's rivals, this war appeared a sham. Pennsylvania officials certainly argued this was the case.[110] And Vandalia's promoters understood what Dunmore was up to. "Can it be possible," Thomas Wharton asked—facetiously—"that Government will let such Men as Cresap . . . go unpunished?" After all, it was rumored Cresap "was making of large Surveys, at the time of this Quarel—and some do not hesitate to say for a Certain Lord." Wharton declared that "every Information We can get, very clearly proves the friendly disposition of the Indians." He understood the implications of Dunmore's provocations. The Shawnees would play into his hands.[111] In fact, it appeared that Cresap's actions—and the other massacres—were part of a conspiracy engineered by Dunmore, Connolly, and their agents like Preston for a landgrab. This was calculated slaughter.[112]

George Croghan understood the nature of the game afoot as well. His fortunes and fortune were tied to the success of Vandalia. If Dunmore won, Croghan was finished. But Croghan was no fool. He played three games of his own and hedged his bets. He planned defenses with supporters of the Pennsylvania interest. He also acknowledged—in some fashion at least—Virginia's sovereignty. And all the while he was using his waning power to keep the peace, a move that would, he hoped, preserve Vandalia. In other words, he tried to use his influence and guile to subvert Dunmore and Connolly's plan.[113]

But when the crisis with the Cherokees and the Shawnees first unfolded, Croghan showed his hand. After Cresap's and Greathouse's misdeeds, a group of Indians arrived at Fort Pitt and told Croghan they would set off "to Alarm the Nations," ensuring "destruction over our Frontiers." Croghan successfully pleaded with them not to take this step.[114] Croghan did not play the peacemaker for altruistic reasons. War, he knew, would imperil Vandalia, driving prospective settlers off. With no militia, no institutional structure, and no government, Vandalia could offer no protection. Violence therefore invited disaster. As Croghan put it, "I have more private property to lose in this country by an Indian war than perhaps any other single subject has at present." He concluded that "an Indian war would ruin my affairs."[115]

He found himself exposed as he cooperated with Pennsylvanians to devise some protective measures. As Vandalia's chief booster, Croghan also wanted to stem the flow of people off the frontiers by offering them some form of protection. But he did so by negotiating in good faith with the Delawares, Shawnees, and Six Nations and by taking prudent measures, not by manipulating a volatile situation. In early June, as he held a series of meetings with Indian representatives, he hired men to protect his property and his home and plantation, which he called Croghan Hall, from Indians and Virginians and, along with some of his friends from Pennsylvania, enlisted scouts to range down the Ohio "in order to protect our fellow subjects from flying down the cuntry as itt appears that a General panick has sazed the whole cuntry."[116]

Perhaps Connolly saw through Croghan. Perhaps not. Nonetheless, hiring the scouts gave Connolly the excuse he needed to pounce on Croghan. He portrayed Croghan's attempt to raise scouts in cooperation with Pennsylvania supporters as treachery and as a challenge to Virginia's authority in the region.[117] Laid up with gout and rheumatism, Croghan witnessed his reputation besmirched and his solid relations with Indians imperiled.[118] In fact, Dunmore laid the whole crisis at Croghan's doorstep. He stormed that Croghan "has strove to sett the Shawnese upon the backs of the Virginians by his insidious and dangerous speeches." Croghan, he alleged, was "the sole author and sole cause of all the present disturbances." Dunmore charged that he had denied Virginia's jurisdiction in the region, though he had accepted a commission as magistrate. "He had constantly acted a duplicate part throughout the whole tenor of his conduct" and was engaged in "complicated malpractices." At least, Croghan stood guilty of this last charge. Dunmore hoped to see Croghan delivered to Williamsburg in irons as "the author of all the disturbances in these parts."[119]

With Croghan discredited and his diplomatic overtures compromised, the Virginians had ensured the Shawnees remained isolated. The work of the surveyors about the Falls of the Ohio had "discontented" some Shawnees, especially the young men. But they would find little support for their grievances. Although some Shawnees had spent a great deal of time trying to bind Indians together in a confederacy to resist white encroachment, these plans had foundered on the resolve of Dunmore. The Cherokees had already been neutralized. The Delawares, who saw the looming storm, would not support them. Their putative patrons the Six Nations, who counseled peace with the Virginians, would "take no part with the

Shawnese."[120] When Shawnee diplomats offered the "war belt" to the Iroquois and "demanded the Hatchet to strike the English," a Mohawk
"threw the Belt back at them."[121] Only some of Logan's Mingoes could be
expected to stand with the Shawnees.[122]

Plans appeared to be coalescing. As the Shawnees steeled themselves
for the inevitable, Dunmore asked Connolly to make preparations for
"marching into the Shawnese Town." He ordered Connolly to instruct the
officers leading the expedition "to make as many Prisoners as they can of
Women and Children" and "to reduce the Savages to sue for Peace."[123]
The people were at a perfect pitch, prepared to vent their spleen on an isolated and vulnerable enemy.[124] In these circumstances, the Shawnees had
little choice but to attack. A few did so in early September. On the Clinch,
Shawnee raiders killed John Henry and took his wife and two children
from their beds, dragging them back to their settlement. Similar small
raids took place throughout the month.[125] The people clamored for revenge. One particular incident illustrated how far the settlers had come. A
boy who was scalped near the Clinch "frequently lamented" before he
died that "he was not able to fight enough for to save his mammy."[126]

Plans for the assault on Shawnee country began at Fort Dunmore.
During the summer, Dunmore left Williamsburg, stayed at Michael
Cresap's father's place, and arrived at Pittsburgh. His entourage from the
East included seven hundred men and "a couple of French horns and a
S——tch piper, with the Union Flag desplayd."[127] Volunteers intent on
booty and land made up Dunmore's force.[128] Ostensibly, he ventured west
to meet with Delawares, Shawnees, Mingoes, and Iroquois, but in reality
he arrived to make final preparations for war. And he would be ready to go
once the scouts, such as Boone, returned with word about the surveyors.[129]
By September, all was in place. On September 11, Connolly declared that
the Shawnees "had a long time since maltreated the Virginians, that the
latter had never scorged them for it, and that now he was come with the
troops of that Province to chastise them." Dunmore then asked Connolly
to call out the county militias.[130]

While Dunmore made ready at Pittsburgh, his agents like William
Christian "continued to exert himself for promoting the expedition as well
as taking care of the Fronteers."[131] Christian faced an immense task. As
well as drumming up support, he had to keep an eye out for surveyors, offering them all the protection they needed to make it back.[132] He also had

to coordinate the movement of men and supplies from all over the West. The county lieutenant for Augusta, Charles Lewis, marched with six hundred men, canoes, and four hundred packhorses carrying fifty-four thousand pounds of flour. Four hundred men came from Botetourt County. One column of twelve hundred men would be led by Andrew Lewis, chief agent of the Greenbrier Company. As Christian said, "the number of men greatly exceeds his expectations." Christian had three hundred men from Fincastle with him. But he thought he would have to requisition more to highlight Fincastle's contribution, even if doing so weakened the county's protective cordon.[133] Dunmore marched west as well with a force of over a thousand troops, who would rendezvous with Andrew Lewis's forces farther west.

Even as they marched to battle the Shawnees, officers still had to strike the balance between fear and hostility. As soon as the troops headed west, they came under attack. John McGuire of Andrew Lewis's column "was badly wounded" in one exchange. Thirty Indians ambushed Dunmore's advance party of four hundred. Four men died. Later others discovered their scalps "hung up like Colours." Although the Shawnees could not produce the same number of fighting men the Cherokees could, one commander reckoned "with their near friends" they could "meet us with about 1200 good men on short warning."[134] To keep the men from fleeing, local officials acceded to the men's wishes about the type of officer who would lead them.[135] Officials also decided "it is not best to say any thing publickly of attacking the [Shawnee] Towns, but only to propose going to Ohio . . . and returning up New River." They were moving west to "chastise," not to conquer. Most troops dreaded the thought of crossing the river or moving "so near the Enemy's Country." Marching north of the Ohio to Shawnee settlements would require staying in the field for a prolonged period of time. Marching north also might reveal that the expedition was less about protection for the frontier than about determining who would rule it. On the other hand, recruiting circulars, which suggested that Shawnee towns might be targeted, declared that vengeance, protection, and plunder were assured by an operation in which "the Earl of Dunmore is Deeply ingaged."[136]

In early October, the main body led by Andrew Lewis arrived at a place called Point Pleasant on the south bank of the Ohio River where it meets the Great Kanawha. The troops did not cross, but made camp. As an officer named William Ingles declared, they thought themselves "a terror to all the Indian Tribes on the Ohio and thus Luld in safety till Sunday the 9th." All hell broke loose after they heard the Sabbath sermon. A hunting party had discovered Indians, who had crossed the river on rafts the night before, a mile away from the camp. Ingles dispatched a detachment and in so doing touched off a larger engagement. The Shawnees "Disputed the Ground with the greatest obstinancey often running up to the very muzles of our Guns where the[y] as often fell Victims to their Rage." The Indians fell back to defensible ground and continued engaging the Virginians.[137] The Shawnees hoped to keep them from their settlements on the Scioto.[138]

"I cannot describe the bravery of the enemy in the battle," Christian contended. "It exceeded every man's expectations." Far from a soft target, the Shawnees had deployed shrewd defenses along the Ohio, placing men on both sides of the river "to kill our men as they would swim over." The "Chief" of the Shawnees facing the Virginians "continually ran along the line exhorting these men to 'eye close and shoot well' and 'fight and be strong.'" The Virginians retreated under the onslaught, at "which the enemy beat back slowly and killed and wounded our men at every advance."[139] With reinforcements, the Virginians finally formed a line. The Indians taunted them, challenging them "to come up and learn to shoot." The Virginians refused to charge but held the line. At nightfall, as they pulled back, some Shawnees called out that "tomorrow they wd have 2000 men for them," and "damnd our people often for 'sons of bitches.'" Others hollered, "'Don't you whistle now' (deriding the fife) and made very merry about a treaty."[140]

The Indians did not return with two thousand. Nor should they have spoken of a "treaty." The two sides had fought to a standstill at Point Pleasant.[141] Meanwhile, Dunmore marched his force north of the river to the Shawnee town of Chillicothe. He learned that the Shawnees had prepared for his arrival, clearing a field of fire around the town, and had "plenty of provisions, ammunition in the greatest plenty."[142] They did not fight. Surrounded by the troops that had marched with Dunmore and those that had fought at Point Pleasant, the Shawnees at the urging of Cornstalk came to terms. They "proposed laying themselves at the Govrs. Mercy and told him to make the Terms and they should be complied with." Dunmore demanded all prisoners and insisted that they were "never more to make war or disturb us." From this point forward, Dunmore informed them, they were never to come over "to our settlements but to Trade."[143] Under the terms of what was called the Treaty of Camp Charlotte, the Ohio River would serve as a new line in the West. To the north would be Indian territory, and the south white land. But unlike the Proclamation Line, which the British drew up to protect Indians from settlers, Dunmore's line would safeguard settlers from Indians.[144]

The expedition proved expensive. By one estimate, marching the men to Point Pleasant and to the Shawnee towns cost £70,000, a fortune by the day's standards.[145] It proved more costly to the men involved. William Christian wrote, "Many of our wounded men died since the Accounts of the battle cam in. I think there were 70 dead." More, he lamented, "will yet die."[146] Christian had seen "many shot in two places . . . some in three." Dunmore's columns did not have to deal with such problems. "His Lordship," Christian learned, "has about 170 beeves and 50,000 of flour for 1300 men." "Perhaps," he hoped, "humanity will induce him to return and come to us." It would not. One officer "had persuaded the Govn. to come here but Maj. Connelly prevented it."[147]

Once he forced the Shawnees to the table, Dunmore did not hesitate to press his advantage in the West. To hold the line, he ordered militia to remain at Point Pleasant as a garrison force "until the Assembly can be applyed to." In other words, he saw the line as a long-term solution. Sovereignty, after all, entails clear boundaries. It also requires unambiguous authority. After he concluded negotiations with the Shawnees, "the Mingoes refused to comply with the terms of the Treaty." Dunmore sent a force of 250 men to a nearby Mingo town. The men killed five and took fourteen women and children prisoner. After they had plundered the town and burned it to the ground, they threatened other Mingo towns with the same fate.[148] Other Indian groups did not prove as foolhardy. The Iroquois, though upset by the treatment of "their oppressed Dependents" at the hands of the Virginians, feared that what had happened to the Shawnees could happen to some of them. The Delawares also "intermeddled little in it." The war further weakened the Shawnees, and with the attacks on the Mingoes they found themselves more isolated.[149]

Dunmore and his agents also saw the war as a vindication of Virginia's claims to the West. To be sure, the Crown remained sovereign. But since Dunmore could now claim he had conquered the area and that he had the allegiance of a people he had protected, Virginians would exercise that sovereignty. Although officials in Philadelphia still regarded the West as theirs, Pennsylvania's nominal claim to the Pittsburgh region suffered a heavy blow. Vandalia for all practical purposes had died.[150] Tied up in London courts and manhandled by Virginians, Vandalia would never become a colony. The failing venture's promoters still planned to entice men and women to the lands that they had argued belonged to the new government, but now they admitted they had lost the bid to bring order to the West. As they tried to sell plots, hoping to salvage some return on their investments of time, money, and hope, they did so from a place called "Pittsburgh, Virginia."[151] The once great scheme to create the great inland colony had degenerated into just another speculative venture.

As Dunmore dispatched older threats, his agents also dealt with a new challenge from North Carolina. William Preston chastised one of his underlings for raising men from the Carolinas to help protect the frontiers. Virginians, Preston suggested, had not fought for the rights of North Carolina settlers.[152] A few months after the battle, Preston reported to Dunmore that a number of men from North Carolina, led by Col. Richard Henderson, planned to settle on Cherokee lands "between the mouth of the Cherokee River and the Great Kanawa." After receiving six wagonloads of goods, Cherokee chiefs had agreed on a sale of lands along the Holston and Great Kanawha rivers and from the Ohio to the mouth of the Tennessee River. This land lay in Kentucky, claimed and now won by Virginia. Henderson planned on selling the land in the spring to "adventurers" for twenty shillings per hundred acres.[153]

Preston understood the nature of this new threat. The price Henderson had set would "induce a great many families to settle there." "When they get possession," he warned, "it may be almost impossible to remove, or reduce them to obedience." Preston promised not to allow the land to be surveyed by the North Carolinians by virtue of Dunmore's surveys and warrants.[154] He also had words with the Cherokees. The Virginians informed one of the chiefs who had made the sale, Little Carpenter, that they had no right to sell the land. Little Carpenter claimed he did not have much choice. "When the young men saw the goods," Preston learned, "they insisted on having them on any terms." He and the other chiefs were obliged to comply with Henderson or "otherwise loose their Authority in the nation, as they hold it on no other foundation than the Loves of the

People." Whether they sold it through love or avarice, the Virginians were determined not to let the deal stand.[155]

By attempting to create order out of the West's disorder, Dunmore, his speculating allies, and western officials now ensured that Virginia stood to control great sections of the West. Dunmore had vanquished the Indians and the hopes of rival claimants with the support of common settlers. Yet he had not done so for their benefit. Indeed, after he defeated the Shawnees, he turned on some of the very people that he needed to reassert control of the West. Just a few months after Dunmore had secured his treaty, his men traveled to the frontier warning people off. Elizabeth Smith, a widow, complained that "soldiers threaten to survey her lands, which her Husband settled upon near six years ago." He did so "contrary to his majesty's Proclamation," but, as Elizabeth Smith argued, "many others did" as well. In this instance, the surveyors relented, allowing Smith to remain.[156] In other cases, they did not relent. Joseph Tomlinson came west with two of his brothers in 1771 "to search for places on the Ohio River." He found a fine patch near a place called Round Bottom. "Finding no claims on that land," Tomlinson and his brothers made several improvements. While he was establishing himself, Tomlinson met George Washington's surveyor, William Crawford, the man who had heard of and condemned the Greathouse massacre as "barbarous." Crawford offered him a job surveying "military lands" between the Little Kanawha and Big Sandy Creek. After some time, the team made its way to Round Bottom, which Crawford intended to survey. Tomlinson asked him not to do so "because himself and his brothers had made improvements thereon and intended establishing settlements on it immediately." Crawford replied that Washington had instructed him to "make a private survey of the land in the Bottom and 'Pledged' his word and honor." Crawford went ahead with his work, trying to convince Tomlinson that the land would remain in his name. Tomlinson, however, had his doubts. He was right to worry. Eventually, Washington claimed possession of Round Bottom on the basis of Crawford's survey. His jobber Michael Cresap, the man who more than any other had helped engineer a crisis to remake the West for Dunmore, "sent out about fourteen hands to settle the round Bottom."[157]

Back in Williamsburg on Christmas Eve, Lord Dunmore reflected on the meaning of the war that would bear his name. Pennsylvanians alleged that he had trumped up the war to benefit himself and his "Land Jobbers." Dunmore denied the charge. But he also justified it. He had brought a semblance or veneer of order to a region where it was sorely lacking. Common settlers, in particular, needed government, not so much to protect them as to restrain them. "They do not conceive that Government has any right to forbid their taking possession of a Vast tract of Country, either uninhabited, or which serves only as a Shelter to a few Scattered Tribes of Indians," he charged. Indians, to be sure, were "but little removed from the brute Creation." The same, he suggested, held for settlers, who "acquire no attachment to Place: But wandering about Seems engrafted in their nature," and who were "equally ungovernable." To keep them in check required "to receive persons in their Circumstances, under the protection of some of His majesty's Governments already established"—Dunmore's Virginia, in other words. He concluded that "this affair, which undoubtedly was attended with circumstances of Shocking inhumanity, may be the means of producing happy effects," including impressing "an Idea of the power of the White People, upon the minds of the Indians."[158]

"It is the general opinion," William Christian declared, "that the peace with the Shawnese will be lasting."[159] The West was still a dangerous place, but no longer the terrifying state of nature that Dunmore sought to mold to his own proposes. The newly won regions proved safe enough for wealthy Virginians to stake their fortunes and futures on them.[160] From this point forward, the militia would be mustered and kept ready to protect these interests. Squatters and Indians were not welcome.[161] Unwittingly, common men and women had a hand in remaking a fallen world and redrawing a more impermeable line between whites and Indians, but they would not claim land on their own terms. In the struggle to remake society out of a competitive state of nature, the strongest and most unscrupulous had won. At least those settlers already in the West had the solace of protection. The Virginians and the Shawnees agreed to ratify a permanent peace settlement in the spring.[162] At that point, and under the broad terms already determined, the new order would formally emerge in the West.

FIVE

Revolution and Uncertainty:
The War of Independence
and Self-Sovereignty

After Point Pleasant, speculators and their jobbers, tied to wealthy patrons in the East and supported by Virginia's government, were poised to set the terms of settlement in much of the Ohio valley. Ironically, of course, common men and women in the West had a hand in this by allowing the wealthy to use them in attempting to reestablish authority. As elites pandered to settlers' fear of Indians, promising a return to order and protection, the people had followed. Ultimately, however, Dunmore would fail to reconstitute sovereignty.

The very moment Dunmore marched on the Shawnees, representatives from the mainland colonies were meeting in Philadelphia in what would be known as the First Continental Congress to discuss a concerted response to Parliament's decision to close the port of Boston, among other measures, in the wake of the Tea Party. The meeting to determine colonial action against what many Americans regarded as intolerable and provocative acts did not bode well for Dunmore's tenure in Virginia. In 1773 and 1774, Dunmore had dissolved the Virginia Assembly when its members voiced support for resistance to British pressure. Then, in 1775, less than a year after the defeat of the Shawnees, Dunmore's actions provoked a crisis in the colony. In that year, he removed Williamsburg's store of gunpowder to a warship when rumors of a rising reached his ears, and he issued proclamations forbidding the meeting of any convention and, most famously, offering freedom to slaves of "patriots." Amid rioting, he fled the capital, allowing the people to declare that much like King James II, he had abdicated his position as governor. A revolutionary convention now ruled Virginia.[1]

Just how long this state of affairs would last no one knew, nor could anyone guess. In other words, with the beginnings of what would become a war of independence, Dunmore's flight threw the West into a state of uncertainty and flux. With so many questions about authority unresolved, men and women—wealthy and poor, Indian and settler, Virginian and Pennsylvanian, American and British—floundered. If the western crisis of sovereignty unleashed a maelstrom of competing interests amid chaos, the beginning of the broader War of Independence and the uncertainty it engendered marked a distinctive and tentative phase of that process.

Although the period of flux begot indecision, the glimmers of something revolutionary were becoming discernible during these years. After Dunmore's fall, leading patriots from Virginia followed his example and sought to restore order on the frontier—and to claim much of it—by curtailing rights of improvement, traditional prerogatives of settlers that had defined the process of frontier development for decades. In this instance, however, some common people would start to make a case for the retrieval of these rights. This cause, of course, would appear more conservative or backward-looking than progressive.[2] Yet something more fundamental was at work. Immediately preceding the War of Independence, settlers had given leave to men like Dunmore and Connolly to reknit the social fabric as they wished. In the midst of the collapse of power and authority in the West and through the crucible of the War of Independence, some people were refusing to allow this sort of thing to happen again.

The shift began to take place as no reliable patrons emerged to recontrol the West in the first years of the War of Independence. With Dunmore's failure, neither the British, the new American government, state officials, nor Indians could reestablish order on their own terms. Even those most likely to prevail, patriot Virginia's leaders, failed. As competition isolated common men and women, estranging them further from competing groups, they grew less inclined to rely on others to reconstitute the bonds of society in their name. The sense among common people that they had no single party to blame for their plight, could count on no one to relieve them, and had no confidence in the ability of any single group to reassert authority allowed the people of the West to begin refashioning the tentativeness and indifference of others into the stuff of their own politicization. This subtle but revolutionary change—the first stirrings of self-sovereignty in a world without sovereignty—represented the stuff of the West's war of independence.[3]

Lord Dunmore's fall from grace in Virginia did not lead to an explosion of violence, but hostilities simmered, and given the general unease gripping the whole continent, the empire, and especially the West, few made daring pronouncements about authority. Uncertainty, of course, generated fear. But it also compounded confusion. Take the case of the Indians in the Ohio valley. Given the way Virginians had treated Indians in places like Kentucky, British officials expected a "General Confederacy against the Rebels."[4] In fact, as one commentator explained, most Indians were "in a great Pannick." Settlers were building forts, surveyors mapped their lands, and no one restrained either. The British could offer no real protection to what Indians called "the big knife."[5] Far from creating a sense of unity or Pan-Indian cooperation, the atmosphere of the period heightened divisions among Native Americans. Older Cherokee and Shawnee leaders, who had witnessed the ravages of more than twenty years of hostility, had seen alliances and allies come and go, and now saw how whites turned against each other, believed that using the uncertainty of the period to declare their own independence invited more disaster. Younger men, who had the most to lose by watching settlers overrun hunting grounds and the most to gain in terms of prestige by launching raids, acted as free agents in the West.[6] In these circumstances, for many Indians "the happy Moment was now arrived when they might do themselves Justice and recover their lost Lands," and small raiding parties fanned out from Cherokee and Shawnee villages without the blessing of their elders to recover hunting grounds and settle old scores, generating sporadic, rather than generalized, violence.[7]

Uncertainty, however, did not only confound Indian responses to the question of order. The British also failed to take concerted action in the West. For their part, the British responded to the new western crisis with caution. Since 1772, they had little active presence in western regions outside the jurisdiction of Quebec. By 1775, they did not plan to reenter that chaotic world. Officials like John Stuart and Guy Johnson kept London informed of developments in the West, urging their overlords to approach the region with care. For the most part, officials followed Stuart and Johnson's lead. British agents would keep a keen eye on rebel movements in the West, hoping, for example, not to allow American adversaries to create a strategic link to the Mississippi and the port of New Orleans.[8]

In fact, the region proved of only marginal interest to the British in the early years of the war and mattered only insofar as it affected the central struggle with the rebels. Neither the Board of Trade nor the ministry thought the time was at hand to initiate a war of liberation for the Indians. Instead, officials ordered commanders to adopt a wait-and-see approach and "to try all means to preserve the general Peace" with the Indians.[9] Instead of retaking abandoned forts or devising a grand western strategy, British officials proposed taking advantage of Indian discontent to harass the rebellious colonies along their edges. Gage believed that the rebels, who had abused the Indians in their greed for land, deserved as much, and wished to make use of the Indians "to distress a people who have acted so wantonly rebellious."[10] But even these moves proved tentative and unformulated.

The more cautious Johnson and Stuart contended that a placid West served the larger goals of winning the war and eventually reintegrating the colonies into the nation. Stuart argued that his deputies should go among the Indians, the Cherokees in particular, and urge them to drive "all agents and emissaries from the Rebells" out of their lands.[11] But he did not see the efficacy of sponsoring Indian raids. "I do not construe this Instruction as an Order to attack the frontier Inhabitants of the provinces indiscriminately," he argued. He would "employ the Indians . . . to distress His Majesty's Rebellious Subjects by all practicable Means, that Government and the Constitution may be re-established in the distracted provinces." Slaughter would not serve these purposes.[12] Guy Johnson agreed. For him, the purpose of any western policy was "to preserve the Indians dependence on, and their attachment to the Crown." He advised continuing to cultivate Indian friendship, but warned against trying to persuade Indians to launch a strategic offensive.[13] At the end of the day, they decided— by default, really—to take what the unsettledness of the West provided.[14]

Henry Hamilton was the exception that proved this British rule. A career soldier who had served in the Seven Years' War, Hamilton became lieutenant governor of Detroit in 1775. His main task was to "keep the Savages in readiness" should military commanders deem their help necessary. Throughout 1775 and 1776 he did just that. In 1777, officials—or so they claimed—decided the time had come to use what "Providence has put into His Majesty's Hands, for crushing the Rebellion."[15] Lord George Germain suggested that "Parties of Indians conducted by proper leaders" should make "a Diversion on the Frontiers of Virginia and Pennsylvania." Good leaders, he hoped, would restrain Indians from committing atrocities and direct them to proper targets.[16] Hamilton received orders to "fill all the lower parts of the Ohio with bodies of savages that should constantly succeed each other." At all times, Indians should be in the field "ready to fall upon the Rebels" and cut off all communications and commerce on the Mississippi.[17] Although it is unclear whether Hamilton paid scalp bounties to Indians—perhaps a myth earning him the sobriquet "the hair buyer"—he indeed offered "presents," such as weapons, ammunition, food, and blankets, to the Indians of the upper Great Lakes region who traveled to and from Detroit, as well as Indians from the Ohio valley.[18]

The results, reflecting the opportunistic approach, proved modest. Indians attacked targets of opportunity but in some cases shot little more than cattle and horses. In 1777, for example, Morgan Jones of Grave Creek reported an attack on his settlement during which Indians killed a mare, stole a few horses, and maimed cattle. "The Cattle," he claimed, "came home with the arrows sticking in them twelve Inches." He and his neighbors tracked the raiding party, but the Indians got away.[19] Though terrifying, such raids usually did not rise above the level of harassment and, when they did, proved isolated. Of course, settlers died, but far fewer than in periods of general warfare. Young Indian men, as it was reported, "were now determined for the King," who was providing some with the tools of warfare.[20] But the nature of what they were doing did not change with British involvement.

Early in the war, the Americans responded to limited raids with limited expeditions. In 1777, as Guy Johnson reported, the "diversion" policy was having some success. Raids along the frontiers of Pennsylvania and Virginia—staged by Cherokees, Iroquois, Shawnees, and Indians from the upper Great Lakes—had forced the Americans "to detach General Hand with some Troops to protect the Frontiers."[21] Americans had indeed dispatched a force under Edward Hand to garrison Fort Pitt. They also sent troops to deal with the raids of young Cherokees. Nearly two thousand men marched to some Cherokee villages, long deserted by the time they arrived. The troops burned the houses they came across and sixteen acres of corn. But they caught few Indians, many of whom simply moved farther west to continue launching their raids. In fact, the only incident worth noting on the entire expedition, which lasted but a month, occurred on the morning of September 1, when a fellow named Jonathan Huff was accidentally shot and killed as he was crossing a creek. Commanders staged raids like this in part to ensure that Indians would not plunge the region into generalized violence.[22]

Indeed, easterners only sponsored such expeditions to keep the West quiet. An American agent even discounted the significance of Indian raids for the tranquillity of the West. He argued that they were infrequent and that those rumored to be in the offing were "not only improbable, but impracticable." Why, he wondered, would Indians from Detroit trek down to the frontiers of Virginia and Pennsylvania? Such reports only "injure the Frontier Inhabitants."[23] Truth be told, the Americans were doing very little to protect the frontiers. British plans of "diversion," of course, could only work if the Americans considered the West significant. But given what they were dealing with in the East, the West did not capture the attention or the imagination of rebel leaders. Both the Continental Congress and the army regarded the West in much the same way the British did, as a backwater to the main theater of operations in the East.

Leaders did not ask what they could do for the West; they asked what it could do for them. In most cases, they hoped to extract men and food from western regions to people and feed the eastern army. From early on, Washington called for western beef to feed the Continental army and for men from the West to bolster troop levels in the East. He and others, in fact, hoped that western "long rifles" aimed by men with skill as marksmen would terrify the British. In 1775, Gage reported that "Emigrants from Ireland have arrived . . . at Philadelphia, where we are informed Arms were immediately put into their hands upon landing. There are many Irish in the Rebel army particularly amongst the Rifle-Men, brought here [to Boston] from the Frontiers of Virginia and Pennsylvania." The great rifleman coup never transpired.[24] Nonetheless, Washington ordered his recruiting officers to scour the frontiers for men.[25] East trumped West. William Grant, a deserter from the Continental army, claimed that easterners insisted that the West was pacified, creating justifications to entice militias raised for western defense to leave and join the army in New Jersey.[26]

A stable West, one supplying men and materials to the East, served a larger goal of independence. The key to that policy, as far as easterners were concerned, was placating the group of Indians closest to settlements of the Pennsylvania and Virginia frontiers, the Delawares. Officials did all in their limited powers to keep the Delawares neutral, signing treaties in 1775, 1776, and 1777, promising goods and friendship for neutrality.[27] Indeed, members of the Continental Congress styled themselves as impartial friends of the Delawares. They understood that tensions existed among the Delaware peoples. Like the Shawnees and Cherokees, young Delawares launched sporadic raids on frontier settlements. But leaders understood that as long as Delaware communities were divided, general war could be avoided.[28] In the meantime, congressmen assured the Delawares that they would not neglect them "when the country shall be restored to quiet to encourage and promote your Civilization by inducing Ministers, Schoolmasters, Tradesmen and Husbandmen to reside among you."[29]

American officials also understood the bind in which Delaware leaders found themselves. At once under British and under American pressure to remain quiet, the leaders also confronted what they called "the foolish young men" in their nation who wanted to war with Virginians, as well as the warriors of other Indian nations who regarded the Delawares as "Virginians."[30] Retaining Delaware friendship, Congress reasoned with a great deal of justification, required fair dealing and a steady supply of goods above and beyond what the British could offer. Americans did not flood Delaware villages with goods—far from it—and Delawares continually complained about "the want of Cloaths."[31] But they did what they regarded as just enough to keep the Delawares from going to war on the frontiers.

Above all, Americans tried to cultivate the friendship of Christian Delawares who lived along the Muskingum River with Moravian missionaries. Neutral and peaceful, these men and women refused to be dragged into the conflict on principle. And these communities proved to be models of the sort of neutrality the new American government hoped to cultivate among the Delawares. Although the men and women would take no part in war, the Moravians who ministered to them provided critical intelligence to American authorities about bands of belligerent Delawares and the hostile plans of other groups of Indians. When rumors swirled of potential attacks, the Moravian David Zeisberger informed the commander at Fort Pitt. Time and time again, he assured the Americans that Delaware leaders "are yet determined to stand fast and not to meddle with the war" and "want to live in friendship with the white People if they only know that the white People has no bad designs against them."[32] Meanwhile, members of Congress assured "the pious Instructor" that "we will afford him every assistance."[33]

Treating groups like the Delawares with dignity, or at least claiming to care about their plight, would ensure that violence would not reach diverting levels. A western commander claimed that Indians and settlers shared a common bond and common destiny. Both were "Countrymen, born and grown up in the same Country." If divided, the British were to blame. "Americans," he declared, "would never have differed with the Indians if they had not been forced to it by the English, when their King ruled America."[34] Mimicking the measures the British had adopted in 1763 in the West, Congress appointed commissioners of trade with the Indians and superintendents of Indian affairs and planned on establishing two stores for trading, one in the heart of Delaware country on the Muskingum, the other near Shawnee lands on the Scioto, mandating fixed prices for goods. Regulating trade would, American officials hoped, "keep them in Peace with the Colonies" and keep the West quiet.[35]

In truth, pious words defined the American approach to the West. To be sure, when the British did not move to reman the forts in the Ohio Country that they had abandoned, Americans did. But supplying the West remained an afterthought. The very worst officers led the troops in the West, and western commanders routinely had insufficient troops at their disposal to protect settlements or supply Indians. The American commander in the West who took over for Hand, Gen. Lachlan McIntosh, envisioned a refurbished Fort Pitt as a hub of the West, bristling with cannon, manned by a large number of troops, and surrounded by smaller forts up and down the frontier. Instead, he would have to make do with little more than a hundred men.[36] The few troops at this and smaller outposts in the region complained on a continual basis of shortages of food, blankets, kettles, and even powder. Barracks, if they existed, were in an appalling state, and some of the posts were "badly situated" and virtually useless for defense.[37] To make matters worse, smallpox struck a disheveled Fort Pitt and the smaller posts along the Ohio and its tributaries in 1777.[38]

The man responsible for implementing this American policy along the frontiers of Pennsylvania and Virginia, therefore, faced a daunting challenge. George Morgan had worked with George Croghan as a trader, had lived in the Illinois Country, had served as a frontier diplomat, and had been a partner in a number of land schemes, including the crippled Vandalia enterprise. As soon as the war broke out, Morgan accepted a position as the chief agent for Indian affairs in the "Middle Department," occupying a position more or less comparable to Guy Johnson's and John Stuart's posts. He reported to a group of officials, largely from Virginia, called the "Commissioners for Indian Affairs." His role involved fostering peace and stability in the West. Congress charged him to convince Indians "of the good wishes and good intentions of the Congress for and towards them, and to cultivate harmony and friendship between them and the whole people," requiring him to adjudicate "all differences and disputes, that shall happen between the Indians and the white people," paying "particular" care that settlers make no "impositions upon the former." White settlers could, after all, corrupt neutral Indians, perhaps driving them into the arms of the British. "Treat all those people," Congress ordered, "with kindness and hospitality; inspire them with sentiments of Justice and humanity." If he did, civility would follow. "Dispose them," his orders concluded, "to introduce the arts of Civil and social life and to encourage the residence of husbandsmen and handicrafts men among them."[39]

He proved the ideal choice for ensuring that the West would not intrude on eastern concerns. In early 1777 he wrote John Hancock, the president of Congress, that the "Western Indians are now altogether quiet." Although raiding parties rarely attacked in the dead of winter, Morgan believed that regular troops could leave their posts for the eastern front without causing any harm in the West. Perhaps, he suggested to Hancock, militia "might readily be induced to enlist in the Continental Service under good officers, for the express purpose of garrisoning those Posts during the War."[40] Morgan's optimistic take on Indian-American relations therefore reflected what members of Congress were hoping to hear. Indeed, he argued that "the most pacific measures with liberal Presents if in our power to make them will be attended with much happier consequences with the savages than our armed forces can produce."[41]

The framers of the Declaration of Independence, of course, gave voice to western issues. When delegates in Philadelphia argued that the king was acting with a "Cruelty and perfidy scarcely paralleled in the most barbarous ages, and totally unworthy the head of a civilized Nation," they understood how these words, steeped in stadial assumptions, would resonate. On the heels of this condemnation, they declared that the king "has excited domestic insurrections amongst us, and has endeavoured to bring on the inhabitants of our frontiers, the merciless Indian Savages, whose known rule of warfare, is an undistinguished destruction of all ages, sexes, and conditions." The British, who had "abdicated Government here," creating a crisis of authority and ushering in a period of grave uncertainty "by declaring us out of his Protection and waging War Against us," had plunged to the level of savages. Much of this was mere rhetoric. That Congress placed the concerns of the frontier men and women at the very end of a long list of grievances, however, is telling. To them, the frontier was a marginal place, and they hoped it would remain so.

Both the British and the Americans, therefore, tended to see the West as peripheral. This, of course, is understandable. Both had armies in the field in the East. Although the British encouraged western raids, and Americans hoped to stop them, they never rose to the level of a general war. The West, to the relief of both parties, remained relatively quiet in the years 1775 to 1778. As long as the region bubbled at acceptable levels of violence, it would not divert attention from where it was due. These were hardly the types of conditions to inspire confidence in the West; but that was the point. Although settlers and soldiers complained, rumblings of discontent and violence did not rise to a pitch that diverted attention from the concerns of the East.

Neither the British nor the American response to the continuing crisis of authority in the West gave much solace to settlers, however justified negligence might have been. Perceiving the West as a place peripheral to a larger war of independence ensured that it remained in a state of gnawing uncertainty, stasis, and simmering violence. With the British equipping Indians and the Americans mouthing friendship, frontier settlers had few good choices. Some settlers supported the British, though in the Ohio valley from 1775 to 1778 such instances were rare.[42] As word spread that the British were equipping the Indians—though not sponsoring large-scale raids—the choice of most became clear. Many, understandably, became cautiously pro-patriot. They would stand against "Tyranny," but that tyranny took the shape of British-supported Indian raids.[43]

Like the British and eastern Americans, men and women out West were concerned with their interests. As a Kentucky settler named John Brown claimed, frontier settlers, too, had subscribed to "the zeal for Liberty." But he conceded that such sentiments centered on concerns that British officials were helping Indians launch raids.[44] Revolutionary ideas, therefore, in this context only made sense as they were refracted through what was happening on the ground. Issues that gripped the imagination of easterners—taxation, representation, constitutional rights, consumption—paled in comparison to the distinctive stresses westerners faced. Because they recognized that simmering hostility was far better than all-out war and were convinced that the British were sponsoring Indian raids, yet were wary of American overtures to Indians, a cautious and conditional patriotism made sense.

In the midst of this general aura of uncertainty, only Virginia's new leaders seemed to have a concerted plan for the West. Admittedly, it was born out of initial confusion. As the crisis between the colonies and Britain worsened—and Dunmore's stock fell—some of his erstwhile allies did not know what to do about the lands Dunmore had secured, finding themselves trapped between a convention that hated Dunmore and a British government that hated many of the speculators.[45] Patrick Henry did not share these concerns. He sent ammunition and powder to the frontier and appointed men like Preston and Christian to play prominent roles in the defense of the West against Indian attacks sponsored by British agents, such as Stuart and Cameron.[46] In other words, Henry did his best to assure people that local elites such as Preston had their best interests at heart. Famous for his "give me liberty or give me death" speech in 1775, a mainstay of the convention, and elected as the independent commonwealth's first governor, Henry had solid patriotic credentials. More than nearly any other Virginian, he also stood to profit from Dunmore's landgrab. While others worried over the uncertain status of the West, Henry forged ahead. Of course, the war in the East remained central to the bid for independence, but with so much of Virginia's money tied into the West, it took on a greater significance than it did for the Continental Congress or the British. In the wake of Dunmore's flight to England, revolutionary Virginians therefore looked to inherit his mantle in the West. Like Dunmore, Virginia's speculating elite, now holding the levers of power in Williamsburg, also believed they could use uncertainty and chaos for their own purposes, namely, transforming Dunmore's claims for the colony of Virginia under the Crown into the state of Virginia's claims.[47]

Opportunities for doing so arose from unlikely sources. After Dunmore's tenure, Richard Henderson of North Carolina, who had purchased a huge swath of land from Cherokees in Kentucky, tried to create his own colony on land claimed by Virginia. To make what was called Transylvania a successful venture, he initially attracted any settlers he could, even squatters, with promises of entering their claims through improvement. He also encouraged another sort of migrant, the petty speculator. Daniel Boone was one such man. Another was George Rogers Clark, a militia captain under Dunmore who had moved west in search of fortune in the period after the British had left the frontier. By 1775, Henderson had begun to change the terms of settlement, demanding quitrents from settlers, raising purchase prices, claiming huge amounts of land for himself and his partners, and warning off squatters. Settled in Harrodsburg, Clark styled himself a champion of the downtrodden seeking traditional rights to competency. Clark appealed to Virginia officials to make good on their claims to the region and protect him and his holdings, sending petitions to the Revolutionary government headed up by Henry and invoking claims of conquest through the Battle of Point Pleasant in part to do so. In response, revolutionary Virginians did what Dunmore had done around Fort Dunmore, creating new counties to sustain the institutions of sovereignty, thereby strengthening the state's declarations to that effect.[48]

Like Dunmore, Virginia's revolutionary leaders understood they could mold the West for their own purposes. They did so in a number of ways. First, they relied on the guile of men on the make like Clark to serve the larger needs of the state. Leaders also sought to create the illusion of consensus in the West. John Stuart complained that Virginia's officials had instigated false rumors that he was calling on the Cherokees to attack and that "the negroes were immediately to be set free by Government, and that arms were to be given them to fall upon their Masters." Stuart understood "that nothing can be more alarming" to all Virginians, east and west, "than the Idea of an Attack from Indians and Negroes."[49] In other words, the very real concerns of easterners and westerners in Virginia, tied to race, could be yoked to the cautiously patriotic sentiments of frontier folk to create a sense of common purpose.

Finally, Henry and other officials with a stake in the Ohio valley seemed intent on allowing the West to teeter between rage and trepidation, anarchy and uncertainty, employing resources only insofar as they protected the state's interests. On the one hand, they whipped settlers into a frenzy of Indian hatred from time to time, using rumor in much the same way Dunmore had, when it suited their purposes. Virginia's leaders also sent troops west when doing so would strengthen their claims to land.[50] To hold on to the state's stake in the West, when Continental troops traveled west to burn Cherokee towns in 1776, Henry ordered Virginia militia to march as well under the command of "Brigadier Lewis," the same man who led one column of Dunmore's victorious army in 1774.[51] On the other hand, Henry's Council also preached the merits of peace and respect for Indians when such a need arose, arguing that Delawares and even Shawnees were "our Faithful Friends and Brethren," who should not be molested.[52] For all his talk of defending the interests of his state writ large, Henry mustered no troops to quell Indian raids as they began in 1777, relying instead on frontier counties to call up fifty men each to send to Kentucky.[53] In 1778, the Council—with Henry at its head—again depended on militia from frontier regions for western defense.[54] Once mustered, the militias did little in these years. John Struthers, a Virginian serving for two months in 1776 near Fort Pitt, recalled "the only military prowess performed during this tour was the capture, or rather finding, of five new bark canoes."[55]

In general, East eclipsed West for Virginians in more ways than one.[56] While they had to balance many concerns, and troops were needed in the East, something else was at work as well, as a speculator named John Bowman learned in 1778. Bowman worried that "Men being scarce" because of Indian raids, he could not make improvements on lands nor sell them. The only remedy he could propose was building forts for protection. The government had other plans. Instead of constructing defensive blockhouses, Bowman was "Ordered by Government to Erect a stockade fourt on the Banks of the Ohio Near sum Salt Spring to afford Protection to such Persons as may be Imployed in Making Salt."[57] Keeping people on the frontier served Virginia's purposes under Dunmore. But not necessarily any longer. Indeed, in 1776 William Christian claimed that the argument to keep people in the West was an aim of "the ministerial gentry." This mysterious group, never named by Christian, "only make use of our people being over the line as a trick to excite the Indians." The times called for resistance to this ploy. If the people remained, he warned, "ruin must overtake them." He advocated a new policy. Gather men, he suggested, "to remove those who would not voluntarily do it."[58]

Times had changed. Settlers' flight hampered Dunmore's plans for conquering the West; however, their flight helped a patriot Virginia's plans for securing it. Squatters now proved more troubling than Indians. As Dorsey Pentecost, a well-connected Virginian with interests in the West, explained, some would "esteem" a general alarm scaring people off as "the best News they ever heard."[59] One such man was John Todd. In 1776, he and other speculators moved out to claim the lands that he had surveyed in western Virginia. He was shocked at what he found. "On my arrival here," he noted, "I found almost all the lands I expected to find vacant either occupied or cabbined so that the Gentlemen along with me must either have returned home again or settled on cabbined Lands."[60] Todd had assumed that entering claims preempted any sort of occupancy right. The future of Kentucky, he argued, was made "weak" and "distracted with the clashing Interests of Cabbinning and Surveying." He knew where he stood. "I am afraid," he informed Preston, "to loose sight of my House least some Invader takes possession."[61] Virginia needed new laws to strengthen the claims of eastern speculators and evict squatters to finalize settlement. Moving the people off the land simplified the process of settlement and forestalled disputes over claims. Fear therefore served an important role.[62]

In other words, Virginia's leaders tended to view settlers in much the same way Dunmore had, as pawns to be shifted about. For example, Henry had plans for those who remained. When he heard a rumor that Indians planned to attack Fort Pitt in the late summer of 1776, John Page, the president of the Council of Virginia, ordered William Fleming to march to protect the fort. "The present Garrison at that Fort," Page asserted, "would be unable to baffle their attempts."[63] Sending militia under the orders of Virginia's Council would serve as a reminder that the region around the fort still belonged to Virginia. Maintaining a claim to this broader region meant securing settlers. In some instances, therefore, Virginians wanted settlers gone, in others they wanted them to hold firm, and in still others they wanted them coming and going. Fewer people would confound speculators' plans for plots already claimed, but men and women were arriving to safeguard sovereignty and purchase land. By 1779, Kentucky in particular reeled in such a profound state of flux.[64]

Virginia's strategy threatened American plans. By unilaterally determining policy for the West, Morgan argued, Virginians had adopted measures "which I fear will be highly injurious to the Interests of the Colonies."[65] To be sure, Morgan was not a disinterested party in the West. He still clung to some hope that the Vandalia scheme would come to fruition. Yet he pointed out a troubling truth: Virginia's interest in land and its aggressive actions would inflame tensions with Indians.[66] Westerners would suffer and, most significant, the West would awaken, imperiling a broader American strategy of not allowing the West to intrude on the eastern war.

Morgan complained about what was going on, suggesting that Virginians were trying to manipulate events out West to solidify their hold on the region.[67] He reported his fears to Congress, arguing that Virginians were claiming the region as theirs but did little to protect it or supply it.[68] Moreover, he doubted the veracity of the many alarms sounded in the West that were scaring people off. To stop these, he asked Congress to appoint "a cool experienced Person of a liberal mind and clear of all Party Views" and who had no interest in "the conquest of Indian Lands."[69] In 1777, he charged county lieutenants of western Virginia with sending "Scouting Parties into the hunting Grounds of our Friends the Delawares." These acts, he claimed, were "premeditated" and aimed at using violence to manipulate events and gain land.[70] At one point, he suggested that allowing the Virginians to do what they wished in the West would play into British hands.[71]

Morgan lost.[72] Acting on a tip and the orders of a magistrate, the commander at Fort Pitt arrested Morgan late in 1777 as a conspirator against the United States. Along with the notable British agents Alexander McKee and Simon Girty, Morgan stood accused of colluding with the enemy by writing letters to Detroit and of consorting with Loyalists. Ultimately, Edward Hand released him, arguing that he found Morgan "a Zealous and faithful Servant to the United States."[73] It turned out that Hand was right to do so. In fact, Morgan had killed a Tory. But his imprisonment ended his days of authority in the West. Before his arrest, Morgan had had the power to call out local militia from Fort Pitt. Under a cloud of suspicion, he lost that authority.[74]

By the summer of 1777, Virginia's initiative in winning the West sent mixed messages to settlers, further clouding an already confused situation. On the one hand, settlers took part in raids sponsored by the government. On the other, officials reined in settlers who wanted to kill Indians without state sanction.[75] Settlers, at once fearing what Indians and the British could do, also had reason to question the motives of the Americans and the Virginians. Cherokees, despite official denials, were still attacking settlements, most likely with the connivance of British agents.[76] Delawares, despite the assurances of their leaders, were also raiding. David Zeisberger informed leaders that parties of Indians were scouting the frontiers, moving between the Ohio Country and Detroit, and attacking targets of opportunity. Mingoes, moreover, were trying to convince Delawares to cast their lot with them. He feared the neutrals could not withstand the pressure to launch attacks.[77] Shawnees, with whom the Virginians and Americans were trying to negotiate a peace, threatened to strike back for the land they had lost as rumors swirled that they were preparing to attack en masse.[78]

Given the atmosphere on the frontier, fear was a reasonable response. Settlers spent much of the year "forted up." Really little more than a few houses surrounded by a stockade to protect people and animals, these complexes grew in number in 1776 and 1777. Although 1776 did not prove an especially bloody year, people in the West lived in a state of anxiety during the summer as small bands of Delawares, Shawnees, Cherokees, and Mingoes launched small raids. William Preston declared "that very soon, this County will be broke up and dispersed." People fleeing crowded the roads. And as he put it, "The Confusion of the People is beyond Description."[79] In 1777, the panic worsened.[80] A fellow named William James summed up what he and his neighbors were experiencing. Though he discussed no attacks in his area in the spring of 1777, he noted that he was writing from a fort. He declared his case "truly piteous for want of support and assistance." The previous year Indians "took my Negroe man Prisoner." His children had left. And he did not want to relive his experience from twenty years before, when he was held by Indians for five years "in Braddock's War."[81]

Events and experience had conditioned settlers to perceive threats all around. And years of rumors had taken their toll. In 1776 and 1777, stories swirled of Indians in the region taking or delivering "the Belt and the Hatchet," pushing some to the edge of sanity.[82] According to one such settler, men and women labored under "the greatest uncertainty" and "the greatest uneasiness of Mind imaginably."[83] A Kentucky settler asked a difficult question of officials. "Why could not 2 or 3 or 500 men be sent if needful, rather than leave so many women and children exposed to savage barbarity; from a state abounding in men," he stormed. "It is," he concluded, "cruel, unfeeling, and vastly unhumane, and unchristian," an insult to his "transalpine brethren."[84]

In the midst of growing insecurity, settlers on the frontier began suggesting that adherence to any government had its limits. As early as 1776, as fears spread, men and women from "an infant, frontier county" refused to allow recruiting officers, who "drained" the region of vital manpower, into the county. They also sent letters to the Committee of Safety in Philadelphia asking if "the safety of the interior parts of the Province would not be better secur'd by adding strength to the frontier."[85] In "West Augusta," Virginia—the region around Pittsburgh—settlers petitioned the House of Delegates to allow the area to become "the fourteenth link in the American Chain." The petition was rejected.[86] A fellow named James McGavock summed up the frustration of the period: "While there is such a powerful parley working for their own Interests back at home, and abroad," meaning easterners tending to the needs of easterners, "justice cannot be done to Common People in this Country."[87]

The uncertainty that defined the region in this period defined how the settlers saw their world, and their inability to defend themselves even during a period not noted for bloodshed epitomized the bind they were in. Thomas McGuire, a spokesperson for the "fort people" of Buffaloe Creek, declared that he and his neighbors could spare no men for a militia draft. With some men guarding the fort, others bringing in crops, and a few chasing Indians in the area, McGuire's resources were spread too thin. In the choice between serving out of walls or hunkering down within them, the people had to opt for the latter.[88] The people of Grave Creek, for their part, declared that they would muster for militia duty only to protect their fort. Their leaders could not persuade them to range.[89]

By 1778, about the only thing certain in the West was the notion that "the frontier at this Juncture seems to be in the greatest Confusion." As another season of fear loomed, some fled, but those "left behind" did not know what to do. They were "reluctant to leave their homes, and afraid to stay."[90] In 1778, William Fleming tried to make Patrick Henry understand the mind-set of people in the West. "The inhabitants of the exterior parts of the county," he reported, "are secured in Forts, and Families further in have gathered to houses, where they thought they could make the best defense." He noted, however, what he called "the unusual behaviour of the Enemy." Indians milled about. But they did "little Mischief." Nor did they murder people, kill cattle, steal horses, or rifle through deserted houses. For a people conditioned on fear, inaction betokened doom. The Indians "make it believed they meditate a heavey stroak," that they wanted "to get a thorough knowledge of the Country." Ironically, though he had experienced attacks, he "never knew such a general Panick amongst the People."[91] Western settlers, in other words, found themselves in a compromised and vulnerable position. Unable to fend for themselves, yet reluctant to trust government officials who failed to appreciate their fears, they were teetering much as they had in 1774 between panic and rage.

In 1778, Virginia's leaders offered a solution out of this bind. For some time, people had been clamoring "to send an army" to "drive away all our enemies who are gathering."[92] If a defensive force was not dispatched to vulnerable regions, like Kentucky, then Detroit, the nerve center of British strategy in the West, presented the clear choice for a strike. Virginians would propose such an expedition, but only on their own terms. About the same time the members of the Assembly of Virginia decided to open a western land office in the fall of 1778, the commander at Fort Pitt asked the governor to call up frontier militia for a period of six months to strike belligerent Indians and then to march on Detroit.[93] Henry declined. It was clear that he did not want to cooperate with Continental leaders if the lands in question rightly belonged—or should belong—to Virginia.[94] Without Virginia's help, Congress was brought to recognize the impossibility of sponsoring an attack on Detroit and in July 1778 "deferred" the expedition "for the present."[95] Virginians would act alone.

The twenty-six-year-old lieutenant colonel George Rogers Clark, who had done great service for Virginia under Dunmore and Henry, devised the commonwealth's plan for securing the West. Clark proposed a bold strike at the British-Indian nexus in the West, claiming Virginia forces could take Detroit and end the Indian menace once and for all. He also had other motives beyond the protection of settlers for doing so. In private, he had sent spies to the Illinois Country and now asked Henry and the Council for the means to take it for the commonwealth. Virginia's Revolutionary government gave Clark its full support. Indeed, Henry went so far as to promise that the state, not the counties, would bear the cost for Clark's march. To keep the home front more secure while the men marched, Henry ordered large amounts of ammunition and flints "for the general use of the S. Western Frontier."[96] He then called up local militia, asking for a sizable force of seven companies made up of five hundred men. In doing so, Virginia was depending on some of the very men who had fought at Point Pleasant for Dunmore.[97]

What followed was one of the extraordinary stories of the war. Clark had declared that Detroit was his ultimate goal. His public orders comported with such a plan, instructing him to recruit men for this and the defense of Kentucky. He also had a secret set of instructions. These directed Clark to march to the Illinois Country. Clark tried to claim that Illinois was the key to the West. He had made the case that the French villages along the Mississippi provisioned Detroit, that British forces there sent Indians to raid Kentucky, and that the region proved critical for keeping an open channel with New Orleans. The third claim had some weight. The first two did not.[98] When he headed west at the Falls of the Ohio, the men questioned him about their objective. Clark informed them that they would aid in the protection of Kentucky and cripple Detroit, but would do so by other means. He planned to secure Illinois first. The militia he was leading suspected foul play. Illinois had no British troops or outposts to speak of, and the Indians there were not attacking the frontier. Clark's only objective, they reasoned, could be a landgrab, to claim this area as Virginia's for easterners. Refusing to be complicit in this scheme, men began deserting and returning home. Clark claimed that "leading Men in the fronteers" were poisoning the minds of common men. Perhaps. Yet he acknowledged that the "populace" in some regions stood against him, suspecting that the governor had sent him west for "some other secret impulses," and that if the men knew at once where they were heading even fewer would have marched. But this much is clear. This type of ploy had worked for Dunmore. For Clark, it did not.[99] Those few who went—about 150 out of a proposed 500—proved the dregs of the West, noted for their heavy drinking and penchant for misplacing horses. Short on every supply, save whiskey, Clark's officers could not even muster enough men to guard the stores. In what one soldier called a "starving situation," even the likes of these deserted.[100]

This is not to say that Clark was not above pandering. Indeed, he took it to new heights. Clark with the militia remaining reached the Illinois settlement of Kaskaskia in July, seizing it and Vincennes as well without firing a shot. Then again, he faced no resistance. Clark informed the French habitants in both places of a treaty signed between the United States and France. To let them, the Indians of the region, and his men know of his resolve, he "took down the English flag . . . wrapped a large stone in it, [and] threw it into the Ouabash." "Thus," Clark intoned, "we mean to treat your father." Clark was staging a piece of theater. After dousing the king's colors, he laid two belts before the Indians of Vincennes, one red, the other green. "If they delighted in mischief and had no compassion on their Wives and Children," he told them to pick up the red belt. If they preferred peace, grab the green. One of the Indians replied that no one could "place good and bad in the same dish," kicking the belts as he did so. Clark responded that "our design is to march thro' your Country and if we find any fires in our way, we shall just tread them out as we walk along, and if we meet with any Obstacle or barrier we shall remove it with all ease." He warned that "the bystanders"—the innocent, in other words—"must take care less the splinsters should scar their face." He finished with a warning, intended more for his men than for the Indians. "We shall then," he promised, "proceed to Detroit where your Father is whom we consider as a Hog put to fatten in a Penn, we shall inclose him in his penn till he be fat, and then we will throw him into the River."[101] Through such acts, Clark, it appeared, had accomplished what he had set out to do. Illinois had been brought into the American fold by a Virginian, and settlers there would be considered "citizens of the Republic of Virginia." And he had held some of his force together with the promise of Detroit.[102]

While he was enjoying the fruits of his costless victory, however, he heard that the British had retaken Vincennes. The lieutenant governor of Detroit, Henry Hamilton, had learned that Clark had marched into the West. Word soon reached British commanders to the east, who feared the rebels were trying to secure a trading route to the Mississippi or trying to link up with the French near New Orleans.[103] Hamilton hastily assembled a force of Ottawas, Chippewas, Pottawatomies, and regulars, took Vincennes without facing much resistance, and sent away most of the Indians with whom he had come, reasoning that if Clark attacked Vincennes again, he would only do so once the winter had ended. In the meantime, he destroyed the fort's billiard table, arguing that the troops had spent too much time playing while Clark was roaming the West.[104] In the spring, Hamilton promised to unleash Chickasaws, Cherokees, Shawnees, Delawares, Mingoes, Wyandots, Miamis, Senecas, Ottawas, Chippewas, and Hurons against settlements in Kentucky and against Clark's force at Kaskaskia. He would stop rebel shipments by promising that "there will next year be the greatest Number of Savages on the Frontiers that has ever been known."[105]

It was not to happen as Hamilton planned. Clark marched on him in the dead of winter. On February 24, when the Virginians arrived at the gates of Vincennes, Hamilton proposed a three-day truce and a secret parley. Seeing that Hamilton had not prepared any defensive works, Clark refused to talk.[106] After his troops had initiated a siege, setting off an eighteen-hour firefight with little damage to either side, a scouting party of fourteen Indians and Canadians was returning to Fort Sackville. On seeing the "English flag flying at the fort," the party discharged its pieces, "an usual compliment with these people." Clark's men shot a few of the party and seized the others, dragging them behind the village, "notwithstanding," as Hamilton declared, "a truce at this moment existed." Clark's troops tomahawked three of the Indians, one of whom, "after having the Hatchet stuck in his head, took it out himself and delivered it to the inhuman monster who struck him." The Virginian struck a second and third time, "after which the miserable spectacle was dragged by the rope about his neck to the River, thrown in, and suffered to spend still a few moments of life in fruitless struggles."[107]

Hamilton was right to use the word "spectacle." For that is what Clark provided his men, or as he put it, an "impression." After tomahawking the Indians, he placed one of the Canadians in chains and ordered one of his men to scalp him. The soldier hesitated. Clark told him to proceed. The Virginian slowly lifted a piece of the scalp with the knife but stopped again. Clark insisted he finish the job. At this point, others intervened, persuading Clark to imprison the man. According to Hamilton, Clark was "reeking with the blood of those unhappy victims." Clark, not Hamilton, was playing the part of monster whose "reason began to be impaired."

Hamilton wisely agreed to surrender on seeing the rage he was facing. Clark then ordered the British commander clapped in irons and "hung the scalps of the Indians killed . . . on the tents of the surrendering British."[108]

The Virginians turned Hamilton into a bogey. Echoing the exact phrasing of the Declaration of Independence, the Council in Virginia condemned Hamilton for offering scalp bounties and for "inciting the Indians to perpetrate their accustomed Cruelties on the Citizens of these States, without distinction of Age, Sex, or Condition." In the declaration, the king stood accused of these barbarous acts. But in the wake of Clark's recapture of Vincennes, Hamilton played the part of the savage, capable of degrading the former French subjects in the area, inciting them to barbarity, and Indians as well. Hamilton was responsible for the mayhem in the West. "Humanity blushes," some of Virginia's leaders declared, "at the conduct . . . in inciting the savages to spill the blood of our defenceless Women and Children whose lives ought to be held sacred by every being who boasts the name of man."[109]

Pinning the blame on Hamilton was a sound strategy for controlling the West.[110] Doing so implied that violence was not endemic to the region or to the period, but was the logical conclusion of Hamilton's fall from civilized behavior and his corruption of susceptible Indians. Hamilton's capitulation therefore gave the veneer of safety, suggesting that once this menace from Detroit was clapped in irons the insecurity of the West would be a thing of the past.[111] For a long time, Hamilton had been the subject of rumor and speculation that he had "given the bloody belt and tomhock to strike the Virginians."[112] Of course, the issue was more complex. Indians were striking of their own accord. Yet in this world of flux and dichotomies, of deepening hatreds, Hamilton became the sum of all fears.

The spectacle of Hamilton, whom Clark's men paraded through frontier settlements in Kentucky, along the Ohio, and around Fort Pitt on his way to Williamsburg, announced to all that Revolutionary Virginia had assumed Dunmore's mantle. Settlers threatened the British prisoners and refused to give them anything more than bear flesh and Indian meal, and only Clark's troops protected Hamilton from their rage. Hamilton saw up close the world of uncertainty he, in part, had helped create. For years living in dread, the common people found some relief in spitting on a scapegoat.[113] While the United States had floundered, Virginians had succeeded.

In many respects, Clark's theatrics served as a culminating act in Virginia's quest for the West. The western state of flux, and the ways settlers responded to it, allowed Virginians to secure Kentucky and retain claims to the region south of Fort Pitt. And now they proposed to make use of this unsettledness to achieve something far more ambitious. "The State of Virginia," Daniel Brodhead, the latest in a series of commanders at Fort Pitt, wrote as Virginians assumed control over Illinois, was "now preparing to acquire more extensive territory by sending a great body of men under Col. (whom they intend to raise to the rank of Brigadier) Clark." Brodhead had hoped American forces would control the West. "But it seems," he lamented, "the United States cannot furnish either troops or resources for the purpose, but the State of Virginia can."[114]

Clark's victory was patriot Virginia's Point Pleasant. Not only were claims in Kentucky to be rationalized and the region around Fort Pitt held, but the commonwealth had gained a new rich region and the trade of the Mississippi and could pursue claims in the northwest, around Detroit, thereby allowing the inhabitants there "to become fellow Citizens of a free State." As Clark wrote to Thomas Jefferson in the fall of 1779, Illinois was the "key" to the West. The other regions depended on it, and luckily it fell "within the state of Virginia."[115] Clark consolidated his holdings in Kentucky and garnered more land through his service to Virginia, as did Henry. What he was on the cusp of doing, by his own estimation, was ending a state of war and returning much of the Ohio valley to something akin to its previous condition, albeit under the jurisdiction of Virginia. Soon after Virginia officials established Illinois County, Clark declared the region pacified and "almost in a state of Nature" yet destined for a "flourishing Trade."[116] Still, Brodhead had his doubts. The West, he argued, was a strange place. In fact, he would not be surprised to see the whole enterprise "fall thro'." After all, he believed "that wise men at a great distance view things in the western country very differently from those who are more immediately acquainted with circumstances and situations."[117]

Brodhead's words proved prophetic. In fact, Clark's—and Virginia's—western enterprise collapsed. For a start, the people of Illinois were not cooperating. Capt. Richard Winston, part of the small force intended to hold the region, considered the inhabitants of Kaskaskia "a set of ignorant asses" who "deserve to be ruled with a rod of iron or droved at the Point of the bayonet." Despite the pretensions of the Virginians to annex the area, the people were still "Strangers to liberty."[118] With time, Virginia's Illinois adventure seemed ill-advised, so much so that the state commissioned a group to look into the mess in 1782. Some believed that the problems lay in "the great Distance from the Kaskasias to the seat of Government," but others recognized that the Virginians' slapdash approach to taking and controlling the region was to blame.[119]

But something far more significant was at work. Clark and other Virginians had tried to use the uncertainty of the period much as Dunmore had done. Like Dunmore, Clark pandered to people's fears, hoping to unleash useful anger and resolve. But by 1779, elites had greater difficulty managing such sentiments, and, as soon became evident, the image of authority that Clark wanted to project proved a mirage. Detroit would not be taken or even attempted. As the commander at Fort Pitt explained to Washington, Clark could not raise men from frontier regions to hold on to Illinois for Virginia's elite. Contrary to what Clark had hoped and claimed would happen with Hamilton's arrest, more raids were coming from Detroit, and the people were still holed up in forts.[120] The continuing violence ensured that little trade was moving up the Mississippi. Moreover, speculators leaving places like Kentucky for Illinois were going missing, possibly as "a sacrifice to the Indians."[121]

In the uncertainty of the West, what the people were refusing to do proved more significant than what they were doing. Given the suspicion people articulated as governments promised but failed to protect them, Clark's pronouncements of peace once the monster Hamilton was in chains must have rung hollow. Clark and the Virginians had not cleared away uncertainty, nor had they reestablished authority. Clark would propose later expeditions against the Shawnees. But only a few "Old Standbys" would turn out. Indeed, Clark and his officers spent more time in courts-martial dealing with desertions than in fighting Indians.[122] It became clear that Clark was doing nothing more than trying to enrich himself as he, his officers, and the standbys "drank very hard while they had any thing to drink."[123] In the midst of the failure of Virginians at this time to pay the high costs order entailed, some of the people were not becoming patriots so much as self-sovereign.[124]

In fact, in these years, alarming sentiments were beginning to grip the West. The land office finally opened in Kentucky. The Land Law of 1779 promised to recognize the claims of settlers who had arrived before 1778 based on improvements they had made. It went further, offering these men and women rights often claimed by speculators. They now would have the opportunity to purchase more land—the right of preemption— for a reduced price. On paper, the law seemed to steer a middle course between the rights to competency of common settlers and the preemptive rights of speculators. In practice, this formulation was designed to be and was a boon to men on the make such as Clark—surveyors, jobbers, and adventurers—and grand Virginia speculators. Virginia land companies, such as the Loyal Company and the Greenbrier Company, did especially well. Rival companies, such as those sponsored by Pennsylvanians, did not. Those who secured patents under Dunmore were also entitled to title. Even Henderson benefited. As long as he was willing to put his claims under Virginia's jurisdiction, he could still hold on to 200,000 acres for himself. In other words, this was a law designed by the wealthy and well-connected to benefit the wealthy or well-connected.[125]

But sales did not go as planned. Petitions from settlers poured into Williamsburg protesting the law. Some made threats. One "combination of people," for example, had formed near the Falls of the Ohio and threatened to seize the entry books of Virginia's land commissioners. Similarly, a group from Harrodsburg clamored to ask Congress to have the law overturned.[126] Some took to ignoring it. John May had hoped that he could claim vacated land in Kentucky, and in early 1779 the prospects looked good. He hoped such land would go for "ready Money," which would mean that only the wealthy could hope to claim it.[127] But as men like May were working under the assumptions of Dunmore's settlement, poorer settlers who had to rely on improvement and did not have ready cash for land were settling where they pleased. May explained that officials had little choice but to accede to the wishes of the squatters. Poorer men and women refused to relinquish what they had and, more troubling, understood that they could demand one-half of a claim if they offered their services to speculators.[128]

Settlers were once more "taking advantage of the Times to establish themselves in good Settlement," a British commander explained. By 1781, these people, not "Virginia troops," were "the Enemies to be apprehended."

Through renewed and unfettered settlement of the West, he feared, "the Enemy are effecting their purpose by degrees Establishing themselves in this Country."[129] Some common settlers, in short, were threatening to turn back the clock by resurrecting the old process of frontier development that the British, Dunmore, and Clark and Henry had imperiled. The attempt to reconstitute a traditional right did not undo elite avarice, force easterners to rethink their approach to the West, or even prove more than ephemeral. But it did betoken a new understanding that in this state of deepening uncertainty, common people would not be easily manipulated.

Such changes had implications not only for the ways that settlers viewed the land but also for how they viewed their betters and themselves.[130] While the people determined not to march with Clark again, some were now taking things into their own hands. William Preston noted a troubling change after the first militia members had deserted Clark at the Falls of the Ohio. Men were organizing themselves. Preston reported with alarm "a scheme that a number of young men have formed of embodying themselves into a Company or two and marching at their own Expense into the Indian Country." While there, they planned to "annoy the Enemy and endeavour for a time to divert him from coming into our Frontiers."[131] Similarly, one of the Virginians sent to Illinois did "openly Declare that all the officers of the State are a Damn'd Set of thieves and Robers only come to this Country to Rob and Pilage the Inhabitants."[132] These sentiments did not signal class warfare, nor did they suggest that conflict between groups was now endemic to the West. These years were marked too deeply by flux and confusion. But they did illustrate that people who were standing alone in the West would begin to rely on their own judgment and refuse to cooperate with those who would place their parochial interests before the people's most basic rights to self-preservation.

Taken together, such incidents of politicization did not necessarily represent a transformative moment or the crossing of some critical threshold. What they did signal was an emerging sensibility that would become more widespread and increasingly manifest in the West as the crisis of sovereignty continued. As it did, incidents would be transformed into patterns of politicization. As two Kentucky speculators put it a year after the Clark debacle, common men and women had become "an ungrateful people" while "Ohio Adventurers" had grown "chagrined with their disappointments in the Land Way." This change had "left us much weaker than we were last spring."[133] The change that was occurring was not so much ideological—as we conventionally understand the term—or discursive, meaning pertaining to language or bundles of ideas, but behavioral.

In some ways, that a war of independence was taking place during these upheavals on the frontier was almost incidental. For ideas that we associate with the war, such as rights or virtue, did not alone empower people or give voice to the voiceless; rather, the ways people tried to negotiate their world, and the nature of that world, created the conditions for an emerging sense of self-sovereignty. What was happening in frontier communities in the late 1770s, then, did not differ that much from what had nearly happened in these types of communities fifteen years earlier in places like Paxton, when settlers who refused to defer to their betters threatened to push the colony of Pennsylvania to the brink. Only sovereign authority had thwarted them. For that matter, what was happening did not differ from what had happened in England a century before, or what would happen in Ireland twenty years later. Aside from the fact that men and women in the Ohio valley were confronting uncertainty for a far longer period of time—in some cases more than thirty years—their plight and their response to it were not exceptional. Politicization began when sovereignty was ineffectual and uncertainty reigned. What set of ideas people would use to make sense of this situation was a different matter altogether, but this much was certain: the ideas that structured the ways they made sense of a troubling world would be drawn from what that world had to offer. But for the present, in this world of failed sovereignty, and the competition that defined it, the actions of common men and women suggested that they were beginning to claim that any new order established, and any authority reinstated, would have to be achieved along lines that they would lay out. As Samuel Wharton explained, some "Inhabitants westward of the Allegany Mountains have by Beat of Drum declared Themselves an Independent State . . . It is said there are 5000 Men, good marksmen who have associated themselves to defend their Independence." They would not be led. "Some of them," he concluded, "have crossed the Ohio and are settling . . . Lands."[134]

Whether true or not, Wharton's observation spoke to a new order emerging in the West. John May noted in 1780 "Scenes of Inequity respecting Land," which he found "really astonishing." As he was trying to locate warrants near the confluence of the Ohio and Green rivers, he saw his hopes for the region evaporating. "There is no such thing as Friendship existing in this Part of the World," he intoned. He could trust no one. "With what a Jealous Eye we view one another, every Man looking upon his neighbour as his Enemy." Order had not come, and it appeared uncertainty would deepen. In such circumstances, May's hopes had to remain a "secret" as "People suspect that there are extraordinary Matters going on."[135] The questions the West now faced were, What sort of authority would be acceptable to men and women? And what would they consider the basis of society, when and if that authority should be constituted?

SIX

Revolution and Violence:
Warring Against Indians
and Reimagining the West

On November 11, 1777, James Hall and at least five other militia-men from western Virginia burst into a cabin at Fort Randolph near Point Pleasant, killing the Shawnee Cornstalk and two of his sons, then mangling their bodies.[1] Cornstalk, of course, had forged the agreement with Dunmore ceding the Kentucky Country to Virginia. In the years after the treaty, he emerged as a voice of caution among the Shawnees, some of whom were launching raids to win back the land that whites had claimed at Fort Stanwix and taken after Point Pleasant. Considered too conciliatory by some of his neighbors, Cornstalk had left the Scioto River valley with his family for less belligerent Delaware settlements farther to the east. A few days before the killing, American military commanders asked him to Fort Randolph to discuss the possibility of some sort of peace treaty with the Shawnees. Neither Cornstalk's benign neutrality, his decision to live among Delawares, nor American protection was enough to spare him.[2]

The slaughter of Cornstalk signaled a new era in a western revolution. Since 1773, the competitive tenor of life in the West had teetered between disorder and uncertain authority, punctuated by moments of violence. Now bloodshed saturated the West. After Cornstalk's murder, a British official noted, "the Indians are not to be pacified."[3] The war in the West had taken a frightening turn, and the British, Indians, and settlers began to kill one another with abandon.

By the early 1780s, violence, not state authority, controlled the Ohio valley. This failure of sovereignty, however, did not make people embrace the cause of independence for the United States with greater vigor. In fact, the transition from disorder to uncertainty to unfettered violence—a change settlers helped precipitate—created greater disaffection with authority; the new violent tenor of the West obviated sovereignty. Men increasingly acted without the blessing of sanctioned authority.[4] Far from deferring to their betters or even following their leads, common settlers had come to reject ineffectual patronage and embrace the power that autonomy and violence conferred in a revolutionary crucible.

Authorities struggled to minimize the damage. Virginia's Council, with the blessing of Governor Henry, acknowledged the nature of "the dangerous Situation of our Western and Northwestern Frontiers, in consequence of the late Murders of Cornstalk and other Shawnese Indians at Fort Randolph," and offered a $200 reward for James Hall's capture for "perpetrating the atrocious and barbarous Murder."[5] William Preston, who had proved his diplomatic skills in 1773 and 1774 by dealing with the Cherokees, sent messages to the Shawnees declaring that the perpetrators would be tried "by our Laws in the same manner as if they had murdered as many white People."[6] For his part, the commander at Fort Pitt sped off to Philadelphia to consult with leaders over what to do.[7]

Officials condemned, but they could not act. Indeed, they had lost the ability to shape events in the West. Alone amid the bloodshed, without patrons, people took things into their own hands, resulting in more appalling incidents. George Morgan warned of a troubling trend a year earlier. "Parties," he had alleged, "have even been assembled to massacre our known Friends." Fearing what whites would do, he went so far as to allow Indian messengers to sleep in his chamber "for their Security."[8] His words proved prophetic. Shortly after Cornstalk's murder, a large party left Fort Pitt in the dead of winter searching for "hostile Indians." They found none. Instead, they killed the brother of Captain Pipe, one of the men responsible for keeping the Delawares officially neutral, two women, and a child. They also took "two Squaws Prisoner." These Indians—"all Delawares"— had lived less than fifty miles from Fort Pitt "in confidence of our friendship," Morgan asserted. Whether or not the intention was to undermine that confidence, Morgan could not say.[9]

Although incidents like the massacres at Fort Randolph and Beaver Creek appeared to be extensions of the grisly work done at Lancaster by the Paxton Boys in 1763, the rationale for butchery had changed by the early 1780s. Settlers no longer killed because they could ill afford to wait for civility to transform Indian societies. In part, they now killed because, in an increasingly violent state of war, most believed that the civility model was fundamentally flawed. By the latter years of the war, settlers had little choice but to deem Indians essentially inferior, for civility no longer proved a reliable measure of superiority. While militiamen from frontier counties were killing women and scalping children, Indians were acting with great reserve. Indians and whites, therefore, had turned the civility equation on its head. In these circumstances, after decades of disorder and as violence escalated, settlers rejected its premises. Behavior no longer betokened development or human worth. Color did.[10]

In 1763, the slaughter of innocents at least raised eyebrows in the West. By 1783, it did not. By that time, settlers were fashioning a new consensus in the West. The process that would make for revolution had plunged the West into a crisis of authority and competition to remake society. Dunmore had been able to bang the anti-Indian drum and have the people do his bidding. They had complied. The uncertainty that followed Dunmore's fall from grace had forced people to fend for themselves, in the process giving them the wherewithal to refuse to be complicit in their own marginalization. Yet as their voice in their own future grew, they created the conditions for a world in which violence and racism would prove the only certainties. Racist violence, in other words, was becoming the new basis of society in the West. The frightening, even modern, vision of the way the world worked would provide the social template for the West, one that speculators, military commanders, and officials in the West would either come to accept or have to tolerate.

It did not take long for westerners to understand the nature of their new world in the aftermath of George Rogers Clark's debacle and Cornstalk's murder. By 1780, bloodshed had escalated not only to new levels but also to new forms. For years, officials, speculators, and settlers had voiced concerns about a "General Indian war," often invoking it as a self-serving threat, a prod to action, or an unjustified fear. Now westerners finally confronted it as reality. For a start, raiding parties had grown in size. In the summer of 1779, American commanders learned that Shawnees,

Mingoes, Wyandots, and a few Delawares had banded together "at the Big River in order to cross and go to war." More than a hundred had set out to "recogniter the banks if clear of White People." Discovering a settlement, this scouting party descended on it, killing a number and taking fourteen prisoners.[11] After a party of at least thirty Indians had killed and scalped two men, a woman, and two children on the Pennsylvania frontier, a settler named George Bush begged Edward Hand for help. He had not seen the raiders, but he feared this was no isolated incident.[12]

Westerners were facing something new and terrifying. Since the War of Independence began, the Americans had tried to keep the Delawares neutral. After the atrocities at Beaver Creek, however, doing so proved increasingly difficult. Delawares had also become, as a British agent put it, "frightened by the incroachment of the Rebels." In fact, Delawares believed that the Americans were treating them as a "Catts Paw."[13] Americans, after all, had not delivered promised goods or weapons, even acknowledging that while the British could clothe Indians "in the most elegant manner," Americans left them naked with nothing "but a little whiskey."[14] Negligence had a price. By 1780, most of the Delawares "declared in favour of the British."[15]

During the summers of 1780 and 1781, word was coming from the West of massive raids by Indians. In August 1781, ministers working with the neutral Delawares along the Muskingum reported that "two hundred and fifty Indians chiefly Delawares and Wyandots were . . . on their way to attack the different Garrisons or posts on this frontier and consequently to destroy the contiguous country." The specter of large-scale raids threatening both forts and defenseless settlements from Delaware country threw western Pennsylvania into a panic.[16] To make matters worse, more Cherokees were also opting for war. As more and more settlers streamed into or near Cherokee country after treaties were signed with Virginians, older chiefs could not restrain younger men. William Christian conceded as early as 1780 that the Cherokees "say they will never treat with us, but retire to the Mountains, and continue the War." Virginia's plans of keeping the Cherokees quiet while they grabbed more of the West, therefore, had failed every bit as much as American plans for the Delawares.[17] "We shall now experience what I have long strove to avoid, a general war with the savages," Brodhead lamented.[18] With few troops, he could do nothing to stop them.

The shifting tide on the frontier had not been lost on the British. They had noted with alarm Clark's march through the West. They had also intercepted a letter from Patrick Henry to the Spanish governor of New Orleans, asking him to send goods to the Americans and informing him that Virginians planned to build forts along the Mississippi.[19] Although these overtures accomplished nothing, they reminded the British that the West could have strategic importance.[20] Beginning in 1779, therefore, in the wake of the Clark fiasco, commanders began to reconsider their approach to the West. About the same time, John Stuart—a man who like Johnson and Croghan had supported the civilizing mission and who long was a voice of restraint—died. With him, British restraint died as well.

Instead of just sponsoring or encouraging raids, the British were beginning to participate in them. As they did, the Hamilton model of British-Indian warfare, the exception before 1778, now became the rule in the West. First envisioned in December 1777, the new model was unveiled by the British on a limited basis in the summer of 1778. In that year, rangers and Indians "destroyed a number of Settlements upon the Frontiers of Pennsylvania."[21] At first, Indians referred to such raids as making "mischief." Alexander McKee, for example, was working with two hundred British troops and with Delawares, Shawnees, and Munsies near the Miami River, building forts and dispatching parties "to do Mischief unto" Americans and their dwindling number of allied Indians. McKee's confederates struck isolated settlements in targeted regions and later tried to destabilize the area around Fort Pitt.[22] These plans also involved securing small outposts held by militia and western Continental forces, such as Fort Laurens.[23]

The results proved as horrific for settlers as they were impressive for the British, and although commanders did not intend to retake the West, disorder festered. Conquering Fort Pitt, though an inviting target, was rejected by the British.[24] Rather, they focused their assaults on smaller outposts. These British "green coats" or "green jackets"—"Red Cloth are to them a great disadvantage, being seen at a great distance"—relied on a mixture of conventional and guerrilla tactics. Since some were American-born or immigrants who had lived or served in the backcountry, they were often skilled at the American way of war.[25] On June 30, 1778, for example, Maj. John Butler—an American-born son of a British officer who had served the Crown as an Indian agent—led a group of five hundred rangers and Indians to a settlement at Wyoming, on the upper Susquehanna River.

Pennsylvanians on the frontier had never encountered a force of this size, and the British and Indians took two forts without firing a shot. On July 3, Butler learned that the rebels were assembling for an attack. "This pleased the Indians highly," he reported, "who observed they should be upon equal footing with them in the Woods." As the Americans marched out, the British torched the forts they had taken to give the impression they were retreating. Instead, the militiamen walked into an ambush. The Indians and rangers lay flat upon the ground in "a fine open Wood" and waited. Then the attack began, Indians from the right and rangers from the left. The battle lasted thirty minutes.[26]

"In this action," Butler noted, "were taken 237 Scalps, and only 5 prisoners." Although it appears that reports exaggerated the carnage, Butler claimed he could not restrain the Indians, arguing "that it was with the greatest Difficulty I could save the Lives of those few." He had lost one Indian and eight rangers. After the engagement, Butler's force allegedly terrorized the adjacent countryside. By his estimation, they destroyed eight forts, burned a thousand dwellings, wrecked mills, and drove off cattle, swine, and sheep. To those who contested, "the Indians gave no Quarter." Butler's trail of destruction wound to other settlements on the Pennsylvania frontier, the more prosperous the better. He struck places "which abound in Corn and Cattle; the Destruction of which cannot fail of greatly distressing the Rebels." Butler's actions were therefore designed to make the Americans do what they hoped not to do. Death and destruction on the frontier—or at least reports to that effect—would force the Americans to look west.[27]

British reports of western engagements followed a basic rhetorical formula. Ranger captains argued that they did "everything in [their] power to restrain the Fury of the Indians from hunting Women and Children or killing the prisoners who fell into their hands," but to no avail.[28] In point of fact, the British used such "savagery" to devastating effect. Rangers often attacked from the front while Indians hit the flanks "with great Fury," putting rebels "into a Rout."[29] In one such incident, as it was reported, the British agent Simon Girty, while scouting forts in Kentucky, led a mixed British-Shawnee force against fifty-five Virginia militiamen heading to Fort Pitt in two boats. Forty-four died, either "kil'd on the shore" or "drounded in the River."[30]

This is not to say that the British merely used Indians. In fact, interests converged in the West. Encroachments in "the Country of Kentuck," for example, gave the British justification for attacking.[31] The British realized that Kentucky, in particular, was "the finest country for new settlers in America" and that in 1780 "one thousand Families" were moving there. Nonetheless, "it happens unfortunately for them, to be the Indians best hunting ground, which they will never give up. And in fact, it is our interest not to let the Virginians, Marylanders, and Pennsylvanians get possession there lest in a short time they become formidable."[32] The revolutionary agenda of Indians to take back their lands, therefore, dovetailed with British strategic imperatives.

Within a year of Butler's raid and Clark's march west, British officials realized the great utility of such a strategic convergence. In the summer of 1779, the British military commander of Quebec, who directed many of the ranger units in the West, argued, "I will as much as I am able (and it will be in my Power) increase the Number of parties I have upon the Frontier." In other words, the coordinated raids had passed their trials.[33] Hamilton's successor at Detroit, Col. Arent Schuyler De Peyster, would be given a free hand in sponsoring raids. In the winter, ranger units stayed in the field, along with young Delawares, Shawnees, Iroquois, and Cherokees, blanketing the frontier, attacking from time to time, and keeping an eye on rebel activity.[34]

Settlers in the Ohio valley lay between the British hammer and the Indian anvil. In the summer of 1781, a settler from Pittsburgh reported that more than a thousand Indians, including many Delawares, and rangers were descending on the region.[35] In 1780 and 1781, Shawnees and Cherokees hit Kentucky, hoping to create as much chaos as possible. The normally unflappable John May feared that "an Army of 600 English and Canadians and 1500 Indians are on their March to attack our Post at the Falls of Ohio," in the process resecuring regions "reduced by Col. Clarke."[36] On reaching the targeted area, attacking forces broke into smaller units, large enough to take forts but small enough to move quickly from settlement to settlement. One portion of the large party destined for the Fort Pitt region in the summer of 1781, for instance, attacked the garrison at Wheeling Creek in September, flying "British Cullars and Demand[ing] the fort to Be SurrenDerred." A "Negro" scout from the fort found out "that the force Consisted of a British Captain and forty Regular Soldiers and two hundred and sixty Indians."[37]

Even if reports exaggerated atrocities, such as the "massacre" at

Wyoming, by 1780 settlers knew to expect bloodshed. "Butler it is said," Arthur Campbell noted, "comes against Kentucky in great wrath. He boasts that he will give no Quarter."[38] Rumors such as these were on the mark. "Accounts from Kentuckey," John May wrote in the spring of 1780, "are dreadful."[39] Petitions streamed in from settlers in Boonesborough and Bryan's Station as fears grew that attacks would "Render this Country a Mere scene of Carnage and Desolation."[40] Indeed, in these years Indians made good on the name by which many knew the country: "Dark and Bloody Ground."[41] In the summer of 1780, Indians and rangers were attacking stations and destroying livestock and crops throughout Kentucky, making the following winter one of great "difficulties," a time during which people feared to stray from their stinking blockhouses.[42] A Delaware leader named Killbuck claimed 300 rangers and 500 Indians, including at least 70 Delawares, raided Kentucky. The numbers thrown out were more or less on the mark. De Peyster had given orders to dispatch 150 rangers and 700 Indians to target settlements along the Licking River, at one site killing—or so it was reported—two hundred men, women, and children.[43]

The Shawnees, eager to gain the title "the Greatest Warriors of all Nations," led the raids.[44] They settled old scores with appalling efficiency. In the summer of 1780, Alexander McKee accompanied a group of rangers and Shawnees to Fort Liberty on the Ohio River. While it rained, the men "raised a Battery of rails and earth, within 80 yards of the fort." They fired two shots with their three-pounders, one cutting a spar, the other lodging in a house. Surrounded by troops and artillery, the besieged in Fort Liberty surrendered without a fight. The officer in charge of the rangers, Lt. Henry Bird, "forewarn'd them that the Savages would adopt some of their Children." While he did so, the Shawnees "rushed in, tore the poor Children from their Mothers breasts, killed a wounded man, and every one of the cattle." The party moved on to a nearby fort. It, too, "surrendered without firing a shot." As Bird explained, "The same promises were made, and broke in the same manner." With the cattle killed, the survivors faced the prospect of starvation in the winter.[45]

To make matters worse, just as the ranger commanders turned a blind eye to Indian violence, they also tried to move as many people as they could into British prison camps.[46] Quebec teemed with men, women, and children captured from the Ohio valley. Captives included infants and the elderly taken from the regions around Fort Pitt, Kentucky, and western

Virginia.[47] In 1780, along the Virginia frontier, for example, the British and Indians captured ten members of the Duncan family, ranging in age from forty to two. The Mahon family, also taken in 1780, included the Widow Mahon, aged forty-eight, her eight children, including Roney LaForce Mahon, aged one and a half, and her daughter-in-law Agnes.[48] Ranger units were ordered to "apprehend any Person or Persons . . . directly or indirectly aiding, or abetting the Rebels," taking family members of suspects as "Hostages" to "prevent their or any part of their Family from taking an active part against His majesty's Government."[49]

From Fort Pitt to the Illinois Country, the West lay in ruins. Indians and rangers working together were visiting settlements with "fire and desolation," as a ranger commander observed, and had "reduced the extensive frontier upon the Ohio, to an heap of ashes."[50] Along the Clinch, for instance, James Roark's family met a particularly grisly fate. On March 18, 1780, Indians scalped seven of his children and his wife. Only one of his girls survived.[51] A settler in Illinois claimed the people "are now altogether without authority"; killers roamed with "impunity."[52] The commander at Fort Pitt surveyed the destruction around the fort in 1781 in the wake of summer attacks. "It is truly disturbing to see how this Country is laid waste," he observed, "and more so to hear the lamentations of Widows for their murdered Husbands and Children, and sometimes the Husbands for his Wife and Children."[53] Bloodshed, not uncertainty or disorder, defined the day.

The violence had expected and unexpected consequences. Unsurprisingly, violence did not discriminate between wealthy and poor. Each settler, regardless of status, saw his "Wife and Children coop'd up in a Garrison, the Staunch of which the Streets of Edinburgh is but an Emblem of." A settler named Matthew Price had learned that "you could not send out your servant 100 yards without having him scalped." He cited five men who had met such a fate within a mile and a half of the fort. To be sure, if violence drew speculator and squatter together, tensions still existed. Price noted "great Divisions amongst the People, being dis-satisfied at the disappointment of getting their lands." Large numbers "from the backcountry . . . expected to have taken what Lands they pleased." But they had to contend with men such as Price, and they were "rather inclined to take up Arms against what they called Tuckahoes, meaning the lower Virginians, the latter of which now begin to gain ground." Nonetheless, although tensions simmered within the forts in 1780 and 1781, it mattered little. Few dared leave them to claim the land, and as a result the conflicts over rights to improvement versus rights to preemption that had defined the late 1770s in places like Kentucky grew less heated.[54]

Unsurprisingly, too, many of Price's neighbors—wealthy and poor— came to despise the British. Yet despite such righteous indignation, the years 1779 to 1782, if anything, witnessed greater vacillation among frontier folk. Far from pushing them further into the patriot camp, British and Indian attacks seemed to inspire indifference to the whole cause of independence, a shift that easterners found troubling.[55] In 1781, a perplexed and furious Pennsylvania official named Richard Peters complained that frontier settlers would not supply forts with food. Some refused to pay taxes, others to support the army, and men raised to serve in the militia were rebelling.[56] A year later, an officer from Fort McIntosh reported that some women seemed to be supporting the British cause. While their husbands hunted, most wives "never went outside the garrison unless for water." But on hearing rumors of another series of raids, a few decided enough was enough and concocted "A Design, to go off to the Enemy."[57] Indeed, as the commander at Fort Pitt wrote in 1780, "I learn more and more of the Disaffection of many Inhabitants . . . [and] The King of Britain's health is often drunk in Companies." If regular troops left, he believed, some would see it as "a favourable opportunity to submit to British government."[58] He wrote Washington asking for permission to order some "disaffected inhabitants" away from Fort Pitt, an area "infested" by 1781.[59]

So pronounced was the trend that Thomas Jefferson demanded something be done. In 1780, Jefferson—now governor of Virginia—was alarmed to discover that some on the frontier claimed by Virginia had grown "so far discontented with the present government as to combine with its enemies to destroy it." Jefferson wanted to spare no expense to capture the disaffected and bring them to trial, promising the government of Virginia would pay for "strong guards of militia" to ensure they did not break out of prison.[60] William Preston scrambled to get to the bottom of the affair. He found that seventy-five men in his region were "disaffected from the present Government" and "had combined to disturb the Peace of this unhappy Frontier." They had, he learned, sworn oaths of allegiance to the Crown and were corresponding with other Tories up and down the frontier. Preston ordered militia captains to "discover all suspected Persons in their respective Companies."[61]

To some extent, British strategy was geared to fomenting these types of

divisions. As they hammered frontier settlements, the British also tried to
entice those suffering to support the Loyalist cause, suggesting that only
the king's army could restore order in a broken world. Much like the strategy the British hit on for the South after the opening stages of the War of
Independence, commanders in the West hoped to create and exploit such
sentiment on the frontier.[62] Officers argued that westerners settled where
they did, in part, to flee "the oppression of Congress."[63] They noted with
great pleasure that Clark failed time and time again to raise any men for
his forays into the West after his first mission, reporting that "the general
clamour of the Country is against Clark for his ill treatment of the militia."[64] Rangers nailed letters to doors of empty cabins, urging settlers to accept British sovereignty.[65] Simon Girty and Alexander McKee, it was said,
brought a store of British uniforms with them "to Cloath the People" of
the frontier.[66] As American commanders learned from the Moravian missionaries on the Muskingum, Girty was corresponding with settlers
around Fort Pitt by dropping off "a Packet of Letters out of a Hollow
Tree."[67] The "disaffected" also sent letters to the British at Detroit "neatly
rolled up in a powder horn."[68]

Even one of the mythic heroes of the Revolutionary frontier flirted
with loyalism. In 1778, Shawnees captured Daniel Boone and a few of his
companions while hunting. They then led him to Detroit, where he
seems to have given intelligence about Kentucky stations. The British
learned, for example, the exact location of the fort at Boonesborough, as
well as how many men defended it. Boone told his captors that the people
"have been so incessantly harassed by parties of Indians, they have not
been able to sow grain, and at Kentucke will not have a morsel of bread by
the middle of June." They had no clothes. Nor did they expect help from
Congress. Many would be prepared, Boone informed them, "to come to
this Place before winter." On learning this, rangers passed out "placarts,"
enticing settlers to declare for the Crown, as they raided.[69] While those
captured along with Boone suffered at the hands of the Shawnees, running the gauntlet naked and sleeping in the snow, the British gave Boone
a saddled horse. After his interrogation at Detroit, the Indians took Boone
back to Chillicothe and adopted him as one of their own, before he escaped back to the Kentucky settlements.[70] Settlers back at Boonesborough
began to wonder what Boone had told the British once a party of more
than four hundred Indians descended on the settlement in August, besieg-

ing the fort for nine days and trying to undermine its defenses and foul its water supply.[71]

Neither Boone's vacillation nor the disaffection of many on the frontier stemmed from fickleness or the cultural degeneration caused by living far from the East; rather, such sentiments emerged once it became clear neither the British, the Virginians, nor the Americans could bring an end to the state of war in the West. Even as the British wondered whether the disaffected acted out of principle or self-interest, they conceded that settlers would "faithfully defend the Country, that affords them Protection."[72] The western revolution had become an elemental struggle. In places like Kentucky, after two years of large-scale raids, bitter winters, and no help from the East, things looked dire. "If no succour is sent to Kentucky," William Christian explained, "and the war with the British continues another Year, it is more than probable the whole of the Inhabitants will be killed, taken to Detroit or driven away."[73] The settlers' War of Independence centered on these harsh realities. As a Kentuckian explained, to understand the West in these years entailed reading "the Book of Lamentations." "This world," he wrote in 1780, "never new human nature so defasd as the unhappy settlers . . . [M]aney of them still remaining in the Wilderness having lost every horse and Cow they were possessed of and hole Families have perishd."[74]

Compounding the problem, no help came from any quarter to defend the frontier. Part of the reason stemmed from "the unsettled jurisdiction" of the West.[75] After Clark's failure, Virginians struggled to come up with funds even for feeding and equipping militias.[76] Pennsylvanians also shirked their responsibilities. As long as Virginia would not act, and "the line between this State and Virginia" was not fixed, Pennsylvania would not help.[77]

Looking for help from American forces seemed a fool's errand. On paper, the Americans possessed a series of forts at strategic points that could be used for defensive or offensive operations. As well as Fort Pitt, troops garrisoned a post twenty-five miles away on Beaver Creek named Fort McIntosh, another at the mouth of the Kentucky River about eighty miles above the Falls of the Ohio, one below and one above the falls, and for a short time a fifth on the Tuscarawas named Fort Laurens.[78] In reality, these proved ineffectual. Troops lacked "Blankets, Shirts, and many other articles of Clothing."[79] At Fort Pitt, most of the three hundred rank and file

were "unfit for the service."[80] Troops complained of endemic food shortages as fraud among the quartermasters was rampant.[81] Even the British
did not see the Americans as a threat. And with good reason. When Fort
Laurens came under attack from Delawares and as officials decided they
had no means to reinforce it, it was abandoned.[82] At that time, as some in-
formers claimed, the whole American force in the Ohio valley numbered
little more than 200. Fort Pitt's numbers had dropped to 110; the rest were
spread around, a few even staying in farmhouses.[83]

Frontier posts, therefore, did little more than struggle to support their
own existence. To be sure, commanders discussed plans for expeditions,
asking county lieutenants to raise volunteers, but these were postponed
again and again.[84] In 1779, Washington ordered western officers to make
plans for an expedition even as he realized that siphoning off men for attacks would leave settlements "exposed."[85] Eventually, he called it off, citing a shortage of men and supplies.[86] By 1780, he had ended all pretense
of sending troops to the West for defense or attack.[87] In the same year,
Brodhead, who had requested county militia to muster for a general attack, informed the men they could stand down. They had not stirred in
any event.[88]

In these straits, the people refused to support Continental troops. Instead of supplying Fort Pitt with beef, settlers drove their cattle into the
mountains. Men refused to march east to serve when called up, and militiamen deserted their posts or did not turn out when ordered.[89] When they
did sell food to the army, they asked "a most scandalous price and indeed
are not willing to part with them at any price for any other than hard
money." With the Moravian Delawares one of the few reliable sources of
supply, leaders considered impressments of goods as the only viable solution but conceded that "at best" getting supplies in this way was "a very disagreeable business."[90] Troops at Fort Pitt discovered that the "Country
Inhabitants" took them for "fools" for serving without pay and "Cowards"
for failing to protect settlements.[91] "The citizen," a settler at Pittsburgh in
1781 found, "is opposed to the soldier."[92] So tainted had the relationship
between fort and country become that an exasperated Brodhead declared,
"I cannot comply with the expectations of my superiors, and at the same
time please a rabble." In 1781, Brodhead resigned.[93]

His replacement, William Irvine, was appalled by what he confronted.
"I have tried to œconomize," he wrote Washington after taking over com-

mand of the western district, "but every thing is in so wretched a state that there is very little in my power." Bringing order to the West was out of the question. "I never saw troops cut so truly a deplorable, and at the same time despicable, a figure," he fumed, adding that "no man would believe from their appearance, that they were soldiers — Nay! It would be difficult to determine whether they were white men."[94] Within a few months of assuming command, Irvine confronted the righteous anger of men who had not been paid for more than two years, had no fuel to keep warm, and were clothed in rags, making them "Utter things much to the Prejudice of the Character of a Soldier."[95] While whispering mutiny, they spent their time "Playing at Long Bullets" in the street of the town near the brew house and gambling.[96]

Therefore, settlers fended for themselves. In August 1781, as a large force of Indians was expected to hit western Pennsylvania, the commanding officer of the Western Department issued a clarion call for the frontier counties. Federal troops would not or could not help them. The people would have to rely on their own wits. "This is the time," Brodhead intoned, "that the friends of this Country Will shine in opposition to the disaffected, and I am Confident that every man, who prefers freedom to slavery, Will step forth, to defend his Property, his innocent Wife and Children or dear Relations."[97] Around this time, more people began arming themselves, refusing to have anything to do with official plans.[98] Yet they did so as they confronted the specter of large-scale attacks. Without help from the garrisons of the West, the people of Washington County, Pennsylvania, withstood massive raids in 1780, 1781, and early 1782.[99] Volunteers from Westmoreland County faced a similar fate, when in the winter of 1781 they lost "so many heads of Family."[100]

John McDonald, a settler in Montgomery County, summed up the sentiments of westerners in 1780 when he said he "would pay no Taxes." Because violence and competition defined the tenor of the times, McDonald claimed "he would loose his life before he would give up his Arms and that there would soon he supposed be a king in every county." He "thought we had been fighting for Liberty but Slavery was the consequence."[101] McDonald gave voice to three lessons learned from the western revolution. First, there could be no allegiance without protection. The failure to choose a side in the War of Independence did not stem from opportunism, but reflected the newfound political confidence of a people who would not be manipulated faced with the realities of life on the frontier. Second, no one could make legitimate claims to authority amid rampant violence. As no patron emerged promising a return to order, the necessity of isolation was transformed into a revolutionary virtue of autonomy. Finally, as bloodshed did not discriminate between wealthy and poor, the greatest divisions looming in the West were between those who suffered and those who inflicted the suffering. In the state of war, as it had taken shape in the West, status, class, or political allegiance did not mark the salient divide on the frontier. In a world defined by violence and the memories of bloodshed in which all parties acted in constrained circumstances, the gap between Indian and white did.

Together these considerations, fashioned in the state of war, formed conditions for any return of sovereignty. They also provided the chief means to order the chaotic world of the West. Put another way, common settlers were laying out the broad contours of a frontier commonwealth, not the form it would take but the imperatives around which it must be organized. In the violent crucible of the West, they clamored for a form of security that cohered to realities of and experience on the frontier. To be sure, they used some of the broad templates of making sense of the world around them that easterners did as well, be these liberal, republican, or some mixture of the two. But an idea of commonwealth rooted in security against Indians, and the need for the state to act in some fashion to guarantee what settlers regarded as a basic right, took shape from the Hobbesian nature of a world from which they could not escape on their own. Sovereignty would have to reflect this frontier commonwealth vision.

The ideas that animated this conception of sovereignty were a different matter altogether. To be sure, Whiggish rhetoric, country ideology, or the civic republican tradition—those stock bundles of ideas conventionally associated with the ideology of the American Revolution—formed much of the basis of western Revolutionary discourse in much the same way they did for men and women from the East.[102] But one idea that ran through all emerging facets of a popular frontier commonwealth vision and lent them all meaning was the hatred of Indians. As settlers were growing increasingly "disaffected," Brodhead observed, "ignorant inhabitants" demonstrated a greater propensity to attempt "to murder" Indians under "our immediate protection."[103] In a world of violence, vanquishing Indians promised order. Settlers articulated this common hatred most eloquently not by their words but through their actions. And in the early 1780s, settlers were speaking volumes with what they did. Indeed, Indian hatred was taking a frightening turn on the frontier as what we could call genocidal attacks on Indian communities grew in number and frequency. For many westerners, the lust for treating Indians to "fire and sword, and no Quarter" represented the only certainty in an uncertain world.[104] A notion of order rooted in racial violence, therefore, would animate the common people's idea of sovereignty.

In the early 1780s, settlers who had sustained years of privation and bloodshed and had recently confronted appalling losses struck out at any Indians they could lay their hands on. Infamously, in 1782, a number of men from western Pennsylvania and Virginia massacred perhaps the only blameless souls on the frontier. Without the blessing of the western garrisons or the governments of Pennsylvania or Virginia, men largely from Washington County under the leadership of David Williamson set off early in the year to destroy the Indians responsible for the raids of the previous summer and for the recent murder of a mother and child. They found what they conceived to be a guilty party at the Moravian mission villages on a tributary of the Muskingum River. At these settlements, the Moravians and the Indians—mainly Delawares—"had built a pretty Town and made good improvements and lived for some years past quite in the style of Christian white people." Here, they farmed like other settlers in the Ohio valley. They had thrived in these years of violence and had in 1781 "a great number of cattle and Swine to dispose of."[105] The Indians claimed to be neutral, but they had some "attachment to American liberty." After all, they had provided commanders at Fort Pitt with intelligence and food.[106] Although the Delawares there proclaimed their innocence, Williamson's party concluded that they had to be lying. After all, they possessed goods, such as kettles and clothing, that only whites could use. They must have pilfered these on raids. Williamson and the men gathered the Delawares from small villages along the Muskingum, assembling them in the mission town of Gnadenhütten, German for the "huts of grace."[107]

Their professed Christianity could not save them. After holding a "trial," the volunteers and their elected officers condemned each and every Delaware to death. Throughout the evening, as the Indians sang psalms and comforted one another, the men from Washington County debated how to kill them. After rejecting burning the Indians alive, they decided to bludgeon and scalp. On the morning of March 7, 1782, troops escorted them into a cabin by pairs. The Delawares did not resist. Williamson's men then smashed the heads of the condemned with wooden mallets, scalping each of them. After the work was done, they burned the huts of slaughter. In all, the Pennsylvanians killed ninety-six men, women, and children.[108] This group of militia also went on to butcher a smaller number of Delawares at Killbuck Island near Pittsburgh later that same year. At this site, they destroyed anything they came across that constituted Indianness, such as wampum. Other units'similarly savaged Shawnee communities, raping women and murdering children.[109]

The killings of "a number of Indians, at or near Muskingum," alarmed eastern officials.[110] The incident also shocked the British. One officer could not believe what had happened. The frontiersmen had "destroyed the poor innocent Moravian Indians, their near Neighbours, who never went to War against them, or any other People." Most damningly, "under the Cloak of Friendship they murdered them in Cold Blood, and reduced their Bones to Ashes that the Murder might not be discovered."[111] Irvine questioned the men involved, but he found "no man can give any account . . . nor will they give Evidence against themselves."[112] However inexplicable, this type of slaughter was becoming the norm in the West.[113]

The following spring, members of the same militia unit responsible for the Gnadenhütten massacre reassembled under a newly elected leader, William Crawford, and marched to destroy other Delawares and Wyandots at Sandusky. "We Want Revenge Appon the Savages for the Enjurys they Dun unto our Brother Soldiers," a petition from frontier inhabitants read, "to proqure as meney scalps from our Enemy and make Sutch Discuverys as can be maid."[114] Once again, the men, volunteers all, had to equip themselves. No one would sponsor them. Irvine only learned of the plans after Crawford had been elected to lead the settlers. Nearly five hundred men from both Pennsylvania and Virginia turned out, all prepared to march the two hundred miles to Sandusky. Most came from Washington and Westmoreland counties in Pennsylvania and Ohio County in Virginia.[115]

Spies, moving ahead of the force, ran into Indians on the fourth of June. As Angus McCoy recounted, "the play of human destruction" and "the powder music" then commenced. For five hours, McCoy and his comrades exchanged fire with Indians and a small number of rangers.

McCoy claimed, "We had some of as brave a men as ever shouldered a gun." Yet courage was not enough. Throughout the night the Indians received reinforcements, encircling the militia, and the fight continued the next day. Toward sundown, Indians fired a volley at the sun to stop it from setting before they finished their work. Many of these Indians, like the victims of Gnadenhütten, were Delawares, but unlike the Christian martyrs, they were neither peaceful nor neutral. The men from Washington County and western Virginia, having buried their dead and bandaged the wounded, beat a retreat, leaving only a fellow named Thomas Ogle, shot in the chest and not long for the world, behind. The Indians pursued them, killing and scalping stragglers. About forty died, but most made their escape.[116]

Colonel Crawford did not. After Crawford had led a small party, including a pilot, his son-in-law, a physician named John Knight, and a few wounded men away from the main group to cover its retreat, Delawares captured them and marched them back to Sandusky. At the village, Simon Girty greeted Crawford, informing him "that the Indians were very much enraged against the prisoners, particularly Captain Pipe one of the chiefs." Captain Pipe, whose brother had died at the hands of settlers, ordered the faces of the men painted black, marking them for execution. Boys and women tomahawked five of the prisoners, including a Virginian named John McKinley who had joined the expedition. After an "old squaw" cut off his head, she kicked it around the ground. Enraged men, women, and children "struck us either with sticks or their fists," Knight recounted. Four others were also tomahawked and scalped.[117]

The dead were the fortunate ones. What was to happen to Crawford would become the stuff of frontier legend. According to one popular account, Delawares stripped Crawford of his clothes, sat him down by a fire, and beat him. "They then tied a rope to the foot of a post about fifteen feet high, bound the Colonel's hands behind his back and fastened the rope to the ligature between his wrists." After Girty told Crawford he would be burned and Captain Pipe made a speech, the men took their guns and shot his body with burning powder "from his feet as far up as his neck," cut off his ears, and thrust burning sticks into his body "so that whichever way he ran round the post they met him with burning faggots and poles." While women threw hot coals on the ground, Crawford begged Girty to shoot him. But Girty would not speak to him. The tortures continued like this for two hours when "at last being spent, he lay down on his belly: they then scalped him." Crawford was not dead yet. A woman grabbed a board, placed hot ashes and coals on it, and "laid them on the back and head after he had been scalped." The Delawares then burned him alive.[118] As he "roasted," Crawford retained enough strength to swear "some great blows would be struck against this country."[119]

The torture of Crawford, the ominous final words he allegedly muttered, and the ways in which the story resonated underscored a critical shift in the West. As a British commander explained, the frontier people had become "a Trecherous and Cruel Enemy, resolved to Destroy the Indians at all Events," adding that "when any of the King's Troops are taken, they are treated as Prisoners of War, but when Indians were taken, they were immediately put to death." Indians, on the other hand, in this case Shawnees, had resolved "to act like Men."[120] When in 1780 settlers from Hanna's Town near Fort Pitt attempted to kill the few remaining pro-American Delawares, it was assumed "that Women and Children were to suffer an equal Carnage with the men."[121] In contrast, Delawares, British officials noted, "shewed a humanity hitherto unpracticed amongst them." While whites savaged the helpless, Delawares were "sparing the lives of such as are incapable of defending themselves."[122] By 1782, Indians as a rule did not normally kill innocent women and children; indeed, at the same time settlers were butchering the Delawares, Indian raiders up and down the Ohio were bringing prisoners to the British. As one British general put it, what happened to Crawford—although westerners would view it as the rule—proved exceptional and stemmed from Delaware outrage over Gnadenhütten. "The conduct of the Indians upon the Ohio last year," he argued, "was very different." Only whites "who improperly call themselves Christians" and who put innocents to death "in a more shameful manner" exhibited such "Barbarity and cruelty."[123]

In other words, frontier settlers had become the savages. They dressed like Indians. They raided and fought like Indians. And most critically, they ritualistically tortured and killed. Although these rituals might have had the veneer of civility—say, resorting to a "trial" to determine the "guilt" of the Moravian Delawares—such rites also created a rationale for dispensing with mercy and civility. Indeed, as a British observer argued, the settlers, not the Indians, were "reviving the old savage custom of putting their Prisoners to Death which with much pains and expence we had weaned the Indians from in this neighbourhood."[124]

Perhaps most significantly, settlers had stopped executing British soldiers, those whom they had in the past labeled as corrupters. Settlers exonerated the British not because they deemed them innocent of manipulation but because they had come to reject a formula that had stipulated savages could be corrupted by others. To be sure, as an escaped captive named John Dodge argued, the British were "Barbarians" who sponsored and led raids in which Indians took the "green scalps" of children.[125] But Indians themselves—or better, nature itself—were responsible for such depravity. Indeed, by 1782 the Paxton Boy logic that settlers could not afford to wait for civilizing influences to take hold made no sense on the frontier. The early modern model of explaining difference, rooted in culture, could no longer explain the world around them. It had been stressed for some time. In this world of all against all, it cracked. Settlers now conceived Indians as innately inhuman, irredeemable, unable to move up the stadial ladder. In fact, for those who killed Indians and those who hated them, immutable physical characteristics, not culture, now determined levels of civility.

Similar transformations, of course, had occurred on earlier frontiers. At each such juncture—say, 1675 and 1676 in New England or the Chesapeake—once settlers had acted like savages and Indians with civility, white men and women confronted troubling realities, causing them to blur or obliterate conventional ways of understanding human difference. Hence, the butchers of Gnadenhütten—just like other Indian killers on other frontiers—slaughtered the civilized Delawares not only despite their civilized ways but also because of them. Something in this process, however, is especially apparent on the frontier at this juncture: more than discourse or self-perception was at issue. The shift in the ways settlers objectified Indians took place as violence became the only certainty in a chaotic world and as settlers—causes and products of that world—struggled to reinvent the terms of sovereignty while they grappled with what was happening to them as well as what they had become. At this time, in this place, no sovereign authority could restrain racist settlers, as had been the case with the Paxton Boys. In the Revolution on the frontier, therefore, race and violence went hand in hand, one feeding off the other. And in such a context and after years of bloodshed, older cultural models could no longer comprehend social reality.[126]

A few months after Cornwallis famously surrendered to Washington at Yorktown in October 1781, the members of Parliament voted to halt offensive operations in America. From this point on, British troops in the West were to engage only in defensive operations. Nevertheless, violence continued even as its character was changing.[127] The unrestrained savagery with which settlers killed was becoming a defining feature of the West. In the wake of Gnadenhütten, Cherokees suffered "wanton bloody outrages," as the settlers who were assembling to confiscate Cherokee land around the Ohio valley proved "truly barbarous and more than savage."[128] Such terms, of course, had become meaningless to describe Indian behavior. By 1781, Daniel Brodhead, who had worked to uphold Delaware neutrality in the war, had grave doubts about the nature of Indians. "Much confidence," he suggested, "ought never to be placed in any of the colour, for I believe it is much easier for the most civilized Indian to turn savage than for any Indian to be civilized."[129]

The Revolution, therefore, was turning the world upside down. And a new order, instituted by what Americans, the British, and Indians referred to as a rabble, began to take shape in 1782. During that summer of tit-for-tat murder, the area around Fort Pitt swirled with racist hatred and righteous anger as Shawnees, Mingoes, Delawares, and Wyandots launched vengeful raids. Much of their attention focused on Hanna's Town, a settlement thirty miles from Pittsburgh on the road to Philadelphia. In July, one hundred raiders killed fifteen settlers in and about Hanna's Town and captured ten more. The people could not defend their homes outside the fort, retreating to the "miserable stockade," while "the enemy possessed themselves of the forsaken houses, from whence they kept a continual fire upon the fort."[130] Indians also devastated a region seven or eight miles around it, killing three to four hundred head of cattle, seventy horses, and "sheep and hogs innumerable."[131] Indians, in other words, were acting with—as one ranger put it—"vigour and spirit . . . daily bringing scalps and prisoners."[132]

The offensive continued through the summer and into the fall. In early September, "Wheeling was in some degree Blockaded." Indians "Kepted skulking about it for five or six days." They seemed to appear "almost in every Quarter," ensuring that the "people of the Country were alarmed beyond conception."[133] After the assault, the large party of more than two hundred broke into smaller groups, destroying settlements, including "a blockhouse on what's called the dutch fork of Buffaloe."[134] In mid-October, Shawnees reportedly killed seventeen men in the area around the Laurel River.[135] Kentucky also experienced renewed attacks.

"This Country," an exasperated John May reported, "is in a dreadful situation, having been almost intirely overrun this Summer by the Indians; and most of the useful men having been killed."[136] As one inhabitant of Hanna's Town believed, "It seems the enemy had determined to make a General attack upon the Frontiers."[137]

As the West descended into the abyss, settlers once more pleaded for help. Attacks had grown so generalized that militia could not move from one area to another, leaving all isolated.[138] Requests came from up and down the frontier for assistance, as many settlements still lay "extremely dangerous to the Enemy."[139] Unless they received protection from "the rage of a savage and merciless Enemy," settlers feared they could not carry on long in the stockades. They needed relief, food, and, most crucially, coordination.[140] They did not want pious words; rather, they demanded experienced "guards," who were capable of more than "defending the spott they occupy," moved into and around the stockades like the one that held fifteen nervous families at Brush Creek.[141]

After years of war, settlers were asking the government for protection on their own terms, trying to pressure officials "to induce our governments to take some effectual steps to chastise and repress [the Indians]." Experience had taught them "that the nature of an Indian is fierce and cruel, and that an extirpation of them would be useful to the world, and honourable to those who can effect it."[142] The people of Brush Creek played upon the "feelings of humanity and Benevolence" that they believed they shared with their white brethren in Fort Pitt, sentiments that could confound the "unabated fury of the Savages," who presumably could not be moved by such human emotions.[143] As a westerner explained, "The anxiety of the People is general for another Expedition." Settlers would raise the men and equip them if government would provide critical help. That support, however, was conditional and had to be used to savage Indians.[144] In Washington County, where many of the butchers of Gnadenhütten had lived, inhabitants also forted up in the summer and fall of 1782, even failing to sow fall crops. But in this case, they did not stir from their forts out of fear. They stayed because they were awaiting word of an expedition. They did not want to miss out.[145] Even inhabitants of Hanna's Town clamored for an offensive. If troops moved with speed and determination, they suggested, the raiders loaded down with booty still might face justice.[146]

No help came. Irvine offered to lead volunteer militias to clear the

West and to act in concert with George Rogers Clark, who was making noises about yet another great western expedition.[147] Clark marched, but only "got a few scalps" at Chillicothe before returning east.[148] John May had hoped that finally the men at Fort Pitt would prove their worth.[149] Washington, however, would release no troops from the East or from Carlisle, fearing hostilities might once again flare up. Instead, American officials asked Pennsylvania and Virginia to send 150 men each to help.[150] True to form, Benjamin Harrison would not send Virginians anywhere near Hanna's Town, arguing that they would "hault at the boundary line." Virginians, after all, defended the interests of Virginia.[151] The long-hoped-for expedition never materialized.[152]

Settlers did not take the news lying down. Despite the failure to mount an expedition, Congress still demanded the people pay taxes "assessed by the late Supply Bill, in Flour delivered at Fort Pitt at the Market Price."[153] The request touched off a firestorm. In Washington County, inhabitants were "associating to oppose taxation and prevent the sheriff from collecting." They also "caused some of their officers to resign their Commissions and threaten those who continue to act with tarring and feathering if they call upon them for any more Militia duty."[154]

Refusal to cooperate with what they regarded as a negligent government represented the only recourse many had to make their voices heard. Near Muddy Creek, for example, men refused to take orders to muster from their commanding officers and county lieutenants. Frontier settlers, of course, had made such refusals in the past. But now they invoked Revolutionary principles. One such county lieutenant struggled to understand this "Poisoning of the minds of the people." If government did not act to suppress such sentiment, he declared, "the Country (at least the frontier) will be ruined."[155] One settler near Pittsburgh, named Irwin, was doing "every thing in his power to obstruct the payment of Taxes." He harangued the people on the issue, going "to daring lengths to advise them to oppose the civil officers . . . by force and arms." So confident was Irwin that his views reflected the sentiments of most of the people that he dared to deliver his message before two justices of the peace.[156]

If government failed to protect and, just as significant, failed to decimate Indians—the form that people insisted sovereignty had to take—the people owed no obedience. At a meeting on Catfish Creek in Washington County, some inhabitants declared what their revolution meant to them.

The people had turned the realities of government indifference and frontier independence into virtues. In a world in which each inhabitant had to struggle without help, each had to "labour . . . all his might to set aside all law and government and depend upon the Virtue of the people for raising and Equiping this County."[157] Rights, of course, included the ability to kill Indians. Virtue could mean the independent spirit to act against government to do so. Violence and indifference had created a new West.

Although no one could claim authority over the Ohio valley by 1782, the parameters of any prospective settlement for the area were becoming clear. The West, as William Irvine observed, was "in a strange state." Settlers had "deliberated" before killing Christian Indians in "cold blood," including children slaughtered "in their Wretched Mothers Arms." Settlers, moreover, continued to kill "friendly Indians" at "the very nose of our Garrison on a small Island in the River." They had "made Prisoners of a Guard of Continental Troops" and warned the commanding officer, Col. John Gibson, "that they would also scalp him." The people feared Gibson "had an attachment to Indians in general." Indeed, "the general and common opinion of the people of this Country is that all Continental officers are too fond of Indians."[158] As one settler put it, after killing a Delaware with an ax, he "would kill every Man that was blacker than a white man."[159]

Common men and women now set the terms of debate in the West. Although the slaughter of the Indians appalled him, Irvine reasoned that whether such behavior "was right or wrong I do not pretend to determine." He had started to appreciate the nature of settler experience. "People who have had—Fathers, Mothers, Brothers or Children Butchered tortured Scalped by the savages—reason very differently on the subject of killing the Moravians," he conceded. Irvine did not excuse the killing, but as violence escalated, he had come to understand the context that gave rise to it. In any event, he knew it was prudent not to follow Gibson's example. He declared, "No man knows whether I approve or disapprove of killing the Moravians." He therefore refused to "express any sentiment for or against these deeds." The massacre, he had gathered, now served as a social barometer.[160]

As far as he could, Irvine acceded to the wishes of the people. After Crawford's death, news surfaced that he had condemned the mission. Irvine tried quickly to convince the people that he had supported the expedition when in fact he had not. As commander of the West, he insisted he had—in an official sense, anyway—"the supreme command of said volunteers." He also circulated a story that Washington "lamented the misfortune of Col. Crawford's death extremely" and had a "particular esteem" for him. This was true. Crawford had, after all, served as a land agent for Washington. But for Irvine, Washington's esteem had utility, tying the American cause for independence, and by extension his command, with the sentiments of westerners.[161] Irvine also backed words with deeds. When, for example, he equipped a small party of Virginians to "go against an Indian Town," and caught an Indian suspected of informing, he "ordered him instantly put to death." Doing such deeds, he believed, would allow him "to gain the confidence and esteem of the people—as they must be convinced that no partiality, favour or affection, to any colour will be shown by me." He understood that on the frontier, issues of "colour" mattered.[162] If Irvine did not harbor the racist ideas of those around him, he understood that in a world where people styled themselves sovereign, he must accede to their commonwealth ideal. If security did not entail hating Indians, it certainly required removing or decimating them.

The frontier revolution made for some strange bedfellows. In 1782, speculators and officials were worried less about surveying and restoring order than staying alive.[163] And some local elites, who lived amid the carnage, adopted the violent racial idea of citizenship that common settlers had embraced.[164] Hugh Henry Brackenridge, a justice of the peace for the Pittsburgh area, rejected the notion that Indians had become more civilized as the war progressed. "It has been said," he declared, "that the putting to death the Moravian Indians has been the cause of the cruelties practiced on the prisoners taken at Sandusky ... Yet it must be well known, that it has been the custom of the savages at all times." At issue for Brackenridge was not how or even if savages could become civil. For him, the question itself amounted to an absurdity. He did not approve the killing of the innocent Delaware women and children and argued that it "must be considered as unjustifiable inexcusable homicide." Nonetheless, in his eyes they were "animals, vulgarly called Indians."[165]

Brackenridge's experience in the West had changed his thinking. Before the war, he had argued that settlers could claim Indian land, but only because Indians did not "improve it" like more civilized peoples. By the early 1780s, however, he had come to believe that settlers did not have to offer any justifications for confiscation. Although Indians possessed "the shapes of men and may be of the human species," in reality they were "Devils." Their degraded culture, which could not change and arose from an animal-like nature, could "justify extermination." They could not be redeemed. Brackenridge had seen whites try to transform young Indian boys in schools. "I do not know one who has even by these means been rendered a useful member of society," he wrote. "They retain," he added ominously, "the temper of their race." Indeed, as he put it, "I am well persuaded, that for a keg of whiskey you might induce any Indian to murder his wife, child, or best friend." Although they had human form, they could not possess human qualities. Consequently, never sign treaties with them, he argued. Take their land without apology.[166]

Like many Americans during this period of transformation, westerners conceived of virtue as the desire "to Lett every local Consideration and private View Give Way to the Public Good." As they surveyed what one settler called "our New Western World," they reflected on the way "it is very evident That our settling this Country Hitherto has been through Many Difficulties and with Loss of many Good Citizens." The "predicaments we have so Long Groaned under"—violence, indifference, uncertainty, disorder—could only be addressed with a new form of "political authority," one that "originates with the Collective Body."[167] At one extreme, a racialized conception of human difference formed the basis of the new western consensus. At the other was the notion that solving the Indian menace represented the minimally acceptable step for bringing order to the West. This narrow spectrum, compressed further as violence continued, defined the limits of the set of shared beliefs that promised to bring the chaos of revolution to an end while also providing the means to make sense of bloodshed. The search for order in the West, therefore, did not only require jurisdiction or authority. Such considerations paled before a new ideological imperative fueled by the certainty of Indian hostility and Indian irredeemability. As westerners grappled with the crisis of 1782, many agreed that this sentiment must form the basis for reconstructing any meaningful notion of society.[168] Officials had little choice but to accede to popular demands for the form that society would take.

It is comforting to romanticize the experience of frontier settlers, to regard them as men and women engaged in the good fight against speculators and those who would manipulate them. It's also just as gratifying to demonize them, to see them as racists who reveled in slaughtering Indians. These characterizations, however, cannot be meaningfully separated. The struggle to ensure that their betters would not exploit them in a context increasingly defined by Indian-white violence made Indian hatred as an animating ideology possible. Each characterization, in other words, emerged as a product of revolution. Empowerment grew as a response to the failure of patrons to restore order amid uncertainty. Race hatred stemmed in part from the isolation and independence of settlers in a world of failed sovereignty. Both spoke to the nature of the violence people confronted and contributed to, reflecting the fractious qualities of a collapsed society divided between Indians and settlers, squatters and speculators, and animated by unfettered competition. The shifts—occurring in tandem, not in tension with each other—in other words, took place within constrained circumstances. As a group of settlers put it in the wake of the killings of 1782, "Since the year 1777 We have lived in a State of Anarchey."[169] Revolutionary change flowed from the implications of this state of war.

The emerging consensus that stemmed from the Hobbesian nature of competition would form the new basis for the reconstitution of society in the West. Dunmore, Henry, and Clark had tried to foist the trappings of authority on the West to claim it for themselves and their allies. After each failed, only the ideas that had emerged by 1782 could offer a meaningful way to order the western world. Ideas, of course, did not take the place of institutions. But they would place constraints on the type of authority that would be acceptable to the new brokers of the West, the people. The contours of the new West that were taking shape in 1782 and 1783 were especially visible in the last engagement of the War of Independence. On August 14, 1782, as the great Indian offensive of that year reached a crescendo, a group of Indians assembled from up and down the Ohio valley captured "a couple of boys" near Blue Licks in Kentucky. Their capture would lead to what one westerner called "one of the most melancholly events that has happened in all this Western Country." A force from Fayette County pursued the raiding party but "was repulsed," losing four men. Two days later, Bryan's Station came under attack from the last joint ranger-Indian expedition of the war, led by the man who witnessed Crawford's torture and refused to put him out of his misery, Simon Girty.[170]

Nearly two hundred men from the region turned out to take on the attackers. Benjamin Logan, who led a party of militia, understood the stakes involved. He marched "Dreading the consequences that might ensue from this precipitate affair."[171] While most believed they were chasing a raiding party that had taken a few boys, more than six hundred Indians waited in hiding, picking the spot to ambush the Kentuckians between the deepest part of the river by the lick and around steep cliffs. "Thus circumstanced," Logan recounted, "the Savages, sure of victory, rushed immediately up and threw our men into confusion." Retreat was impossible. Moreover, "many were killed after they were made prisoners, as they were seen tied." The combined British-Indian force routed the Kentuckians, killing seventy-seven, many after surrendering.[172]

Logan begged for help. He asked the governor of Virginia. He did not bother asking Irvine at Fort Pitt, who had proved useless. Logan found himself in the role of making the request because, as he put it, "all our magistrates heave been killed except three." Poor and wealthy, squatter and speculator, had died. He did not plead for support, however, for "defensive" purposes. The time for such actions had long since passed. "Unless you can go to their towns and scourge them," he warned, "they will never make a peace; but on the contrary keep parties constantly in your country to kill." Logan claimed that 470 people had been captured by joint ranger-Indian parties over the past three bloody years. While many of the men "were taken to Detroit," the women were "retained among the Indians as slaves." Despite British promises to return prisoners, these captives would "never get through Indian country" unless the Indians were decimated. The inhuman savages could not be party to civilized behavior and, as such, could not be treated with it. Savage them, Logan insisted.[173]

Although the violence was continuing even though the War of Independence had come to an end, settlers dared to reimagine a West that had seemed lost only ten years earlier. Daniel Boone, who fought at Blue Licks, prophesied that a new Kentucky lay on the horizon. In 1784 he was quoted as saying, "Thus we behold Kentucke, lately a howling wilderness, the habitation of savages and wild beasts, become a fruitful field; this region, so favourably distinguished by nature, now becomes the habitation of civilization." The eradication of savages and beasts would represent a watershed, "a period unparalleled in history, in the midst of raging war." In the West lay a new world, one without Indians. "Where wretched wigwams stood, the miserable abodes of savages," he concluded, "we beheld the foundations of cities laid, that in all probability, will rival the greatest upon earth."[174]

Gone from this narrative were Boone's vacillation, western disaffection, and the conflict between squatter and speculator, as well as the memories of Dunmore, Henry, and Clark. In the chaotic state of war, men and women imagined a new, ordered state of nature, a new start for the West, but one only conceivable given the defining bloodshed and uncertainty of the Revolution. Indeed, the memories of violence and the new race hatred that had emerged from it offered the only certainties and bases of order for this state of nature. As one Indian put it in 1784, in this new West only the realities of "White Flesh" and "Red Flesh" had withstood the furies of revolution and taken on new meanings from them.[175]

PART III

American Leviathan

The final cause, end, or design of men, who naturally love
liberty, and dominion over others, in the introduction of that
restraint upon themselves, in which we see them live in commonwealths, is the foresight of their own preservation, and of
a more contented life thereby; that is to say, of getting themselves out from that miserable condition of war . . . This is the
generation of that great Leviathan, or rather, to speak more
reverently, of that *mortal god*, to which we owe under the *im-
mortal God*, our peace and defence.

—Thomas Hobbes, *Leviathan*, chapter 17

SEVEN

South and North:
Envisioning Commonwealth
on the Frontier

The growing western consensus over the fate and nature of Indians in the Ohio valley was epitomized by the continuing call to defend the West even after the war had ended. In early 1783, settlers pleaded with eastern officials to construct forts at the mouths of the Kentucky, Licking, and Limestone rivers. Because many westerners had come to believe that the nefarious nature of Indians compelled them to attack even in the absence of the active work of British provocateurs, settlers hoped the state of Virginia and the federal government could coordinate a plan to garrison the forts with a company of regulars and militia, supplying them from "the neighbourhood of Fort Pitt."[1]

Virginia's Council responded that fort construction never justified the expense. "Fatal experience has shewn us," Benjamin Harrison argued, that forts did not deter Indian attacks or protect settlers.[2] As the British had learned in the early 1770s, forts were, as a board of western commissioners argued, "of Little use in covering and defending a Country situated as it is against an Enemy who carry on a war in the Manner the Indians do."[3] The plea for protection, critics charged, seemed to stem from an irrational impulse and reflected the self-serving motives and prejudices of common settlers.[4]

For westerners, however, the utility of forts lay in their significance as symbols. Forts made sovereignty manifest. Yet in different contexts, they stood for distinctive sovereign imperatives. The British had manned theirs, in part, to safeguard Indians so as to keep the peace. Dunmore had ordered forts constructed to placate settlers so as to use them for war. Now westerners wanted them to savage Indians so as to end the state of war. In the context of a world still disordered, forts also served as useful barometers of eastern resolve to understand and perhaps even to protect the West, to view it as an integral part of the United States and not as a place apart. Although by 1783 settlers did not have a coherent program for the reinstitution of order in the West, they understood that protection buttressed all other rights and had to be the basis of any society that emerged from the ferment of revolution. Thus the issue of forts underscored a critical truth in the West: while the War of Independence had ended and eastern society had returned to some semblance of normalcy, westerners still foundered in disorder and bloodshed and desired security. The end of the War of Independence, as a Kentuckian put it, should have been "an event of great joy," as settlers "anticipated a suspension of their Indian wars, but in this they were mistaken."[5] They still existed in a state of war, a point easterners failed to grasp or resolve.

"There is nothing more common," *The Pittsburgh Gazette* noted in 1786, "than to confound the terms of the American revolution with those of the late American war. The American war is over, but this is far from being the case with the American revolution. On the contrary, nothing but the first act of the great drama is closed."[6] In the West, still mired in uncertainty and chaos, the Revolution continued. After the war had ended, westerners still faced the task of forging an enduring Revolution settlement or, put another way, securing the commonwealth. Doing so entailed overcoming significant obstacles. First, violence continued. Second, governments in the East failed to assert the authority they claimed. Third, after 1784 two "Wests," in fact, existed side by side. North of the Ohio River, the federal government claimed sovereign authority, while to the south Virginia did. Finally, any emerging order had to conform to the western consensus being brokered by common men and women. In the West, Indians could not be considered redeemable, or they had to be moved out. Settlers, who were empowered as sovereigns by the ferment of revolution and who had laid out the conditions for the restoration of sovereignty, certainly were demanding as much.

Understanding these challenges and figuring ways to overcome them represented the terms for imagining a frontier commonwealth and, by implication, the conditions for the integration of the West into the nation. In pressing the East to "protect" the West, settlers both wealthy and poor from north and south of the Ohio River were transforming the basic terms of a consensus into a coherent vision. By the early 1790s, as chaos dragged on for nearly ten years after the signing of the Treaty of Paris, settlers, speculators, squatters, and frontier officials argued that "protection" meant more than defending westerners from an inherently savage enemy. The plea for protection became the organizing principle for a West struggling to devise standards for landownership, to ensure that the Ohio valley had outlets for trade, to guarantee that the region did not descend into conflict between wealthy and poor, and, of course, to defend lives, liberties, and property from continuing violence. They were beginning to argue that only the state could deliver them from their state of war and its attendant evils.

This frontier commonwealth vision grew to encompass both settlements south of the river and those sponsored by the federal government north of the river. Ironically, of course, elites were articulating an understanding of social integration that common men and women had envisioned in the crucible of revolution. Defending the West, for men and women on the frontier, implied ridding the region of Indians, and by the early 1790s nearly all westerners subscribed to protection as the fundamental right of society, even those who had migrated to the West from self-described "enlightened" eastern areas.

At the end of the War of Independence, the issue of sovereignty in the West still bedeviled settlers, speculators, and officials. State authorities debated each other over boundaries as Virginians made grand claims to the whole of the Ohio valley and those from "landless" states argued otherwise. Dunmore's conquest of the Shawnees in light of the Treaty of Fort Stanwix, in part, gave Virginians a solid argument for undisputed title to Kentucky, the area south of the Ohio River. But the failure of Virginia's leaders to restore and maintain order in Illinois, in part, weakened their claims to areas north of the river. Eventually, the federal government under the Articles of Confederation won jurisdiction north of the Ohio River, as Virginia ceded its interests there. Here Congress would supervise any settlement, adjudicate any disputes with Indians, and organize any plans for development. By 1784, Virginians had won concessions in regions they ceded to the United States, but they retained control of the

Kentucky district despite much grumbling. The Ohio valley, therefore, was divided into two sovereign territories.[7] And eastern states, such as Pennsylvania, acceded to this arrangement, issuing proclamations prohibiting their citizens from measuring, settling, surveying, or claiming lands to the north and west of the Ohio River, as well as recognizing Virginia's right to jurisdiction south of the river.[8]

But such arrangements poorly mirrored the reality of life on the frontier at the end of the war. For the most part, although these disputes about sovereignty in the Ohio valley and their resolution captured the attention of officials out east, they proved academic for most settlers. Sovereignty, after all, had meaning only insofar as Virginia and the United States acted to bring order to the regions west of the mountains. Until security came, the particulars of jurisdiction mattered little.[9]

Certainly, Virginia's authority south of the river did not bring stability to the region. To be sure, with the end of the war Virginians in the West attempted to return to normalcy. For a start, speculators once again tried to resume their activities. Ebenezer Zane, for example, had laid out and sold many lots around Wheeling for $25 to $50 for three-quarters of an acre. Here he raised corn, wheat, rye, barley, rice, and flax.[10] Andrew Lewis, an old standby, won a "vast" grant of nine thousand acres near Point Pleasant for his services during the war, and William Christian eyed lands near the Beargrass.[11] George Washington retained his lands on the Round Bottom seventeen miles below Zane's plantation and resolved to order his holdings in the West by collecting rents and warning off squatters.[12] Despite his failures and continuing problems with the bottle, George Rogers Clark, of course, had won an enormous grant near the Falls of the Ohio for his troubles during the war.[13] Daniel Boone picked up where he left off as a jobber.[14] And John May, along with his backers out east, tried his damnedest to corner the market on settlement and preemption warrants in Kentucky.[15]

Some places in the West, such as Lexington, took on the outward trappings of eastern society in the wake of the war and were fast becoming pockets of civility in a sea of insecurity. In 1787, a visitor named Mary Dewee found "the society" of Lexington "very agreeable."[16] Through the purchase of teacups and the finer things in life, some Kentuckians and western Virginians were trying to consign the violent past to oblivion.[17]

Try as they might, however, even residents of Lexington could not escape the past. Years of violence, chaos, and uncertainty had transformed the West, and were continuing to do so. Speculators did not have free rein to evict squatters or take any land of their choosing. Indeed, they tended to act in a chastened fashion, understanding, as Patrick Henry certainly did, that the "custom of the country" had changed since 1774.[18] In Kentucky, common settlers now asserted their right to a share of the land, a privilege their more wealthy neighbors had at least to respect. By granting rights to both settlement and preemption claimants, officials had privileged the access of jobbers to land but also created a sense of confusion that some settlers exploited. In 1788, Christopher Greenup, for instance, who lived in Danville, complained that "some Persons has seized possession" of a lot he owned in Lexington and were "cutting and carrying off the Timber." Possession, he feared, meant more than his legal claims.[19] Another fellow named John Mills learned as much a few years later when the lot he purchased from a wealthy speculator named Israel Ludlow was "something Incumbered in consequence of a M. McConnels Improving." Although the wealthy and opportunistic claimed land, the McConnells of the world, some feared, might inherit too much of the earth.[20] Surveyors had to tread carefully in these circumstances. Because they inevitably fell afoul of what they called "settlement and preemption claimants," disputes arose, making it difficult if not "impossible," as one argued, to complete their work.[21]

Although the western crisis of sovereignty had not overturned power relations in the Kentucky district, it did carve out a space for common men and women to keep a step or two ahead of the wealthy. Despite the hold speculators and jobbers had on the land, guaranteed by Virginia land acts, people kept migrating to the region, hoping to use uncertainty to their advantage. In 1787, a "vast multitude" of men and women were streaming into Kentucky "through the Wilderness."[22] They also came in down the Ohio River. An American officer posted to the Ohio valley noted—with some alarm—that "from the 10th of October 1786 until the 12th May 1787, 177 Boats, 2689 Souls, 1333 Horses, 766 Cattle and 102 Wagons, have passed Muskingum bound for Limestone and the Rapids."[23] The pace picked up the following year. In June 1788, he cataloged 308 boats and over 6,000 men and women with their horses, cattle, and hogs who had passed down the river over the previous six months. "The emigration," he declared, "is almost incredible."[24] Most he regarded as "vagabonds," an almost feral people eager to kill an Indian if given a chance and heedless of authority.[25] Many, by all accounts, were desperate and desperately poor.[26]

William Christian learned in 1784 that he could not ignore rights, be they traditional or progressive, that arose in the vortex of competition and violence when his "Beargrass Tenants now refuse to pay any rent at any rate." He had little hope of getting his money as "they are as grand villains as live on earth."[27] Easterners journeying west came face-to-face with the new realities of life there. As one put it, "artful Cunning" men, who showed no deference to their betters and who "make no Appearance of being worth much property," were claiming land in Kentucky.[28] One traveler making his way down the Ohio River in 1792 with a few Indians noted "the inhabitants of the city of Limestone manifested a very unfriendly spirit." He feared for his life as men on horseback assembled on the riverbank uttering "many threats." Farther down the river, he passed a number of Kentucky boats filled with militiamen, who "cursed us vehemently." A light cavalry officer tried to "pacify the people" but, unable to do so, advised the easterner to "proceed as soon as possible."[29] The prudent policy in a West where deference had disintegrated, therefore, was live and let live.

Unsettledness therefore ensured fluidity. A few settlers became petty speculators, taking advantage of continuing chaos and rights to preemption to lay claim to more land than they needed for a competency. Landgrabs of this sort, of course, made sense in such a competitive environment. Others squatted near the edges of more settled regions, risking life and limb in the hopes of claiming land through improvement. Others still, who had settled in areas where claimants had warned them off, moved north across the Ohio River to the even less stable regions, where they created squatter communities. Those who traded opportunity and competency for relative security lived as tenants in more densely settled areas such as the Beargrass. In other words, although two-thirds of men and women living in Kentucky by the late 1780s did not own land, landlords did not have a free hand to dictate the terms of land settlement.[30] In 1784, for example, Harry Innes, a well-connected migrant from Virginia, claimed a thousand acres on a branch of the Green River only to find it was also claimed by a man who had lived in the region for far longer.[31] No doubt, Virginia officials and wealthy westerners attempted to control the settlement of those arriving in the region after the war had ended. In the fluid West, however, these attempts would create legendary legal troubles for the next fifty years in Kentucky as people claimed overlapping plots. Such disputes, of course, spoke to continuing conflict between those who had land and those who wanted it. They also betokened an openness that revolution continued to foster.[32]

If the wealthy or those aspiring to be were not going to make a killing anytime soon on renting land or selling plots, trade, then, became crucial. Prospects, however, were not bright. In the Ohio valley, as one migrant put it, "there is no money," leading him to believe that only "industry and frugality . . . may save our property."[33] In Wheeling, he found "Hangers on plenty," poorer people on the land. "Oh that they had cash to match their curiosity," he mused.[34] Merchants, in fact, could not "dispose of their goods," and by 1789 some feared that two out of three traders in Kentucky would close shop. That is, unless they could get their goods to New Orleans.[35]

The Ohio valley formed an integral part of the larger Mississippi River system. Settlers understood that trade would prosper only if produce went downriver. "Now we know by experience," a Kentucky booster asserted, "that forty tons of goods cannot be taken to the Falls of Ohio from Philadelphia under sixteen hundred pounds expence." The river route offered hope. "By improvements on the Mississippi," he argued, "goods can be brought from New Orleans to the Falls for the tenth part of that expence."[36] In 1787, a settler in Fayette County, Kentucky, believed that "the public mind seems most attracted to our Commercial prospects, of which the navigation of the Mississippi is our main hope."[37]

More times than not, the river was closed to westerners. No sooner had the Americans signed the Treaty of Paris, acquiring the region west of the mountains as far as the Mississippi, than the Spaniards who controlled the land west of the river refused to allow American boats to carry goods to New Orleans. If the Spanish relented, as one settler prophesied, areas like the Beargrass in Kentucky would be "a fine Country in a Short time." Without Spanish permission to use the Mississippi, "I think we shall ever remain poor."[38] Moreover, without the use of the river, as a Kentucky grandee argued, not only would the West become "valueless," but "Kentucky will be subject to domestic discord." Trade could ameliorate elite discontent over the murkiness of any land settlement and make even the meanest plots profitable. In fostering markets, trade could also inculcate habits of diligence in inhabitants often deemed indolent by eastern elites. The river, therefore, was a key to order and authority.[39] The issue united the wealthy and the poor; indeed, it seemed one of the bases for an uneasy accommodation. "By all appearances, the people will become so strong in the course of a little time, as to force a Trade at all events," an American official in the West warned.[40]

Westerners therefore tried to press the federal government to sign a commercial treaty with Spain. In pushing for this concession, however, they faced opposition and indifference. Harry Innes asked one of his friends out east to track down and rebuke John Jay, who allegedly had argued "that the Western people had nothing yet to export, and therefore the Cession of the Mississippi would be of no injury to them." Jay's politics did not bother Innes; rather, what he perceived to be Jay's eastern prejudice did. As Innes wrote, allowing the Spaniards to stymie western trade "would be unjust because it would be sacrificing one part of the community to . . . another and depriving the Western Country of that inestimable right, equal liberty, which was secured to us by the revolution." Innes ended his letter with a warning, one born out of experience in the West during the war. "If Congress takes upon herself this power [to cede navigation of the Mississippi]," he offered, "she may with the same propriety deprive us of the navigation of the Ohio or any of its branches" and "stretch her arbitrary hand to private property and upon the same principle of reasoning from one usurpation to another reduce us to a state of Vassalage."[41]

Concerns about land and trade played out against the backdrop of continuing violence. From 1783 to 1786, Indians still launched raids, many retaliatory, on settlements filled with those who would look to exterminate them. At this time, in fact, British-allied Iroquois attempted to create a new confederation of western nations to halt American encroachment. The confederation had some early successes. In 1785, for instance, Shawnees, Miamis, and Cherokees killed and scalped "several adventurers, settlers on their land."[42] Certain areas suffered more than others. Some settlers reckoned that the mouth of the Scioto, on Shawnee land, was "the most dangerous point" in the Ohio valley.[43] According to Daniel Boone, the Limestone proved a likely site for an ambush.[44] Regions around the Wheeling area also became a favorite target for raids, "as there is nothing separates it from the Indian wild, 200 miles in width, and the whole stretch of the continent in extent."[45]

Usually, the poorest—those living in the most "exposed" and marginal areas—bore the brunt of raids.[46] The wise kept dogs out to warn of attacks.[47] The foolish failed to take such measures. On June 29, 1785, according to a popular captivity narrative, Frances Scott of Washington County in Virginia greeted a large body of armed men heading to Kentucky. Feeling safe on that sweltering evening, she and her husband and four children left the door to their cabin open. Indian raiders arrived that night, shooting her husband. They then "stabbed and cut the Throats of the 3 youngest children in their Bed, and afterwards lifted them up and dashed them down on the floor" at the foot of their mother. They also tomahawked the eldest girl, aged eight. The raiders took Frances Scott captive, marching her for thirty-two days and giving her no more than sassafras leaves and cane stalks to eat. While washing her daughter's blood off her apron in a stream, she made her escape, subsisting alone in the woods for a month before finding help.[48]

Indians also stymied surveying. "I have located both your warrants," a frustrated surveyor in relatively peaceful Lexington explained, "but the places where they are Entered in is too dangerous."[49] John May had surveyed some plots along the Ohio River, but others could not be approached because, as he put it, "the Indians have been more troublesome." Indians complicated an already confused series of land arrangements. May worried that some of his claims would "be lost out" unless surveyed soon. But in early 1786, he had no great hopes. The Indians were "dispersed through almost every Part of the Country where our Land lies," making it "impossible to proceed in surveying for several Months past."[50] George Washington, who hoped to travel to his lands on the Great Kanawha and restore them to order, similarly could not because of Indian raids.[51]

In 1785, elites did not necessarily accept the notion that all Indians should be wiped out. They saw it as undoable and impolitic.[52] But these views began to change in 1786. In early April of that year, William Christian, who had cooperated with Dunmore and Patrick Henry in their bids to dominate the West, had "fallen a sacrifice to their barbarity." Indeed, Patrick Henry was writing his "Dear Brother"—actually, his brother-in-law—about the state of his "Family" lands in Kentucky as Christian lay dying. Indians had launched attacks in the Beargrass, and Christian died as he led a force pursuing the raiders. In 1786, raiding parties were not only hitting exposed areas like the Limestone and Licking settlements and the falls but also attacking more orderly regions like Jefferson County, the region around Lexington.[53]

Kentuckians believed that the federal government would have to act for peace to come. Although the Treaty of Paris won Americans the trans-Appalachian West, the British refused to relinquish control of a number of their forts until the Americans repaid some of their prewar debts to British merchants and reimbursed Loyalists for property confiscated.[54] They also did so because they feared Indian violence if they surrendered their posts to the Americans. And although the British had publicly asked Indians to stop attacking exposed settlements in December 1782, the raids continued with covert British support.[55] Like Spanish control of the Mississippi, British occupation of posts on sovereign American territory, for some, demonstrated the shameful impotence of the new nation. For westerners, however, who feared the British were trying to facilitate and coordinate Indian raids, the issue was more elemental.[56] It did not center on national honor or even territorial integrity. Such concerns mattered only insofar as they demonstrated once again the failure of easterners to address western concerns.

Indian attacks, impatience with the federal government, or even the uneasy accommodations over land did not turn Kentuckians into a "people." On the contrary, well-to-do settlers in Lexington saw their neighbors as a rabble. A slave-owning transplant from Virginia found herself "Surrounded by People that has been brought up so differently from myself that when Sick and Low spirited their Company only disgusts." She exclaimed, "O what would I not give to be blessed with a sensible agreeable woman for a Neighbour that had been brought up tenderly as I have myself."[57] These "principal" settlers, though, tended to view Indians in the same light as poorer settlers living in exposed settlements did. "These devils will never be easy, until they are extirpated," argued one wealthy settler after learning of an attack in 1789. "Facts," he averred, "are stubborn things." And the "proper trade" of the "yellow devils" consisted of "cruelty and bloodshed."[58]

Indian hating and its utility in pressuring eastern officials to act gave the wealthy and the poor a basis for understanding each other and acting in unison to reestablish society in the West. All in the Ohio valley knew that "it is not very material to us here whether the Indians treat or not, for they . . . will continue to do mischief on our frontier settlements."[59] In light of common suffering at the hands of a commonly demonized enemy, the wealthy valorized the actions of the poor. In 1789, for instance, as Wheeling reeled from raids, a story circulated of the bravery of the two Johnstone "lads." After two Indians in "Christian dress and wearing beaver hats" captured the boys, aged ten and twelve, they "retired into the wilderness" and made a fire, a boy tucked under the arm of each. The boys, however, did not sleep. Spying the chance, "they concerted a plan of killing the Indians and escaping." The older boy grabbed a gun, passed it to his brother, and told him to fire "when he saw him, the elder, strike the tomahawk into the head of the other savage." The plan worked. On learning of their deeds, "a number of the stoutest and bravest men" mustered "to go on a hunt" for other Indians.[60] The widely agreed-upon lesson was twofold: even the poorest possessed honorable virtues; and Indians, even if they dressed in a civilized manner, were little better than animals.

In places like Kentucky and western Virginia, elites had another reason to subscribe to this essentialist vision. Many of them owned slaves. John Breckinridge, who had moved to Kentucky in the midst of Indian raids with "fear and trembling," realized that his fortunes rested on the backs of his "Negroes." An aspiring lawyer, Breckinridge sent twenty slaves ahead of him to Kentucky to prepare his settlement, and then hired them out when he did not use them on his plantation. In a region economically hamstrung, the labor of his slaves proved one of the few reliable sources of income as he sought to climb Kentucky's social ladder.[61] Patronizing notions of the nature of slaves, therefore, dovetailed with the frontier belief in the irredeemable nature of Indians. Kentucky would be dominated by whites, blacks would provide the labor, and Indians existed as a cultural glue, since the hatred of them was fast becoming a basis for order.

In 1783 and 1784, stories were making the rounds pointing to this emerging confluence.[62] In 1783, six Indians attacked an isolated homestead. "There being no man about the house but a negroe man who lay out the Door between Sleep and Wake, a little Girl first discovered them. and ran in the house crying Indians." Like the alert and crafty Johnstone boys, she understood what was happening. As the slave and the girl's mother awoke, one of the Indians grabbed the girl. Without thinking, the "Negro presented his gun," forcing the Indian to release the girl. A struggle ensued. The slave "drew his fist and in two or three strokes stun'd the fellow." Grabbing the Indian's "War Club," he then "gave him a lick on the side of the head which knocked him Down." The little girl and her mother finished the work with a broadax and an iron bar. In an ending almost like that of "Little Red Riding Hood," in which the woodsman scares off the wolf to save the maiden, a nearby hunter heard the fracas and fired a shot at the other five Indians trying to get into the house. They all fled. "Thus," the writer concluded, "was a large family Saved from Savage Barbarity."[63] In this instance, the loyal inferior thwarted the nefarious savage for the benefit of the poor settler.

Unsurprisingly, therefore, Kentuckians did not only tolerate but celebrated Indian killers. In September 1786, George Rogers Clark proposed a two-pronged offensive against confederated Indians, leading one force against settlements on the Wabash. His men abandoned him once more, and the attack failed. A month later, Benjamin Logan from Lincoln County raised 790 men to march against largely empty Shawnee towns. He encountered no opposition, burning two hundred cabins and fifteen thousand bushels of corn. One militiaman claimed, "We skelpt all we catch'd." In fact, the force killed eleven Shawnees and took away thirty-two prisoners before returning to Limestone.[64] During the raid, a Shawnee chief named Malunthy did not run away. "Having confidence that he would not be hurt" by the Kentuckians, he stood outside his cabin and "displayed the thirteen stripes," as well as a copy of a treaty that he had signed on behalf of his people with the Americans at Fort Finney.[65] The troops took him as a "prisoner of war." A few days later, under orders to bring no harm to prisoners, Col. Hugh McGary of Mercer County tomahawked him, even though McGary acknowledged him "one of the Chiefs or King of the Shawnese." He wanted to kill any Indian he could get his hands on, screaming at one point that "by God, he would chop . . . down" anyone "who should attempt to hinder him from killing them at any time."[66] McGary was considered a hero by the people. Though he was court-martialed for disobeying orders, his actions were "highly approved of in Kentucky," and the American flag the dead Shawnee had waved "is displayed as a Trophy upon Lexington court house."[67]

Such raids alone would never address all the concerns of westerners. One old hand declared, "I am clear of opinion that Military force only can make permanent Treatys with Indians and circumscribe their Bounds." Chastisement was not enough. "That force," he explained, "must march into their Country and lay Waste their Towns and Awe them by a standing force on the spot."[68] What was at issue was the disjunction between the expectation of peace with the end of the war and the reality of continuing violence, as well as the state's inability or reluctance to address it. In western eyes, the government was "trifling . . . with some of the savages."[69] Harry Innes condemned the government for inaction: "The Troops on the banks of the Ohio between Fort Pitt and the rapids are of no consequence to us." It was clear that "Congress do not mean to give us that protection, which as part of the Federal Union we are entitled to."[70]

Protecting the lives, liberties, and property of westerners—or establishing the basis for order and society—meant opening the Mississippi, clearing out the British, and conquering the Indians. But protection, Innes complained, "we never received from any quarter." George Rogers Clark "from his long intemperance was rather inadequate," and the governor of Virginia, though willing, proved unable. The American superintendent of Indian affairs, Gen. Richard Butler, seemed to favor Indians over settlers and "appears to have fixed a prejudice in his breast by no means consistent with a man in office, against the people of Kentucky." Finally, "the position of Troops on the Ohio, and the conduct of the commander, serve only to convince us that those troops never were intended for our protection, but to prevent settlements on the Federal lands." In other words, what Innes summed up as "Three negatives over us" ran headlong into the central tenets of a frontier commonwealth vision rooted in security, an efficacious state, and the demonization of Indians.[71]

Given the conditions with which they struggled, westerners tended to view broader issues that affected them and all Americans, such as the debate over the Constitution, through this all-encompassing lens of protection. Officials from the states and the federal government claimed that "our western friends, beyond the Allegheny, may be assured, that we shall not be unmindful of their interests" while drawing up the document in Philadelphia in 1787.[72] Westerners did not necessarily believe this. To be sure, they understood that the merits of the Constitution rested on how well it balanced power and liberty. However, they interpreted these concepts in light of the way easterners protected the interests of the West. Some lent their support to the Constitution, as they hoped that a more powerful government no longer enfeebled by the "Imbecility of Congress" under the Articles of Confederation could finally act with authority in the West.[73] One opponent of the Constitution, however, feared that the new, powerful government would ensure that the East would continue to dominate the West.[74] In other words, the terms "anti-federalist" and "federalist," as they are conventionally understood, made little sense for the West. Although some supported the Constitution and others did not, a democratic settlement, in the context of continuing Revolutionary violence, did not necessarily preclude an efficacious state. In the West, liberty and power were not always at odds.[75]

Kentuckians made these sentiments known in a number of ways. First, some threatened to use the Spanish presence in the region to leverage the federal government to act. For some settlers in the far western reaches of the Kentucky district, the area closest to Illinois and the Mississippi, doing so made a great deal of sense.[76] From as far away as Louisville "the threats of the Savages" induced people to flee west of the Mississippi for Spanish protection, "apprehensive that an attempt would be made by the Indians to burn the Village."[77] Rumors spread of "inhabitants of Kentucky" in general, and of one "Mr. Connolly" near the falls in particular, who were planning to secede from the Union.[78] Others tried to instigate a war between the United States and Spain to force open the Mississippi.[79] Second, some proposed making the district of Kentucky another region of federal jurisdiction like the Northwest Territory.[80]

Finally, many pinned their hopes on statehood. The case was simple. Virginia had offered little help to Kentucky.[81] In the face of the failure of any authority to take control of the West, only Kentuckians could look after their interests and "safety." Proponents for the new state had a simple agenda. Not only would it provide for some type of defense, but its "first and principal object must be the opening of the Mississippi." Unless Kentuckians had "free navigation," the "fertility of their soil will not avail them," and "their land will rather decline than rise in value." The most powerful justification for making Kentucky a state stemmed from the distinctiveness of western experience. "The thirteen old states," a booster wrote, "are . . . bounded by the ocean on the East." Not so the West, which was "readily exposed to hostile incursions, and on the North and South [surrounded] by two powerful European nations, who watch their progress with a jealous eye." And just as the eastern states had "gained their independence" through "a great expence of blood and treasure," so, he concluded, was the West continuing to earn its independence.[82] Making Kentucky a state would ensure that one set of officials—state authorities—had western interests at the top of their agenda.

Statehood or no statehood, Kentuckians still found themselves in a chaotic world, which an American commander summed up as "principally owing to the want of a government."[83] By 1787, Lexington had now become the target of Indian attacks. "The distressed situation of this Part of the State," a frustrated and furious county lieutenant named Alexander Bullitt charged, "is now arrived to such a Point as to make further Temporizing of any kind with the Indians Inevitable Destruction." What bothered Bullitt more, however, was news that at a time when Kentuckians were convinced that the Indians of the Ohio valley "are united" in an active offensive, "Gen'l Butler, the Indian Agent for Congress," was spreading the word that "most of the Tribes are Pacifically Inclined." "Will they not conclude," he stormed, "that we have no Government at all and that the Salvation of the District Depends upon Erecting one as soon as possible." With no protection, there could be no sovereignty.[84]

On paper at least, north of the river lay a different world. In 1784 and 1785, as members of Congress passed land ordinances establishing the region north and west of the Ohio River as federal land, they envisioned an Ohio that would not resemble the sordid mess that the area south of the river had become. Ultimate sovereignty, in theory, lay with the federal government, which through a flexible and elegant plan mandated how new states could be created in lands secured through the War of Independence. The new system emerging from the land ordinances, in theory, also allowed for unfettered western expansion.[85] More than power was at stake. As officials of the federal government tried to get out from under the crushing debt of the War of Independence, they laid out the Northwest Territory as a virtual "land bank" for repaying debt while allowing orderly settlement. Slavery would not exist north of the river. As states that had historic claims—real and imagined—to the region "reserved" some lands as they relinquished sovereign claims, the federal government also made the first attempts to free the northwest from Indians. In 1785, at Fort McIntosh, officials met with Delaware, Wyandot, Chippewa, and Ottawa representatives to treat for peace and secure land in Ohio for settlement. The following year, emissaries from the Shawnees did likewise at Fort Finney. In return for cessions north and west of the river, Indians could expect to be treated with "Lenity and Generosity."[86] The more famous Northwest Ordinance of 1787 inscribed the relationship between land and Indian treaties into law. "The utmost good faith," the ordinance read, "shall always be observed towards the Indians, their lands and property shall never be taken from them without their consent." The act went on to declare, "In their property, rights and liberty, they shall never be invaded or disturbed." The ordinance's goal was to settle the region while maintaining "peace and friendship" with the Indians.[87]

At first, it seemed the plan for ordering and exploiting much of the West would work. Well-connected easterners soon took advantage of the ordinance. John Cleves Symmes, a judge from New Jersey, purchased land from the United States for a settlement near the north bend between the Miami rivers. He hoped to attract "respectable" people to his settlement, offering them relatively inexpensive land if they promised to move to the region within two years. In doing so, Symmes targeted soldiers, ministers, and schoolmasters, the type to bring "civility" to the region. In the meantime, he assured them that he had the promise of the secretary of war, Henry Knox, to protect the settlements. Symmes then sold off larger tracts of his purchase to other prominent émigrés from New Jersey, who founded settlements called Columbia and Losantiville, later to become Cincinnati.[88] No sooner had Symmes arrived than Knox made good on his word, ordering the dispatch of a party of troops "for the protection of his intended Settlements."[89]

French migrants established a settlement farther east across the Ohio River from Point Pleasant called Gallipolis. They had arrived from France having purchased, or so they believed, land from a defunct French enterprise called the Scioto Company. After hearing of their plight, federal officials offered them land in the Northwest Territory, hoping such generosity would in some way repay a debt the new nation owed to France. More critically, doing so would establish what they regarded as the right type of settler in the West, a good counterweight to the type of people who lived across the river.[90]

New Englanders similarly envisioned a new world to the west. Under the ordinance, private joint-stock companies and individuals could redeem their now depreciated Continental certificates for land in the region. The Ohio Company was organized in Boston in 1786 along these lines. The company's associates agreed to "raise a fund in continental certificates for purchasing LANDS in the western territory belonging to the United States." A share cost $1,000 in certificates or $10 in gold or silver, and no shareholder could buy more than five shares.[91] As the 1787 ordinance was under debate, a group of New Englanders bought a million and a half acres of land lying roughly between the Muskingum River and the Scioto valley. Led by veterans of the war, officers all, they hoped to establish a new, orderly settlement with its headquarters at the confluence of the Muskingum and the Ohio. On April 7, 1788, 48 settlers landed at the spot, followed by nearly 150 more over the course of the year.[92] As the first settlers spent the following summer constructing not only their homes at their new settlement, which they called Marietta, but also the works of a civilian fort known as Campus Martius, officials scouted out promising plots for future settlement.[93]

These were heady times. And these members of the company hoped to establish a settlement where the principles of the Revolution—their readings of it, in any event—would flourish. Rufus Putnam, one of the organizers of the company and soon to be a brigadier general in the army, took control of the settlement and called its first grand jury.[94] One of the first measures passed for bringing order to the territory spoke volumes. The territorial governor, Arthur St. Clair, issued a proclamation banning "the use of intoxicating liquor in the Northwest Territory." Until peace could be achieved with Indians, authorities were authorized to seize "all spirituous liquors in the hands of private citizens."[95]

Officers of the company wanted only the best and brightest to settle Ohio.[96] Good people would bring good government. "Many of our associates," a settler declared, "are distinguished for wealth, education and virtue; and others, for the most part, are reputable, industrious, well informed planters, farmers, tradesmen and mechanics."[97] Unlike, say, Kentucky, which was enmeshed in a complex pattern of conflict and accommodation between squatters, jobbers, and well-connected speculators, the associates of the Ohio Company created the conditions for a much simpler and less contentious land settlement. Some settlers, to be sure, were wealthier than others, but none were destitute. Although land was distributed through a company, few owned more than twelve hundred acres. The men and women who settled in Ohio, therefore, were poised to create a more egalitarian society than the one to their south. A society without the cravenly rich or the desperately poor would allow the settlement to prosper. In the wake of the Revolution, these New Englanders suggested, the habits of industry for the lower orders would complement the abilities of the better-off and more virtuous to knit together a more perfect society than the one they were leaving.[98]

Like their Puritan forefathers, the new patriarchs of Ohio realized that disorderly Indians could destroy order and imperil their republican errand into the Ohio wilderness. Unlike their Puritan ancestors, however, the New Englanders at Marietta tried their best to get along with Indians in the region.[99] Trouble may come, one prominent settler warned during a Fourth of July speech, but if it did, "it is our duty as well as our interest to conduct towards them, with humanity and kindness." As settlers were in the process of "reducing a country from a state of nature to a state of cultivation," they had to "endeavor to cultivate a good understanding, with the natives, without much familiarity."[100]

Accomplishing this mission required dutiful vigilance. In particular, it meant ensuring that the wrong sort of person stayed off their grant, which all agreed meant keeping out those Virginians who were streaming in across the river from Kentucky.[101] In other words, one of the foundations for accommodation in Kentucky—the movement of squatters north of the Ohio River—imperiled order in Ohio. New Englanders styled themselves a more enlightened set than those who lived across the Ohio River. In the minds of the men and women who settled Marietta, the Ohio River divided two distinct worlds.[102] The North in their eyes stood for enlightened principles, civilized society, and orderly rule. The South did not. And officials north of the river feared that the fertility of land there "very much attracts the attention of these fellows who wish to live under no government."[103] While some Kentuckians and transplanted Virginians made murmurs of declaring themselves "not only independent of the State of Virginia, but of the United States altogether," the "New England settlers are very industrious" and were creating a settlement both "strong and very secure."[104]

By the close of the 1780s, the New Englanders had succeeded in developing a society of what one visitor called "considerable taste." Settlers had cleared between six hundred and seven hundred acres of land. They had beehives and vegetable gardens and were raising all sorts of crops.[105] By 1788, the founders of the Ohio colony were planning an elaborate Fourth of July celebration, including a banquet in honor of the governor and the officers of the garrison that would feature barbecued venison, buffalo steaks, bear meat, and a "great pike" caught by a prominent settler.

Those who shared the feast, therefore, had tamed the West.[106] At Marietta, as opposed to the rest of the western world, "Gay Circles of Ladies, Balls, etc." were held. "These were the changes," a proprietor of the company noted, "which this three years ago Wilderness has undergone."[107]

Here the federal government also established its beachhead of the West. Named after the military commander of the territory, Lt. Col. Josiah Harmar, Fort Harmar had arisen just across the Muskingum from Campus Martius and Marietta. Much like the settlement in its shadow, the fort was, as one settler believed, "very handsome." Within its bastioned walls, settlers encountered Indians who came and went to treat with military commanders. In fact, he found all he met at the fort, including the Indians with whom he dined, "very sociable."[108] Small numbers of troops fanned out from this fort to garrison smaller posts along the Ohio and its many tributaries. Order was the order of the day. Authorities had less rarefied reasons than the associates of the Ohio Company for securing order in the region. They wanted to avoid the sordid landgrabs, and the subsequent squabbling, that had defined the early Kentucky experience.

Good management and a small but vigorous federal presence in the region could also forestall a dreaded and expensive Indian war. Indeed, troops had orders to protect the company's surveyors from Indian raiding parties "and at the same time to avoid hostilities with the Indians."[109] Henry Knox, the secretary of war, proposed a new approach to dealing with Indians in the wake of the War of Independence. Hoping to attach them to the new American government, Knox argued that Indians could no longer be treated unjustly. Conquering Indians, he calculated, would require twenty-five hundred soldiers and cost about $200,000 per year, an unreachable sum. Preaching justice and cost-effectiveness, he wanted to revive Sir William Johnson's system of accommodation, hoping to transform Indian culture over time by doing so. It was too late to save Kentucky, but it wasn't too late to save the Northwest.[110]

Unsurprisingly, army officials preached the same message of order that company directors did. Much like how the British had conceived Indian policy in 1763, men like Harmar realized that maintaining peace with neighboring Indians would keep costs down and keep the frontiers quiet.[111] Harmar and his subordinates were eager to inform the government that in 1785 the Delawares and Wyandots in the region seemed "friendly" and that the Shawnees "make great professions of peace" even as he admitted to others that "the Indians down the river, viz. the Shawnees, Miamis, Cherokees, and Kickapoos have killed and scalped" several Virginians.[112] Men such as Harmar and St. Clair understandably did all in their power to "brighten the chain" of friendship with Indians, going so far as to hold regular discussions with disaffected groups. Therefore, without a hint of irony, Harmar could inform Henry Knox, "I am endeavoring all in my power to conciliate the minds of the Indians," and at the same time, to make sure that the region served its larger purpose of helping the government stave off bankruptcy, could order his troops to "cover the Continental surveyors" who worked Ohio.[113]

The gravest threat to this plan came from the poorer sort who were streaming into the West. Masterless men, Harmar feared, could undo the soundest policy. "These men upon the frontiers," Harmar argued, "have hitherto been accustomed to seat themselves on the best of lands, making a tomahawk right or Improvement, as they term it, supposing that to be sufficient Title." Harmar believed "them in general to be averse to federal measures, and that they would wish to throw every obstacle in the way to impede surveying of the western Territory."[114] Federal troops therefore took a vigorous approach to warning off squatters.[115] As early as 1785, troops moved throughout the region north and west of the river destroying cabins and ordering people to leave behind the corn they had planted. In one such instance, Ensign Ebenezer Denny gave a family two weeks to quit its claim because one child lay sick with a snakebite. Nonetheless, after the child recovered, the family was instructed to leave the region and tear down its own cabin. Such magnanimity proved exceptional. On one mission in August 1785, Denny reported that he had torn down twenty-three cabins.[116] Troops would not only "dispossess" such individuals but also "severely chastise them for their insolence, and defiance of the Supreme Authority."[117]

Squatters resisted this new Ohio vision, arguing that such evictions flew in the face of the principles that animated popular conceptions of commonwealth. In the Ohio Country, settlers claimed to be "true and faithful subjects of the common wealth of America, and are as we have always been ready to venture our Lives in the common defense of the same"—that is, "presuming hitherto we were in our present circumstances and state safe under the protection of Government." Yet "to our great surprise we have received advice that an armed party are on their way with orders from Government to dispossess us and to burn and destroy our dwellings."[118] Some cooperated, some pleaded for mercy, others resisted.[119]

Harmar and his men were playing a dangerous game. William Irvine, the former commander at Fort Pitt, tried to give Harmar an idea of the types of people with whom he was dealing. From hard experience, Irvine had learned — and come to appreciate — "this world, at least this new part of it, is in almost a state of nature." People had no government and they followed no rules, seizing any and all "valuable spots." "You are," he warned, "in a delicate situation." The people regarded Harmar as a puppet of land jobbers. Dislodging people or "prevent[ing] intruders" was one thing. "The destruction of property," however, would be regarded as an act of war.[120] Governments in the past, after all, that had tried to treat Indians in a straightforward fashion and that had privileged Indians over settlers had reaped whirlwinds.

Governments in the past had also hoped to foster good relations with Indians, but they could not control the types of people that Mariettans now called "Virginians" from threatening the arrangement. Harmar found it incredible that "the prevailing opinion of the people in general on the frontier" was "that it's no harm to kill an Indian."[121] And they treated the troops who protected Indians with equal contempt. When a fellow named Armstrong got his hands on a soldier charged with removing settlers from the northwest side of the Ohio River, he had him "Stripped to the Skin and tied up to a post for . . . at least 3 hours and a half under frequent Showers and cold wind."[122]

At the same time, officials in Ohio invited Indians to settle in the region that they had warned white settlers to steer clear of. Indeed, peaceful Indians in some instances could "be assured of the friendship and protection of the United States."[123] And while squatters saw their fields burned to the ground, such Indians would receive corn. To add insult to injury, federal officials like Josiah Harmar believed that the tension between illicit settlers and Indians could create more order in the region. "The circumstance of a few adventurers (settlers on the Indian lands) down the river, having been kill'd and scalp'd, has had a good effect," Harmar argued. "It has halted them in their rapid emigration."[124] He also contended that white Indian killers should "be executed in the presence of the Indians."[125] Harmar, in other words, did not see Indians like the squatters he sought to evict.[126]

Creating a world free from Virginians therefore proved crucial to both the government's and the company's plans for Ohio. And in reality, for all the grand plans of order implicit in the land ordinances, this was the chief means by which the state asserted its sovereignty. It did not do so by conquering Indians. On the contrary, the enlightened principles that animated Marietta's founding, the associates hoped and believed, would naturally lead to better relations with Indians. And elites in the territory pinned their hopes on this approach. Hostility to Indians did not derive from a "natural" animosity between two races. On the contrary, wise rule, enlightened principles, the right sort of settler, and vigilance, the company leaders argued, would deliver them from the sorts of troubles with Indians that nearly every settlement in British North America had experienced. In fact, they boasted their plan was already reaping dividends less than a year after initial settlement. The Indians' "depredations since the last year, have been trifling," a settler argued, "and their murders few in number." Indeed, Indians seemed to cause more problems for the unruly men and women across the river.[127] Rufus Putnam believed that the slaughter of Virginians, while tragic, was understandable. Virginians stole horses from Indians from time to time. Indeed, "a Gang of Robbers" was working over the Indians in western Virginia settlements.[128] North of the river all appeared different. "The kind and friendly treatment of the Indians by the first settlers," argued a Mariettan, "has conduced greatly" to relations "without blood-shed" and to settlement "without opposition."[129]

The northwestern settlers expected and hoped to achieve nothing short of creating a "new" New England in the Ohio wilderness. Because most settlers of Marietta came from the East, they did not have, according to Putnam, "those prejudices against the natives which commonly arise from long wars with them" and could therefore enjoy "the prospect of peace and tranquility to the frontiers."[130] And as late as 1790, it seemed to be working. During the summer of that year, Delawares and Ottawas came in and out of Marietta, trading deerskins and meat for corn.[131] The settlements were thriving, Rowena Tupper declared, and "our Buildings are decent and comfortable."[132] They had, it seemed, triumphed in overcoming nature and creating society. Tupper exclaimed, "The Indians appear to be perfectly friendly [and] their encampments are in sight of our Buildings."[133] This errand seemed to be succeeding. "Are we, indeed, in a wilderness?" another settler asked. "The contemplation of the scene before me, would almost lead me to distrust my sense."[134]

The New Englanders should have paid more attention to their senses. The world around Marietta swirled with Indian-white hostility. In 1789, Indians "according to their custom," as Harmar put it, had taken "the Liberty of Killing and scalping defenceless people, now and then," including a number at Judge Symmes's settlement.[135] In May 1790, a settler in Ohio County complained that "the present Behavior of the Indians to us is very alarming." In one month's time, he explained, "they have killed two persons, taken five prisoners burnt ten houses stole a number of horses and killed Cattle."[136] Even just a few miles from the Muskingum, seven or eight people had been killed by Indians just a few years before the settlement of Marietta.[137] The following year a Mrs. Moore and her eldest daughter were "scalped their ears cut off and their arms and then ham stringed and threw into the fire and Burnt to death."[138]

Such atrocities were to be expected. Settlers from Kentucky to western Pennsylvania were, after all, encroaching on lands that Native Americans regarded as their own. Officials had two treaties in hand that said otherwise, but the 1785 Treaty of Fort McIntosh and the one signed at Fort Finney with some Shawnees the following year were hardly worth more than the paper they were written on. The treaties ceded much of the Ohio valley to American settlement, but even the signatories conceded that most Indians viewed them as worthless and fraudulent. The same could be said of the 1789 Treaty of Fort Harmar, which amounted to a desperate attempt to try to keep the fictions of the older treaties alive. Violence therefore would and did occur, and settlers would have to contend with "disturbances."[139] But if bloodshed could be kept to acceptable levels, combative Indians could be diplomatically and militarily isolated. The key, as the architects of this policy noted, was to rein in only those groups of Indians that seemed to contest settlement or who refused to come to the negotiating table.

From time to time, local officials took up the cudgel against such Indians but not with an eye to conquest. In 1790, because of what Henry Knox called "incursions of small parties of Indians on the western frontier," the government had authorized the dispatch of spies at government expense. But when, in Knox's estimation, the trouble had passed, the authorization for spies "is to be considered as having ceased and terminated."[140] In that year, Harmar also led a small force largely composed of militia, most of which came from Kentucky, against some Indians from western Ohio who had been attacking Ohio valley settlements. Harmar had orders not to launch a far-reaching offensive but "to act offensively against the Shawnese and outcast Cherokees joined with them, inhabiting north west of the Ohio." Knox instructed him to seek out "banditti" and act with the "highest œconomy."[141]

The attempt failed. In what one participant called "helter skelter" fighting, Harmar's force lost about a hundred militiamen and seventy-five regulars. They killed no more than one hundred Indians. But they had failed to pacify the "banditti."[142] On the contrary, the Indians seemed more aggressive after the campaign than before. The problem, a court of inquiry found, lay with militia from Kentucky.[143] As Kentuckians seemed to understand, Harmar's campaign did not amount to an attempt to conquer Indian land or even to rationalize the fraudulent and now forgotten treaties with Indians in the wake of the War of Independence. Rather, it was an attempt to "chastise" wayward Indians, to bring them back into line.[144]

In this western world of seething hostility, the question these New Englanders faced was this: could they keep a larger world at bay, or could the ideology of Indian-white relations they constructed keep pace with reality? The answer was no. And they would learn of the fate of their errand in 1791 at a place called Big Bottom.

In the years after the initial founding of Marietta, company associates sponsored smaller settlements nearby. Since those were to be limited in scope, the associates hoped Indians in the region—and many of these were Christian, peaceable Delawares like the martyrs from Gnadenhütten— would not be alarmed. In the autumn of 1790, the company permitted thirty-six men to settle on the bottom about thirty miles above Marietta on the east bank of the Muskingum on what were called donation lands.[145] The men came from Massachusetts, Rhode Island, Connecticut, and New Hampshire. At this time, the company sponsored similar settlements at a number of points on the streams feeding into the river, including Belpre, Waterford, and Wolf Creek. Each settler received one hundred acres of land, which he was expected to improve within a few years.[146]

Therefore, the settlement at Big Bottom was a rather modest affair. The young men erected a blockhouse of large beech logs. Not far from the blockhouse, two settlers, Francis and Isaac Choate, built a cabin and began clearing the woods. Up from the bottom, two Virginians named Asa and Eleazar Bullard already had settled in a cabin.[147] Although the region around them swirled with violence and despite the warnings of experienced hands, the settlers at Big Bottom demonstrated little vigilance and even less sense. A few weeks after their arrival, the weather had turned bitterly cold, and the river had frozen over a few days before Christmas. Because clay also froze in these conditions, they did not chink between the logs. They rarely posted sentries. They did not even leave their dogs outside the blockhouse to sound an alarm. Settlers also did not construct palisades around the blockhouse, even though on the opposite bank of the river ran an old Indian path from Sandusky to the mouth of the Muskingum. Perhaps they thought they were immune to the bloodshed engulfing other frontier settlements. We will never know.[148]

On the afternoon of January 2, a raiding party of Delawares and Wyandots from the Upper Sandusky area—the same peoples who had tortured and killed Colonel Crawford—traveling on the old path encountered the settlement on the opposite bank of the river. The Big Bottom settlement, apparently, had not been their objective. But it proved a target of opportunity. Later in the day, the twenty-five young men broke into two parties and crossed the frozen river on foot. The smaller party entered the Choate cabin in a friendly manner and sat down for dinner, before seizing the men and restraining them with leather thongs. The Choates submitted without resistance. Meanwhile, the larger party headed to the blockhouse undetected. One raider smashed open the door while others ran in. They had found the occupants at supper. From outside, other Indians aimed their guns between the unchinked logs and shot a few men by the fire. The wife of one of the Virginians, Isaac Meeks, resisted. She attacked one of her assailants with an ax, which she plunged into his shoulder. She was quickly killed, as were the others in the blockhouse. One young man tried to escape by a window but was shot as he clambered on the roof. The only survivor was Philip Stacy, who hid under some bedding in the corner of a room. He was discovered after the killings, and the raiders spared his life and took him along with the two Choates as a captive. All told, twelve persons perished in the attack.[149]

The raid seemed to precipitate more attacks throughout the Ohio valley. On January 10, two hundred Indians attacked a small station called Coleraine on the Great Miami near Judge Symmes's settlement, shooting flaming arrows and besieging it for twenty-five hours.[150] By March 1791, officials up and down the Ohio valley from Pennsylvania to western Virginia and Kentucky reported fresh outrages.[151] As one frontier settler put it while attacks seemed to be multiplying throughout the Ohio valley, "We can Expect nothing but an Indian War."[152]

The Big Bottom massacre revealed, by the standards of a West still mired in war, the flawed foundations of Ohio. Only after the massacre did settlers in Ohio interpret isolated incidents up and down the frontier as part of a larger design. After Big Bottom, the reasoning went, the "horror committed by the savages . . . multiplied upon all points of the Ohio. There is not a single doubt," white Ohioans now believed, "that all the Indians are agreed to make war and destroy all the settlements formed on the right bank of La Belle Riviere."[153]

On this point, they were right, and they were wrong. The Indian confederation in their midst was indeed making war on white settlements throughout the region. But Ohio Company settlers could not admit that they represented part of the problem. By their logic, any attack on Ohio Company land had to be part of a general war against Americans in the West. Their minds could not grasp the possibility that Indian raids could have been caused by the New Englanders in Ohio. "Our prospects," Rufus Putnam lamented, "are much changed. Instead of peace and friendship with our Indian neighbors a hored Savage war Stairs us in the face."[154] Officials scrambled to prepare adequate defenses for what they feared awaited the Ohio colony. They appealed to the federal troops in the region for help. They sent out spies of their own. They refitted hastily built palisades. They removed women and children from exposed outposts.[155] It became clear that they, too, existed in a state of war.

In this brief window of time, regions north and south of the river—no matter which government claimed them—had more in common than areas east and west of the mountains. The transplanted New Englanders therefore had ready allies.[156] Even before Big Bottom, Kentuckians and westerners in general had complained of the failure of eastern governments to protect western settlements.[157] But after the events of the early 1790s, the tone of westerners became more shrill and alarming. Elites in Marietta wasted little time in petitioning the government for protection. Putnam issued a terse and harried letter to Secretary of War Henry Knox pleading for help. Only government could solve the problem. "I consider

the event," Putnam wrote, "as a forerunner to other attacks of a more serious nature and which may involve us in complet ruin unless prevented by
Government imediately taking measures for our protection."[158]

In other words, after Big Bottom, officials at Marietta discovered a newfound appreciation for the sentiments of Kentuckians. Indeed, common
settlers, especially those who had suffered at the hands of Indians, now
proved useful. Ohio officials could no longer "be silent," as they put it,
while others were being killed. The officers of the company now conceded, "it is with pain we have heard the cruel insinuations of those who
have been disaffected to the Settlement of this Country." They continued,
"It is not possible that those men who have pursued into these woods
that path to an humble competence . . . should be doomed the Victims
of a Jealous policy." That policy, which had been sponsored and supported by men like Harmar and Putnam, was now revealed for what it was.
Although these men had argued that the death of Virginians served a
larger purpose of deterring squatters, it now seemed unjust to use "the
mangled bodies of their friends exposed as a Spectacle to prevent emigration."[159]

It's at this moment, as interests converged, bridging lines of class and
region, we can say that a coherent "western vision" rooted in popular notions of commonwealth emerged. And the one idea more than any other
that yoked areas north of the river to those to the south was protection.
"The first principle of society," Harry Innes declared, "is mutual protection."[160] In short, easterners had to see things the way westerners did and
had to acquiesce to what was fast becoming a coherent vision. The East
had a responsibility for "protection," insofar as it would "preserve the lives
and property of many of our fellow Citizens" in the West.[161] These were
the wages of union. As Ohio's New Englanders learned, they, too, were entering a world of darkness and a place still at war. Although they had comforted themselves with the notions that they were fashioning a "society"
and that they were not infringing on Indian lands, they, too, lived in a
world defined by violence and shaped by the past. After Big Bottom, they,
too, called for the opening of the Mississippi and the removal of the British
from the West.[162]

As a rule, most of the New Englanders of Ohio did not embrace the
racist ideas of, say, Hugh Henry Brackenridge. Nonetheless, they now realized, as Kentuckians had for some time, that only the state could end the

state of war. The federal government had "to take effectual means to bring the natives to Submission." This notion, moving beyond chastisement to conquest, was the foundation of any frontier commonwealth.[163] New Englanders now agreed with westerners south of the river that only the removal of Indians, not squatters, could sustain protection. As they now argued and, eerily, as their ancestors had believed in the seventeenth century, bringing an end to chaos, uncertainty, and violence entailed subduing Indians. On the eve of the Big Bottom affair, as tension gripped the Ohio valley, Putnam had already sensed what the answer was. "As to Indian matters, we are fearful that the spring will open a general attack on the frontier unless prevented by Government carrying a war into the enemy's country," he insisted. Because Indians had not "had a sufficient drubbing," preemptive war offered the answer. The inhabitants of Ohio, as much as those from Kentucky, he wrote Washington, "have as great a claim to protection as any under the Federal Government."[164]

No protection, therefore, meant no society.[165] Without the most basic right, which preceded all others, the markers of civility could never emerge in the region. That is, civility for whites. While men such as Harry Innes rejected the notion that Indians could ascend the stadial ladder because of their innate inferiority, they still argued that the evolutionary pattern held for even the meanest white settlers. If New Englanders did not share Innes's sentiments about Indians, they had to admit that only without them could Ohio graduate from its present unsettledness. Protection therefore promised to usher in a new age for a new West. On the other hand, if government did not protect, all were still sovereign unto themselves.[166] Common men and women on the frontier had embraced this reality and transformed it into a virtue. Now it became a defining feature of the region.

Along with the commonwealth ideology, a common understanding about land and the right to improvement also appeared to be taking shape north and south of the Ohio River. South of the river, settlers, jobbers, and speculators had forged an uneasy accommodation in which conditions allowed the poor in some cases to stay a step ahead of the wealthy. North of the river, a place never as volatile and more egalitarian, squatters and company settlers did not see eye to eye, nor would they. But Indian war obviated violent contention. Although each earlier attempt to restore order in the West had entailed stymieing the right to improvement, by the early

1790s the state of war in the West would not allow officials and the wealthy to do what they pleased with the land. But neither was a final settlement of the land question imminent. In the western world, the issue remained unsettled. In both Kentucky and Ohio, conflict over land did not disappear; rather, for the moment it was comprehended within the western commonwealth vision.

EIGHT

West and East:
The Limits of Commonwealth
on the Frontier

In July 1789, a westerner shot a Delaware named George Washington, igniting a firestorm. According to reports, "vagabond Whites from the neighbourhood of Wheeling" ambushed and wounded Washington while he was hunting on the Muskingum. The shooting scandalized officials. George Washington knew and enjoyed the respect of the governor of the Northwest Territory, Arthur St. Clair. Josiah Harmar, the American military commander of the West, dubbed George Washington "a truly confidential Indian," going so far as to say, "I believe there is not a better Indian to be found." A deserter from the army named Lewis Wetzel had gunned him down for no other reason than that he was an Indian. While hoping Wetzel would "be hanged up immediately without trial," Harmar had him arrested and held at Marietta.[1]

He should have hanged him. Soon after his arrest Wetzel escaped under suspicious circumstances, fleeing for Kentucky. He then settled in Limestone, the area from which Benjamin Logan had marched his murderous militia. As luck would have it, a month after the murder, a company of American troops in three boats, led by Capt. William McCurdy, stopped at the settlement at midnight during a rainstorm as they were heading down the Ohio River to Post Vincennes.[2] On arrival and without apparent rhyme or reason, soldiers entered a number of houses without permission, harassing the inhabitants, stealing food, and tearing up gardens. Worse still, two soldiers named Lawlor and Delaney broke into a house, seized a settler, and grabbed his money. They then "dragged him down the Bank to the Boats some pulling him by his Hands while others held his Heels." After the victim slashed at one of his captors with a knife, other soldiers joined the two, beat the man, and tied him fast in one of the boats.[3] When residents complained to McCurdy, he shot back that "all the Inhabitants of Limestone were a pack of damned Beggars and Villains."[4] After all, the man the troops had seized was Lewis Wetzel.[5]

After the night of plunder, the citizens of Limestone sought restitution and justice. Kentuckians wanted McCurdy arrested, the soldiers who rampaged through their town punished, and Wetzel freed. But a general court-martial acquitted the troops of all charges.[6] The men, it found, had not robbed Wetzel, nor had they treated the people of Limestone any worse than they deserved.[7] "All kentucky is in an uproar about it," an officer declared.[8] The whole affair served to "stir up the animosities between the troops of the United States, and the citizens of the district."[9]

The tangled story of George Washington, Wetzel, and McCurdy revealed the extent of a growing rift of incomprehension between the East and the West. And it did so because in this tale the name Washington mattered far more than the fact that a Delaware bore his name. Washington the figure and the image epitomized the fictions that the new government would act as a fair arbiter and that by trading his sword for a plowshare, he had signaled an end to the Revolution, secured for better or worse by the new Constitution.[10] The trappings of authority so bound up in his image, however, could not obscure the reality of the failure of authority in the West.

The rifts between East and West, perception and reality, and expectation and experience had coalesced to forge a frontier commonwealth ideal based on the idea that only the state could provide security. By the 1790s, however, in some regions of the West, men and women would wait no longer and took it upon themselves to put an end to revolutionary chaos despite and because of the illusory image of the state's power. In doing so, these people would declare themselves a "society." Some turned their backs on eastern authority out of a sense of frustration. Others sought to reconstitute the bonds of order out of a newfound conviction to act for themselves. These individuals understood that although geographically "the Allaghania mountain" formed "the back bone of America or of the United States," the range, in fact, towered as the physical manifestation of the gulf between western concerns and Atlantic interests that had grown so wide that no reconciliation on the terms of easterners seemed possible.[11] Only if the East bowed to western demands for protection, especially when it came to conquering and displacing Indians, could peace come.

Western Pennsylvania emerged as the epicenter where men and women enacted the western vision and turned resistance into a blueprint for the creation of commonwealth. Here discontent with the continuation of violence, uncertainty, and chaos took more violent forms than in Kentucky or Ohio, where common settlers had forged tacit, if uneasy, agreements with regional elites and where consensus over the principle of protection emerged without conflict. Not so in Pennsylvania. Here settlers did not hammer out an accommodation with speculators or with local elites. Complaints in general fell on deaf ears. In this context, common settlers acted for themselves to re-create sovereignty. In so doing, they led the West in putting into practice what had been articulated.

In fact, they went further. Western Pennsylvanians embraced the commonwealth ideology, arguing like others that Indians had to be removed or eradicated, that with violence society could not exist, and that the state's fundamental role was to protect its citizens. The particular pressures that gripped western Pennsylvania, however, added another element to the idea of frontier commonwealth, giving birth to a variation on a common theme that would imperil not only the United States but also the consensus that animated the West. The most radical settlers argued that the right to improvement had to be at the heart of any land settlement. And they threatened violence and independence to achieve this end. In a region beset by unresolved conflicts between squatters, jobbers, and eastern speculators—and reeling from Indian raids and the perceived indifference of eastern government—the common people of western Pennsylvania became the leading edge of western discontent, as some settlers from other regions of the Ohio valley voiced their support for pursuing a new understanding of property rights. They also represented its outer limit, in that such resistance threatened the very bases of accommodation in other regions of the West.

Taken together, the events that illustrated the extent to which a group of westerners were prepared to go in reconstituting society on their own terms are better known as the Whiskey Rebellion.[12] Although labeled a rebellion, insurrection, or epilogue to the American Revolution, the violent protests of frontier settlers in the early 1790s are better considered a final chapter of the western revolution that, as a witness to the events put it, "burst forth with an explosion, that . . . electrified the whole United States."[13] In the process, westerners were transforming a commonwealth vision into a political reality, one that more comfortably rested on the body of a dead Indian named George Washington than on the be-knighted image of the living president named George Washington.

The explosion of the West in part stemmed from the failure of the American government to address the Indian issue on western terms. In the wake of Harmar's limited campaign of chastisement and what Ohioans and Kentuckians interpreted as the raids that culminated in the Big Bottom incident, westerners once again insisted that order could only come to the Ohio valley through a war of conquest. Men and women had borne long enough "all the cruelties of a savage Warr" and demanded that the "general Government would be turned towards quieting the hostile tribes of Indians." Harry Innes informed Henry Knox in no uncertain terms that "Indians have always been the aggressors, that any incursions made into their country have been from reiterated injuries committed by them." He called for a general war. And if Knox did not act, westerners would. "Volunteer expeditions," he warned, "will be carried on into the Indian Countries upon the principles of Protection, and self-Preservation, and Government will not be able to counteract them."[14]

The government responded. In the summer of 1791, Arthur St. Clair, the governor of the Northwest Territory, led another expedition of chastisement, hoping to isolate the groups of Indians responsible for raids. Writing from Fort Washington outside Cincinnati, St. Clair informed the county lieutenants of western America that they were now "authorized by the President of the United States to embody at the Expense of the United States as many Militia, by voluntary enlistment or otherwise as the Law directs."[15] At first, it looked as if the government was going to make good on its promises. Knox ordered supplies from Fort Pitt sent to exposed frontier regions.[16] In August, St. Clair then asked officials of the Kentucky district to send their most experienced fighters.[17] In doing so, he hoped to relieve tensions in the Ohio valley by striking what were known as "renegades" without unduly alarming other Indians. On a larger scale, though, this amounted to a mission, much like Harmar's, to chastise in hopes of civilizing.[18]

Instead, an army not up to the task was about to encounter an effective, organized, and experienced force. St. Clair's troops were commonly understood to be riffraff. Moreover, the government had mismanaged the affair from the start. The army was "badly cloathed, badly paid, and badly fed" and supplied with "very bad powder."[19] Capt. Samuel Newman, who made the trek out West during the summer with eighty-one men, four women, and at least one infant from the East, cataloged a march of folly. Within two days of leaving Philadelphia, he had four men flogged; three days later he dismissed the wife of one of his soldiers for sneaking canteens of rum to the men; and a week later he drummed another out of camp for the same offense. Newman almost reached his breaking point with Patrick Powers. Guarding a number of prisoners confined for drunkenness, Powers persuaded the men to desert with him. For his pains, he received fifty lashes tied to a wagon wheel.[20]

Men such as these did not stand a chance. And a confederation of Indians led by the Miami war chief Little Turtle routed them in October, killing over six hundred.[21] Only one regiment, a contemporary wrote, "knew how to fight" and how to lead a bayonet charge. The rest, as he put it, were "idle and dissipated, picked up along the shores and grog shops of the Towns and Country."[22] The problem, as far as settlers were concerned, again lay with what they regarded as the resolve of a federal government that sought to secure order and authority in the West by sponsoring a policy—chastisement—and an ideology—civility—that westerners had soundly rejected.

After the St. Clair debacle, settlers were, as one put it, once again living in "Dread of the Tawny Enemies who frequently Infest the Good people."[23] Government officials, however, still insisted on treating with the enemy. In the wake of the defeat, officials initiated negotiations with a number of groups. However just and wise such a policy may have been, in the context of a West clamoring for general war, it served to alienate people further. One negotiator argued that the key to pacifying the West lay in "mak[ing] known" that the United States "in no wise desired to wage a bloody war with them, but on the contrary were ready and willing to make a peace which should in every respect be in accordance with the laws of justice and humanity."[24] Knox declared that as treaty negotiations began, "all hostile incursions of the White Inhabitants into or near the Indian Country North of the Ohio should be absolutely prohibited."[25] Another hero of the War of Independence and now western commander, Gen. Anthony Wayne, similarly warned westerners to forgo "any hostile attempts" against any Indians lest they compromise the president's attempt to conclude "a General Peace."[26] Forbearing "all Hostility," as an official put it, demonstrated Washington's inclination "to spare the Effusion of human Blood." Treaty negotiations grew from "that Humanity which distinguishes his Name." Washington, therefore, had decided to "give the misled and deluded Tribes of Belligerent Indians, a last Opportunity to save themselves, by an honourable and substantial Peace."[27]

Two of the men charged with meeting with Indians in 1792 — Rufus Putnam, who was set to travel to Vincennes, and James Wilkinson, who met representatives at Cincinnati — no doubt found themselves in a bind. On the one hand, as representatives of the United States, they had to treat Indians in an honorable fashion, suggesting that "there is no difference between us and you!" On the other, having lived in Kentucky and Ohio during years of violence, they tended to view Indians as a breed apart, as "coppercolored Brethren," as Wilkinson put it.[28] One of the men on a similar peace mission to Sandusky, Col. John Hardin, knew full well that hostilities could not be ended by another treaty. Settlers would not stand for treating with what he regarded as "a cruel savage enemy."[29]

He was right. Settlers did all in their power to hamper any treaty. When, for example, one of the chief Indians negotiating with Putnam died immediately after the talks and "every military honor was shown him and three salutes fired over his grave," a group of men visited his grave that night, dug up the body, and dragged it through the streets. Notices of a reward for the apprehension of the desecraters were circulated. Frontier settlers tore these down, and the men were never caught.[30] Negotiations, unsurprisingly, had come to naught.[31]

No place suffered more during this period, and contained more recalcitrant settlers, than western Pennsylvania. What bothered settlers here as much as anything was the gap between the promise and the reality of the region. Though travelers testified to the beauty and fecundity of the area, in exposed places, such as much of Washington County, visitors encountered a strange mix of promise and perdition, the permanent and the ephemeral. The town of Washington had a courthouse and jail and some "handsome" log houses. Yet the settlers had not taken stumps out of the road. Nearby was "a little stockade for the defence of the neighbourhood" with several log cabins within its pickets.[32] Another visitor, not as sanguine, noted that some settlers lived in houses "not much better than a stye."[33]

Pennsylvania suffered from the same problems as the rest of the Ohio valley. As one western Pennsylvanian put it, "the situation we are in with respect to trade and commerce" required that settlers press the government "whereby the *natural* advantages of our country may be made free and secure to us." Spanish control of the Mississippi River left frontier men and women "destitute of any market for the produce of our soil."[34]

Without trade, civility had not flourished. Col. John May, who had enjoyed the lavish Fourth of July festivities in 1788 at Marietta among the West's elite, found the one he spent in western Pennsylvania along "the dismal Monongahela river" the following year depressing. Far from hopeful toasts to Washington and the Delawares, he lifted a glass to these thoughts: "In this world of disappointments, let us take what enjoyment we can get. 'Let us eat and drink for tomorrow we die.'"[35] While Marietta was enjoying the short-lived fruits of society, Pittsburgh was beset with poverty.[36] It was a town of extremes, mimicking the East yet mired in the West. One day a woman moving from Philadelphia to Lexington, who passed through the town, dined on biscuit, cheese, and wine with Colonel Butler and Captain and Mrs. O'Hara. The next, she reported, "the Town [was] all in arms." A report came in "that a party of Indians [were] within twenty miles." The local militia scrambled to assemble as drums beat men to arms. The whole scene, which, she concluded, made "a very disagreeable appearance," reminded settlers and visitors that violence swirled outside the confines of the town.[37]

Concerns about authority plagued the region. The area contained advocates of Virginia, friends of Pennsylvania, champions of a new western government, and "the enemies to all."[38] Most frustratingly, common men and women contended with what they perceived as the indifference of those eastern leaders who could legitimately claim sovereignty, officials from Pennsylvania. In the wake of the Big Bottom incident, when settlers killed a number of Indians on Beaver Creek, authorities in Pennsylvania, far from supporting calls for eradication of Indians, had issued a proclamation offering the princely sum of $1,000 for the arrest of the killers even as Indians were attacking up and down the Ohio valley.[39]

Like other frontier settlers, western Pennsylvanians also contended with a steady stream of Indian attacks after the War of Independence concluded.[40] Throughout the Ohio valley the pace of the raids picked up in 1790. In May of that year, for example, Indians waylaid nine boats heading down the Ohio River.[41] In 1792, the most exposed regions in western Pennsylvania had a "very troublesome" time with the Indians.[42] Absalom Baird from Washington County considered the attacks after the St. Clair debacle the worst he had ever seen. Well-garrisoned Pittsburgh did not come under attack, but many outlying areas, especially Washington County, did. Indians were also attacking settlements near Laurel Hill and were even threatening vulnerable regions just to the west of Carlisle in the mountains. As raids mounted, settlers rushed a letter to Governor Thomas Mifflin, asking for any help from state or federal authorities he could muster. The state, settlers alleged, did nothing, and federal troops were stationed out West but were "loitering amongst them as nuisances."[43]

Through these experiences, the common people of western Pennsylvania, much like the rest of the Ohio valley, harbored a "great aversion to those wretches," the Indians.[44] Some of them, of course, had butchered the Christian Indians at Gnadenhütten. Others condoned the atrocity.[45] So race-addled had the settlers in western Pennsylvania become that some Indians considered it the most dangerous region of the Ohio valley. In 1790, a Seneca complained to "the Fathers of the Quaker State" of the people who lived outside of Pittsburgh, pleading with officials in Philadelphia to "fix some person at Fort Pitt, to take care of me and my people." Whites in the area had killed and maimed a number of his people over the past few years. Of the "thirteen fires," he believed, only Pennsylvania would defend Indians on the frontier. Ironically, the state would have to do so by confronting its own citizens, the most racist on the frontier by his reckoning, evidenced by "the repeated robberies, and in the murders and depredations committed by the Whites against us."[46]

In many ways, therefore, the tenor of life in western Pennsylvania differed little from that of other areas in the Ohio River valley after 1790. All dealt with actual and perceived eastern hostility and indifference, Indian raids, and economic marginalization. Yet although the situation in western Pennsylvania resembled that of Kentucky, and to a certain extent even Ohio, the region differed fundamentally from the other areas. Unlike Kentucky, no accommodation between settlers and speculators appeared on the horizon. To be sure, men such as William Irvine and Ephraim Douglas, ensconced in or near Fort Pitt's protective walls, had tried to create the image of sympathy for the masses. They did so, however, not out of conviction or a sense of common threat or purpose, as had been the case in Kentucky and in Ohio, but because they feared the chaos that racist settlers in places like Washington could unleash.

In the years after the War of Independence, friction was increasing between haves and have-nots. Many of the greatest speculators and landholders, in these years of uncertainty, were becoming wealthier while the poor faced greater demands. In fact, the number and influence of large landowners, the wealthiest of whom were often absentees, were growing in the late 1780s and early '90s. In the region, the top 10 percent of the population saw their landholdings increase by nearly 50 percent from the 1780s to the early '90s. By this time, these men controlled 35 percent of the land. One named John Nicholson, who served as Pennsylvania's comptroller general, owned 3.7 million acres of land. Wealth, in other words, was becoming concentrated. At the same time, the percentage of landless settlers was on the rise. In some townships, more than half of all settlers had no land. For those who did, the average acreage of the typical farm had fallen from a hundred acres in the 1780s to fifty acres by the mid-1790s. As population surged in the period after the War of Independence, with the number of settlers in the West nearly doubling during the 1780s, more and more desperate men and women labored as tenants.[47]

If anything, the poorer were suffering more in the late 1780s than they had during the relatively freewheeling days of the war, when they had a bit of freedom to settle where they wanted. In fact, settlers found themselves caught between the avarice of jobbers and the greed and indifference of landowners, who were aided and abetted by local officials. In the 1790s, for instance, William Bingham, who claimed more than one million acres in the region, hired a surveyor and would-be jobber named John Adlum to look after his lands. For his troubles, Adlum received a percentage of the profits from sales, as well as unsold lands.[48] At times, Adlum had to evict his own kind. During the early 1790s, men from Greensburg marched west to the Allegheny River and the French Creek country "to seize lands by what they called improvements, and to prevent those who had bought and paid the state for it, from surveying the lands." Even after "the indians took the liberty of skinning a few of the heads of those who went for the purpose," a number continued to grasp what land they could. "Those improvements," Adlum wrote, "were made by girdling a few trees, and driving four forked sticks in the ground, and laying two poles across in front and rear of the forks and covered them with bark." Although they employed the methods of squatters, these were aggressive jobbers, working either for themselves or for a wealthy patron.[49]

Squatters in western Pennsylvania, like those in Kentucky and Ohio, no doubt found what land they could amid competing interests and groups as they tried to scratch out precarious existences.[50] Yet fluidity in these years in this region did not allow tensions to dissipate. Rather, fluidity heightened tensions. Those who had ties to eastern merchants and credit, the very wealthiest, drove competitors out of business and used their connections to amass wealth and land. The many, on the other hand, suffered. Squatters faced eviction, and common settlers had to endure mass foreclosures and at times debtors' prison. In these years, amid economic stagnation, wealthy landowners—many from outside the area—did not relent, demanding cash that was hard to come by to satisfy debts and pay rents. At times, up to 40 percent of settlers in western Pennsylvania faced some sort of foreclosure.[51] This distinctive dynamic, not accommodation, defined relations between an increasingly absent wealthy and a growing number of poor in western Pennsylvania, ensuring that safety valves were hard to find.[52]

Elites in the region, unsurprisingly, were walking a fine line. On the one hand, they had to contend with settlers who refused to defer to their judgment, as a gap was looming between the experiences of leading officials, some of whom enjoyed national or statewide reputations, and those of the landless.[53] On the other, minor local officials, whose influence did not extend beyond their local worlds, even some of whom sympathized with their neighbors, had little power to protect settlers from eastern actions or from the failure of government to defend western interests. In the 1780s, in some less developed places, like Washington County, elected justices of the peace could empathize with their poorer neighbors. Though better off, they, too, struggled with a failed economy, insecurity, and violence. By 1790, however, when the state's new constitution stipulated that justices would be appointed for life, such bonds were attenuated. In a world dominated by absentees, who had little or no experience with western chaos, the landless lost their voice.[54] As a prescient local official in Pittsburgh understood, the "fate" of authorities with muted powers was "intimately connected" with the fortunes of Indians.[55] Each confronted common men and women inflamed by Indian hatred and animated by the impotence and hostility of authority. Fittingly, in some areas, visitors were advised to carry pistols, as locals had a habit of carrying "large clubs" when they went out.[56]

Experience and outlook, therefore, distinguished common settlers from many of their more prominent neighbors and from easterners. "In these scenes of horror" during the war, as the inhabitants of an outlying county in Pennsylvania wrote in 1786, "we were your frontier. Our blood answered for yours. Our hazard and unparalleled distress purchased your safety." Speaking for all frontier settlers, they argued that they "had stood between you and the tomahawk and scalping knife, and diverted the inhuman strokes from you." Since they had confronted an irredeemable enemy, no one could deprive them of land they had earned a right to hold. "Your government," the group told Pennsylvania officials, "hitherto, have been extremely earnest to cram their laws down our throats," laws devised to protect the claims of the wealthy and to ignore the rights of those who had sacrificed. In confronting such "great evils," exacerbated by Indian raids, men and women had a duty derived from the principle of "self-preservation" to resist.[57]

Trapped between Indian anger, eastern indifference, and the unsympathetic hostility or sympathetic impotence of local officials, western Pennsylvanians had few certainties in life. Perhaps the most critical and revealing was whiskey. Indeed, the cult of whiskey symbolized the fortunes of the region. For these westerners, distilling whiskey made good sense. In a region with rich land but little trade and money and no way of moving bulky goods over the mountains or downriver, whiskey proved a valuable commodity. Whiskey production also offered small farmers a means to use crop surpluses in some sort of profitable way, and it could almost stand in as a form of currency. "In some respects," as a resident of the region noted, it "answered the place of money." Whiskey proved extremely easy to distill and was therefore the perfect lazy man's product.[58] But whiskey had other uses, less practical but no less significant. For starters, western Pennsylvanians drank a great deal of it. During the war, when the army needed a strong drink for troops, many in western Pennsylvania began distilling it. In the years thereafter, even as demand dried up, manufacturing continued as "general consumption became exceedingly great" in the West.[59] "In the neighbourhood of Pittsburgh," a writer calling himself a traveler noted, "almost every other farm has a still-house on it, where the people assemble and drink away their health and estates."[60]

Whiskey played one other critical role in western Pennsylvania. The production—and consumption—of whiskey underlined the sense of alienation, anti-authoritarianism, and violence that permeated many of the poorer settlements. After all, "the eating of hominy," Ephraim Douglas claimed tongue in cheek, "is as natural to us as the drinking of whisky in the morning." Whiskey underscored the common people's contempt for a wider world that looked down on frontier inhabitants as unruly and as uncivilized as the Indians around them.[61] As a settler calling himself "A Farmer" argued, whiskey defined what they were, what they were not, and the growing distance between the two as the East failed to protect the West. "I have often thought that for all the advantages this Country has heretofore obtained by their representatives," he declared, "they might as well have sent my neighbour Duddy Dougherty, who never drinks whiskey but by the quart. I am sure Mr. Dougherty would have done us no harm."[62]

The tensions gripping Duddy Dougherty's world—East versus West, wealthy versus poor, Indian versus white—were revealed in one unexceptional encounter. On March 18, 1786, Richard Butler, commissioner for Indian affairs, stopped at the settlement of Ligonier on his way down the Ohio for a conference with Indians. At a place called Irwin's, Butler tried to get some breakfast. Inside he encountered four locals, all justices of the peace for Washington County at a time when they were still elected by the people. He also met one Col. James McFarlane, "as the people called him," Butler patronizingly added. Butler could not believe these men could be officials. All were still drunk from the evening before, the conclusion of a successful Saint Patrick's Day. The visit did not go well. The hungover so-called colonel, as Butler noted, "began to interrogate us in a very impertinent manner and made use of some very coarse observations." McFarlane condemned Butler and his mission, declaring "an absolute determination to be at War with the Indians." He also lambasted "the State of Pensa for not giving relief to the frontiers when distressed by the Indians." By Butler's reckoning, McFarlane, although a veteran of the

War of Independence, was "Severe and ill bred," and his drunken partners acted in ways "unbecoming decent men." Butler "pushed on without breakfast."[63]

Western Pennsylvania was a troubling corner of a larger troubled western world. A writer offering advice to American farmers looking to settle the region simply said do not go. "You will," he warned, "be exposed to great danger of being killed by the Indians on your way to those places," adding that "you will labor for little, or nothing." By the end of the 1780s, Pennsylvania was no longer the "best poor man's country," a place where common settlers could keep a step ahead of the wealthy and gain competency. If you must go, he concluded facetiously, "chuse lands for a settlement that are near those navigable waters that *run towards* the Atlantic ocean and which are within the jurisdiction of the United States." And above all avoid the "banditti" in the region, or those disaffected from the state and federal government.[64]

It did not take much to set the "banditti" off. And on March 3, 1791, they found their excuse. On that day, with bipartisan support Congress passed an excise on distilled spirits. Much like the British had done in the mid-1760s to pay for victory in the Seven Years' War, the Anglophile secretary of the treasury, Alexander Hamilton, decided that selective taxation could fund the new nation's debts from a war of independence and shore up the government's credit. Hamilton saw a responsible level of debt as beneficial to an infant state. Taxing the wealthiest members of society, however, was not part of such a strategy. Tariffs levied on imports imperiled relations with merchants, as did taxes on planters' lands. An excise on the production of distilled spirits, however, would provide revenue while not alienating the better sort. Large distillers, it was hoped—with justification—would pass the burden on to the consumer.[65]

In the West in general, collection did not go smoothly. The commissioner of the revenue, Tench Coxe, whose job it was to oversee the execution of the excise, reported that within a year of its application many citizens cooperated. Easterners in particular displayed "no appearance of opposition" and, if they did so, relented once a collector arrived. Coxe found "the excise system really beneficial to the landed interest. It is also true that the greater part of the Town distillers and of the principal distillers in most of the well populated Counties, consider the system as favourable to their Business." The West presented a different story. "In the four Western Counties of Pennsylvania," Coxe reported to Hamilton, "the prejudices and opposition are such as almost to defeat the execution of the revenue laws." Settlers in the four northwest counties of Virginia, likewise, were dragging their feet. He also noted "pretty strong discontents" in the frontier sections of North Carolina, the district of Kentucky, and South Carolina.[66]

While many frontier settlers resisted by not paying the excise, the poorer sort of western Pennsylvania—those whom a local official referred to as a "landless body of men"—resorted to violence.[67] Of course, the excise imperiled what westerners saw as valuable "family manufactures."[68] But more important, by targeting whiskey—the drink and symbol that defined them—it threatened a way of life and a means to make sense of a troubling world and their marginal place in it. Soon after the passage of the excise, settlers "threatened the town" with what they called "Tom the Tinker."[69] Handbills nailed to trees and published in newspapers announced his impending "visit," declaring that "his mettle is hot, and his ladle up ready for casting."[70] For any person who "rendered himself obnoxious" by obeying the new law, Tom the Tinker would cut his still to pieces, an act he called "mending." His followers appeared at the homes of "cowards and traitors" in the night, with blackened faces or disguised as Indians, asking not "'Are you Whig or Tory?' But, 'Are you a Tom the Tinker's Man?'"[71] He declared each exciseman to be a "cheating son of a bitch" and promised that anyone who showed support for the excise would "have his house torn down and demolished."[72] Thus, Pennsylvanians responded to the excise much like the Black Boys had when confronted by what they regarded as British appeasement of Indians.

Although they relied on "traditional" forms of protest, the whiskey men drew upon the lessons learned during their own period of politicization. Insecure in their lives, liberty, and property, they argued that the revenue scheme contradicted the rationale of the western commonwealth vision in its many guises. A writer styling himself "Republican" argued that the West bore disproportionate burdens with the excise. He declared to easterners, "You must convince me . . . that it is justice to excise our principal article of trade, which generally serves as a substitute for cash, and that yours should go free." Westerners demanded, "You must shew me, that there is no justice in demanding contributions from the citizens for the support of government in proportion to their wealth and benefits they enjoy." The self-styled Republican ended his defense of resistance to the new law by arguing, "When you reconcile these things with the principles of liberty and freedom, equality and justice, and with the rights of mankind, then I will not only be ashamed, but even confounded; I will then renounce republican principles, and become your convert."[73]

Through experience and Revolutionary ideology, a trenchant opposition to the excise emerged, allowing issues that had animated revolutionary ferment on the frontier to blossom into something more troubling. Drawing upon older forms of opposition, western settlers began creating committees of correspondence to communicate common concerns, to draw up plans for concerted resistance, and to keep each other apprised of strategy.[74] Committees, intimidation, and ostracism, of course, had been key features of urban campaigns to repeal British legislation in the years before the War of Independence. Now in the West, groups of citizens, as a critic put it, were "constantly forming and binding themselves to each other to oppose it [the excise] at every stage, and to make joint expense of any costs or damages that may accrue."[75] Committeemen also made it clear that their grievances extended beyond the excise. Their complaints also stemmed in part from "our want of markets, and the scarcity of a circulating medium."[76]

At issue for these committees was nothing short of their experience during revolution and the commonwealth vision that had emerged from it. By funding debt through excise, the government edged toward tyranny. Such schemes were "contrary to the ideas of natural justice . . . [and] subversive of industry by common means, where men seem to make fortunes by fortuitous concourse of circumstances rather than by economic virtues and useful employment." In these circumstances, as had happened twenty years earlier, power rested "in the hands of a few persons who may influence those occasionally in power to invade the Constitution." Challenging both federalist and anti-federalist notions of political economy and invoking opposition writers popular during the 1770s such as John Trenchard and Thomas Gordon, westerners argued that the tax would "discourage agriculture, and a manufacturing highly beneficial in the present state in the country."[77] Restating a lesson learned through the process of revolution, they argued that sovereignty did not reside with the state and insisted, "We are the people, and . . . Congress are only our servants."[78]

In the summer of 1794, a renewed fervor gripped the West as men and women resurrected symbols that had animated the first instances of resistance to British rule. Most conspicuous of these was the erection of liberty poles. When westerners heard that farther east in Carlisle judges were assembling to hear cases in the excise dispute, two hundred men marched into the borough before the fleeing judges. As the judges left, the men erected one liberty pole near the courthouse, where they burned Pennsylvania's chief justice in effigy, and a second near the front door of a man arrested for resisting the excise. On it, they placed a placard with the words "Liberty and Equality." Throughout the night, they cheered, drank, and "fired many vollies," hoping they could "effect another revolution." Excise taxes were, as one pole man put it, "damned Laws and would be pulled down and they had Backing sufficient to do it," adding that "he had a good Gun and could shoot damned straight."[79] The next morning a justice of the peace for the borough cut the pole down. Nonetheless, the people erected a larger pole in the same spot, decorating it with a red Sons of Liberty flag, and placed "armed men from the country to the number of from 60 to 100" to stand guard through the night.[80]

Erecting a liberty pole followed a ritualistic formula. The assembled first voted to put up the pole, after which axmen were selected to find and prepare a suitable tree. The ceremony was then followed by speeches justifying the act. In one such instance, a citizen of Derry announced at the town's pole raising, "We should never be a happy people or enjoy our liberties until the present Congress were all executed."[81] At Carlisle, a revolutionary declared that such acts were necessary. "The People in the West," he argued, "had better Separate themselves from the Government of the U. St.," and the West "had better form a government for themselves who had no President, no King."[82] One went so far as to declare, "The Government had Carried themselves too high and must be taken down."[83] Next, those assembled chose symbols and phrases for the pole. In the summer of 1794, at one such meeting, a party of "68 or 69 people" met in a tavern to consider erecting what one called a "Whiskey Pole" in a town square. John McGrath proposed that the flag for the pole "have an Irish harp joined to it."[84] McGrath lost. His idea of using Irish symbolism was overruled, and other imagery graced the flag. After speeches and deliberations had ended, armed sentries, guarding the pole and disarming those opposed, worked in shifts throughout the night.[85] The first and last steps in these rites often involved whiskey.[86] As each vote was taken and after the pole went up, whiskey was passed around, and all present were handed a jug and asked if "they would drink whiskey without excise."[87] Drinking served as a sign of commitment. Those who did not indulge were suspect, those who did compatriots.[88]

Liberty poles appeared throughout the frontier as men and women used mass meetings and ritualistic speeches as opportunities to air their grievances.[89] Caught up in the frenzy, men and women rode off to neighboring towns to tell of news and to erect new poles. After erecting a pole in Franklin County, five hundred men headed to neighboring towns to do the same. A group of armed men from Chambersburg confronted them on the way, asking the pole men who was in charge. One replied that "they had no officers, they were all as one." Another chimed in that "they would set up the Pole if the Devil stood at the Door," claiming "the Constitution was over" and "no Law could ever punish them."[90]

Those westerners who decried the frontier's disorder but did not favor the whiskey men's prescription for it suggested that perhaps the rebels were going too far. William Findley, a leading Republican from the region, sympathized with the commonwealth vision but not the version favored by the poor in western Pennsylvania. Findley considered the rebels "persons of violent passions and little discretion." Some with "a latent predisposition to violence" had whipped into a frenzy "the ignorant and obstinate part of the people, which was the class that now gave most trouble."[91] Another lampooned the rebels as a drunken lot paying homage to a character modeled on a stereotypical Indian war chief derisively called "Captain Whiskey." The captain, as the paper put it, relied on the "power of his all conquering monarch, whiskey, and of the intrepidity of the Sons of St. Patrick in defence of their beloved bottle." While the critic began to see the merit in sending an army to suppress such lawlessness that differed little if at all from Indian incivility, Captain Whiskey responded that the army should be sent against the Indians.[92]

By the 1790s, the actions of the whiskey men seemed a dangerous anachronism. At the time the Constitution was adopted, federalists and anti-federalists alike had reached a broad consensus about the American Revolution. For better or worse, it was over. In one sense, of course, as they conspired to shunt Tom the Tinker to the margins, easterners made the claim that they—and not westerners—were the legitimate guardians of the Revolution's legacy. But they were saying something more by labeling the violent protests as "insurrection." In the East, revolution had ended. In the West, it had not. Even as the federal government and states made claims to sovereignty and authority that in the West did not yet exist, westerners wanted to dictate the form of the Revolution settlement for the West. Easterners rightly sensed that if they were allowed to do so, this would have implications for the broader nation.

While those in the East who favored a more liberating Revolution settlement agreed with some of the aims of westerners in the 1790s, they denounced Tom's violent tactics and the use of Revolutionary symbolism.[93] As the Democratic-Republican Society in Philadelphia put it, "Passion instead of reason assumed the direction of their affairs, disorder and disunion were the consequences."[94] Similarly, New York's society condemned the western Pennsylvanians for resorting to violence and for being "too hasty."[95]

While Republicans at least sympathized with some of the grievances of the rebels, those who favored a Revolution settlement rooted in efficacious government had no such qualms and tried at every turn to claim that the Revolution should be relegated to memory. Federalists or Nationalists, as they were called, tried to restore order and elite rule to a society that had reeled from violence and the financial chaos of the 1780s. Some wrote the whole episode off in the West as "the passions of the ignorant" inflamed "by Whiskey and seditious speeches."[96] Others saw more than liquor to blame. "A very few in Philadelphia had kept the fire up by Writing" letters, one of the authorities alleged, which had the effect of "stir[ring] up the minds of the People."[97] Turning the old Revolutionary equation of liberty versus power on its head, Alexander Addison, the appointed president of the Courts of Common Pleas for the counties of western Pennsylvania, argued that "in the choice of anarchy and tyranny, the last, as the least evil will be preferred."[98] After all, a number of the whiskey men wanted nothing less than "the people of the Western Country to wedge war against the United States."[99]

The people themselves suggested that they were using the symbolism of the War of Independence and invoking its memory because of the parallels between their case and that of patriots twenty years earlier. They rejected the impotent form of sovereignty that was being foisted on them, an authority without real authority and the pious yet hollow promise of domestic tranquillity and common defense. As practiced, eastern concepts of sovereignty would ensure that they would never escape the state of war. They therefore had to be resisted. As one writer put it in 1794:

> *Their liberty they will maintain,*
> *They fought for't, and they'll fight again . . .*
> *In furious rage quite desperate grown,*
> *They'll turn the cont'nent upside down,*
> *They'll damn your fine new constitution*
> *And make a terrible confusion.*[100]

Yet their agenda also moved beyond the oppositional or destructive. In turning their backs on eastern models of sovereignty, they began imagining their own. The watchword of the West emblazoned on placards may have been "liberty," but order was their goal. Indeed, it's fair to say that the westerners engaged in agitation were the true friends of order. They were attempting through resistance to end the chaos of the endemic state of war in the West and reconstitute society. By 1794, however, they insisted on establishing a society on their own terms.

Committees of correspondence therefore represented more than holdovers from or imitations of forms from the War of Independence. Within the framework of these committees, agitators also devised their own models of government and society more attuned to the sympathies of the frontier. Electing officers and drawing on the local militia structure to organize, they created their own frames of government, far more responsive to popular concerns than the new federal government. "We the people of Hamilton's district," one western constitution read, "in order to form a speedy communication, between ourselves" and other regions, and to create "a more perfect union to ourselves and our posterity, do ordain and Establish this constitution for the district of Hamiltons." Power, to "be vested in a society," was shared by a council elected every six months and a president voted in every nine months. Every male over the age of eighteen served as an elector. "This Constitution of the government of the society," as it was called, created structures to adjudicate disputes, "to encourage able teachers for the instructions of youth," and to "encourage the industrious, and promote the man of merit."[101] Western Pennsylvanians also created their own courts and elected their own officials at the county level for multicounty meetings.[102]

As William Findley argued, associations "of a more permanent nature commenced" in late 1793 and early 1794. Often formed from militia regiments, such as the one at Mingo Creek, they were "frequently attended by three hundred persons." In the absence of genuine authority, these associations provided it. "The rules of this institution, and various powers which it is reported to have exercised," Findley wrote, "imitated the language, and assumed the forms of regularly constituted authority." To him, they were mimicking forms that emerged in places like Massachusetts on the eve of the War of Independence. But such analogies miss the point. In 1774 and 1775 in Boston, in the midst of chaos, revolutionaries introduced their own versions of social institutions as the prevailing ones rooted in British sovereignty had ceased to function. Westerners in 1793 and 1794 were engaged in a similar process. Out of the necessities of a state of war, they sought to give institutional form to the autonomy that the period of violence and uncertainty afforded.[103]

Republicans in the East had joined similar societies during the early 1790s. But in the West, these groups planned and coordinated campaigns of intimidation and violence. Veterans of the Pennsylvania line traveled the roads of the West "all armed with guns and pistols, all painted like Indians," or "in women's clothes" to accost collectors of the hated tax.[104] They tarred and feathered collectors, stripping them before binding them naked to trees. Tom the Tinker's men burned officials in effigy and did the same for settlers who housed collectors.[105] "The plan," as one witness put it, was "abuse the officers secretly and by this means deter others from serving."[106] One Washington County man, who dared in public to declare that westerners could hardly expect the aid and protection of the government if they failed to follow the law, was "Imediatley Branded . . . with Tar and Feathers [and] one half of his head close shaved."[107] In other words, they were enforcing the rules of their society, standards designed to deliver them from violence and chaos.

While whiskey served as a potent symbol of this aspirant society, the images that played a similar role for the post-Revolutionary East had little resonance. Western "rioters," as one official called them, had "fired many shots through the signs hung out of the President's head."[108] As neighbors of Tom the Tinker's men warned that such iconoclasm was beyond the pale of acceptable behavior, increasingly insurgents responded, as did one man in the West, that George Washington could "kiss his backside."[109]

In the summer of 1794, as committees formed and as Tom the Tinker visited collectors, the situation in the West and for the whole country had reached a stage of crisis. Isolated incidents out West coalesced into a "tone of unreflecting madness, and drew into its vortex many persons of good morals."[110] On July 16, one hundred armed men launched a "daring and cruel" attack on the Allegheny County home of the inspector of the excise, Gen. John Neville, the man who had cooperated with St. Clair in his failed campaign of chastisement and who also was a major landholder in the region. A day later, five hundred appeared again before his house "with Drums and in all the Military pomp and parade," exchanged fire with federal troops, and burned Neville's house to the ground.[111] The attackers, in fact members of the Mingo Creek association from Washington County, were led by the same McFarlane who had condemned Richard Butler's mission of peace to the Indians. McFarlane, the local official who had empathized with his neighbors yet had no leverage over state or federal authorities, lost his life in the skirmish.[112]

With the attack, the first concerted attempt of western Pennsylvanians to redeem their fallen world, leaders called for the West to awaken. Local associations sent out circulars and called for an assembly of westerners to meet. Their members resigned themselves to the fact that "it is therefore now come to that crisis, that every citizen must express his sentiments not by his words but his actions." The committeemen asked settlers to do so not as American citizens but as members of a new imagined community formed in the crucible of revolution and created in the image of frontier commonwealth. "You are then called on," the circular read, "as a citizen of the western country, to render your personal service, with as many volunteers as you can raise."[113] In late July, members of western committees assembled on Braddock's Field outside Pittsburgh. Vivid reminders of appalling violence still littered the site. Up to seven thousand westerners trampled the bones of Indians, Britons, and Americans still thinly buried on the ground. They also assembled amid trees that bore the signs of a battle that took place forty years earlier.[114]

Numbering now between three and four thousand, the Whiskey Boys "marched to Pittsburgh with an Intention," as one critic alleged, "to burn the town, considering the inhabitants are friends to the Laws."[115] Pittsburgh, of course, represented a place apart in the West, a town like Washington that suffered from eastern indifference but that unlike Washington did not lie on the most exposed fringes of the frontier. Filled with officials impotent to rectify their own situation and with those who gave conditional allegiance to the western cause, Pittsburgh served as a vivid reminder of the peculiar nature of western Pennsylvania's state of war. The whiskey men claimed to march for weapons and for allies, hoping in particular that they could seize arms in the town's federal arsenal and convince federal troops to join their cause.[116] In doing so, "they considered the conduct of Congress in seizing British posts, arms, etc., while they remained colonies . . . to be a precedent perfectly applicable to their case."[117] Tom the Tinker's men demanded that all who supported the excise leave the town. The people of Pittsburgh, "awed into silent submission" by the demonstration of force, acquiesced, offering food, liquor, and best wishes for their "brethren" in the "common cause."[118]

The Pennsylvanians struck a responsive chord. Some settlers in Kentucky, western Virginia, and even as far off as Ohio were claiming their cause "connected" and were making plans "to convene together in order to determine for Peace or war."[119] In a number of ways, members of Democratic-Republican societies in Kentucky now saw the cause of western Pennsylvanians as their cause as well. "Nature," one Kentuckian wrote, "has done everything for us; Government everything against us." Although Indians with British support raided to "murder our wives and children," the central administration also trampled their rights. Westerners argued, "We are too distant from the grand seat of information; and are too much hackneyed in the old fashioned principles of 1776, to receive much light from the . . . new fashioned systems and schemes of policy, which are the offspring and ornament of the present administration."[120] The excise proved the straw that broke the proverbial camel's back. The country was still "infested with savages" and languishing with little trade. "We can make Whisky," a Kentuckian wrote in 1793, "but we cannot make money."[121]

In fact, frontier disturbances seemed to be spreading. In isolated incidents, settlers attacked the home of "an Officer of the United States" in Morgantown, Virginia, and whiskey poles went up in Hagerstown, Maryland.[122] A few men and women in Cincinnati gave "aid, assistance, and comfort" to the rebels in Pennsylvania.[123] During the summer when western Pennsylvanians were marching on Pittsburgh, some settlers in Kentucky began to organize for resistance, and a few went so far as to suggest that if their struggle failed to succeed, they would "renounce the allegiance to the United States and annex themselves to the British."[124]

Within the broad confines of the commonwealth consensus, in other words, the Pennsylvanians had allies. "Western America," members of one committee thundered, "has a right to expect and demand that nothing shall be considered as a satisfaction, that does not completely remove our grievances." They again trumpeted that westerners had rights to protection, asserting "that the attainment and security of these our rights, is, the common cause of the western people, and that we will unite with them that may be most expedient for that purpose."[125] Westerners, in fact, drew a distinction between a virtuous West and a pernicious "Atlantic influence," one dulled by luxury and ignorance. "The principles of our confederation," the settlers in Lexington wrote, "have been totally perverted by our Atlantic brethren," and that "luke-warmness and indecision no longer [could be] countenanced." "Nothing," they warned, "but the spirit of 1775 [could] counteract" what they called "eastern fraud."[126] Since the government would not protect them, they would take it upon themselves. Emboldened by the whiskey men, one Kentucky committee suggested equipping a ship to sail down the Mississippi and dare the Spaniards to stop it and federal officials to support the bold act. They would then get the proof they needed "whether they will be compelled to abandon or protect the inhabitants of the western country."[127]

The "rebellion," in fact, formed the spear point of western conviction, drawing together discontents focused on the issue of protection and giving them a menacing edge. In 1794, justices of the peace in Ohio County, near Wheeling, refused to prosecute a man named John McCormack suspected of engaging in rebellion.[128] Similarly, a justice of the peace for Belpre, Ohio, named Griffin Greene informed Winthrop Sargent that he had to resign his office. Greene believed that he "could never tend to the assistance of oppression, and more especially, that class of men, that earn their scanty living by hard labour." More important, he could not serve in an official capacity when his neighbors did "not suck in the sweets of the general Government, to their aid." Continuing Indian attacks cost westerners dearly, and now they had to pay an excise with no expectation of protection. Without protection, he suggested, there could be no government, nor were people required to abide by the fiction that one existed.[129]

Indeed, it's fair to say that as the death toll from Indian raids mounted and as resistance to the excise grew, the first signs of a new sensibility rooted in a "western nation" began to emerge. In an "Address to the Inhabitants of the United States West of the Allegany and Appalachian Mountains," members of the Democratic Society of Kentucky charged that the federal government exhibited "a neglect bordering on contempt" for western protection. Although they had hoped that the new government under the Constitution would have the "requisite energy" to safeguard the frontier, they found instead that only "our brethren, on the Eastern Waters, possess every advantage."[130] By 1794, westerners had to concede the "degraded and deserted situation of this Country, both as to its commerce and protection." They resolved that "the inhabitants of the Western Country have a right to demand, that their frontiers be protected by the general government."[131] The question they began to entertain was which "general government," that of the East or one of their own making. Patriotism, they warned, "like all other things, has its bounds," and "attachments to governments cease to be natural, when they cease to be mutual."[132]

Westerners had bided their time in a world of disorder until the day a government was strong enough to deliver them from such a fate. That day had come, but the government had not acted. If government did not "procure" this right for them, they would grasp it themselves.[133] To make good on these principles and to see if western ideas of society could form the basis for a new government, westerners began clamoring for more committees of correspondence to be created to "give and receive communications on these subjects" with other frontier regions.[134]

In imagining the contours of a new nation, westerners had history, sentiment, and common enemies on their side. As sufferers at the hands of Indians, they had a mythic history of self-sacrifice, binding them together through experience and memory. After all, all westerners believed that they had colonized what they called "this distant and dangerous desert." Each and every one of them, at least in their own minds, had "fought for and acquired" their lands.[135] Moreover, under the rubric of protection, they had an animating ideology that could bind wealthy settlers in Lexington to poor squatters in Washington, Pennsylvania. Increasingly, and as the crisis progressed, westerners had come to define themselves against an eastern "other," those who lived on "Eastern Waters" and benefited from the American government's "local" prejudice.[136]

On August 14 at a place called Parkinson's Ferry on the Monongahela, representatives from committees of correspondence formed throughout western Pennsylvania and the counties of western Virginia convened to discuss their plans and to announce their will to create a western society of their own. As a steady rain fell, men on horseback brandished a six-striped red and white flag, the same type of flag that the Sons of Liberty had flown in the years before the War of Independence, now representing the resolve and unity of six western counties. In a great field before the single house at the site, a crowd asked passersby, "Are you for Congress or for Liberty?"[137] The assembled erected a liberty pole with a marker reading "Liberty and no excise, and no asylum for cowards or traitors."[138] At the early sessions, one westerner argued that men and women on the frontier should establish a committee of public safety, "whose duty it shall be to call forth the resources of the western country, to repel any hostile attempts that may be made against the citizens, or the body of the people."[139] They would defend their sovereignty. Others talked about framing a new declaration of independence.[140]

Sovereignty, of course, involves space. And what these men and women assembled on the Monongahela were doing was transforming a sentiment of popular sovereignty into a political reality and a virtual, imagined commonwealth into a nation. Through eastern indifference and hostility, Indian attacks, a virulent racism, and popular political mobilization—all symptoms, causes, and effects of revolution—a consensus formed among common men and women that had become the basis for a western vision, eventually a western society, and now a western nation. Some may have pressed for secession. But threatening to leave one nation proved less significant than inventing the basis of another. For the meeting at Parkinson's Ferry focused on the western answer to western problems, how the West would bring an end to its revolution. "The time is now come," Kentuckians informed Pennsylvanians in the summer of 1794, "when we ought either to relinquish our claim, to those blessings proffered us by nature, or endeavour to obtain them at every hazard." As "Inhabitants of Western America," they had become "Fellow Citizens" of a new land of promise, one only within their grasp to realize. The West was a place "uncontaminated with Atlantic luxury, beyond the reach of European influences," where "the pampered vultures of commercial countries, have not yet found access."[141]

To officials, the western situation was spiraling out of control. William Bradford feared the meeting at Parkinson's Ferry would lead to "civil war."

"The insurgents," he believed, "will have time to strengthen themselves — to circulate the manifests they are preparing — to tamper with the people of Kentucky — to procure Ammunition and to overawe or seduce the well-affected." He worried that the militia could not overwhelm them and was "not to be depended on." Westerners were writing letters to other militia regiments, claiming all in the West should support the cause. The allegiance of four western counties in Virginia to the federal government looked suspect. If these regions that were "filled with a great number of hardy woodsmen" cooperated with those assembled at Parkinson's Ferry, the government would be in a "dangerous" position.[142] Colonel Butler, the man who had condemned and lampooned the fallen McFarlane, now feared his ilk. It seemed to him the "Whole Country would rise." In a panic, he called up all available troops from western outposts to the Pittsburgh area.[143]

Settlers from Washington, who claimed a new allegiance to the "Western Country" and had tried to "convince the people of Kentucky that we feel ourselves the same people with them in many of the most important political considerations," faced significant obstacles in cementing a union.[144] In western Pennsylvania, at this moment of crisis, security and protection had meanings beyond the commonwealth vision, further fueling radical claims but also straining the bonds with other westerners. The formal petition that emerged from the meeting at Parkinson's Ferry denounced large landowners for their avariciousness, as well as the government for permitting individuals and companies to dictate the terms of settlement.[145] A local named William Bonham decided the time had come for war. "More men," he believed, "[were] engaged in the present opposition than was at the Beginning of the Revolution between Britain and America."[146] Bonham saw the issue as one of political and economic justice. Eastern policies were "oppressive on the poor people." Speculators and "Land Jobbers," as he called them, "should pay the taxes." The right to improvement in these circumstances was imperiled. Because the government did not recognize these rights, "the only remedy," in Bonham's mind, was "to Nip the United States in the Bud." "A Revolution in this country," he intoned, "was necessary."[147]

In the summer of 1794, western Pennsylvanians insisted that any government existed to uphold and guarantee the values of its society. On the Pennsylvania frontier, where no accommodation between wealthy and poor lay on the horizon, inhabitants tried to enshrine a system of land distribution that ensured the poor would have access to property. In Pennsylvania, some citizens resolved "that the mode of selling Back Lands in great quantities to companies is unjust and improper, because it is destructive of an essential principle in every republican government." In western society, government had a role to encourage "the equal division of landed property . . . so far as is consistent with that encouragement due to industry." Doing otherwise would "alienate the affections of common people" from government. And only popular sovereignty, not as fiction but as fact, could guarantee order. "All civil authority," these westerners claimed, "originates with and is derived from the people in a republican government." Moreover, "every law made by the representatives not agreeable to the voice of those from whom they derive their authority is tyrannical and unjust."[148]

In other words, while the Pennsylvanians stood as the apogee of a broader western commonwealth, they also revealed its limits. To be sure, some western Virginians, men who represented the fifth and sixth stripes of the rebels' flag, condemned "men of wealth . . . engrossing lands profusely."[149] But although the Ohio valley bubbled with intrigue and possibilities, Pennsylvanians would have a difficult time moving beyond a six-striped flag. Like the Sons of Liberty, the men from western Pennsylvania envisioned a new form of sovereignty. But they would challenge the very basis of the broad appeal of commonwealth in other regions of the Ohio valley beyond the four western counties of Pennsylvania and two counties of western Virginia. Common men and women in both Kentucky and Ohio, of course, struggled with the same concerns that infuriated common Pennsylvanians. They, too, were beset by jobbers, speculators, or companies. They, too, hoped to gain rights to improvement. But in Kentucky and Ohio, local elites and common settlers had comprehended potential conflict over land within their understanding of commonwealth. Such a process had not gripped Washington County.[150]

Nonetheless, some frontier inhabitants in America were employing the symbols, rituals, violence, and rhetoric of their revolution and the War of Independence to cobble together a coherent but troubling ideology of independence and equality. Swigging whiskey and shouting liberty, they unleashed a bloody campaign to make political processes more accountable to common people, to open the West up to trade and opportunity, to provide ready access to land for the landless, and to try to force the government to wage a race war against Indians to achieve these goals. The state's role, as they saw it, was to sustain this contentious and contradictory vision. In so doing, as John Marshall put it, they "threatened to shake the government of the United States to its foundations."[151]

Easterners like Marshall pointed with a great deal of justification to the American Revolution, comparing the threatening antics of Tom the Tinker to what they regarded as the purer actions of the liberty men of the 1770s. But the analogy obscures what in fact was going on. Patterns of resistance in western Pennsylvania and Virginia paralleled those of the War of Independence not only through mimicry but because the West was still contending with the disorder of revolution. In these circumstances, they used their own rituals and forms of association to create the conditions for the reemergence of society and perhaps to serve as markers of a new nation. Like many people caught in the throes of revolutionary ferment, they had little choice but to manipulate the notion of sovereignty. As the East, in their minds, continued to pay lip service to western pleas for protection — and all that the term represented for westerners — settlers had to create the stuff of sovereignty, which of course entailed rejecting eastern projections of authority and eastern models of order, as well as eastern interpretations of the American Revolution and War of Independence. This agenda inspired fear in the East. Easterners therefore framed the birth pangs of a western society as an "insurrection" not so much to deny westerners a claim to the legacy of the War of Independence as to keep the debate focused on issues that would obscure the essential and troubling truth that animated the Whiskey "Rebellion."

NINE

American Leviathan:
The Covenant for Commonwealth

In 1793, as the West was beginning to erupt, Harry Innes received an extraordinary letter from a famous acquaintance. Thomas Jefferson, who was serving as secretary of state, predicted that 1794 would prove a momentous year. "It is very interesting to the US to see how this last effort for living in peace with the Indians will succeed," he wrote. "If it does not," he reckoned, "there will be a great revolution of opinion here as to the manner in which they are to be dealt with." With negotiations breaking down amid the pressures and prejudices of the West, the future did not appear bright for Indians. With rebels combining to resist the East, the future looked uncertain for the United States. Indeed, Jefferson concluded, "This summer is of immense importance to the future condition of mankind all over the earth: and not a little so to ours."[1]

Jefferson's words proved as prophetic as they did cryptic. In the new West, animated by a vision of frontier commonwealth, Indians and society could not coexist. Arthur Campbell, who had lived through the darkest days of the war in the Ohio valley, longed for order. Men and women were not designed for "the primeval state of the world," a place defined by a time "previous to his entering into a state of society." Although fallen creatures, people still had the right to live without uncertainty and violence. "Notwithstanding this degradation of our species," a moral morass Campbell had lived in for some time, "we feel ourselves to be beings of an order more inclined to society than solitude, more delighted with the exercises of benevolence and humanity than with injustice and cruelty."[2] In not asserting its sovereignty, the state had failed to bring the commonwealth into being. Campbell insisted that the impotence of government "over the Ohio, is become truly alarming, for instead of crushing a predatory banditti at once, they have increased their strength, and we have now to contend with a powerful confederacy secretly abetted by our natural enemies the British." Commanders had exhibited "too much of a Quaker spirit." Paxton Boy–like attitudes—what Campbell called "the force of the big knife" and which he regarded as "popular"—were needed. After all, he was convinced that Indians were not fit for society through "the love of shedding innocent blood."[3]

Westerners—even those inclined still to view Indians as redeemable—believed that nothing less than the state securing the West by vanquishing Indians and removing them from white settlement areas could rescue it from disorder. As William Findley discovered, during a long revolution, "there was an unavoidable relaxation of morals, and of the execution of the laws." At the same time, "the country was cruelly wasted by perpetual savage depredations." Settlers had conflated one with the other. Chaos, they now argued, stemmed from the Indian menace around them, a force they could not conquer without federal help and direction.[4] As a western Virginian put it, "Factious spirit" had "prevailed too much in this country." He worried if anything could "reconcile the minds of the people to the government."[5] George Rogers Clark observed that "it is a pity that the Blood and Treasure of the people should be so lavished when one campaign properly directed would put a final end to the war." Ironically, by 1793 only aggressive action tending to some final solution for the West could "establish a Harmony between us and the Indians" and, he might have added, between settlers and the government.[6]

So Jefferson was right. Americans were experiencing "a great revolution of opinion" in 1793 and 1794. And because of this, Indians would face a cataclysm. Much like the British had in the 1760s, thirty years later the American government found itself in a difficult position west of the mountains. Officials could not placate settlers and do justice to Indians. But the analogies between empire and nation end here. The British had to reckon with angry settlers intent on killing a people they regarded as uncivilized but redeemable. During the intervening years, settlers had asserted their sovereignty, articulated a vision and program for change, and come to see Indians as essentially inferior or at least unfit to live among whites. Agitation in the early 1790s crystallized these dynamics and gave them a political thrust, challenging the foundations of the new nation. At the moment whiskey men were threatening to create an independent western commonwealth, government officials pushed Indians out of the Ohio valley, establishing a new line over which Indians could not trespass. Unlike the British, therefore, Americans proved willing to decimate the Indians to retain the West. Thus settlers achieved their ideal of protection and obtained the preconditions for a white society to flourish.[7]

Although they won their commonwealth, only the state, as settlers had argued for some time, had the resources to end the state of war and complete revolution. Government officials, of course, had interests in securing the West, be they driven by ideology, power, or wealth. Some regarded the West as a nagging problem that had to be solved for order to prevail throughout the nation after the tumult of revolution.[8] In other words, interests converged in securing the Ohio valley. The American nation, from its origins rooted in western empire, was not predestined. Nor for that matter was it only conceived in the East. It was also imagined and constructed on the periphery as a creative response to the collapse of sovereignty and the violent competition implicit in its reconstruction. Only as common people and the state reached an agreement over the West could meaningful sovereignty be established. Through the process of East and West creating a common Revolution settlement, common settlers prevailed in accomplishing commonwealth on their own terms. Yet although the people claimed ultimate sovereignty, only the state could assert that sovereignty and, in so doing, give it meaning. The process of giving birth to Leviathan, therefore, was an act of co-creation.

The national state would police the bounds of commonwealth. Doing so entailed controlling the lines that separated whites from Indians with troops and forts, thereby accomplishing what the British would or could not. Protecting boundaries also required ensuring that more radical interpretations of commonwealth, those beyond the limits of western or national consensus, met a fate similar to that of the Indians. The hopes of the whiskey men for a commonwealth vision rooted in the right to improvement and curtailing the prerogatives of wealthy speculators and jobbers were not to be fulfilled. Trivializing their activities as an "insurrection," the state's officials would unleash Leviathan to establish the limits of commonwealth. Nonetheless, in an informal fashion the state would support the movement of common settlers streaming west in search of competency. As the federal government reconstituted order, a land settlement, rooted in ambiguity, would emerge as a Revolution settlement, rooted in racial clarity, took shape.[9]

Taken together, the events of 1794 and 1795 represented the stuff of covenant to create commonwealth. The new settlement that emerged formalized older arrangements from the colonial period over access to land, which privileged the wealthy but provided outlets for the poor. Indian hatred, too, an ephemeral phenomenon in colonial America, became a lasting foundation of the nation. And a democratic culture tied to patterns of disaffection from the colonial and Revolutionary periods became codified. Covenants, of course, involve negotiation. And all actors in the West, with the exception of Indians, won and lost in the bargain. Even the state, whose officials wanted orderly settlement or elite rule, would have to recognize the efficacy of popular political mobilization. Although the state asserted sovereignty, the people would remain empowered, and the savagery of whites—now in the service of the state—would be valorized.

As Hobbes had argued more than a century earlier in a place far away during an eerily similar period of ferment, "Covenants without the sword are but words and no strength to secure a man at all." The types of negotiations over land, race, and the meanings of sovereignty in which men such as George Croghan and William Robertson engaged to create an empire did not differ all that much from the ones concluded between the likes of Jefferson and Innes to create a nation. But one failed while the other prevailed because of what Campbell called the "big knife" of Leviathan. Hobbes also understood that the nature of the covenant required "every man" to declare, "I *authorize and give up my right of governing myself to this man, or to this assembly of men, on this condition: that thou give up thy right to him, and authorize all his actions in like manner.*"[10] Common people had to accede to Leviathan for it to be brought into being. For in much the same way common people, acting as insecure subjects, toppled an empire, common people, acting as secure citizens, created the nation.

The covenants that underscored the return to sovereignty also stood as the ideological boundaries of the new nation. In the Ohio valley, Indians were removed, garrison government held sway, settlers and speculators had reached a tacit understanding based on continuing flux, and order was replacing disorder. This was not Dunmore's settlement, one wholly achieved from above. Rather, it took shape during the Revolution and sprang from the desires of common men and women. In other words, the western society taking shape in the 1790s grew out of the nature of frontier violence and uncertainty, the ways people acted in that context as they made sense of it, and the negotiations that ensued. Just as the process of revolution cohered to the distinctive ways western society disintegrated, its reconstruction conformed to the constraints and visions for society that emerged from the Revolutionary crucible. Only as the state and settlers constructed a covenant based on these realities could a revolution be declared over, the commonwealth born, and an American Leviathan sovereign.

The terms of the covenant to create commonwealth were established by two armies that moved west in 1794. One marched to crush what officials had called an excise "rebellion" in western Pennsylvania. As they feared that the spirit of insurrection against federal authority had spread to other regions, Washington and Hamilton decided to strike the area around Pittsburgh. The choice did not prove difficult. The region lay closest to the then national capital of Philadelphia. But more important, officials recognized that western Pennsylvania had become "the grand Warpost of Sedition," the center of a potential site of western sovereignty.[11] In the summer of 1794, as officials of the federal government initiated talks with western Pennsylvanians, they were also readying to assert their own vision of sovereign limits over the West. Washington himself put his stamp on the expedition, visiting the troops in Carlisle amid a great deal of pomp and ceremony. Awed troops showed him an "affectionate regard" and saw him almost as a "Parent." It was a moment that one member of the army considered "a sublime instance of the cheerful subordination of citizens to the call of their Chief for the support of law and order."[12]

The army sent against Tom the Tinker, however, differed little from those sent out West before. "Brother," an outraged westerner warned, "you must not think to frighten us with fine arrayed lists of infantry, cavalry, and artillery, composed of your water-melon armies taken from the Jersey shores." These "would cut a much better figure in warring with the crabs and oysters about the capes of Delaware" than in battling veteran westerners, many of whom had served on the frontier during the war.[13] A great number of those watermelon troops would have preferred to stay on the shore. Men unfit for service experienced the "most horrid and Fatigueing Marches" with mud sometimes up to their knees as they crossed the mountains.[14] One officer had to issue extra gills of whiskey to keep the troops contented.[15] As the troops passed Sideling Hill, considered the worst ascent on the trip, they were now moving into a "Hell" filled with "devils." Those who took the affair seriously either deserted or were tempted to join the insurgents. "If it had not been for whiskey," a participant observed, "many a poor fellow would have given up."[16]

Nonetheless, the watermelon troops prevailed. They did so not through prowess but because a general western rising that the whiskey men had hoped for failed to materialize. These men, in fact, stood alone against the wealthy in western Pennsylvania and the government of the United States as the type of commonwealth they were imagining proved beyond the pale. They also could not rally the disaffected in Kentucky and Ohio, those on the margins who had forged tacit and conditional alliances with local elites in the face of the Indian menace. What the whiskey men clamored for, although it had great appeal among common people throughout the West, could not unite the frontier at this moment. As the army made its way to Pittsburgh, passing Sideling Hill, Braddock's Field, and the fort itself, the "rebels" ran for the hills. Only a small handful of men perished on the campaign, a few by accident, others by sickness. From such august beginnings, the whole affair fizzled out.

The anticlimactic end of the rebellion and the nature of the army that marched west in 1794 obscured something more consequential at work. In that year, a second army marched west, but this one was not formed to "chastise" recalcitrant savages or savage whites. In 1792, President George Washington recalled Anthony Wayne, a veteran of the Revolution, out of retirement to train a force for the rigors of frontier warfare. Unsurprisingly, westerners, who could not conceive that the government would act to secure them, feared that another weak army was preparing to take on the Indians of the Ohio valley and that chastisement once again was the aim. Even as rumors swirled of an expedition, men and women were threatening to leave the frontier. Many believed that the governments of the United States and, in this case, Pennsylvania would not even supply them with much-needed ammunition, never mind mount a campaign of conquest.[17] "The period is now at hand," an exasperated settler wrote to an officer, "that this settlement must absolutely evacuate if no support can be had." He and his neighbors "have lived with great Patience in expectation of help before this time." That expectation had consistently gone unmet. He juxtaposed his sense of unease with news of the "insurgents," who were marauding through the West "without repulse."[18] Perhaps the mention of the rebels served as a veiled warning: if the government would not act against Indians, chaos would continue not only for the West but for the whole nation as well. Nonetheless, having witnessed debacles before, few in the West, especially in western Pennsylvania, wanted to lift a finger for the army.[19]

Many also had misgivings about the appointment of Wayne. Although he was noted for his ferocity, some also remembered him as the man who put down—in ruthless fashion—a mutiny of the Pennsylvania line during the war. Some westerners, mainly of the "old soldier" variety, were "striking" over Washington's choice of commanding general.[20] A group of Kentuckians made the point that Wayne's appointment "Obliged us to give up all expectations of succour from the General Government." Regardless of the commander, "the system of warfare," they stormed, "which is pursued at present by the United States will never humble the Indians or induce them to consent to make a lasting peace."[21]

On this count, they were wrong and they were right. On the one hand, precedent and perception pointed to a feeble and unsympathetic response by government. In fact, it seemed that the state could only act with relative resolve when reining in what it regarded as the excesses of the commonwealth vision. On the other hand, about the time Jefferson was talking about "a great revolution of opinion" and as officials were dispatched to negotiate with Indians, federal officials had decided to act. Washington's administration had asked Congress to set aside $1 million for the War Department to raise and train a proper force of five thousand regulars. This was no army of chastisement. This "Legion of the United States," in fact, was created to conquer. In so doing, it would lay out the other terms of the covenant for commonwealth.[22]

Wayne's army, better prepared than both St. Clair's force and the watermelon troops, proved unlike any assembled in the West since the Seven Years' War. Indeed, it's fair to say that the army sent to put down the insurrection achieved what it did because a much more formidable force was also striking in 1794. The West had teetered between at best a civil war and at worst another war of independence. And until disorder was addressed, the threat of both would continue to loom. The "Affections and Attachments" of settlers, an eastern friend of Arthur Campbell's argued, had to be "governed and regulated by right Reason." The West had reeled from "a sudden and violent Transition from one Extreme into another." As the Ohio valley confronted a "Civil War," he prayed that the government would "not at this Time be embued in the Blood of their Brothers and Fellow-Citizens." He saw a new future. "Let us accompany Wayne to fight the Savages," he pleaded, "let us oppose with manly Vigour those without and within those who would oppress and enslave us." Only this course would stave off "anarchy, endless Confusion and Misery."[23]

Easterners were beginning to understand these sentiments. Indeed, with Wayne's appointment the government planned an expedition "calculated upon a much larger scale." John Brown found that "the augmentation of the Military establishment is alarming to many," especially to a people still harboring deep-seated fears of a standing army.[24] Officials still placed conditions on any military action. The army training would only be unleashed if and when negotiations with Indians broke down.[25] But if and when that happened, Indians would face a determined and well-funded force. "The public will have but one mind" if negotiations faltered, Wayne declared, "as to the vigor with which the War shall be pursued."[26] He argued that no government could fail to prepare for war as Indians continued to attack "whilst we are holding forth the olive branch, and inviting them to peace, upon the most humane and liberal principles." That policy, he conceded, had not worked.[27]

By the end of the summer of 1794, some believed that "war appears . . . to be inevitable—for there is no alternative." Although many still wanted to chastise the Indians, some were beginning to show impatience over the "manner the president means to treat with them." The time had come "to have adopted the language they use with us," the discourse of war.[28]

The temper of the West was changing. American officers stationed at Pittsburgh had worried that weapons, stored at blockhouses as deterrents against Indian attacks, would fall into the hands of the whiskey men. But no longer. As Wayne's legion mobilized, and "as the insurgents have lost that systematic opposition which they were at one time likely to make," such fears "greatly subsided." Cannon could be used for its intended purposes.[29]

The legion, which cared little about stages of development, would conquer through total war. One official in the West had warned the Indians, even as they mocked him "with a universal roar, *vulgarly called farting*," that Wayne would crush them. Most critically, Indians would receive no quarter. Those who resisted "would inevitable be put to death." His army was filled with "*Veterans well disciplined*, and commanded by officers of undoubted courage and, experience, and numbers of whom served in our revolutionary war, and were used to hard fighting." Wayne, he argued, "knows no fear, and there will be no approaching him in any direction with impunity." Even "civilized" Indians had reason to tremble. Wayne would "turn on them" and destroy their homes and "all their comforts."[30]

On August 20, 1794, Wayne once again proved himself "that Thunderbolt of War."[31] On that day, his army defeated a confederation of Native Americans on the Maumee River at a place called Fallen Timbers. The battle did not amount to a mythic victory. "The loss on both sides was trifling," John Breckinridge wrote. Nonetheless, the expedition achieved a level of success greater than that imagined under the earlier campaigns of chastisement. Breckinridge wrote, "As it is the first stand the arms of the U. States have ever made against the Indians, I think it will produce good consequences."[32] The troops maintained discipline, defeating the Indians by holding their ground and executing a frightening bayonet charge. Federal troops treated Indians with a hitherto unknown ferocity. One, for instance, cut off the heads of two Indians with two strokes. Others cut them down as they tried to flee to a nearby British post. A racially charged fury also defined some of the fighting. Enraged soldiers, for instance, savaged those British they found—white men—because they were dressed like Indians.[33]

At Wayne's headquarters at Greenville in the Ohio Country, Indians learned of the nature of their new world. The defeated Ohio valley Indians assembled there embodied all stages of development from the savage to the civilized. A visitor to this "Grand Parade" of humanity named David Barrow, a Baptist minister, noted that some Indians spoke "tolerable English" and French, while others epitomized "human nature without disguise unassisted by the arts." Both were surrounded in Greenville by a growing number of American troops, as more and more continued to travel west. Barrow trembled at the attitudes of American officials and soldiers, some of whom had embraced the sentiments of the settlers around them. "I well remember," he recounted, "to have heard many of the whites swear if they could catch one of them out, they would kill them as soon as a deer."[34] Whites had become the savages of the West.

The resulting treaty reflected these by now prevalent attitudes. It established a firm line well north of the Ohio River separating Indian lands from white lands, with the confederation promising to "cede and relinquish forever all their claims" to much of the Ohio valley. Wayne drew this line not to keep settlers from Indian territory—the rationale behind the British Proclamation Line—but to keep Indians from white lands. The treaty therefore won much of what would be the state of Ohio and a southern section of what would be the Indiana Territory for white settlement. But as Indians began leaving the Ohio valley after the battle, it effectively made nearly all of Ohio and Kentucky and all of western Pennsylvania and Virginia a no-go area for Indians. For settlers, it promised the "joy of an uninterrupted peace with the Indians." Unsurprisingly, after the treaty "the party spirit" settlers had felt against Wayne was "declining."[35]

While Wayne wielded the "big knife" of sovereignty, officials also addressed other issues that had kept the West, as settlers argued, in the state of war. Some feared that although the Indians had been defeated, the British would remain, continuing to pose a threat for the West. William Preston, writing his brother John from Greenville, declared that most of those assembled for the treaty expected "an uninterrupted peace with the Indians." He added, however, "tho how long this will continue God only knows as the Brittish are useing all their art to send them to war again by giving them much larger presents than they used to do." Although the British did not allow fleeing Indians to enter their fort near Fallen Timbers for fear it would rekindle hostilities with the Americans, they were "repairing the Fort at Detroit"—the old nerve center of the British-Indian alliance—and did not intend "to deliver it up."[36] Most troubling, "the extraordinary appointment of Jay," a person John Breckinridge called "the evil Genius of this country," as the chief American negotiator with the British, did not inspire confidence in government resolve to finish what it had started in the West.[37] Because of disputes between the executive and the legislative branches, problems over personalities, and Jay's reputation, westerners expected more delays.[38] Settlers also feared that the government was doing little about the Mississippi and that the factious nature of politics in the East would bring the process of negotiations to a halt.[39] So although a western peace appeared on the horizon, other concerns threatened "the common cause of the Western People," especially "the tame submission of the general government" to Britain and Spain at the expense of the frontier. "Protection," after all, still represented the "grievance of the greatest magnitude."[40]

By 1795, however, the government would meet western demands for protection and address the consensual ideas behind frontier commonwealth in nearly all their guises. On November 19, 1794, John Jay signed a treaty of friendship with Britain that, although compromising American sovereignty and independence in foreign affairs, guaranteed the British would leave the frontier. Even if Indians still wanted to fight, in other words, they would receive no support in doing so. In the minds of westerners, the departure of the British from the West ensured the years of worry had ended. About the same time, Thomas Pinckney's diplomatic mission to Madrid secured free navigation of the Mississippi for westerners. As agitation over western concerns was reaching a crescendo, therefore, federal officials were responding with vigor on a number of fronts.[41]

Including the manner in which they would defend the western settlement. The Treaty of Greenville stipulated that in the midst of Indian country, the United States would maintain forts and the lands surrounding them. These included nearly every significant portage east of the Mississippi, key trading posts as far west as the "Chikago river," soon-to-be-abandoned British forts and posts, and the confluences of major rivers. Indians also relinquished 150,000 acres of land "near the rapids of the river Ohio" for George Rogers Clark and "his warriors." Between all ceded lands east and west of the treaty line, "the people of the United States" would enjoy a "free passage."[42] Here sovereignty would be made manifest. William Preston reported that detachments of the army remained in the West after the conclusion of treaty negotiations. They were "building a Garrison [and] it is thought that two or three Forts will be built before they return."[43] After Fallen Timbers, most frontier counties reported that they had sufficient protection.[44] County militias were "mustered out," even from what had been regarded as exposed regions, with the exception of a number of "Woodsmen."[45]

In other words, federally administered garrison government would control the West. Eventually, Detroit became a depot for the transit of troops to administer and safeguard the expanding frontier. And under Jefferson's presidency, the army would number thirty-two hundred troops, most stationed in the West. The new American government thrown into a crisis over western demands had learned from the British example. Although supporting a standing army seemed anathema to the principles of the War of Independence, officials understood that western land had to be held by a visible and credible force that would maintain the integrity of the line and the government's claims to sovereignty. Government could not rely on the good faith of Indians or the deference of white settlers.[46]

Officials of all political stripes had their motives in conquering the West. Some believed that only if the new nation expanded across space could they keep the republican experiment alive. Sooner or later, therefore, Indians would have to be removed or would have to embrace the broader culture. Others with less well developed ideas concluded that order had to prevail to rein in the excesses of revolution. These sought not so much to win the West as to quiet it and, in so doing, create the conditions for incremental and orderly settlement. Ends and means, therefore, converged in the conquest of the confederacy of Ohio Indians. In the process, however, the state met the conditions laid out by westerners for the return of sovereignty, effectively ending the perception that the East would not or could not secure the West. After the two armies had marched, western Americans perceived the first signs of "a Permanent Peace." Although they remained cautious, for the first time in many years they sensed a hopeful future. "We are now never without a Party of the hostile Indians amongst us," a soldier at Greenville reported to those at home. These, however, were not raiding but arriving "for a permanent treaty." He knew "the Indians too well to trust to any thing they may please [to] advance." Still, he had a newfound faith in the federal government. Senators, he had heard, would keep "the army upon its Present Establishment" in the new West. He noted that the following fall he and his comrades would "march to Sanduskey and there erect a Garrison." The selection of Sandusky was fitting and telling. By choosing it, Americans were claiming that never again would whites be tortured by Indians in the Ohio valley. The symbolism of place could not have been lost on Indians. Near the place where vigilantes had slaughtered innocents, the federal government would now protect settlers.[47]

After the suppression of the rebellion and Wayne's defeat of the Indian confederacy, a traveler to the West noted that "the people in this quarter appear perfectly quiet, and much more friendly than in November last." He continued that "they talk but little politics, and excise is scarcely ever mentioned," and "the utmost tranquility seems to prevail." The visitor did not attribute this turn of events to the "victory" of Washington's army over the whiskey men. Rather, he suggested that the treaty with the defeated tribes was the source of newfound optimism in the West.[48] As an observer had prophesied in 1792, "The strong arm of the Union ought to be outstretched to protect all its citizens, and nothing will effect that protection, on the Western Frontiers, but carrying devastation into the hearts of the Indian Villages."[49] That arm was now outstretched.

Some feared a return to chaos after Wayne's victory. Speculators and settlers, or so it was believed, would resume their fight over access to land, or states would try to employ squatters to claim territory. The competition that defined the western revolution, in other words, would continue. Nothing of the sort happened.[50] The West, in fact, graduated from its state of war. Timothy Pickering declared in 1796 that the days of chaos had ended at last. The Ohio valley, he argued, enjoyed "universal quiet."[51] He was right. The man whom one officer at Fort Washington called "Thy Solomon" had transformed the West. Wayne had ensured that the most hostile Indians were preparing to move not only beyond the Greenville line but beyond the Mississippi as well.[52] As Indians left, more settlers entered. "Indeed," as John Brown put it, with Wayne's victory, "the prospect of migration to the westward exceeds any thing ever known before."[53] William Preston, a long veteran of the West's troubles, summed up the changes that were transforming the Ohio valley. In December 1795, he wrote a friend that Wayne was leaving the frontier for Philadelphia. The fight for the West had ended. Preston wished his friend good luck in his "speculative pursuits" and wished "that when we meet again fortune may place us in a situation to spend the balance of our days in ease free from the cares and toils of War and injury."[54]

Within a remarkably short period of time, westerners were constructing the outward signs of society. In March 1795, to cite just one example, Kentuckians wrote a letter "to the People of the Atlantic States of America" for help. The plea no longer focused on protection. Nor did it claim westerners as a distinct people of a sovereign western nation. Rather, these

Kentuckians saw themselves as one with easterners, though with distinctive claims to the blessings of society and with a distinctive mission in the unified nation. The West, they argued, was "an infant country" just delivered from chaos in dire need of godly ministers and "the defusion of Literature." What had been luxuries during war became necessities during peace. Hoping to establish a "seminary of learning" named the Kentucky Academy, they asked for contributions for what would become the country's first trans-Appalachian college, Transylvania University. They knew that trade would come and the state would become wealthy. But as it did, they needed pastors who would help the people make sense of the trappings of wealth. "You are fully apprized," they confidently declared, "that neither Physicians, Lawyers, states-Men nor Spiritual Guides can exercise their functions with propriety, without that Superior degree of knowledge which is most easily and surely obtained in seminaries of learning." They therefore needed donations from their "fellow citizens of the Atlantic States." They had a special claim to this aid. Their bloodshed had earned it. The sacrifices of westerners, they believed, had benefited the whole nation and would continue to do so. "Multitudes of you or your posterity will shortly share the advantages" that had been wrought by western sacrifice.[55]

The West, of course, did not enjoy a period of perfect harmony. Tensions still existed between individuals and groups. Settlers still robbed and killed. People still lived with fear. But these remnants or stains of violence now represented aberrations, not the rule. In November 1795, for instance, a resident of Morgantown complained that a number of settlers from Kentucky were stealing horses. Following the treaty, as Indians were heading west, Alexander Buchanan and Charles Schoolcroft planned on robbing them. Although they were warned their actions might "irritate the Indians," they "persisted and went on," stealing three horses and selling them. Peace, therefore, was not perfect. But as trade began to flourish and peace seemed secure, the years of unfettered violence and disorder ended.[56]

The new cultural parameters of western society were becoming discernible a short time after Wayne's victory. Most conspicuously, Indians, such as the group robbed of their horses, would bear the cost of peace. A man named Logan understood what the future would hold for Indians. A nephew to and namesake of the famous Logan whose kin whites had savaged on the eve of Dunmore's War and who then began a campaign of retribution, the younger Logan vowed never to take up arms against settlers again. Resignation, rather than fear, encouraged him to take this path. When a jobber turned petty official from the East encountered Logan, he "was astonished to see the tears rolling down his manly cheeks very copiously." This Logan was suffering from what he called "a disease of the mind" ever since the Americans had "laid *us and the British on our backs.*" In the meantime, he feared, the power of the whites would grow and that of Indians would continue to diminish.

Violence and uncertainty would continue for Indians. Although the easterner tried to argue that the whites "were not so savage," Logan knew "that it is otherwise." "You have destroyed our towns and sometimes by surprise," he countered, "and you never spared any." The official asked Logan to give him one example. Logan gave him "a look of *surprise and indignation.*" He had only to mention one place: Gnadenhütten. "There was a town on the Muskingum river, settled by some of your good white people amongst the Indians," he explained. These whites were not like the rest who headed west. They "had persuaded a number of indians to cease going to war, to cultivate the ground, and to worship the Great Spirit, after the manner of these good white men, and not after the manner the indians used to." They had embraced the mantle of white-defined civility. "And what became of them?" Logan asked.

Although for whites the West had been redeemed, Logan could never know salvation. The jobber asked after his famous uncle. That Logan, the nephew replied, had died eight years earlier. He had killed him. The younger Logan said that "it was the order of the nation." His uncle's eloquence, reputation, and skills as a warrior, the nation had believed, would have brought quick and certain ruin to Indians. Ironically, of course, ruin had come nonetheless. "He was a very, very, great man," he declared, and "I am ready to die."[57]

Easterners were beginning to appreciate that irony. Dead or nonthreatening Indians, such as the famous Logan, indeed possessed greatness. But those living like his nephew were destined for oblivion. While some easterners believed Indians "incapable of civilization," officials such as Washington and Knox, though dispatching Wayne west, still believed that Indians could with time be civilized.[58] Thomas Jefferson, famously, had written that in terms of capacity Indians equaled whites. In fact, he employed stadial theory to do so, demonstrating its utility to explain American development and culture. Jefferson agreed with scholars like William Robertson, a man whose work he knew and admired, as well as Francis Hutcheson, who had a great influence on his thinking, that Indians and whites shared a common human sensibility. While these Scots had the Highlands, a place noted for its barbaric people, as a laboratory for their "conjectural" history, Jefferson and the Americans had the West and its savages.[59] "Civilization," Jefferson believed, alone made men different. And whites "in equal barbarism" would act as Indians. In fact, in some ways Indians surpassed whites. As a people, they regarded "eloquence in council, bravery and address in war" more highly than European cultures. Indeed, they had produced an orator the equal of Cicero, the very man whom the young Logan had killed.[60]

But the ground had shifted since 1763, when such views enjoyed widespread acceptance. There is, of course, an ebb and a flow to Indian hating. After all, the tensions of 1675 and 1676 had given way to the long peace of the early eighteenth century. But at this juncture settlers had come to hate Indians and consider them irredeemable at a critical time. At the moment this wave reaching tidal proportions through decades of violence crashed, local elites had either subscribed to the views of common settlers or dignified their ideas with tacit approval. In fact, in the bid to maintain order in the West, federal officials were now acting to sustain this vision. In other words, essentialist ideas—ephemeral as they might have been in the past—gripped the imagination of a nation when negotiations were taking place to bring revolution to a close, to make sovereignty meaningful, and to create commonwealth. In the 1760s, stadial theory when applied to the American West held that Indians and whites should be kept apart to safeguard Indians so as to civilize them. In the 1790s, the same sets of ideas held that whites and Indians had to be separated to protect whites so as to safeguard order. In Croghan's and William Johnson's world, nearly all assumed that men and women, including Indians, could move up the stadial ladder or that cultures could progress over time with the right influences. By the 1790s, the stadial formula in practice could only work for whites. For the British, the idea of civility could stand as a protection for Indians, and served as the foundation of empire. A generation later, the idea of civility ensured the removal of Indians, a notion that would animate a nation. Francis Hutcheson, whose ideas lay at the heart of stadial assumptions, had conceived of the moral sense to refute Hobbesian assumptions of human behavior and understanding. Ironically, many of these same ideas, espoused now by luminaries such as Jefferson, harbored very different implications in part because of the Hobbesian nature of the revolutionary West and the ways in which common people had made sense of that world.[61]

After the Paxton Boys had finished their murderous spree, Benjamin Franklin had caught a glimpse of this future, but he derided it as too far-fetched to believe. Franklin had viewed the combination of essentialist and stadial visions of humanity as an absurdity. In his estimation, a world in which "white Christians" acted like "savages" amounted to an aberration, something to be condemned because it contradicted nature's law. Because "whites" had acted as "savages" on a regular basis for thirty more years, the absurd had become reality. In Jefferson's America, this reality had come to define the tacit agreement holding the new nation together in which Jefferson reasoned like a supporter of the Paxton Boys, unwilling or unable to wait for civilizing influences to take hold, and common settlers had become what Franklin had hardly dared to imagine, racist monsters. Although Jefferson did not share the racist assumptions—at least when it came to Indians—of the settlers living to the west, he had reached the same conclusions about the future of Indians. They could not stand in the way of western expansion. Not surprisingly, Jefferson would be the first president to imagine an America east of the Mississippi completely free from Indians.[62]

At the very moment that western assumptions about Indians converged with eastern aims for the West, settlers and speculators, easterners and westerners, were also forging a land settlement.[63] To be sure, in the aftermath of the rising of the whiskey men, it appeared that the land would be inherited by the wealthy. In western Pennsylvania, the place where common settlers, speculators, and jobbers fought over rights of improvement, wealth grew even more concentrated as a smaller number of men engrossed more of the land once peace and security had come. Mobility and tenancy would define the lot in life of the poorer sort.[64]

The apparent triumph of the wealthy obscured a more subtle process at work, one that defined the nature of land settlement emerging in the Ohio valley both north and south of the river, as growing numbers of settlers streamed in hoping to claim land once peace was formalized. In Ohio, federal officials for all intents and purposes did away with the right to improvement. Hoping to raise revenue off the region once war had ended, the government passed the Land Act of 1796. The act doubled the amount of money each acre had cost under the Land Ordinance of 1785 but maintained the minimum sale allotment, thus keeping poorer men and women from gaining rightful title to a great deal of valuable land near prospective towns and markets. Ironically, the regions won over to white settlement by the Treaty of Greenville would fall under the purview of the act. To pay off federal debt and keep the land jobbers attached to the fledgling state, the government, in fact, pandered to speculators. In 1800, officials relented after they had failed to raise significant revenues, decreasing the sale allotment and allowing settlers to purchase land on credit after placing a sizable deposit. Land would be sold through public auction. While poorer settlers could rarely hope to raise the money to purchase land under such a scheme, the government enshrined the right to preemption, the boon of speculators and jobbers. The land acts therefore mimicked Virginia's land settlement in Kentucky. Orderly settlement, it was hoped, would attract the right sort of settler and accomplish the government's goal of revenue and stability. To oversee the process, the state created a sizable administration in the West.[65]

Similarly, in Kentucky wealthy settlers consolidated their hold on the land as soon as peace came. With the opening of the Mississippi and the departure of Indians, the Bluegrass quickly was transformed from a wilderness to a settled society that resembled hierarchical Virginia. At the top reigned planters, and at the bottom were slaves, who were displacing white tenants as the region's labor force. Poorer whites owned less and less land as the Bluegrass became more and more developed. In the Green River region, by contrast, squatters sought and received relief in 1795 and 1797. But over time, through preemption rights that these relief acts and another in 1800 guaranteed, those willing to amass more land than was needed to earn a competency began to dominate the region. This, too, became an area defined by slave labor, concentrations of wealth, the market, and landlessness. As this happened, the right to improvement was no longer recognized. In both the Bluegrass and the Green River, those many who tried to claim land through "traditional" rights had to face down those few who made and executed the law.[66]

All throughout the West, the jobbers and those most attuned to law and the market would win the West. Some gained land through provisions such as the Virginia land law of 1779. Some were able to purchase federal land on credit. Some received land bounties as veterans or, the lucky few, donation lands. The rest, those less fortunate, less savvy or well connected, or less ruthless, would have to labor as tenants or move. Neither the federal land acts nor the commercial development of Kentucky, therefore, stopped squatting. Far from it. In fact, the land settlement of the Ohio valley encouraged those seeking competency to move west of the Ohio Country onto Indian lands. The years of peace, therefore, heightened restlessness and mobility throughout the Ohio River valley. Like land under the old process of frontier development, that available under the new system would lie on the edge of western settlement, and settlers would once more serve as a "hedge" between white areas of settlement and Indian lands. The new system thus formalized an older informal arrangement. In other words, although poorer men and women had few possibilities of settling on their own terms in established regions, they could still stay one step ahead of the wealthy if they were willing to move farther west.[67]

But common men and women would no longer stray onto Indian land alone. They were now preceded by troops and surveyors, agents of the state and the market. During times of stress, such as the War of 1812, squatters farther west of Ohio would once again use the window of unsettledness to claim land. Although government officials formally warned them off and condemned them as "evil disposed persons," at the same time, as the number of those staking claims through improvement grew to unmanageable proportions, they granted amnesties or relief. In these instances, a grateful nation would once again reward those who along with the army stood against the savage foe, valorizing the common settler but consigning succeeding generations to the same rootlessness.[68]

The 1795 settlement ensured that the right to improvement would not be formally recognized but tacitly and grudgingly tolerated from time to time. The new land arrangement recognized those who confronted Indians, those willing to move beyond accepted bounds who paved the way for commercial development. Certainly settlers saw things this way. "The first adventurers to this then disart country," a 1794 remonstrance to the General Assembly of Kentucky read, "were imperiled hither with the view and expectation of acquiring lands for themselves and their posterity." These people had "sought out, fought for, and maintained the country, after having spilt their best blood, and encountered inexpressible distresses and difficulties." True, officials from Virginia had recognized the rights of the first adventurers, those who had suffered during the years of darkest violence. More recent settlers, who likewise had sacrificed throughout the "Indian wars," argued they were entitled to land as well. The "unequivocal consent of all," the political foundation of the state of Kentucky, mandated land "for rescuing a country from the Hands of savages." After all, those with the largest claims, just as much as the squatter, could lose out to "the modern tricky land jobber," who would "beggar the innocent, the unwary and the meritorious first adventurers."[69]

The relationship between citizens and western lands inscribed in the Treaty of Greenville reflected the formalization of ambiguity and unsettledness. In it, Indians agreed to relinquish lands they sought to sell in the future to the federal government. Only the state had this right. The state would determine where settlement would occur; its citizens did not have a free hand to settle where they pleased. "Such citizens or other persons," the treaty stipulated, "shall be out of the protection of the United States."[70] The British had tried to accomplish the same goal by declaring that men and women who moved beyond the Proclamation Line into non-subject regions surrendered their privileges as subjects, including the right to protection. The region beyond the American line was still a place of incivility. But whereas officials of the empire tried to but could not stop settlers from moving over the line, the new nation's officials had interests in allowing settlement on Indian lands. In this context, the words of the treaty had little practical meaning. An ambiguous land settlement in which formal prohibitions did not mesh with what was happening on the ground, in fact, served the interests of the state in promoting orderly settlement. Common settlers proved a useful vanguard. Unsettledness, in short, created the conditions of settledness in the West as it prepared the way for expansion.[71]

Jefferson's famous "empire of liberty," therefore, took shape from the covenant. Indian territory, in fact, formed a safety valve for the nation, allowing the land settlement to retain its now formalized informal character. The promise of limitless land ensured that conflict over property could be blunted and minimized the possibility that chaos, such as that unleashed by the whiskey men, would return. With troops stationed in the West, citizens in perpetual motion, and surveyors and officials seeking the next cession, an expansionist empire of liberty not only jibed with ideological imperatives. It also made practical sense, guaranteeing that the covenant between various participants in the Ohio valley and between East and West would not be broken. Empire in the West was the ransom paid for the birth of a nation.

The state not only established the limits of commonwealth by refusing to allow it to stray beyond the western consensus but also acted as its arbiter or umpire by codifying the trade-offs of covenant. A democratic political culture, for example, which had blossomed in the disorder of revolution, became a foundation of the American West at the time of settlement. Common whites and those local elites who had come to see eye to eye over Indians would ensure that universal manhood suffrage became the rule, not the exception, as trans-Appalachian states entered the Union. Even in Ohio, where landholding qualifications for voting were established by the Northwest Ordinance, settlers would demand and win a more egalitarian settlement, allowing virtually all white men to vote. In Kentucky, the legal confusion over landholding and the uneasy accommodation worked out between settlers and officials combined to ensure that all white men would enjoy the franchise regardless of property owned or tax paid.[72] Moreover, officials from states like Pennsylvania recognized the rights of westerners to equal representation within state legislatures, an issue that had nagged frontier settlers since the end of the Seven Years' War.[73] Even the meanest settlers had inherent claims to life, liberty, and property as whites.

They had something more. Settlers had earned such rights through their sacrifice. The political rights of the poorer sort, rooted in an ability to stand up to manipulation, therefore proved as fundamental as Indian hating to the culture of the West and the larger Revolution settlement. In fact, as Alexis de Tocqueville later recognized and as officials had to acknowledge in the 1790s, democracy meant more than voting rights. It had become "a habit of the heart," which in the context of the western revolution was refined through disaffection with authority, rituals of violence, and the creation of a coherent ideology. In the post-Revolutionary West, the wealthy could not afford to ignore or manipulate the now-politicized people around them. Through their revolution, the poor did not inherit the earth or the levers of state; but they could claim a right to the margins of each.[74]

Settlers beheld a new West. Noah Linsly, traveling from Morgantown to Marietta in 1797, saw the West as others had seen it a generation before, as an idyllic state of nature. "The Western Counties of Penna. are very hilly," he wrote, "but the land is in general very good." He also discovered a nascent society in the West: "The inhabitants are a mixture of every thing; but not altogether so rough and uncivilized as I expected to find them." He found even the settlers of Washington a "well informed, agreeable people." Here the "practice of Law" flourished, a development that none scarce imagined only a few years before. Many were still "indolent and poor." Linsly, however, expected this to change. Lands in the region were selling between $4 and $8 an acre, a price sure to entice the industrious. For the wealthier, hundred-acre lots on the Muskingum were going for $500. Linsly's West, in other words, represented the best of two worlds, a land of promise and a land of fulfillment.[75]

America's future lay there. In 1804, an easterner named James Gibbons made the trek over the mountains to Ohio. On first seeing the Ohio River, he could not believe his eyes. "The Ohio," he declared, "is a beautiful stream of water, I think the handsomest I ever saw." He also saw opportunity. While gazing at the river, he "contemplated in Idea the future grandeur of this western world — when the stream should be covered with vessels spreading their canvass to the wind, to convey the produce of this fertile country to New Orleans and across the Atlantick Ocean." Of this, he had no doubt. "Every thing that our Country produces," he gushed, "grows here with a luxuriousness unknown to us." All a family needed, he argued, was a tent in which to sleep, a little money to purchase land far to the west, and some time to build a cabin and plant some seeds. Cheap land, he conceded, would not be simple to find. It would require some work, but by his reckoning even the poor had a place in this "New Canaan."[76]

The elements missing from these accounts, however, proved as telling as those described. Neither Gibbons nor Linsly made mention of troops garrisoning the West, whose presence underscored the order they assumed. The lengths the poorer sort would have to go to claim land of their own were not clear. Nor did either discuss Indians even in passing. The western world without Indians that Daniel Boone had begun to imagine at the close of the War of Independence had come to pass. If the frontier had reverted to a state of nature as society began to flourish, it had done so having lost its innocence, its idyllic character now tempered by the violence that begot it, the absence of Indians the most conspicuous sign of that past. The West had fallen but now was redeemed by the blood and chaos of revolution. Indians, of course, as Boone understood, served as the chief sacrifice. The western world once again enjoyed peace, but one now ensured by the presence of soldiers, the absence of Indians, the movement of a politicized citizenry, and silence about each of these.

Some understood the complex mix of promise and perdition that animated the West. In 1797, Elias Backus wrote a letter to a friend in Philadelphia to complain of the place to which he had ventured. The place he had settled named Belle Isle near Marietta swung "from the pleasures of society, to the horrors of solitude." Here he encountered a society of sorts, but one not to his liking. "Surrounded by a sett of tenants ruder than the savages themselves—and consoled in these misfortunes, by the melancholy moanings, of the midnight owl," he longed for the "agreeable scenes" of the East "when we skimmed the cream (and sometimes the broth) from society."[77]

Such contradictions defined the new West. In 1795, David Barrow, traveling through the Ohio Country as he left his native Virginia for Kentucky, noted wagonloads of families venturing over "the most western verge of this august pyramid of nature," Laurel Hill, where they beheld "a most delightful prospect." Animals grazed on "a delightful plain checkered with rich farms." The fact that common men and women lived off the plenty of western Pennsylvania "entirely exempt from the horride cause of negro slavery" delighted Barrow. The issue of slavery, he suggested, divided and distinguished regions north and south of the Ohio River in fundamental ways. A different, though related, curse "absolutely inconsistent with every idea of republicanism as well as humanity and christianity," however, blighted both banks of the river. Settlers, he discovered, still "pretend[ed] to ascendancy one over another." They considered Indians "hardly of the same species." Their "prejudices and interests" were such that they could not "impartially think and reason on the subject." Barrow preached the old and by-now-irrelevant theme of civility. "Do not the men," he asked, "decently cover their nakedness [with] breech clothes and the women with shrouds?" The customs of Indians, he argued, "are not more extra ordinary than are practiced by our nymphs and fops in this most enlightened and Christianized age." If they attacked with savagery, "who provoked them to these acts of cruelty?" he asked. The "white Christians" had "learned them" savage ways by crossing "the boundary lines."

Barrow sensed a direct link between the evils of slavery and anti-Indian racism. "If the Indians whip and cruelly treat the whites; it is no more than the whites serve the blacks," he argued. Kentuckians, especially, who owned slaves had only reaped what they had sown. Even the meanest white enjoyed the right to "suffrage." And these he found the most cruel of the species. They wanted not peaceful coexistence with Indians but the peace that came with domination. Westerners could not accept what he regarded as a self-evident truth. "For my part," he wrote, "upon calm reflection I think man is man in every age, in every clime, in whatsoever dress whatever color or circumstance; and all are alike good . . . and equal by nature." All could be "reformed," presumably even racist whites.

Yet even Barrow could not perceive how the utilitarian ways he viewed the West excluded Indians from its future. Because of the recent past and the new nation's appetite for the wealth of the West, Indians, he conceded, would have to live with their own "boundaries." After all, the regions open to whites were destined to become a "rich property in the greatest proportion that is to be found in the whole of North America if not the whole world," and settlers would travel here "beyond numeration." Although he did not mention why common people would have to move restlessly from place to place, the implications were clear for Indians. The use of the Mississippi "would open a sufficient door to all the western world." Social development inevitably would reach its most advanced stage. In the future, his descendants would find "first rate buildings and occupied with as polite inhabitants as are to be found in any part of the United States or perhaps in the known world." The West had a special role to play in the providential plan. "It appears to me that this country is designed by the great parent of the universe as the seat or stage of some of the last scenes," he declared.

Although Barrow believed the West was still "the dark and bloody ground," he argued that this old name for the region, one with violent connotations that summed up the past thirty years in the Ohio valley, could be made anew. "The growth of trees in those countries," he asserted as he redefined the famous phrase, "is so luxurious that they form a shade so universal and add thereto the darkness of the soil." In this new world, the past held new meanings. Unlike Jefferson, he condemned slavery without equivocation and saw a link between it and the treatment of Indians. But like Jefferson, he had to accept—however reluctantly—that the future of Indians had been written by frontier settlers he condemned and lionized in the same breath and by his own assumptions of national progress and expansion. He could live with the West's contradictions, in other words, even as he disparaged or ignored them.[78]

Easterners may have condemned this new West, but they also were drawn to its curiosities, to those who had shaped its distinctive features. One such curiosity was Thomas Cresap. Thomas, of course, had been the father of Michael, the man who in popular memory had touched off Dunmore's bid for the West. The elder Cresap had also worked as a gun for hire on the frontier as a young man in the 1730s. When Benjamin Smith Barton ran across a person he took to be Thomas Cresap in 1799, he "was then in his 103 year," though some, he hastened to add, asserted that he was 110. According to Barton, the old colonel lived in Old Town on the western border of Maryland and Virginia along the Potomac and "was perfectly blind" and nearly deaf. Still, "he was continually declaiming, in the most violent language against the Indians." Although no Indians lived near Old Town any longer, Cresap could not escape the past. Barton must have seen a ghost. Thomas Cresap had passed away years earlier. But as Barton's experience illustrates, the memory of Cresap and that of his son would live on even as the West progressed. Although the Cresaps remained as relics of a revolution now passed, killers in the abstract who spoke to a bygone age, they and their ilk had won and inherited the West.[79]

Speculators and officials may not have liked the contours of the new West, but they could do little to change them. Similarly, settlers had to settle for much less than they had hoped. But such give-and-take was in keeping with the covenant that had brought revolution to a close. The West was distinctive, and the government would guarantee it remained that way. The world Indians now inhabited, hemmed in and pressed farther west, proved more pernicious than any Dunmore or Connolly could have imagined. The boundary line would move. The essentialist logic of its erection, including the new system of land settlement, as well as the hard bargaining that went into reconciling East and West, dictated as much. Henry Knox tried to wash his hands of the whole affair, but to no avail. "A future historian," he wrote, "may mark the causes of this destruction of the human race in sable colours." The common people of the West had pushed for this to happen. Yet he understood the dilemma he and others

faced and how the government had to act. "Although the present government of the United States cannot with propriety be involved in the oppro-
brium," he argued, "yet it seems necessary . . . that some powerful
attempts should be made to tranquilize the frontiers, particularly those
south of the Ohio." The people, after all, "loudly demand the interference
and protection of government."[80]

Knox claimed that government acted almost as an "invisible hand" in
the West, quietly responding to the people. Federal authorities had reacted
to popular sovereignty, as he suggested, but not in the way he implied. The
state did not act as an impartial and unwilling participant in the business
of holding a nation together. He and others had made a choice to see the
world like westerners rather than lose the West, a choice that even British
imperialists had not made. Americans had signed the awful covenant. After years of upheaval, during which no empire, nation, or state could impose its authority on the West, only an American Leviathan had brought
an end to the Ohio valley's state of war, creating the conditions for a new
society to emerge.

A fellow by the name of John Gano, who had moved to the area
around Cincinnati in 1787 and witnessed the final years of revolution, saw
the fruits of the federal government's hand in the stark transformations in
the offing by the end of the 1790s. With the Treaty of Greenville, he argued, as "hostilities ceased, and the settlements began to increase rapidly
every thing relating to them put on a new aspect." What he called "a laudable ambition and emulation" prevailed. People still competed in the West
but to see "who should open the most Land for cultivation get the first fruit
and raise the most grain pork and Beef." Settlers built mills. "The change
was great," he announced: "From alarm, Danger, and Death which the
inhabitants was exposed to, peace plenty and bright prospects of wealth
and happiness began to open to view."

Though the luxuries of the East "began to find their way into the
wilderness," while the land of the wealthy, close to towns, grew in value,
common men and women were destined to "move to the frontiers where
land was cheap and game plenty." This necessity that emerged from revolution took on the cast of virtue in the new West. "The woodsman or
hunter," Gano believed, "tho he often undergoes the most severe hardship
and privations and exposed in every way cannot be reconciled to the
Labours of the husbandman or farmer." Experience and inclination

did not equip him for the settled life. "He would prefer mounting hills passing Vales fording nay swimming streams half starved to following the plough and taking his regular refreshment and rest." In the new West, the value of common whites hinged on embracing what had been considered a barbarous or even savage existence. These characteristics, formerly an empire's curse, now became a nation's strength. In this post-Revolutionary society of sorts, human worth no longer depended on cultural development. With the fracturing of the older notion of civility, the white savages that Gano described owed their place in society to their skin color. Gano concluded that "this may be considered in some measure as the depravity of human nature." But he saw something else at work. Indians, he argued, had been right but in ways they dared not imagine. What had happened in the West "makes the Indian adage good. Can't make [an] Indian [a] White Man, but soon make [a] White Man [an] Indian."[81]

This tale that white savagery won the West, of course, proved just as absurd as the racist notions that gave rise to it. Only the participation of the state accomplished the task. Yet transforming the trade-offs and realities of revolution into the myth of its settlement gave even the poorest living on the edge of subsistence and society a stake in the new world arising in their midst and the new nation now united. Such fables that Gano peddled made the uncomfortable contradictions of the frontier revolution reconcilable. Durable and potentially explosive divisions, such as those separating who could afford to settle near towns and those who had to move, softened in the telling of such stories. Other divisions, all too easy to acknowledge for a people who had suffered years in a state of war, hardened. Pushing Indians out of the new West allowed even the meanest settlers a privileged position in a post-Revolutionary society and in the Revolutionary memory. With even civilized Indians excluded from the West and from memory, only white savages remained. However savage they had become, they had done so in the service of white civilization. In reality of course, the government concluded this sordid business. But white settlers had also pressed officials to follow this course, and in this way they became the quintessential heroes of the American Revolution.[82]

By the end of the War of Independence, a French settler in America named Hector St. John Crèvecoeur was already sensing what these types of people meant to the nation and its character or identity. "What, then, is the American, this new man?" he famously asked. He was a citizen of "the most perfect society now existing in the world." The old distinctions of rank and status that defined European culture had no meaning here. Rich and poor alike enjoyed "a pleasing uniformity of decent competence." America was becoming the seat of a new civilization, "a new social system," and "a new race of men." Perhaps, he argued, the most distinctive person to emerge from a war of independence that was giving birth to this exceptional society was the frontiersman. Settlers, far removed from government, were still living in a stunted society, trapped in what Crèvecoeur called "often a perfect state of war; that of man against man, sometimes decided by blows, sometimes by means of the law." On the "extended line of frontiers," visitors encountered "barbarous rudiments." Here, as Crèvecoeur put it, "many families exhibit the most hideous parts of our society." Yet they and their customs had a critical role to play in the new nation. Savagery and barbarism were needed to clear the land for more "industrious" sorts. They then would "recede still farther." As he argued, "Such is our progress." In other words, for civility to take hold for the nation as a whole, some had to remain in primitive states. "The impure part," he argued, "serves as our precursors or pioneers."[83]

Sovereignty entails a history. It also depends on myth.[84] The sacrifices of these people, suffering and embracing an ennobling savagery, made America as an idea possible. Only a people "ferocious, gloomy, and unsocial" wedded to "lawless profligacy," reflecting the rude wildernesses they conquered, could tame the continent. Ironically, Crèvecoeur added, these people who hated the Indians appeared most like them. "The manners of the Indian natives," he wrote, "are respectable compared with this European medley," which lived in "sloth and inactivity," a "mongrel breed, half civilized, half savage." Yet they were in other respects the ideal Americans. They lived in "the unlimited freedom of the woods," free from the intrusion of government. As the "freeholder" took the place of the white savage, America came into being. Their anti-authoritarian, violent, and even racist values—indeed, their "degeneracy"—jarring to polite society and frightening to those unaccustomed to them, proved critical for the peace and stability of the whole.[85]

Of course, from a European perspective, what happened to the Indians was tragic. Crèvecoeur did not share the racist attitudes of common settlers or of slave owners like Jefferson. Indeed, like many of his contemporaries, he believed "men are the same in all ages and in all countries. A few prejudices and customs excepted, the same passions lurk in our hearts at all times." The cultures of Indians and white savages both reflected the worlds they inhabited. But visitors like Crèvecoeur could not disentangle one dynamic from the other. Freedom for whites, who could reject civility if they wished, entailed subjection of Indians, who could embrace civility to no avail. Whether nature or nurture compelled Indians to savagery, he could not say for sure. By the time he was writing, however, the issue was becoming moot. The freest Americans could only become so as long as Indians had no future. Because of this, "time will efface those stains" of the atrocities committed by settlers. We should therefore, he cautioned, "wink at these irregularities" that defined the culture, so-called society, and the crucial role of the frontier settler.[86]

Myth not only makes contradictions manageable. It also forgets. Forgotten by 1795 were vacillation and class animosities. Opportunity and promise, not outcome, drove this society, in which mobility would continue to be necessary for competency. Forgotten was the manipulation by elites. Settlers now believed that their independent spirit marked their earliest days on the frontier. Also forgotten was the true nature of the horrors settlers had inflicted on Indians. They had killed Indians, but in the service of a larger good, or so the argument went. Sanding off the rough edges of reality from the frontier revolution sanitized what had happened as it romanticized those who participated in atrocities. Doing so, of course, helped erase the psychic trauma of the terrors settlers had experienced and meted out. But selective memory accomplished something else. Because the western world had profoundly changed in a short period of time, images of bloodshed receded into the past as Indians receded west. These acts and these people belonged to another time.[87]

Consigning much of the recent past to oblivion and varnishing other aspects of Revolutionary experience valorized settlers and justified their state of development. It turned Indians into irredeemable peoples in theory and in fact, as it allowed the Revolution to end and made a national settlement possible. As Crèvecoeur argued with some insight, the frontier had a special role to play in a distinctive nation. "Our little society," he wrote in the voice of a western settler, "united in perfect harmony with the new adoptive one, in which we shall be incorporated, shall rest, I hope from all fatigues, from all apprehensions, from our present terrors, and from our long watchings." Through the competition for "self-preservation . . . the rule of Nature," they had created a new world, as well as a new nation.[88]

Lost in the mists of myth was also the nature of that Leviathan that had emerged from the covenant between people and state. Only those, it seems, who were not privy to the covenant, but were the objects of it, could see the contradictions and silences that brought commonwealth into being for what they were. When Judge Symmes had proudly displayed the coat of arms of the United States to visiting Shawnees, explaining the significance of the symbols and how they demonstrated the peaceful intentions of the Americans, the visitors were appalled. One of the Shawnee captains responded, "Let me also give my explanation, perhaps it will come nearer to the truth than yours." Why pick the eagle, he asked, if the government of the United States promised to act as an impartial arbiter in the West? He could think of "good, innocent birds" that would be more appropriate. "There is the dove," he argued, "which would not do harm to the smallest creature." The eagle, however, was "the largest of all birds and the enemy of all birds. He is proud, because he is conscious of his size and strength." The eagle, he continued, "looks down disparagingly upon all birds." Talons spoke of the bird's "hostility." Worse still were the implements of war the eagle held in its talons, arrows and rods. "Now tell me," he asked, "have I not spoken the truth?"[89]

In 1832, "Citizens of the Western Country" called on "citizen soldiers, and those who were engaged with us in regular service" in George Rogers Clark's expeditions, to meet for the fiftieth anniversary of the ineffectual 1782 march. On November 4, 1782, they had promised to meet fifty years later "at Old Fort Washington," now the thriving port town of Cincinnati. These were the few men who had decided to march with Clark after the debacle of 1778 and 1779 and the desertion of most of his force, those few who had been called his "Old Standbys." To those living in the Ohio River valley, these were the men who had laid the groundwork for "the conquest of the Western Country from the British and savages." The standbys hoped their past would be an example for the future. "The few surviving race of us," they wrote, "who are now standing on the verge of the grave, view with anxious concern the Welfare of our Common Country." They had played a critical role in a liberating revolution. They had "fought against British oppression and savage cruelty," both of which a younger generation of Americans could only imagine, "to secure to your own posterity, the blessings of liberty, religion, and law."

Their sacrifice, they tried to convince themselves, had brought society. And civility had its price. They had killed as savages and had died at the hands of savages to secure a democracy, one in which by this time all white men had a political voice. "We will meet," the veterans informed younger men and women, "and we will tell you what we have suffered if you will listen: we will admonish you face to face to be as faithful, as we have been to transmit those blessings unimpaired to your posterity; that America may long, and we trust forever remain a free sovereign, independent and happy Country."[90] Tellingly, they made no mention of the defining features of the Clark campaigns, the manipulation of poorer settlers by the wealthy, the landgrabs, the savage treatment of Indians to pander to the prejudices of white militia, and the resulting widespread disaffection from the patriot cause. Missing also was the preeminent role the government played in securing the protection that now defined the West and ensuring that the memory of revolution that these westerners harbored would remain inviolate. The bargain struck that ended the Revolution mandated that such realities be vanquished from memory.

Of course, divisions within regions in the Ohio valley remained and had grown in significance since 1782. North of the river, slavery did not exist. South, it did. Only with the security provided by the sword of Leviathan, of course, did such critical distinctions matter. Only with the commonwealth secured could north meaningfully differ from south in the West. But for one moment, these old veterans wanted to tell those who now lived in the Ohio valley that a generation dying away had led a revolution that rose above these looming divisions to create a unified western vision of society that transformed a whole nation. By doing so, of course, they had a hand in healing an east-west divide at the expense of a growing north-south rift. But in the heady days of 1832, when the veterans met for the last time to remember and forget, both of these divisions, one in the past, the other in the future, seemed worlds away. For their mythic sacrifice, unfettered by the reality of the past, they wanted one last chance to "take a final adieu to meet no more until we shall all be assembled in a world of spirits." On the fiftieth anniversary of what should have been a forgotten expedition, these men could believe that they had created America. And in many respects, they were right.

George Rogers Clark's Monument

O n November 3, 1921—long after the veterans who had met in 1832 passed to "a world of spirits"—Mrs. Paul Goodloe McIntire, a former Charlottesville schoolteacher and wife of a leading philanthropist, and the New York sculptor Robert Ingersoll Aitken unveiled a group of bronze statues dedicated to the memory of George Rogers Clark. Three groupings, including Indians, Clark on horseback, and armed men skulking behind Clark, were mounted on a Stony Creek granite base emblazoned with the inscription "Conqueror of the Northwest." Amid much fanfare and in the presence of local dignitaries, professors, and students, the two "pulled the cord" and dedicated the epic monument to the University of Virginia. "There was," as the local newspaper explained, "some little hitch, as the Indians were inclined to seclusion, but with a little aid they were finally shown to the world."[1]

Speeches extolling Clark followed. The president of the university accepted the monument to "a hero, a pioneer, and a conqueror" as a token to the "great men, great governmental ideas, and great unselfish spirit" that had brought America into being. The statues were, a local professor declared, a "monument of pride, enlightenment, and inspiration—a monument erected as a memorial to the daring adventures and dauntless courage of George Rogers Clark." Their unveiling spoke to "the tribute we love to render" to the "continental exploits of giant men," those who were "sent forth on their high missions and fateful destinies by the prophetic wisdom of Thomas Jefferson." These giants had "saved vast reaches from the grasp of England—a nation once hostile to our new born liberty, now blessedly banded together with our own country in the moral leadership of all nations, to the end that peace on earth may reign." The nature of that empire, as well as of the state of war that followed its collapse and created the conditions for a Clark to emerge, was now lost in the mists of time and myth.[2]

The historian who delivered the keynote address cast Clark as the man "who led the vanguard of the great Westward movement—'Carving a cross on the wilderness rim.'" He had channeled the force of "the rude borderers of the West," men referred to as "a set of uncivilized Virginia woodsmen armed with rifles." He saw in Clark the nation's past and its destiny:

> "Jamestown and Plymouth were the cornerstones of the foundations upon which the great fabric of the United States has been built up; and the United States is today one of the dominant factors in the history and in the future of the world of men." Whether engaged in the conquest of the Northwest, the final winning of the World War, the creation of a League of Nations . . . America, young, strong, and hopeful, is still a nation of pioneers:
> Have the elder races halted?
> Do they droop and end their lesson, wearied over there beyond the seas?
> We take up the task eternal, and the burden and the lesson, Pioneers! O Pioneers![3]

The citizens of Charlottesville were not alone in hailing their hometown hero. In 1921, as the sesquicentennial of Clark's march to Vincennes lay on the horizon, Americans were rediscovering Clark, defining his deeds as mythic, and erecting suitable monuments to his memory. Boosters of a memorial to be constructed in Vincennes lauded the 1778 expedition as one that had "resulted in the addition of seven great states to the Union and made possible its extension across the continent." Clark spoke to their present as he never quite had in the past, not even in 1832, when the veterans tried to convince a wider West of their significance. Nor in 1879, the centennial of the capture of Fort Sackville, when the stories of his exploits failed to capture the attention of a nation.[4]

Public commemoration, of course, memorializes contested memory. Representations of figures from the past tell us much more about who we are than what these individuals were or what they accomplished. Acts of commemoration, historians tell us, also entail struggles for supremacy within the communities in which they take place. The wealthy, for instance, commission statues as a way of legitimating their roles in society, while those on the margins use the openness of such moments when the past is revisited to assert their participation in the canonization of memory. Certainly, the Clark monument, centered on the great man, celebrated the likes of its benefactor, Paul Goodloe McIntire. In another sense, however, American public art lionizing "pioneers" proves the exception to this rule. In fact, works like the Clark monument, which speak to a past in which ordinary men and women undoubtedly played critical roles, blunt conflict and create a middle ground that obscures tensions in the present. In commemorating the Revolutionary frontier, in other words, men and women reenact covenant. The conquest of the West, as the citizens of Charlottesville agreed, defined the commonwealth's greatness and began with them, with giants like Clark and the nameless souls in his shadow.[5]

Consensus does not betoken reality, though. The groupings are of types that spoke to the hopes, fears, and needs of those assembled. The Indians, standing before Clark and thus in the way of inexorable progress, appear as noble or cowering savages, people trapped in a state of nature that no longer can be. The West's future was not theirs. Clark, astride his horse, looks trim, handsome, young, unafraid. With his hand beckoning the way forward to those behind him, he seems to represent destiny. The only feature distinguishing his image from European equestrian statues is the fur mantle he wears, a vestige of the land he would continually conquer in popular memory. Clark's future, in reality, did not prove much brighter than that of the Indians he confronted. His troubles with the bottle and bouts of depression caught up with him, and in 1809 he collapsed from a stroke. Paralyzed on the right side, he later fell into a fireplace, burning one of his legs so badly that it had to be amputated. In 1818, with his mind gone, he died broken and disfigured, a nearly penniless ward of his brother-in-law William Croghan, the nephew of the long-since-dead George Croghan.[6]

The most interesting grouping of the three, and the most telling, memorializes those faceless men behind Clark. Those who met in Cincinnati in 1832 would not have recognized themselves in these statues. And perhaps that was the point. These figures appear almost as hybrids, white savages or civilized Indians, people of indeterminate race. They wear European clothes and brandish the weapons of civilization; yet the hair and features of some suggest the Indianness Clark confronts. They look menacing yet cautious, aggressive but eager to follow Clark's lead in conquering the West. Their position implies that civility follows in Clark's wake. As the group marches west and conquers the savagery without and within, redemption is assured. The ennobled Clark, then, acts as *primum mobile*, the redeemer of the common man and the leading be-knighted edge of civilization. For those assembled at the unveiling, the lesson was clear. The extinction of savage culture went hand in hand with white civility. One ensured the other. And this dynamic was mediated by the illusion of deference to elites like Clark. In this moment memorialized, images, cultures, and races blend together, relegating a revolution defined by essentialist hate and unfettered popular sovereignty to a forgotten past that had served as midwife to this more enlightened present.

In the statue, therefore, a fable of how America came to be, what it meant, and how it differed from the other nations of the earth becomes frozen in time. And we still cling to this fable. Whether we celebrate or condemn founders such as Clark, we need the illusion of their omnipotence either in creating or in forestalling revolution to define "who we are." We struggle over the memory of what such narratives mean, but in our mythic conceptions of the past and our Revolution we ultimately agree that the founders bear responsibility for what we have become. Men like Clark stand in as proxies for the exceptional nature of America, something to be decried, celebrated, ignored, but not understood. What we cannot admit in our memory are the true faces of the group behind Clark, the hybrids, lest they reveal the complex fissures in the nation for what they are: contradictions renounced through covenant and commonwealth and rationalized by Revolutionary and frontier mythmaking. Their facelessness represents to us a peculiarly American vision of a transnational modernity, one rooted in mobility, compromise, and hybridity—born of revolution and war, but tempered by the need to make sense of savagery and whiteness. The monument testifies, silently, to how processes of frontier and revolution, global in scope and universal in time, intersected and then played out in an American context.[7]

The Clark monument attempts to obscure the transnational nature of what went on in America in the haze of exceptionalist symbolism. Ultimately, this paradox, as well as our inability to come to terms with it, sustains the covenant or social contract that we have agreed upon as American citizens. Paradox holds us together; indeed, the heat of contention focused on the likes of Clark does not divide but unites, further reinforcing the myths that define "who we are." Fittingly, the Clark monument, which is constructed of these materials, still stands, while the Quick monument, which eschews ambiguity, does not.

The Leviathan, too, conspires to obscure the past. The state, of course, has no place in the Clark monument. Yet its absence underscores its critical role in maintaining commonwealth. The state's complicity in myth is laid bare from time to time, most visibly when officials forget the terms of covenant. At those moments, the men behind the horse rise up and appear for what they are, complex, frightening, liberated men who have consented to their hybridity and their marginal roles in memory so as to have a place in the present.[8]

Notes

INTRODUCTION: TOM QUICK'S MONUMENT

1. For Tom Quick and what follows, see James Eldridge Quinlan, *The Original Life and Adventures of Tom Quick, the Indian Slayer* (Deposit, NY, 1894), 16, 37–38, 98; Willard Sterne Randall and Nancy Nahra, *Forgotten Americans: Footnote Figures Who Changed American History* (Reading, MA, 1998); and Vernon Leslie, *The Tom Quick Legends* (Middletown, NY, 1977). For an intriguing look at all things Quick—recent newspaper articles, popular recordings, history, Delaware voices, and a petition titled "Bring Down the Tom Quick Monument"—see the Web site tristateunity. veneziale.net/tom%20quick/index.htm.

2. Robert Wiebe, *Who We Are: A History of Popular Nationalism* (Princeton, NJ, 2001).

3. James Eldridge Quinlan, *Tom Quick, the Indian Slayer* (Monticello, NY, 1851).

4. James Allerton, *The Hawk's Nest* (Port Jervis, NY, 1892), 221–22, cited in Leslie, *Tom Quick Legends*, 19.

5. Leslie, *Tom Quick Legends*, 22, 45, 155.

6. Frederick Jackson Turner, "Contributions of the West to American Democracy," in *The Frontier in American History* (New York, 1920), 249, 253, 248.

7. Turner, "The Old West," in *Frontier in American History*, 121, 107, 106, 104.

8. Noel Paul Stookey, "Tom Quick," *Something New and Fresh* (1978).

9. See, for instance, Gary Nash, *The Unknown American Revolution: The Unruly Birth of Democracy and the Struggle to Create America* (New York, 2005).

10. Edmund Morgan, "The Other Founders," review of *The Unknown American Revolution*, by Gary Nash, *New York Review of Books*, 22 Sept. 2005.

11. Daniel Richter, *Facing East from Indian Country: A Native History of Early America* (Cambridge, MA, 2003). On the changing definitions, see Gregory Nobles, *American Frontiers: Cultural Encounters and Continental Conquest* (New York, 1997); the introduction to Andrew Cayton and Fredrika Teute, eds., *Contact Points: American Frontiers from the Mohawk Valley to the Mississippi, 1750–1850* (Chapel Hill, NC, 1998); Jeremy Adelman and Stephen Aron, "From Borderlands to Borders: Empires,

Nation-States, and the Peoples in Between in North American History," *American Historical Review* 104 (1999); and Eric Hinderaker and Peter Mancall, *At the Edge of Empire: The Backcountry in British North America* (Baltimore, 2003).

12. Nobles, *American Frontiers*, xi. See, for instance, Thomas Bender, ed., *Rethinking American History in a Global Age* (Berkeley, CA, 2002); and Joyce Chaplin, "Expansion and Exceptionalism in Early American History," *Journal of American History* 89, no. 4 (2003).

13. See Gordon Wood, *The Radicalism of the American Revolution* (New York, 1991) and *Revolutionary Characters: What Made the Founders Different* (New York, 2006), 26–27. Alan Taylor, who has argued that the proponents of this approach have tended to embrace or at least not quibble with the exceptionalist label, has also contended that they have a difficult time integrating the experiences of common people in their studies. See Alan Taylor, *Writing Early America* (Philadelphia, 2005), 214–36.

14. As J.G.A. Pocock argues, "Hobbes's formula does not go to the heart of the seventeenth-century experience of civil war, which was that men fight each other not merely because there is no sovereign to stop them, but because an existing sovereignty has disintegrated and they must fight each other in the effort to reconstruct it." *The Discovery of Islands: Essays in British History* (Cambridge, UK, 2005), 122.

15. On the ethnically mixed composition of places like western Pennsylvania, see Thomas Slaughter, *The Whiskey Rebellion: Frontier Epilogue to the American Revolution* (New York, 1986), 66; and Eugene R. Harper, *The Transformation of Western Pennsylvania, 1770–1800* (Pittsburgh, 1991), 5–6, 174.

16. Three of the best studies that deal with the Ohio valley during the period of the Revolution suggest this is the case. See Fred Anderson and Andrew R. L. Cayton, *The Dominion of War: Empire and Liberty in North America, 1500–2000* (New York, 2004); Richard White, *The Middle Ground: Indians, Empires, and Republics in the Great Lakes Region, 1650–1815* (New York, 1991); and Eric Hinderaker, *Elusive Empires: Constructing Colonialism in the Ohio Valley, 1673–1800* (New York, 1999).

17. See, for example, Edmund Morgan, *American Slavery, American Freedom: The Ordeal of Colonial Virginia* (New York, 1975).

CHAPTER 1: DRAWING THE LINE

1. "The Opinions of George Croghan on the American Indians," *Pennsylvania Magazine of History and Biography* 71 (1947), 152–59.

2. Karen O'Brien, *Narratives of Enlightenment: Cosmopolitan History from Voltaire to Gibbon* (Cambridge, UK, 1997), 156–60.

3. Stewart Brown, "William Robertson and the Scottish Enlightenment," in Stewart Brown, ed., *William Robertson and the Expansion of Empire* (Cambridge, UK, 1997), 7–35.

4. Eliga Gould, *The Persistence of Empire: British Political Culture in the Age of the American Revolution* (Chapel Hill, NC, 2000).

5. The ideology of the "first British Empire" is a peculiarly understudied topic. To be sure, nearly every study of the American Revolution looks at the ideas that made Britain tick after 1763. But most of these treatments study empire only insofar as it ex-

plains the American crisis. Bernard Bailyn's *Ideological Origins of the American Revolution* (Cambridge, MA, 1967)—the best treatment of the subject—readily comes to mind. When scholars do consciously look at "empire," they either present in-depth studies of the commercial makeup of empire or view empire as an assemblage of political ties and institutions. The best of the former is T. H. Breen's *Marketplace of Revolution: How Consumer Politics Shaped American Independence* (New York, 2005). The latter is the stuff of the old imperial school of early American history, works by scholars such as Charles McLean Andrews and Lawrence Henry Gipson. When it comes to the ideology of what we would consider territorial empire, most, understandably, focus on the nineteenth century and the "second British Empire." The most notable study here is C. A. Bayly's *Imperial Meridian: The British Empire and the World* (London, 1989). The second empire, after all, lasted a great deal longer than the first. David Armitage's *Ideological Origins of the British Empire* (Cambridge, UK, 2000) would seem to fill the gap, but his study really looks at the late-seventeenth- and early-eighteenth-century maritime arrangements that animated British ideological thought. Certainly, during this period, we could not call the empire territorial, such as would emerge after 1763. Similarly, see Anthony Pagden, *Lords of All the World: Ideologies of Empire in Spain, Britain, and France, c. 1500–c. 1800* (New Haven, CT, 1998). *The Oxford History of the British Empire* (New York, 1998) might finally have touched off a reappraisal of this notion of empire, pressing scholars to view the empire in America after 1763 in much the same way the nineteenth century is studied. See, for instance, the book by one of the editors of the series, P. J. Marshall, *The Making and Unmaking of Empires: Britain, India, and America, c. 1750–1783* (Oxford, UK, 2005).

6. "Proclamation of October 7, 1763," in Clarence Alvord and Clarence Carter, eds., *The Critical Period, 1763–1765* (Springfield, IL, 1915), 39, 41.

7. *The Expediency of Securing Our American Colonies* (Edinburgh, 1763), in Alvord and Carter, *Critical Period*, 147, 134.

8. Thomas Gage to Lord Hillsborough, 5 Jan. 1769, CO 5/87, 5, Public Record Office, London.

9. William Smith, *An Historical Account of the Expedition Against the Ohio Indians* (Philadelphia, 1765), 67–68; Henry Bouquet to Gage, 31 May 1764, Bouquet Add. MSS, 21637, 27, British Library, London.

10. "Proclamation of October 7, 1763," 43.

11. "Plan for the Future Management of Indian Affairs," 1763, CO 5/65, 123–32.

12. Notes on the Proclamation Line, 10 May 1766, CO 5/84, 114.

13. "Proclamation of October 7, 1763," 43.

14. "Distribution of Troops, 1763," in Alvord and Carter, *Critical Period*, 5–7.

15. On this theme, see Fred Anderson, *The Crucible of War: The Seven Years' War and the Fate of Empire in British North America* (New York, 2000), 566, 570.

16. Ibid., 274–79. The best treatment of the political maneuvering behind the royal proclamation remains Jack Sosin, *Whitehall and the Wilderness: The Middle West in British Colonial Policy* (Lincoln, NE, 1961).

17. Burke, *Speech on Conciliation with America*, 1775 (New York, 1898). On this theme, see Breen, *Marketplace of Revolution*.

18. R. A. Humphreys, "Lord Shelburne and the Proclamation of 1763," *English Historical Review* 49 (1934), 244. On this earlier vision of maritime empire, see Armitage, *Ideological Origins of the British Empire*. Also see Eric Hinderaker, *Elusive Empires: Constructing Colonialism in the Ohio Valley, 1673–1800* (New York, 1997), 168; Gordon Wood, *The American Revolution: A History* (New York, 2002), 21–22.

19. Great Britain Board of Trade, *Journal of the Commissioners for Trade and Plantations from January 1759 to December 1763*, 31 Oct. 1763 (Nendeln, Liechtenstein, 1970), vol. 11, 401.

20. Notes on the Proclamation Line, 115. Also see Verner Crane, "Notes and Documents: 'Hints Relative to the Division and Government of the Conquered and Newly Acquired Countries in America,'" *Mississippi Valley Historical Review* 8 (1922), 371.

21. Crane, "Notes and Documents," 371–72.

22. Sosin, *Whitehall and the Wilderness*; Hinderaker, *Elusive Empires*, 165, 168.

23. Humphreys, "Lord Shelburne and the Proclamation of 1763," 241, 255; Anderson, *Crucible of War*, 566.

24. "Distribution of Troops, 1763," 5–7.

25. Gregory Dowd, *War Under Heaven: Pontiac, the Indian Nations, and the British Empire* (Baltimore, 2002); and especially Daniel Richter, *Facing East from Indian Country: A Native History of Early America* (Cambridge, MA, 2003), 209.

26. Dowd, *A Spirited Resistance: The North American Indian Struggle for Unity* (Baltimore, 1992).

27. Gage to Bouquet, 15 Oct. 1764, in Louis Waddell, ed., *The Papers of Henry Bouquet* (Harrisburg, PA, 1994), vol. 6, 663.

28. William Trent journal at Fort Pitt, 24 June 1763, Historical Society of Pennsylvania, Philadelphia (hereafter cited as HSP). On this, see Elizabeth Fenn, *Pox Americana: The Great Smallpox Epidemic of 1775–82* (New York, 2001).

29. Amherst memorandum, 16 July 1763, in Waddell, *Papers of Bouquet*, vol. 6, 315.

30. Amherst to Sir William Johnson, 27 Aug. and 30 Sept. 1763, in *Pennsylvania Archives*, 2nd ser., vol. 6, (Harrisburg, PA, 1877), 587, 598.

31. Bouquet to Gage, 20 May 1764, George Croghan Papers, file 7, HSP. For this interpretation, see Dowd, *War Under Heaven*.

32. William Johnson, "A Review of the Progression, State of the Trade, Politicks, and Proceedings of the Indians of the North District," 16 Nov. 1767, CO 5/58, 189–90.

33. Johnson to Lords of Trade, 20 Aug. 1766, in E. B. O'Callaghan, ed., *Documents Relative to the Colonial History of the State of New York* (Albany, NY, 1856), vol. 7, 852.

34. Earl of Halifax to Amherst, 18 Oct. 1763, in *Pennsylvania Archives*, vol. 6, 599–600. Also see Bouquet to Richard Peters, 5 Oct. 1761, *Pennsylvania Magazine of History and Biography* 33 (1909), 224. The chief architects of the royal proclamation recommended the measure only after word of Pontiac's War had reached London. See Humphreys, "Lord Shelburne and the Proclamation of 1763," 252.

35. Gage to Halifax, 9 Dec. 1763, in Clarence Carter, ed., *The Correspondence of General Thomas Gage with the Secretaries of State, 1763–1765* (New Haven, CT, 1931), vol. 1, 2; Richard White, *The Middle Ground: Indians, Empires, and Republics in the Great Lakes Region, 1650–1815* (New York, 1991), 270, 308. This interpretation of "enlightened empire" was a critical element of Lawrence Henry Gipson's multi-

volume study of the British Empire in America. See in particular volumes 9 and 10 of *The British Empire Before the American Revolution* (New York, 1961–70).

36. The phrase "Celtic fringe," of course, is Michael Hechter's; see *Internal Colonialism: The Celtic Fringe in British National Development* (Berkeley, CA, 1975). If some English writers were moving beyond culture to explain difference during this period, it could be argued that ethnicity was being used as that marker. See Colin Kidd, *British Identities Before Nationalism: Ethnicity and Nationhood in the Atlantic World, 1689–1830* (Cambridge, UK, 1999).

37. Jim Smyth, *Making the United Kingdom* (Harlow, UK, 2001).

38. Dror Wahrman, *The Making of the Modern Self: Identity and Culture in Eighteenth Century England* (New Haven, CT, 2004), 91–92; Nicholas Canny, *Making Ireland British, 1580–1650* (Oxford, UK, 2001); Smyth, *Making the United Kingdom*; Eammon O'Ciardha, *Ireland and the Jacobite Cause, 1685–1766: A Fatal Attachment* (Dublin, 2000); Robert Clyde, *From Rebel to Hero: The Image of the Highlander, 1745–1830* (East Linton, Scotland, 1995).

39. Wahrman, *Making of the Modern Self*, 86–87; Laura Brown, *Ends of Empire: Women and Ideology in Early Eighteenth-Century English Literature* (Ithaca, NY, 1993).

40. Michael Brown, *Francis Hutcheson in Dublin, 1719–1730: The Crucible of His Thought* (Dublin, 2002); Evan Radcliffe, "Revolutionary Writing, Moral Philosophy, and Universal Benevolence in the Eighteenth Century," *Journal of the History of Ideas* 54 (1993), 221–40; Daniel Carey, "Method, Moral Sense, and the Problem of Diversity: Francis Hutcheson and the Scottish Enlightenment," *British Journal for the History of Philosophy* 5 (1997), 275–96; and Daniel Carey, "Reconsidering Rousseau: Sociability, Moral Sense, and the American Indian, from Hutcheson to Bartram," *British Journal for Eighteenth-Century Studies* 21 (1998), 25–38.

41. O'Brien, *Narratives of Enlightenment*, 118, 122, 131–34; quotation is from 101. Nicholas Phillipson, "Providence and Progress: An Introduction to the Historical Thought of William Robertson," in Brown, *William Robertson*. On the four-stage theory, see Ronald L. Meek, *Social Science and the Ignoble Savage* (Cambridge, UK, 1976).

42. O'Brien, *Narratives of Enlightenment*, 94; quotation is from 103. Michael Hont, ed., *Wealth and Virtue: The Shaping of Political Economy in the Scottish Enlightenment* (Cambridge, UK, 1983).

43. Burke cited in David Armitage, "The New World and British Historical Thought: From Richard Hakluyt to William Robertson," in Karen Kupperman, ed., *America in European Consciousness, 1493–1750* (Chapel Hill, NC, 1995), 67.

44. Armitage, "New World and British Historical Thought," 63.

45. C. A. Bayly, "The British and Indigenous Peoples, 1760–1860: Power, Perception, and Identity," and Phillip Morgan, "Encounters Between British and 'Indigenous' Peoples, c. 1500–1800," in Martin Daunton and Rick Halpern, eds., *Empire and Others: British Encounters with Indigenous Peoples, 1600–1850* (Philadelphia, 1999).

46. Canny, *Making Ireland British*; James Axtell, *The Invasion Within: The Contest of Cultures in Colonial North America* (New York, 1985); Roxann Wheeler, *The Complexion of Race: Categories of Difference in Eighteenth-Century British Culture* (Philadelphia, 2000); Wahrman, *Making of the Modern Self*; P. J. Marshall and

Glyndwr Williams, *The Great Map of Mankind: British Perceptions of the World in the Age of Enlightenment* (Cambridge, MA, 1982); Kathleen Brown, "Native Americans and Early Modern Concepts of Race," in Daunton and Halpern, *Empire and Others.* Linda Colley makes the point that Amherst represented a glaring exception to this rule and in no way should we consider his views normative. See *Captives: Britain, Empire, and the World, 1600–1850* (London, 2002), 186.

47. Harry Gordon journal, 1766, CO 5/85, 62–63. See also J. H. Elliott, *The Old World and the New World* (Cambridge, UK, 1970); and Anthony Pagden, *The Fall of Natural Man: The American Indians and the Origins of Comparative Ethnology* (Cambridge, UK, 1986).

48. *Expediency of Securing Our American Colonies*, 148, 144, 151, 152. This writer saw the West as a sort of safety valve in much the same way that organizers of the Virginia or London Company conceived the Chesapeake a century and a half earlier. James Horn covers this theme in *Adapting to a New World: English Society in the Seventeenth-Century Chesapeake* (Chapel Hill, NC, 1994).

49. George Croghan private journal, Fort Pitt to the Illinois Country, 1765–66, George Croghan Correspondence, Cadwalader Collection, ser. 4, 2–21, HSP. Croghan saw this "State of Nature" through the lens of commodification, another way in which Europeans had viewed the New World. See William Cronon, *Changes in the Land: Indians, Colonists, and the Ecology of New England* (New York, 1983).

50. Gordon journal, 1766, 62–63.

51. Humphreys, "Lord Shelburne and the Proclamation of 1763," 244.

52. Edmund Fitzmaurice, *Life of William, Earl of Shelburne, Afterwards First Marquess of Lansdowne, with Extracts from His Papers and Correspondence* (London, 1912), 2, 4, 8.

53. Jim Smyth, "'Like Amphibious Animals': Irish Protestants, Ancient Britons, 1691–1707," *Historical Journal* 36 (1993); Canny, *Making Ireland British.*

54. Humphreys, "Lord Shelburne and the Proclamation of 1763," 250.

55. The paper is published as an appendix in ibid., 259, 261.

56. Ibid., 259.

57. Fintan O'Toole, *White Savage: William Johnson and the Invention of America* (New York, 2005); and Kerby Miller, David Doyle, et al., eds., *Irish Immigrants in the Land of Canaan: Letters and Memoirs from Colonial and Revolutionary America, 1675–1815* (New York, 2003), 461–76.

58. Board of Trade to Johnson, 5 Aug. 1763, in *Pennsylvania Archives*, vol. 6, 585–86.

59. Johnson to Board of Trade, 25 Sept. 1763, in *Pennsylvania Archives*, vol. 6, 593.

60. Johnson to Lords of Trade, 24 May 1765, in Alvord and Carter, *Critical Period*, 506.

61. Johnson to Board of Trade, 25 Sept. 1763, CO 5/65, 117–22.

62. William Johnson, "Review of the Trade and Affairs of the Indians in the Northern District of America," in O'Callaghan, *Documents*, vol. 7, 953, 960; Johnson to Board of Trade, 25 Sept. 1763, in *Pennsylvania Archives*, vol. 6, 593.

63. Johnson to Lords of Trade, 13 Nov. 1763, in *Pennsylvania Archives*, vol. 6, 603. From time to time, he called Indians of the West "subjects." For instance, in a letter to Amherst, whom he despised, Johnson agreed with Amherst that some Indians were an "unworthy People past reclaim, and who instead of being treated with, should be

brought to Condign Punishment." Fair treatment, however, "would most Effectually Convince the Indians, that they are now English Subjects." These words must have galled Amherst, and perhaps that was the point. Johnson to Amherst, 30 Sept. 1763, in Alexander Flick, ed., *The Papers of Sir William Johnson* (Albany, NY, 1925), vol. 4, 210–11.

64. Johnson to Board of Trade, 25 Sept. 1763, in *Pennsylvania Archives*, vol. 6, 595.
65. Johnson, "Review of the Trade and Affairs," 958.
66. "Johnson on the Organization of the Indian Department," 8 Oct. 1764, in Alvord and Carter, *Critical Period*, 335.
67. Johnson to Lords of Trade, 8 Oct. 1764, in Alvord and Carter, *Critical Period*, 323.
68. Johnson, "Review of the Trade and Affairs," 957.
69. Johnson to the Earl of Shelburne, 15 Jan. 1767, in O'Callaghan, *Documents*, vol. 7, 891.
70. Johnson to Lords of Trade, 13 Nov. 1763, in *Pennsylvania Archives*, vol. 6, 608.
71. Johnson to Lords of Trade, 20 Jan. 1764, in *Pennsylvania Archives*, vol. 6, 616.
72. Johnson to Shelburne, 15 Jan. 1767, in O'Callaghan, *Documents*, vol. 7, 893.
73. Johnson, "Review of the Trade and Affairs," 959.
74. Johnson to Hillsborough, 26 June 1769, CO 5/70, 234. On this theme, see James Merrell, *The Indians' New World: Catawbas and Their Neighbors from European Contact through the Era of Removal* (Chapel Hill, NC, 1989).
75. Johnson, "Review of the Trade and Affairs," 968.
76. Ibid., 967.
77. "Johnson on the Organization of the Indian Department," 329, 327.
78. *Expediency of Securing Our American Colonies*, 159.
79. Johnson, "Review of the Trade and Affairs," 970, 969.
80. Hugh Blair quoted in O'Brien, *Narratives of Enlightenment*, 124.
81. Nancy Rhoden, "William Smith: Philadelphia Minister and Moderate," in Nancy Rhoden and Ian Steele, eds., *The Human Tradition in the American Revolution* (Wilmington, DE, 2000), 61–67.
82. Smith to Johnson, 16 March 1767, Society for the Propagation of the Gospel Papers, vol. 15, 185–86, Lambeth Palace Library, London.
83. Barton to the secretary, 6 Dec. 1760, in William Stevens Perry, ed., *Historical Collections Relating to the American Colonial Church* (New York, 1871), vol. 2, 294–95. Barton is also quoted in Stephen Conway, "War, Imperial Expansion, and Religious Developments in Mid-Eighteenth-Century Britain and Ireland," *War in History* 11 (2004), 145.
84. Barton to the secretary, 8 Nov. 1756, in Perry, *Historical Collections*, vol. 2, 276.
85. Linda Colley makes the case that people such as Croghan from cultural marchlands of the British Isles had a remarkable ability to see Indians as redeemable, given their personal history and experience as "victims." Raised up from poor and alienated positions, they could empathize with others in that condition. See *Captives*, 190. Fintan O'Toole makes a similar case for Sir William Johnson, arguing that his status as an Irishman and convert from Catholicism allowed him to live a "liminal" existence defined by an almost multicultural sense of tolerance. See *White Savage*.
86. Croghan to Johnson, 24 Feb. 1764, in Flick, *Papers of Johnson*, vol. 4, 339–41.

87. Croghan to Johnson, 10 March 1764, in Flick, *Papers of Johnson*, vol. 4, 362.

88. Great Britain Board of Trade, *Journal of the Commissioners*, 7 June 1764, vol. 12, 65–66.

89. Croghan to Lords of Trade, n.d., in *Pennsylvania Archives, vol. 6, 622.*

90. Croghan to Johnson, n.d. 1765, George Croghan letter book, file 272, Craig Manuscript Collection, Carnegie Library, Pittsburgh.

91. "John Jennings's 'Journal from Fort Pitt to Fort Chartres in the Illinois Country,' March–April, 1766," *Pennsylvania Magazine of History and Biography* 31 (1907), 155–56.

92. Croghan private journal, 18.

93. Gage to Hillsborough, 6 Jan. 1769, CO 5/87, 29.

94. Bouquet to Gage, 15 Nov. 1764, in Waddell, *Papers of Bouquet*, vol. 6, 704.

95. *Expediency of Securing Our American Colonies*, 139, 147, 136.

96. Gage to Halifax, 9 Nov. 1764, in Carter, *Correspondence of Gage*, vol. 1, 44.

97. *Expediency of Securing Our American Colonies*, 135, 137, 148, 150, 157. Greg Dowd refuted this older and pernicious notion that the Indians could not have staged Pontiac's "Rebellion" without French help. See *Spirited Resistance*.

98. Colley, *Captives*, 198.

99. Johnson to Lords of Trade, 16 Nov. 1765, in O'Callaghan, *Documents*, vol. 7, 776–77; Croghan to Lords of Trade, n.d., in *Pennsylvania Archives*, vol. 6, 619; Johnson to Lords of Trade, 24 May 1765, in Alvord and Carter, *Critical Period*, 507; Johnson to Board of Trade, 25 Sept. 1763, in *Pennsylvania Archives*, vol. 6, 594.

100. Croghan to Johnson, 12 July 1764, Croghan Papers, file 1, 1–4.

101. Croghan to Johnson, 24 Feb. 1764, in Flick, *Papers of Johnson*, vol. 4, 339–41.

102. Johnson uses the term "new system" to describe the management of the West in the wake of the royal proclamation. Johnson, "Review of the Trade and Affairs," 963.

103. "Plan for Imperial Control of Indian Affairs," 10 July 1764, in Alvord and Carter, *Critical Period*, 273–80. Stuart seems to have had a personal history much like Johnson's. He worked closely with and had the respect of the Cherokees, and he had been married to a Cherokee woman. Indeed, Linda Colley argues that this Scot better reflects the ways the British considered Indians than, say, Amherst. See *Captives*, 186.

104. Stuart to Lords of Trade, 1 April 1767, CO 5/58, 111.

105. "Plan for Imperial Control of Indian Affairs," 273–80.

106. Gage to Halifax, 9 Dec. 1763, in Carter, *Correspondence of Gage*, vol. 1, 2.

107. *Expediency of Securing Our American Colonies*, 160–61.

108. Johnson to Lords of Trade, 30 Aug. 1764, in Alvord and Carter, *Critical Period*, 307.

109. "Proclamation of Gage to the Inhabitants of the Illinois," 30 Dec. 1764, in Alvord and Carter, *Critical Period*, 395–96.

110. On the duties and travails of such go-betweens, as well as the cultural insularity that ultimately determined their failure, see James Merrell, *Into the American Woods: Negotiators on the Pennsylvania Frontier* (New York, 1999).

111. Croghan to Johnson, 12 July 1764, Croghan Papers, file 1.

112. Croghan to Johnson, 18 Jan. 1767, Croghan Papers, Letters and Documents, file 5, 1–2. The term "middle ground" was coined by Richard White in *The Middle Ground*.

113. Croghan private journal, 7.

114. Croghan to Johnson, 18 Jan. 1767, Croghan Papers, Letters and Documents, file 5, 4, 6.
115. Croghan to Johnson, n.d. 1765, Croghan letter book, file 272, Craig Manuscript Collection.
116. Copy of a treaty between John Bradstreet and the western Indians enclosed in a letter from Bradstreet to Bouquet, 14 Aug. 1764, in Waddell, *Papers of Bouquet*, vol. 6, 605.
117. Gage to Henry Seymour Conway, 28 March 1766, in Carter, *Correspondence of Gage*, vol. 1, 86.
118. Bouquet to Gage, 16 March 1765, Gage Papers, American Series, William Clements Library, University of Michigan, Ann Arbor.
119. "An Early Record of Pittsburgh," *Pennsylvania Magazine of History and Biography* 2 (1878), 303-5.
120. Gage to Halifax, 14 April 1764, CO 5/83, 143; Bouquet to Gage, 20 May 1764, in Waddell, *Papers of Bouquet*, vol. 6, 543.
121. Minutes of a conference with the Six Nations and Delawares at Johnson Hall, 29 April 1765, CO 5/66, 244; "Early Record of Pittsburgh," 303-5.
122. Bouquet to Gage, 20 May 1764, in Waddell, *Papers of Bouquet*, vol. 6, 543.
123. "A Reexamination of Gershom Hicks," 19 April 1764, in Waddell, *Papers of Bouquet*, vol. 6, 522.
124. Deposition of Corporal James Berry, 22 Feb. 1764, Haldimand Add. MSS, 21682, 73, British Library; William Grant to Gage, 24 Feb. 1764, and deposition of Corporal James Berry and five private men, 22 Feb. 1764, Gage Papers.
125. Extract of a letter from Johnson to Gage, 17 Nov. 1763, Gage Papers.
126. Gage to Johnson, 30 Nov. 1763, Gage Papers.
127. Bouquet to Gage, 20 May 1764, in Waddell, *Papers of Bouquet*, vol. 6, 543.
128. Gage to Shelburne, 13 June 1767, CO 5/85, 127.
129. See, for example, Gage to Halifax, 10 Aug. 1764, CO 5/83, 172-73; and Gage to Shelburne, 24 Aug. 1767, CO 5/85, 157.
130. Gage to Shelburne, 30 Jan. 1768, CO 5/86, 35.
131. Shelburne to Gage, 13 Sept. 1766, CO 5/84, 179.
132. Gage to Halifax, 21 Jan. 1764, in Carter, *Correspondence of Gage*, vol. 1, 13.
133. Gage to Croghan, 21 March 1766, Croghan Correspondence, file 8.
134. Johnson to Lords of Trade, n.d. 1765, CO 5/66, 268.
135. Gage to Halifax, 13 Dec. 1764, CO 5/83, 221.

CHAPTER 2: CROSSING THE LINE

1. In the 1730s, Pennsylvania officials had fraudulently taken lands in the area from Delawares and, in the process, forced many to move west into the Ohio Country. While Pennsylvanians hoped to steer immigrants to these lands, Connecticut speculators also had laid claim to the region. In fact, so heated had this debate become that as authorities in America had tried to devise a united colonial front to Indian aggression at the outset of the Seven Years' War, unity foundered in part as leaders from the two colonies could not take their minds off of competing claims in the region for the sake of a common defense. The failed Albany Plan of Union foreshadowed the con-

flicts that were to come. On these complicated themes, see Michael McConnell, *A Country Between: The Upper Ohio Valley and Its Peoples, 1724–1774* (Lincoln, NE, 1992); and Timothy Shannon, *Indians and Colonists at the Crossroads of Empire: The Albany Congress of 1754* (Ithaca, NY, 2000).

2. "The Apology of the Paxton Volunteers Addressed to the Candid and Impartial World," 7, Historical Society of Pennsylvania, Philadelphia (hereafter cited as HSP).

3. John Elder to John Penn, 24 Aug. 1763, John Elder Papers, Dauphin County Historical Society, Harrisburg, PA.

4. "Apology of the Paxton Volunteers," 7.

5. Ibid.

6. Ibid., 9.

7. For the idea of liminality and the Paxton Boys, see Thomas Slaughter, "Crowds in Eighteenth-Century America: Reflections and New Directions," *Pennsylvania Magazine of History and Biography* 115 (1991), 3–34. On the idea of this moment as the first, crucial step toward a policy of ethnic cleansing, see Daniel Richter, *Facing East from Indian Country: A Native History of Early America* (Cambridge, MA, 2003), as well as Richter and William Pencak's introduction to *Friends and Enemies in Penn's Woods: Indians, Colonists, and the Racial Construction of Pennsylvania* (University Park, PA, 2004), ix, x, xvi, xviii. Peter Silver similarly argues that ethnic identification paled before whiteness by 1763. The Paxton affair signaled the critical transition. See "Indian-Hating and the Rise of Whiteness in Provincial Pennsylvania" (Ph.D. diss., Yale University, 2000), 233, 239.

8. Benjamin Franklin, *A Narrative of the Late Massacre in Lancaster County* (Philadelphia, 1764).

9. On this story—and the many myths associated with Franklin—see Gordon Wood, *The Americanization of Benjamin Franklin* (New York, 2003).

10. Lord Halifax to Gage, 10 March 1764, CO 5/83, 48, and Gage to Halifax, 12 May and 7 Jan. 1764, CO 5/83, 151, 38, Public Record Office, London.

11. Gage to Halifax, 12 May 1764, CO 5/83, 151. See also Penn to Gage, 31 Dec. 1763 and 5 Jan. 1764, and Gage to Penn, 10 Jan. 1764, Gage Papers, William Clements Library, University of Michigan, Ann Arbor.

12. Henry Bouquet to Gage, 2 May 1764, Bouquet Add. MSS, 21637, 16, British Library, London.

13. John Joseph Schlosser to Gage, 9 Feb. 1764, Gage Papers.

14. "Apology of the Paxton Volunteers," 18.

15. Sir William Johnson to Lords of Trade, 20 Jan. 1764, in *Pennsylvania Archives*, 2nd ser. (Harrisburg, PA, 1877), vol. 6, 617.

16. Joseph Shippen to James Burd, 3 Jan. 1764, Native American History Collection, Clements Library.

17. Johnson to Lords of Trade, 28 June 1766, in E. B. O'Callaghan, ed., *Documents Relative to the Colonial History of the State of New York* (Albany, NY, 1856), vol. 7, 838.

18. Johnson to Lords of Trade, 16 Nov. 1765, in O'Callaghan, *Documents*, vol. 7, 776.

19. Gage to Halifax, 8 June and 13 July 1764, CO 5/83, 163, 168; Bouquet to John Bradstreet, 5 Sept. 1764, Bouquet to Gage, 9 June 1764, Bouquet Add. MSS, 21637, 58, 30.

20. James Livingston to Bouquet, 5 June 1764, Bouquet Add. MSS, 21650, 238.

21. John Reid to Bouquet, 26 July 1764, Bouquet Add. MSS, 21650, 371.

22. William Johnson, "Review of the Trade and Affairs of the Indians in the Northern District of America," in O'Callaghan, *Documents*, vol. 7, 964.

23. Johnson to Lords of Trade, 20 Aug. 1766, in O'Callaghan, *Documents*, vol. 7, 853.

24. Indeed, while Colonel Bouquet was readying for an expedition into Shawnee country, his subordinate Colonel Bradstreet was signing a treaty with them. Bouquet upbraided Bradstreet for signing a treaty without approval, yet Gage had sent him out to extend peace feelers. See Bradstreet to Bouquet, 14 Aug. 1764, and "Minutes of an Indian Treaty," 12 Aug. 1764, in Louis Waddell, ed., *The Papers of Henry Bouquet* (Harrisburg, PA, 1994), vol. 6, 603–7.

25. See "List of Prisoners Deliver'd Up by the Shawnese Indians . . . and Arrived at Fort Pitt," 5 Jan. 1765, and William Murray to Bouquet, 31 Jan. 1765, Bouquet Add. MSS, 21651, 127, 156; Andrew Lewis to William Preston, 20 Dec. 1764, William Preston Papers, Draper MSS, ser. 2QQ, 58–59, Historical Society of Wisconsin, Madison. David Hay to Bouquet, 29 Oct. 1764, Bouquet Add. MSS, 21651, 28. On captivity and the reluctance of captives to return to what had been their homes, see Linda Colley, *Captives: Britain, Empire, and the World, 1600–1850* (London, 2002); and John Demos, *The Unredeemed Captive: A Family Story from Early America* (New York, 1994).

26. Johnson, "Review of the Trade and Affairs," 964. Also see George Croghan's report of a series of meetings with Delawares and Shawnees, 6 April 1765, CO 5/66, 87–92.

27. Johnson to Henry Seymour Conway, 28 June 1766, CO 5/66, 148–50.

28. Johnson to Board of Trade, 20 Aug. 1766, CO 5/67, 61. See also Johnson to Board of Trade, 20 Aug. 1766, in O'Callaghan, *Documents*, vol. 7, 852; and *Minutes of a Conference, Held at Fort-Pitt, in April and May, 1768* (Philadelphia, 1768), 5.

29. Shelburne to all the governors on the continent, 13 Sept. 1766, CO 5/66, 143–44.

30. Johnson to Lords of Trade, 28 June 1766, in O'Callaghan, *Documents*, vol. 7, 837; Johnson, "Review of the Trade and Affairs," 964.

31. Stuart to Lord Hillsborough, 3 Jan. 1769, CO 5/70, 105.

32. Most perplexing, as Johnson lamented, were the ways in which settlers "despise those in peace whom they fear to meet in War." Johnson to Conway, 28 June 1766, CO 5/66, 148–50.

33. Johnson to Lords of Trade, 16 Nov. 1765, CO 5/66, 300.

34. Gage to Halifax, 8 June 1765, in Clarence Carter, ed., *The Correspondence of General Thomas Gage with the Secretaries of State, 1763–1765* (New Haven, CT, 1931), vol. 1, 61.

35. Johnson to Conway, 28 June 1766, CO 5/66, 148–50.

36. Johnson, "Review of the Trade and Affairs," 965.

37. Hillsborough to Stuart, 31 July 1770, CO 5/71, 11. Also see extract of a letter from Penn to Gage, 15 Dec. 1767, CO 5/86, 17.

38. Gage to Hillsborough, 7 Oct. 1772, CO 5/90, 78.

39. Settlers, some have argued, would recognize how living like Indians had changed them. And they would lash out at those who reminded them of their declension and, by our parlance, their "liminality." On the issue of liminality and whiteness—and the ways modern concepts of race would be constructed—see Jane Merritt, *At the Cross-*

roads: Indians and Empires on a Mid-Atlantic Frontier, 1700–1763 (Chapel Hill, NC, 2003); and Nancy Shoemaker, *A Strange Likeness: Becoming Red and White in Eighteenth-Century North America* (New York, 2004). Some argue that gender anxieties also contributed to the creation of whiteness. On this, see Krista Camenzind, "Violence, Race, and the Paxton Boys," in Pencak and Richter, *Friends and Enemies in Penn's Woods*, 201–20.

40. Stuart to Hillsborough, 12 June 1772, CO 5/73, 164.

41. Bernard Bailyn makes this argument to come to terms with the troubling behavior of frontier men and women in *The Peopling of British North America* (New York, 1986).

42. Although the British government had not made specific plans for the region, one Virginia official declared in 1767, "I understand the Illinois will be settled and formed as separate governments." George Mercer to members of the Ohio Company, 21 Nov. 1767, *William and Mary Quarterly* 1 (1893), 201. On the wranglings of traders and speculators and the line, see Jack Sosin, *The Revolutionary Frontier, 1763–83* (New York, 1967).

43. Johnson to Lords of Trade, 24 May 1765, in Clarence Alvord and Clarence Carter, eds., *The Critical Period, 1763–1765* (Springfield, IL, 1915), 501; George Croghan private journal, Fort Pitt to the Illinois Country, 1765–66, George Croghan Correspondence, Cadwalader Collection, ser. 4, 1, HSP.

44. Fort Pitt Trading Post daybook, 1765–72, account entries for March through June 1765, Historical Society of Western Pennsylvania, Pittsburgh.

45. Memorial of licensed traders of South Carolina to Stuart, 21 May 1767, CO 5/58, 140; Francis Fauquier to Stuart, 21 Nov. 1767, CO 5/69, 133.

46. Johnson, "Review of the Trade and Affairs," 960.

47. Johnson to Lords of Trade, 8 Oct. 1764, in Alvord and Carter, *Critical Period*, 323.

48. Morgan to partners of Baynton, Wharton, and Morgan, 5 April 1768, George Morgan letter book, 1767–68, 118–21, HSP.

49. Croghan private journal, 18.

50. Johnson, "Review of the Trade and Affairs," 972.

51. "The Humble Memorial of Phineas Lyman, Esq., on Behalf of Himself and the Rest of the Officers and Soldiers of the Several Corps of American Provincial Troops," CO 5/67, 183; Gage to Conway, 22 Feb. 1766, CO 5/84, 64–65; "Articles of the Mississippi Company," 1763, in Alvord and Carter, *Critical Period*, 19–29. On these schemes, see Sosin, *Revolutionary Frontier*, 28–34. Johnson participated in the western rage for land. By 1766, he had joined Croghan in a Pennsylvania-based concern that had broadened beyond the membership of the "suffering traders" called the Illinois Company. In 1764, he had floated the idea of establishing some sort of government in Illinois. "The importance of speedily possessing the Illinois . . . is a matter verry much at heart," he wrote at that time. Two years later Johnson got in touch with some members of the board, informing them that "several gentlemen of fortune and character in the province of Pennsylvania" contacted him "for erecting a colony at the Illinois." See "The First American Movement West," 6, transcripts from the Gratz Papers, 1750–1850, William Vincent Byars Collection, HSP; Johnson to Lords of Trade, 26 Dec. 1764, in Alvord and Carter, *Critical Period*, 394; Johnson to Conway, 10 July 1766, CO 5/67, 91.

52. Croghan to Benjamin Franklin, 12 Feb. 1768, and Croghan to Johnson, 30 March 1766, Croghan Correspondence, files 29, 32; "First American Movement West," 6, 15.

53. See Eric Hinderaker, *Elusive Empires: Constructing Colonialism in the Ohio Valley, 1673–1880* (New York, 1997); Thomas Perkins Abernethy, *Western Lands and the American Revolution* (New York, 1937).

54. Wharton to Croghan, 4 Sept. 1770, Croghan Correspondence, file 31.

55. "Articles of the Mississippi Company," 19.

56. Johnson to Lords of Trade, 8 Oct. 1764, in Alvord and Carter, *Critical Period*, 325; Mercer to members of the Ohio Company, 21 Nov. 1767, 200.

57. See, for example, *The Expediency of Securing Our American Colonies* (Edinburgh, 1763), in Alvord and Carter, *Critical Period*, 141, and "Articles of the Mississippi Company," 19–29; Croghan to Johnson, 18 Jan. 1767, George Croghan Papers, Letters and Documents, file 5, HSP.

58. Croghan to Johnson, 27 Dec. 1765, CO 5/66, 114–15.

59. "Humble Memorial of Phineas Lyman," 183.

60. Wharton to Croghan, 24 Dec. 1772, Croghan Correspondence, file 31.

61. Croghan to Wharton, 2 Nov. 1771, Croghan Correspondence, file 29.

62. "Articles of the Mississippi Company," 27.

63. Wood, *Americanization of Benjamin Franklin*; Eric Hinderaker and Peter Mancall, *At the Edge of Empire: The Backcountry in British North America* (Baltimore, 2003), 143. On Hillsborough's career, see Peter Marshall's entry in the *Oxford Dictionary of National Biography* (Oxford, UK, 2004–6).

64. Croghan to Johnson, 12 July 1764, and Johnson to Lords of Trade, 8 Oct. 1764, in Alvord and Carter, *Critical Period*, 464, 325.

65. Croghan to Johnson, 30 March 1766, Croghan Correspondence, file 32.

66. See, for instance, Wharton to Croghan, 4 Sept. 1770, Croghan Correspondence, file 31.

67. For the way this process worked in the eighteenth century, see Patrick Griffin, *The People with No Name: Ireland's Ulster Scots, America's Scots Irish, and the Creation of a British Atlantic World, 1689–1764* (Princeton, NJ, 2001); Richard Beeman, *The Evolution of the Southern Backcountry: A Case Study of Lunenburg County, Virginia, 1746–1832* (Philadelphia, 1984); and Bailyn, *The Peopling of British North America*.

68. The best analysis of this pattern is Warren Hofstra, *The Planting of New Virginia: Settlement and Landscape in the Shenandoah Valley* (Baltimore, 2004). Also see Fred Anderson and Andrew Cayton, *The Dominion of War: Empire and Liberty in North America, 1500–2000* (New York, 2005), 109, 133.

69. Indeed, much of the eighteenth century between the Great Peace of 1701 and the outbreak of the French and Indian War in 1754 can be referred to as the long peace on the borders of Pennsylvania and Virginia. See Anderson and Cayton, *Dominion of War*.

70. James Lemon, *The Best Poor Man's Country: A Geographical Study of Early Southeastern Pennsylvania* (Baltimore, 1972); Hofstra, *Planting of New Virginia*.

71. On the war, see John Oliphant, *Peace and War on the Anglo-Cherokee Frontier* (Baton Rouge, LA, 2001). The tensions gripping the region in the years before the

Revolutionary War are covered in Marjoleine Kars, *Breaking Loose Together: The Regulator Rebellion in Pre-Revolutionary North Carolina* (Chapel Hill, NC, 2002).

72. Undeniably, Thomas Perkins Abernethy cast a jaundiced eye at the activities of speculators, but he saw this dynamic at work in the peopling of the West. See *Western Lands*, 13. Carl Bridenbaugh, while highlighting the settlement of backcountry regions east of the line, underscored the tensions and growing population in those areas that led to the push to move west. See *Myths and Realities: Societies of the Colonial South* (New York, 1952), 121, 123-24, 139.

73. Lords of Trade to His Majesty, 7 March 1768, CO 5/59, 61-62.

74. David Ross to Alexander Cameron, 20 Dec. 1768, CO 5/71, 65.

75. "Articles of the Mississippi Company," 26.

76. Johnson to Lords of Trade, 13 Nov. 1763, in *Pennsylvania Archives*, vol. 6, 607.

77. Johnson to Lords of Trade, 24 May 1765, in Alvord and Carter, *Critical Period*, 503.

78. Ibid., 503-4. See also Johnson to Shelburne, 16 Dec. 1766, CO 5/67, 266-69.

79. Wharton to Croghan, 24 Dec. 1772, Croghan Correspondence, file 31.

80. Deposition of Joseph Tomlinson, n.d., Thomas Cresap Family Papers, 26, Miscellaneous Manuscripts Collections, Library of Congress, Washington, DC; Sosin, *Revolutionary Frontier*, 28, 34.

81. See, for example, extract of a letter from Cameron to Stuart, 27 June 1770, CO 5/71, 31.

82. James Tilghman to Croghan, 24 June 1771, Croghan Correspondence, file 23.

83. Johnson to Gage, 14 Feb. 1765, Gage Papers.

84. John Armstrong to Croghan, 26 March 1765, Croghan Correspondence, file 2.

85. Cresap to Horatio Sharpe, 15 July 1763, Cresap Family Papers.

86. William Trent journal at Fort Pitt, 1763, 2-3, HSP. For a study of the violent nature of the Seven Years' War on the Pennsylvania frontier, see Peter Silver, "Indian-Hating and the Rise of Whiteness in Provincial Pennsylvania."

87. Livingston to Bouquet, 16 July 1763, in Waddell, *Papers of Bouquet*, vol. 6, 317.

88. "Return of Persons Killed or Taken by Indians in the Department of Fort Pitt," 5 Sept. 1763, in Waddell, *Papers of Bouquet*, vol. 6, 410-11.

89. John Brown to Preston [1764], Preston Papers, ser. 2QQ, 50-51.

90. "List of Indian Traders and Their Servants Killed or Captured by Indians," 5 Sept. 1763, in Waddell, *Papers of Bouquet*, vol. 6, 412-13. The best study of how the world of such go-betweens fell apart at the time of the Seven Years' War is James Merrell's *Into the American Woods: Negotiators on the Pennsylvania Frontier* (New York, 1999).

91. "List of Traders Killed by Indians," Dec. 1763, in Waddell, *Papers of Bouquet*, vol. 6, 489-90.

92. James McCullough diary in Kerby Miller, David Doyle, et al., eds., *Irish Immigrants in the Land of Canaan: Letters and Memoirs from Colonial and Revolutionary America, 1675-1815* (New York, 2003), 172-78.

93. Livingston to Bouquet, 16 July 1763, in Waddell, *Papers of Bouquet*, vol. 6, 317.

94. Johnson, "Review of the Trade and Affairs," 959.

95. "Apology of the Paxton Volunteers," 1-4, 6, 8, 9-10.

96. Ibid. For the political debates surrounding the Paxton affair, see the published and unpublished accounts and diatribes reproduced in John Dunbar, ed., *The Paxton Pa-*

pers (The Hague, Netherlands, 1957); and Alison Olson, "The Pamphlet War over the Paxton Boys," *Pennsylvania Magazine of History and Biography* 123 (1999), 31–55.

97. Bernard Bailyn, *The Ideological Origins of the American Revolution* (Cambridge, MA, 1967), 336.

98. "Apology of the Paxton Volunteers," 1–4, 6, 8, 9–10.

99. "The Cloven Foot Discovered," "A Declaration and Remonstrance of the Distressed and Bleeding Frontier Inhabitants of the Province of Pennsylvania," and "An Historical Account of the Late Disturbances Between the Inhabitants of the Back Settlements of Pennsylvania and the Philadelphians," in Dunbar, *Paxton Papers*, 86, 108–9, 128.

100. On this notion of race idioms, see Joyce Chaplin, *Subject Matter: Technology, the Body, and Science on the Anglo-American Frontier, 1500–1676* (Cambridge, MA, 2001); and John Wood Sweet, *Bodies Politic: Negotiating Race in the American North, 1730–1830* (Baltimore, 2003), 8, 110, 115, 272.

101. William Smith, *An Historical Account of the Expedition Against the Ohio Indians* (Philadelphia, 1765), 1–2.

102. Barton to the secretary, 16 Nov. 1764, in W. S. Perry, ed., *Historical Collections Relating to the American Colonial Church* (New York, 1871), vol. 2, 369.

103. Thomas Barton, *The Conduct of the Paxton-Men, Impartially Represented* (Philadelphia, 1764), 6, 8, 14, 29.

104. Ibid., 29, 24.

105. Thomas Barton, *Unanimity and Public Spirit* (Philadelphia, 1755), preface, xiv, 4, 10, 12, 15.

106. Miller, Doyle, et al., *Irish Immigrants in the Land of Canaan*, 487–99; J. P. Myers, "Thomas Barton's *Unanimity and Public Spirit* (1755): Controversy and Plagiarism on the Pennsylvania Frontier," *Pennsylvania Magazine of History and Biography* 119 (1995), 225–48.

107. Johnson to Lords of Trade, 26 Dec. 1764, in Alvord and Carter, *Critical Period*, 393.

108. Andrew Lewis to William Christian, 4 Aug. 1764, Bullitt Papers, William Christian Correspondence, Filson Historical Society, Louisville, KY.

109. Gage to Conway, 6 May 1766, in Carter, *Correspondence of Gage*, vol. 1, 91. See also Johnson to Lords of Trade, 28 June 1766, in O'Callaghan, *Documents*, vol. 7, 838.

110. Dror Wahrman, *The Making of the Modern Self: Identity and Culture in Eighteenth-Century England* (New Haven, CT, 2004), 87, 117.

111. Smith, *Historical Account*, 3.

112. "Petition of Cumberland County Inhabitants to Governor Penn," March 1765, in Waddell, *Papers of Bouquet*, vol. 6, 777–79.

113. On this theme, see *A New Song in High Vogue in Northampton County* (Philadelphia, 1771), which lauds the Paxton Boys.

114. Johnson to Lords of Trade, 26 Dec. 1764, in Alvord and Carter, *Critical Period*, 392.

115. Ibid., 393.

116. On this, see Johnson to Lords of Trade, 8 Oct. 1764, in Alvord and Carter, *Critical Period*, 334.

117. Johnson to Conway, 28 June 1766, in O'Callaghan, *Documents*, vol. 7, 835.

118. Johnson to Shelburne, 14 March 1768, CO 5/69, 164.

119. See, for example, George Morgan's Journal of a Trip Down the Ohio, 1767, 7, 25–26; Morgan to partners, 20 July 1768, 191–93, Morgan letter book, 1767–68, HSP; Croghan private journal, 15; Johnson to Shelburne, 23 Dec. 1767, CO 5/58, 220–22; abstract of a talk from the Cherokee Indians to Stuart, 29 July 1769, CO 5/71, 63.

120. McConnell, *A Country Between*, 12–13; James Merrell, afterword to Pencak and Richter, *Friends and Enemies in Penn's Woods*, 262.

121. By far the best account of what was happening in Native communities west of the line during this period is Richard White's *Middle Ground: Indians, Empires, and Republics in the Great Lakes Region, 1650–1815* (New York, 1991).

122. Bouquet to Gage, 22 Dec. 1764, Bouquet Add. MSS, 21637, 82–83.

123. Bouquet to Sharpe, 20 Dec. 1764, Bouquet Add. MSS, 21637, 84.

124. Sharpe to Bouquet, 11 Jan. 1765, Gage Papers.

125. Bouquet to Gage, 22 Dec. 1764, Bouquet Add. MSS, 21637, 82–83.

126. William Johnson, "A Review of the Progression, State of the Trade, Politicks, and Proceedings of the Indians of the North District," 16 Nov. 1767, CO 5/58, 192.

127. Johnson to Lords of Trade, 28 June 1766, in O'Callaghan, *Documents*, vol. 7, 838.

CHAPTER 3: ABANDONING THE LINE

1. Johnson to Lords of Trade, 20 Aug. 1766, in E. B. O'Callaghan, ed., *Documents Relative to the Colonial History of the State of New York* (Albany, NY, 1856), vol. 7, 851–52.

2. Luke Gibbons, *Edmund Burke and Ireland: Aesthetics, Politics, and the Colonial Sublime* (Cambridge, UK, 2003).

3. A number of historians, while admitting the pressures brought to bear by settlers on imperial governance, favor interpretations that point to a British failure of will or resolve in making the West a just place. Understandably, with colonial boycotts in place with the Townshend duties, doing so proved difficult. On this, see Jack Sosin, *Whitehall and the Wilderness: The Middle West in British Colonial Policy* (Lincoln, NE, 1961). Gregory Dowd, in *War Under Heaven: Pontiac, the Indian Nations, and the British Empire* (Baltimore, 2002), doubts the British ever had plans to deal with Indians fairly. Richard White, in *The Middle Ground: Indians, Empires, and Republics in the Great Lakes Region, 1650–1815* (New York, 1991), concludes that failing to provide adequate resources imperiled the "middle ground" approach. Eric Hinderaker suggests that common whites played an important role in weakening British resolve. He also argues that speculation, engaged in or sponsored by officials, also compromised the system. See *Elusive Empires: Constructing Colonialism in the Ohio Valley, 1673–1800* (New York, 1997).

4. Gage to Lord Hillsborough, 1 July 1772, CO 5/90, 41, Public Record Office, London.

5. Bouquet to Horatio Sharpe, 20 Dec. 1764, in Louis Waddell, ed., *The Papers of Henry Bouquet* (Harrisburg, PA, 1994), vol. 6, 739.

6. For a taste of the kinds of goods that would be used, see the Baynton, Wharton, and Morgan section in the Fort Pitt Trading Post daybook, especially the entry for George Croghan of 1 March 1765, Historical Society of Western Pennsylvania, Pittsburgh.

7. William Murray to Gage, 3 March 1765, Gage Papers, American Series, William Clements Library, University of Michigan, Ann Arbor.
8. Deposition of Elias Davison, 11 March 1765, Gage Papers.
9. Deposition of Robert Allison, 11 March 1765, Gage Papers.
10. Deposition of Davison, 11 March 1765, Gage Papers.
11. Deposition of Allison, 11 March 1765, Gage Papers.
12. Charles Grant to Bouquet, 9 March 1765, Gage Papers; Nathaniel McCullough to Bouquet, 7 March 1765, Bouquet Add. MSS, 21651, 204, British Library, London.
13. Grant to Bouquet, 9 March 1765, Gage Papers. The justice of the peace had little choice but to let them go. As one local put it, "Otherwise . . . it would have Produced a Civil War," or at least "run the Risque of loosing a great many Innocent Peoples lives." Thomas Barnsley to Gage, 11 March 1765, Gage Papers.
14. Bouquet to Gage, 29 March 1765, Gage Papers.
15. John Armstrong to Croghan, 26 March 1765, George Croghan Correspondence, Cadwalader Collection, ser. 4, box 5, file 2, Historical Society of Pennsylvania, Philadelphia (hereafter cited as HSP).
16. The goods, a British military commander charged, had been sent "with a view to a Market, and open the Trade at Fort Pitt before Permission should be given." Gage to Bouquet, 21 March 1765, Gage Papers.
17. Bouquet to Gage, 10 April 1765, George Croghan Papers, file 8, HSP; John Penn to Gage, 22 March 1765, Gage Papers.
18. Gage to Croghan, 4 April 1765, Gage Papers. Also see Bouquet to Gage, 29 March 1765, Croghan Papers, file 8.
19. Croghan to Franklin, 12 Dec. 1765, CO 5/66, 83–85.
20. Johnson to Lords of Trade, July 1765, in Clarence Alvord and Clarence Carter, eds., *The Critical Period, 1763–1765* (Springfield, IL, 1915), 522–23; Johnson to Gage, 27 April 1765, in Alexander Flick, ed., *The Papers of Sir William Johnson* (Albany, NY, 1925), vol. 4, 732.
21. Samuel Wharton to Johnson, 14 April 1765, in Flick, *Papers of Johnson*, vol. 4, 713; Judith Ridner, "Relying on the 'Saucy' Men of the Backcountry: Middle Men and the Fur Trade in Pennsylvania," *Pennsylvania Magazine of History and Biography* 129 (2005), 133–62; Josiah Davenport to Johnson, 27 March 1765, Indian Affairs Commissioner Papers, Gratz Autograph Collection, HSP; Johnson to Croghan, 8 April 1765, Croghan Correspondence, box 6, file 33.
22. Croghan to Franklin, 12 Dec. 1765, Croghan Papers, file 8.
23. Armstrong to Croghan, 26 March 1765, Croghan Correspondence, box 5, file 2.
24. Davenport to Johnson, 27 March 1765, Indian Affairs Commissioner Papers. Also see Robert Callender to Bouquet, 11 March 1765, in Waddell, *Papers of Bouquet*, vol. 6, 764; Nathaniel McCullough to Croghan, 7 March 1765, Gage Papers; Bouquet to Gage, 19 March 1765, Bouquet Add. MSS, 21637.
25. Thomas Rutherford to Bouquet, 27 June 1764, Bouquet Add. MSS, 21650, 272.
26. "Petition of Cumberland County Inhabitants to Gov. Penn," March 1765, in Waddell, *Papers of Bouquet*, vol. 6, 778–79. Greg Dowd argues that, as opposed to the Paxton Boys, the Black Boys did not harbor anti-Indian attitudes (*War Under Heaven*). At the time, Johnson thought otherwise. "The Frontier Inhabitants of

Pennsylvania, Maryland and Virginia," he wrote, "having attacked and destroyed the Goods which were going to Fort Pitt . . . did form themselves into parties, threatening to destroy all Indians they met, or all white people who dealt with them." Johnson continued that they "marched on" to lands beyond the Proclamation Line "where they declare they will form a settlement in defiance of whites or Indians." Johnson to Lords of Trade, 1765, CO 5/66, 268–70.

27. Croghan to Bouquet, 12 March 1765, Bouquet Add. MSS, 21651, 214.

28. Johnson to Lords of Trade, 22 Nov. 1765, CO 5/66, 323–25.

29. Johnson to Lords of Trade, 28 June 1766, CO 5/66, 337–40.

30. Croghan to Bouquet, 12 March 1765, and Bouquet to Gage, 16 March 1765, in Waddell, *Papers of Bouquet*, vol. 6, 766, 768.

31. Morgan to partners, 5 April and 20 July 1768, George Morgan letter book, 1767–68, 113–14, 118, 191–93, HSP.

32. Johnson to Henry Seymour Conway, 28 June 1766, in O'Callaghan, *Documents*, vol. 7, 835.

33. John Stuart to _____, 8 Aug. 1766, CO 5/67, 102.

34. Abstract of a letter from George True, 21 Jan. 1767, and Alexander Cameron's talk to the Cherokees, 9 Feb. 1767, CO 5/58, 99, 100.

35. Johnson to Lords of Trade, n.d. 1765, CO 5/66, 270. On this theme, also see Johnson to the Earl of Shelburne, 14 Aug. 1767, CO 5/68, 168.

36. Lords of Trade to Shelburne, 23 Dec. 1767, CO 5/58, 220–22.

37. William Johnson, "Review of the Trade and Affairs of the Indians in the Northern District of America," in O'Callaghan, *Documents*, vol. 7, 964.

38. Johnson to Conway, 28 June 1766, in O'Callaghan, *Documents*, vol. 7, 836.

39. Croghan to Johnson, 12 July 1766, Croghan Papers, file 1.

40. "The Mutiny Act, March 24, 1765," in Alvord and Carter, *Critical Period*, 485; Gage to Hillsborough, 7 Oct. 1769, CO 5/87, 168.

41. Johnson to Shelburne, 1 April 1767, CO 5/58, 115.

42. Johnson, "Review of the Trade and Affairs," 964.

43. Answer from the headman of the Lower Creek Nation to a talk sent to them by John Stuart, 19 Sept. 1767, CO 5/59, 135.

44. Gage to Shelburne, 5 April 1767, CO 5/85, 86–87.

45. Gage to Conway, 22 Feb. 1766, in Clarence Carter, ed., *The Correspondence of General Thomas Gage with the Secretaries of State, 1763–1765* (New Haven, CT, 1931), vol. 1, 84; Gage to Shelburne, 12 March 1768, CO 5/86, 48.

46. Johnson to Conway, 28 June 1766, CO 5/66, 148–50.

47. Johnson to Lords of Trade, 22 Nov. 1765, 31 Jan. 1766, CO 5/66, 323–25, 330. Also see Gage to Conway, 6 May 1766, in Carter, *Correspondence of Gage*, vol. 1, 91.

48. Johnson to Lords of Trade, 22 Nov. 1765, 31 Jan. 1766, CO 5/66, 323–25, 330.

49. See, for instance, the parallels Johnson draws between his tenants on the New York frontier and eastern insurgents. Johnson to Lords of Trade, 28 June 1766, CO 5/66, 337–40.

50. Johnson to Lords of Trade, 20 Aug. 1766, CO 5/67, 61. Also see Johnson to Shelburne, 16 Dec. 1766, CO 5/67, 266–69.

51. Gage to Conway, 23 Sept. 1765, in Carter, *Correspondence of Gage*, vol. 1, 68.

52. Gage to Conway, 21 Dec. 1765, CO 5/84, 13.

53. Hillsborough to Johnson, 12 Oct. 1768, CO 5/69, 240–41; Hillsborough to Gage, 15 July 1769, CO 5/87, 119.

54. Gage to Conway, 6 May 1766, in Carter, *Correspondence of Gage*, vol. 1, 90.

55. Gage to Shelburne, 22 Jan. 1768, CO 5/86, 11–12.

56. Croghan to Franklin, 12 Feb. 1768, Croghan Correspondence, box 5, file 29.

57. Johnson to Shelburne, 14 March 1768, CO 5/69, 163. For this episode, also see White, *Middle Ground*, 348–49.

58. Croghan to Gage, 17 Feb. and 14 April 1768; Croghan to Johnson, 7 Feb. 1768, George Croghan Correspondence, file 29.

59. Gage to Shelburne, 30 Jan. 1768, CO 5/86, 35.

60. Johnson to Shelburne, 14 March 1768, CO 5/69, 163. Croghan to Gage, 17 Feb. 1768; Croghan to Johnson, 7 Feb. 1768, Croghan Correspondence, file 29.

61. *Minutes of a Conference, Held at Fort-Pitt, in April and May, 1768* (Philadelphia, 1768), 5.

62. Johnson's instruction to Croghan, 5 March 1768, Croghan Correspondence, file 23.

63. Croghan to Thomas Wharton, 7 May 1768, *Pennsylvania Magazine of History and Biography* 15 (1891), 430; Croghan to Penn, 27 March 1768, Croghan Correspondence, file 29.

64. Letter on Frontier Intelligence to John Wilkins, March 1768, Croghan Correspondence, file 29. The goods made it to Fort Pitt with a strong escort of British troops. They also had to protect Croghan "from the Frontier People who have threatened his life." See Gage to Shelburne, 24 April 1768, CO 5/86, 68.

65. Gage relating substance of what Croghan encountered in letter to Hillsborough, 15 May 1768, CO 5/86, 87. Also see Gage to Hillsborough, 18 June 1768, CO 5/86, 113.

66. Richard White argues that at this juncture, the British tried to reestablish the middle ground, condoling Indians and following Indian diplomatic protocol. Arguably, men like Johnson and Croghan never abandoned this approach, even if the imperial plan was centrally administered. Instead, they saw the middle ground not as an end of empire but as a means to make it work. What was new at this juncture was the reliance on the Iroquois to make the failing middle ground work in even the most rudimentary and pro forma fashion. See *Middle Ground*, 346. Although the imperial plan had gone ahead by 1764, the ministry and Board of Trade stipulated that Johnson and Stuart should consult Indians on the parameters of the final boundaries of the Proclamation Line. The Lords of Trade expected that minor adjustments would result and hoped that the finished product would reflect the realities of settlement. If large groups of Indians lived on the eastern boundary of the line, or if large pockets of white settlement jutted into Indian territory, common sense dictated slight shifts in the line. In 1768, as officials reckoned with the specter of more killing and illicit landgrabs, they used this rationale and the now-tarnished covenant chain to redraw the line in a radical fashion, even as the Board of Trade acceded to much smaller adjustments. See Sosin, *Whitehall and the Wilderness*, 163. They believed that they had some justification in doing so. After all, the Iroquois asserted that the Ohio Country belonged to them by "conquests" made a century earlier and that they had permitted the groups living there now to settle on their sovereign lands. Subsequent treaties, such as the Treaty of Easton in 1758, reasserted Iroquois su-

premacy over the region west of the mountains. Moreover, the Iroquois claimed that they had also "conquered" the Cherokees. Relying on the Iroquois in this way created useful fictions that officials could exploit to try to salvage some order in the West. On this, see Johnson to Lords of Trade, 16 Nov. 1765, in O'Callaghan, *Documents*, vol. 7, 777; Gage to Shelburne, 27 May 1767, CO 5/85, 117; Johnson to Stuart, 1766, CO 5/67, 9–11; Fred Anderson, *The Crucible of War: The Seven Years' War and the Fate of Empire in British North America* (New York, 2000), 274–80.

67. Johnson to Hillsborough, 23 Oct. 1768, CO 5/69, 306. The discussion of the conference that follows can be found in "Proceedings of a Treaty held . . . at Fort Stanwix," Oct. and Nov. 1768, CO 5/69, 314–34. Also see Hinderaker, *Elusive Empires*, 168; Sosin, *Whitehall and the Wilderness*, 165–80; and Alan Taylor, *The Divided Ground: Indians, Settlers, and the Northern Borderland of the American Revolution* (New York, 2006), 40–45.

68. Gage to Hillsborough, 9 Sept. 1768, CO 5/86, 170–71; "Proceedings of a Treaty held . . . at Fort Stanwix."

69. Sosin, *Whitehall and the Wilderness*, 175.

70. Ibid., 172.

71. Croghan to Franklin, 12 Dec. 1765, CO 5/66, 83–85; Eric Hinderaker and Peter Mancall, *At the Edge of Empire: The Backcountry in British North America* (Baltimore, 2003), 147; Sosin, *Whitehall and the Wilderness*, 146, 175.

72. Redrawing the line in this fashion would, Johnson hoped, "have the effect to prevent the fatal consequences of an Indian war that seems at present to threaten the middle colonies, by giving satisfaction to the Indians in a point most essential to their interests, without confining the settlements of His majesty's subjects to too narrow limits." Lords of Trade to Shelburne, 23 Dec. 1767, CO 5/58, 220–22; Gage to Shelburne, 29 April 1767, CO 5/85, 108. White concedes that officials salved their consciences by believing they were working for peace (*Middle Ground*, 351).

73. Gage to Hillsborough, 5 Jan. 1769, CO 5/87, 3–4.

74. Johnson to Shelburne, 3 Dec. 1767, CO 5/69, 50–51.

75. Sosin, *Whitehall and the Wilderness*, 171–77; Woody Holton, *Forced Founders: Indians, Debtors, Slaves, and the Making of the American Revolution in Virginia* (Chapel Hill, NC, 1999), 10.

76. Johnson to Shelburne, 14 March 1768, CO 5/69, 163–64.

77. Petition to the Speaker and Gentlemen of the House of Burgesses by the Inhabitants of New River in Augusta County [n.d., but from late 1760s or early 1770s], William Preston Papers, Draper MSS, ser. 2QQ, 115, Historical Society of Wisconsin, Madison. On this, see Hinderaker, *Elusive Empires*, 171.

78. Thomas Lewis to Preston, 17 Aug. 1768 and 14 Jan. 1769, Preston Papers, ser. 2QQ, 105, 106.

79. George Rogers Clark to Jonathan Clark, 9 Jan. 1773, Jonathan Clark Papers, Draper MSS, ser. 1L, 9.

80. David Ross to Alexander Cameron, 20 Dec. 1768, CO 5/71, 65. Also see Stuart to Hillsborough, 20 Jan. 1770, CO 5/71, 52.

81. Croghan had conceded that he did not think the scheme stood any chance of success

during his trip to London when he lobbied the Board of Trade for Johnson's plan for the West. See Croghan to Johnson, 14 April 1764, in Flick, *Papers of Johnson*, vol. 4, 397.

82. Sosin, *Whitehall and the Wilderness*, 186.

83. "The First American Movement West," 9–17, transcripts from the Gratz Papers, 1750–1850, William Vincent Byars Collection, HSP; Ohio Company Papers, vol. 1, 39, 82, 85, Etting Collection, HSP.

84. Holton, *Forced Founders*, 3–10; Hinderaker, *Elusive Empires*, 163, 171–72; Sosin, *Whitehall and the Wilderness*, 175, 189.

85. Croghan to Thomas Wharton, 7 May 1768, *Pennsylvania Magazine of History and Biography* 15 (1891), 430.

86. Sosin, *Whitehall and the Wilderness*; Samuel Wharton to Croghan, 4 Sept. 1770, Croghan Papers.

87. Hillsborough to Johnson, 12 Oct. 1768, CO 5/69, 240–41. Sosin, *Whitehall and the Wilderness*, 178; Hinderaker, *Elusive Empires*, 168.

88. Lords of Trade to His Majesty, 25 April 1769, CO 5/70, 195–96.

89. Any lands granted in the West, the ministry had demanded, had to be made "to the King in Trust for" individuals. But, as a lobbyist argued, "the Question of *Right* does not depend upon those Words, but on the Grantors having an inherent and undoubted Power to grant the Lands to Us, as well as to the King, and on our Rights as *Subjects*." Samuel Wharton to Croghan, 4 Sept. 1770, Croghan Papers.

90. Ibid.

91. When Shelburne had a formative voice in American affairs — before 1768, that is — he supported this policy because he believed that the movement of whites west could not be checked. See Sosin, *Whitehall and the Wilderness*, 158–59.

92. Stuart to Hillsborough, 12 Feb. 1769, CO 5/70, 124.

93. Petition to the Speaker and Gentlemen of the House of Burgesses, 115. On the Cherokee response, see Gage to Hillsborough, 17 Aug. 1768, CO 5/86, 148–49; White, *Middle Ground*, 322.

94. Hinderaker, *Elusive Empires*, 168.

95. Anderson, *Crucible of War*, 274–80.

96. Guy Johnson to Hillsborough, 20 June 1768, CO 5/69, 212, and 14 Aug. 1770, CO 5/71, 93.

97. Stuart to Hillsborough, 2 May 1770, CO 5/71, 105.

98. Gage to Stuart, 16 Oct. 1770, CO 5/72, 41.

99. Jacob Sommerhill to Stuart, 10 Nov. 1768, CO 5/70, 107.

100. Johnson to Hillsborough, 26 Aug. 1769, CO 5/70, 277; Gage to Hillsborough, 17 Aug. 1768, CO 5/86, 146; abstract of a letter from John Watts, Indian interpreter, to Stuart, 17 May 1770, CO 5/71, 33; abstract of a letter from Richard King to John Caldwell, 1 Feb. 1771, CO 5/72, 173–74; Gage to Hillsborough, 9 Oct. 1768, CO 5/86, 196–97; Stuart to Hillsborough, 5 March 1771, CO 5/72, 165.

101. Johnson to Hillsborough, 18 Feb. 1771, CO 5/72, 183.

102. Abstract of a letter from King to Caldwell, 1 Feb. 1771, CO 5/72, 173–74.

103. Cameron to Stuart, 9 Aug. 1772, CO 5/72, 420.

104. Johnson to Hillsborough, 29 June 1772, CO 5/72, 394–95.

105. Mayor of Fort Pitt to Gage, 22 Jan. 1772, Gage Papers.
106. White argues that officials had a difficult time keeping the middle ground operating because officials in London would not furnish the necessary goods. He claims that, in fact, some common settlers—but a minority by his estimation—kept some sort of middle ground alive. These, however, were mainly a few unlicensed traders, a number of captives, and missionaries. Most whites, he believes, rejected cultural accommodation. As he says, any viable middle ground had to be "diplomatic" and did not as a rule extend to "day-to-day life." See *Middle Ground*, 315–39. James Merrell, on the other hand, who questions the utility of the middle ground approach, sees Montour as a symbolic figure in that regard. See *Into the American Woods: Negotiators on the Pennsylvania Frontier* (New York, 1999). Another historian who seems to share Merrell's ambivalence about the concept—albeit exploring a different region from White's study—is Alan Taylor in the aptly titled *Divided Ground*. Both suggest that if the middle ground ever existed, it had certainly fallen apart by the time of the Revolution.
107. Gage to Hillsborough, 7 Oct. 1772, CO 5/90, 78. Also see "Copy of a Speech Sent from the Chiefs of the Delawares . . . Living on the Ohio to the Governors of Pennsylvania, Maryland, and Virginia" [late 1771], CO 5/90, 5–6.
108. Croghan to Gage, 2 Nov. 1771, and Croghan to Samuel Wharton, 2 Nov. 1771, Croghan Papers, file 31; Gage to Hillsborough, 4 Dec. 1771, CO 5/90, 3–4. On Croghan's activities—as well as rival Virginia plans—see Hinderaker, *Elusive Empires*, 172–73; Sosin, *Whitehall and the Wilderness*, 181–210.
109. Hillsborough to Gage, 4 Dec. 1771, CO 5/89, 181. Also see Sosin, *Whitehall and the Wilderness*, 220–21. For the justifications used, see Gage to Wilkins, 9 March 1772, Gage Papers; Gage to Hillsborough, 16 June 1768, CO 5/86, 107; Hillsborough to Gage, 24 March 1769, CO 5/87, 73–74.
110. Gage to Hillsborough, 7 Oct. 1772, CO 5/90, 77. Hinderaker, *Elusive Empires*, 170–71; Sosin, *Whitehall and the Wilderness*, 155.
111. Gage to Hillsborough, 16 June 1768, CO 5/86, 107. As early as the late 1760s, as the system began breaking down, Hillsborough had considered abandoning forts (Sosin, *Whitehall and the Wilderness*, 211). Moreover, they could not fulfill even their most rudimentary function, providing defense. See Gage to Lord Dartmouth, 5 May 1773, CO 5/90, 145.
112. Gage to Henry Hamilton, 24 Feb. 1772, Gage Papers; Gage to Hillsborough, 7 Oct. 1772, CO 5/90, 77. As almost a perverse metaphor for the failure of the imperial plan, even the work of dismantling the fort did not go smoothly. For this fascinating story, see the following letters in the Gage Papers: Gage to Hamilton, 14 March 1772; Charles Edmonstone to Gage, 23 March 1772; Gage to Edmonstone, 9 April, 10 May, 31 Aug., 17 Dec. 1772; Edmonstone to Gage, 24 Dec. 1772. After a great number of headaches, and the incompetence of a junior officer, "this fort was abandoned and demolished 20th Nov. 1772." See "List of Officers Who Have Commanded at the Out Posts from 25 Dec. 1771 to 24 Dec. 1772," Gage Papers, Proclamations and Documents.
113. John Penn, "A Message from the Governor to the Assembly," 16 May 1769, CO 5/87, 138. As early as 1768, the members of the Board of Trade considered the idea of

giving colonies a larger role in running the West. When the original plan for the frontier was adopted, it was done so, in part, "to counteract the Designs of the French." That threat had never materialized. The board therefore proposed to entrust "the Indian Trade, and all other Indian Affairs to the Management of the several Colonies." Lords of Trade to His Majesty, 7 March 1768, CO 5/69, 61–62.

114. Sosin, *Whitehall and the Wilderness*, 187, 205.

115. Samuel Wharton to Croghan, 24 Dec. 1772, Croghan Papers, file 31; Dartmouth to Stuart, 2 Sept. 1772, CO 5/73, 249; memorial of the Grand Ohio Company at the Court of St. James, 11 Aug. 1772, Ohio Company Papers, vol. 1, no. 40. Hinderaker and Mancall, *Edge of Empire*, 144, 150.

116. Hillsborough to Johnson, 1 July 1772, CO 5/73, 154.

117. Gage to Dartmouth, n.d., CO 5/90, 114; McKee to Gage, 26 Nov. 1772, CO 5/90, 116.

118. Stuart to Dartmouth, 4 Jan. 1773, CO 5/74, 22.

119. Johnson to Dartmouth, 4 Nov. 1772, CO 5/74, 5–6.

120. Ibid., 6–7; White, *Middle Ground*, 340.

121. Gage quoted in Sosin, *Whitehall and the Wilderness*, 222.

122. Gage to Hamilton, 30 Aug. 1772, Gage Papers.

123. Frederick Haldimand to Dartmouth, 3 Nov. 1773, CO 5/90, 214.

124. On this, see George Morgan's Journal of a Trip Down the Ohio, and Morgan to partners, 16 Dec. 1767, Morgan letter book, 1767–68, 7, 25–26, 52–53; Hinderaker, *Elusive Empires*, 171, 175; "Rev. John Ettwein's Notes of Travel from the North Branch of the Susquehanna to the Beaver River, Pennsylvania, 1772," *Pennsylvania Magazine of History and Biography* 25 (1901), 208–19.

CHAPTER 4: REVOLUTION AND CHAOS

1. "Extracts from the Journal of John Parrish, 1773," *Pennsylvania Magazine of History and Biography* 16 (1892), 443–48.

2. "A Journal of Two Visits Made to Some Nations of Indians on the West Side of the River Ohio by Rev. David Jones, 1772 and 1773," 7, Indian Papers Collection, Historical Society of Pennsylvania, Philadelphia (hereafter cited as HSP).

3. Paul Wallace, ed., *Travels of John Heckewelder in Frontier America* (Pittsburgh, 1985), 118–19. Also cited in Anthony F. C. Wallace, *Jefferson and the Indians: The Tragic Fate of the First Americans* (Cambridge, MA, 1999), 7.

4. "Opinions Regarding the Grant to William Trent, 1775," 6–7, HSP.

5. "Journal of Two Visits," 15.

6. William Doack to William Preston, 22 Sept. 1774, William Preston Papers, Draper MSS, ser. 3QQ, 101, Historical Society of Wisconsin, Madison.

7. Woody Holton argues that the Indians—by virtue of living in the West—and the British—by virtue of their intransigence—encouraged elite Virginians to pursue this aggressive policy and, in part, helped force them to push for independence. See *Forced Founders: Indians, Debtors, Slaves, and the Making of the American Revolution in Virginia* (Chapel Hill, NC, 1999).

8. It is fair to say that this is the prevailing image we have of elite machinations on the

frontier before, during, and after the War of Independence. Elites conspired to thwart all comers in their quest for unbridled control of the region—and won. For the best treatments of this theme as it relates to this period and region, see Steven Aron, *How the West Was Lost: The Transformation of Kentucky from Daniel Boone to Henry Clay* (Baltimore, 1996), and Holton, *Forced Founders.*

9. Robertson to Preston, 21 March 1774, Preston Papers, ser. 3QQ, 14.

10. "Intelligence Received from Christopher Long, who was sent Express from the Illinois," 24 June 1772; and John Stuart to Thomas Gage, 5 July 1773, Haldimand Add. MSS, 21672, 49, 97, British Library, London.

11. Stuart to Lord Dartmouth, 5 Aug. 1773, CO 5/74, 152, Public Record Office, London.

12. Stuart to Dartmouth, 24 Aug. 1773, CO 5/74, 159.

13. Abstract of a letter from Alexander Cameron to Stuart, 21 July 1773, CO 5/74, 161.

14. William Johnson to Dartmouth, 16 Dec. 1773; abstract of a letter from Cameron to Stuart, 11 Oct. 1773, CO 5/75, 29, 9.

15. Cameron to Stuart, 25 Aug. 1774, CO 5/75, 222.

16. Frederick Haldimand to Dartmouth, 7 Sept. 1774, CO 5/91, 160.

17. Holton, *Forced Founders,* 10.

18. Edward Johnson to Preston, 2 July 1774, Preston Family Papers, 826, Virginia Historical Society, Richmond.

19. "The First American Movement West," 25, transcripts from the Gratz Papers, 1750–1850, William Byars Collection, HSP.

20. Edmund Winston to Preston, 13 March 1774, Preston Papers, series 3QQ, 12. On Washington the western speculator, see Fred Anderson and Andrew Cayton, *The Dominion of War: Empire and Liberty in North America, 1500–2000* (New York, 2005), 104–59.

21. Holton, *Forced Founders,* 30–31.

22. Stuart to Dartmouth, 3 Jan. 1775, CO 5/76, 31. See also "Opinions Regarding the Grant to William Trent, 1775," 6–7; and John Brown to Preston, 25 Nov. 1771, Preston Papers, ser. 2QQ, 129.

23. Johnson to Haldimand, 30 Sept. 1773, Haldimand Add. MSS, 21670, 82.

24. In fact, he advocated a policy sure to undermine his power further. As agents in the South were reporting the murder of white and black settlers on the Georgia frontier and the scalping of Virginians farther north, Johnson argued that an Indian in custody for killing a man near Lake Ontario should be released as a gesture for the murder of a number of Indians by settlers. Johnson had a point. No Indian in the Ohio Country near a white settlement was safe. But the timing of this proposal would be sure to inflame tensions. Johnson to Dartmouth, 2 May 1774, and Dartmouth to Johnson, 6 July 1774, CO 5/75, 107, 135. On the earlier killings, see Cameron to Stuart, 1 March 1774, CO 5/75, 81.

25. Arthur Campbell to Cameron, 20 June 1774, CO 5/75, 206.

26. Thomas Wharton to Samuel Wharton, 30 Nov. 1773, Thomas Wharton letter book, 1773–84, 2, Wharton Family Papers, HSP.

27. Croghan estimate cited in letter from Thomas Wharton to Thomas Walpole, 23 Dec. 1773, Wharton letter book, 2. On the numbers coming in, see Anderson and Cayton, *Dominion of War,* 149.

28. Thomas Wharton to Walpole, 31 Jan. 1774, Wharton letter book, 18–19.

29. Thomas Wharton to Samuel Wharton, 17 May 1774, Wharton letter book, 41.

30. Thomas Wharton to Walpole, 23 Dec. 1773, Wharton letter book, 2.

31. See, for example, *A Proclamation by the Honourable John Penn,* 14 *July 1774* (Philadelphia, 1774) for the capture of the murderer of the "friendly Indian" Joseph Wipey in Westmoreland County.

32. *A Proclamation by the Honourable John Penn, 12 Oct. 1774* (Philadelphia, 1774).

33. Croghan to Haldimand, 4 Oct. 1773, Haldimand Add. MSS, 21730, 307.

34. "Turmoil at Pittsburgh: Diary of Augustine Prevost, 1774," *Pennsylvania Magazine of History and Biography* 85 (1961), 121.

35. Ibid., 142.

36. Dunmore quoted in Eric Hinderaker and Peter Mancall, *At the Edge of Empire: The Backcountry in British North America* (Baltimore, 2003), 157.

37. Dunmore's proclamation cited in *A Proclamation by the Honourable John Penn, 12 Oct. 1774.*

38. "Turmoil at Pittsburgh," 123.

39. Michael McConnell, *A Country Between: The Upper Ohio Valley and Its Peoples, 1724–1774* (Lincoln, NE, 1992), 269; Anderson and Cayton, *Dominion of War,* 148–49, 153–54; Thomas Perkins Abernethy, *Western Lands and the American Revolution* (New York, 1937), 77–78.

40. Deposition of Samuel Whitesitt, 7 Feb. 1775; deposition of John Carnahan, 8 Feb. 1775; deposition of James Kinkead, 13 Feb. 1775, Northern, Interior, and Western County Papers, HSP. Dunmore also, it should be noted, asked his followers to resist but to avoid "tumults" if at all possible. See Dunmore to John Connolly, 25 April 1774, *Documents of the American Revolution* (Shannon, Ireland, 1972), vol. 7, 96.

41. *Pennsylvania Archives,* 2nd ser. (Harrisburg, PA, 1877), vol. 4, 573; "Turmoil at Pittsburgh," 133.

42. Deposition of Devereux Smith, 10 Feb. 1775, Northern, Interior, and Western County Papers.

43. "Turmoil at Pittsburgh," 129.

44. William Campbell to William Christian, 12 July 1774, William Christian Correspondence, 408, Bullitt Family Papers, Filson Historical Society, Louisville, KY. See also Reuben Gold Thwaites and Louise Phelps Kellogg, *Documentary History of Dunmore's War* (Harrisonburg, VA, 1974), 50–51. This source, first published in 1905, it should be noted, has to be handled gingerly, especially when gauging Dunmore's culpability for the war. Though working with "selected" documents, Thwaites and Kellogg claim that "a study of contemporary documents will convince any fair minded student of history that Lord Dunmore acted in this episode with disinterested discretion" (xxvii, xxiv). Abernethy similarly views Dunmore as a relative innocent in the whole affair, in this case a pawn of greedy Virginia speculators. Then again, *Western Lands and the American Revolution* takes aim at such men. "A study of land speculation," he writes in the book's preface, "does not present an altogether flattering picture of the 'Fathers' of the Revolutionary period . . . [A]ctions speak louder than words and . . . public professions should be checked against private activities." The book, in other words, views the activities of speculators with a jaundiced eye, letting Dunmore off the hook. See *Western Lands,* 99, viii. Historians since do not see

things this way. Anderson and Cayton, for example, counter that Dunmore was behind much of the activity, including the Bullitt surveys. *Dominion of War*, 148.

45. Richard White, *The Middle Ground: Indians, Empires, and Republics in the Great
Lakes Region, 1650–1815* (New York, 1991), 356; Christian to Preston, 22 June
1774, Christian Correspondence, 408; Preston to Christian, 27 June 1774, Preston
Papers, ser. 3QQ, 47.

46. See, for instance, "Petition of William Preston, Surveyor of Fincastle County, 18 July
1775," Preston Family Papers, 889; and Dunmore to surveyors of Fincastle County,
6 Nov. 1773 (and any number of similar letters in this series granting land to veterans), Preston Papers, ser. 2QQ, 151.

47. Dunmore to Arthur Campbell, 9 Feb. 1774, Arthur Campbell Papers, folder 1, Filson Historical Society. See also Anderson and Cayton, *Dominion of War*, 148.

48. Christian to Preston, 11 May 1774, Preston Family Papers, 813.

49. Holton, *Forced Founders*, 31.

50. See, for instance, Shad. Vaughan to John Floyd, 25 April 1774, Preston Family Papers, 811.

51. Thomas Wharton to Samuel Wharton, 5 July 1774, Wharton letter book, 48.

52. Johnson to Dartmouth, 22 Sept. 1773, enclosed letter of 28 June 1773, CO 5/74,
171, 173.

53. Extract from Alexander McKee journal, 8 March 1774, CO 5/75, 142.

54. Johnson to Dartmouth, 22 Sept. 1773, enclosed letter of 28 June 1773, CO 5/74,
171, 173.

55. Thomas Wharton to Walpole, 31 Jan. 1774, Wharton letter book, 18.

56. See "First American Movement West," 25.

57. "Turmoil at Pittsburgh," 128, 130. Anderson and Cayton, *Dominion of War*, 148–49.

58. Hinderaker and Mancall, *Edge of Empire*, 158; "Turmoil at Pittsburgh," 128.

59. McConnell, *A Country Between*, 270; Benjamin Hill, ed., *Executive Journals of the
Council of Colonial Virginia*, vol. 6 (Richmond, 1966), 555, 557.

60. James Robertson to Preston, 4 Dec. 1773, Preston Papers, ser. 2QQ, 155. If settlers supported Pennsylvania or Vandalia, forts or surveys meant little or nothing. According to
a speculator, settlers were "as free as any buck a-goin." Holton, *Forced Founders*, 30.

61. Daniel Smith to Preston, 22 March 1774, Preston Papers, ser. 3QQ, 15.

62. Arthur Campbell to Dunmore, 14 Dec. 1773, CO 5/91, 122; deposition of Isaac
Thony, 12 Feb. 1774, CO 5/75, 169; copy of a talk from William Preston of Virginia
to Cherokee Indians, 11 June 1774, CO 5/75, 204; Preston's Address to the Cherokees, 11 June 1774, Preston Family Papers, 823.

63. Dunmore to Stuart, 5 April 1774, CO 5/75, 170.

64. Arthur Campbell to Cameron, 20 June 1774, CO 5/75, 206–7.

65. Alexander Lewis to Oconostota, 9 June 1774, CO 5/75, 202.

66. Arthur Campbell to Preston, 20 June 1774, Preston Papers, ser. 3QQ, 40.

67. Arthur Campbell to Preston, 22 June 1774, Preston Papers, ser. 3QQ, 41.

68. Ibid.

69. Cresap worked as Croghan's part-time agent in the Vandalia scheme, trying to entice
settlers to Vandalia lands. On occasion, he also served as a jobber for George Wash-

ington. Throughout much of 1773 and 1774, he had "been on a scout against the Indians inhabiting the country about the Ohio." Thomas Wharton believed he was busy "locating a large Quantity of Lands," but for whom he was working was unclear. "Turmoil at Pittsburgh," 146, 148; Haldimand to Dartmouth, 1 June 1774, CO 5/91, 153; Thomas Wharton to Walpole, 31 May 1774, Wharton letter book, 46.

70. Thomas Wharton to Samuel Wharton, 17 May 1774, Wharton letter book, 41–42.

71. See, for example, Wallace, *Jefferson and the Indians*; Daniel Richter, *Facing East from Indian Country: A Native History of Early America* (Cambridge, MA, 2003), 213–14; White, *Middle Ground*, 361.

72. Guy Johnson to Dartmouth, 12 July 1774, CO 5/75, 149; William Johnson to Dartmouth, 20 June 1774, CO 5/75, 139–40.

73. Extract from McKee journal, 143. Eric Hinderaker, *Elusive Empires: Constructing Colonialism in the Ohio Valley, 1673–1800* (New York, 1997), 190.

74. White, *Middle Ground*, 357.

75. Wallace, *Jefferson and the Indians*, 3.

76. Extract from McKee journal, 144; Wallace, *Jefferson and the Indians*, 3, 6.

77. Guy Johnson to Dartmouth, 26 July 1774, CO 5/75, 151. Guy Johnson, alas, was a shadow of his late uncle. Hardly cut out for the stressful and complex job, he eventually was relieved of his duties. For a discussion of Guy Johnson, his abilities, and his inabilities, see Alan Taylor, *The Divided Ground: Indians, Settlers, and the Northern Borderland of the American Revolution* (New York, 2006).

78. Arthur Campbell to Cameron, 20 June 1774, CO 5/75, 206–7.

79. Hinderaker, *Elusive Empires*, 191.

80. Preston to Christian, 27 June 1774, Preston Papers, ser. 3QQ, 47.

81. Arthur Campbell to Preston, 1 July 1774, and Preston to Christian, 2 July 1774, Preston Papers, ser. 3QQ, 50, 51.

82. Preston to Edward Johnson, 2 Aug. 1774, Preston Family Papers, 836.

83. Christian to Preston, 22 June 1774, Bullitt Family Papers, 408; Hinderaker, *Elusive Empires*, 192; Thwaites and Kellogg, *Documentary History of Dunmore's War*, 33–35.

84. "Petition of Colonel Christian to the Honourable the President and the Gentlemen of the Convention," 3 Jan. 1776, Preston Family Papers, 912.

85. William Campbell to Christian, 12 July 1774, Christian Correspondence, 408.

86. Preston to Joseph Cloyd, 29 June 1774, Preston Papers, ser. 3QQ, 49.

87. Arthur Campbell to Preston, 1 July 1774, Preston Papers, ser. 3QQ, 50.

88. Woods to Preston, 5 July 1774, Preston Papers, ser. 3QQ, 56.

89. Bryce Russell to Preston, 2 July 1774, Preston Papers, ser. 3QQ, 52.

90. Christian to Preston, 4 July 1774, Preston Papers, ser. 3QQ, 54.

91. Joseph Floyd to Preston, 14 April 1774, Preston Papers, ser. 3QQ, 17. See also James Robertson to Preston, 5 July 1774, Preston Papers, ser. 3QQ, 55. Officials feared, in particular, that the Clinch and Holston valleys would be abandoned in the summer of 1774. See Thwaites and Kellogg, *Documentary History of Dunmore's War*, xii.

92. Preston to Christian, 27 June 1774, and William Russell to Preston, 26 June 1774, Preston Papers, ser. 3QQ, 47, 46.

93. Arthur Campbell to Preston, 28 Aug. 1774, and Robertson to Preston, 11 Aug. 1774, Preston Papers, ser. 3QQ, 85, 73.

94. Christian to Preston, 22 June 1774, Christian Correspondence, 408; William Russell to Preston, 26 June 1774, Preston Papers, ser. 3QQ, 46.

95. It emerged that the Cherokees had never murdered the traders and the two messengers. "Nothing," Christian reported, "was to be feared." Christian to Preston, 9 July 1774, Christian Correspondence, 408. On this theme, also see Arthur Campbell to Preston, 9 July 1774, Preston Papers, ser. 3QQ, 58.

96. Christian to Preston, 22 June 1774, Christian Correspondence, 408.

97. Christian to Preston, 4 July 1774, Christian Correspondence, 408.

98. Smith to Preston, 8 July 1774, Preston Papers, ser. 3QQ, 57.

99. The complicated and duplicitous nature of what officials were up to was epitomized by their uses of Crabtree. After the negotiations with the Cherokees and the news about the messengers and traders, Preston faced the difficult task of placating the Cherokees and appeasing settlers for the purpose of empowering speculators. Crabtree stood at the intersection of these conflicting goals. The people had rallied to him. At one point, therefore, Christian advised Preston "to encourage Crabtree to go in search of the Surveyors." Allowing him to go "might serve to atone for his guilt in killing the Cherokee." Using Crabtree, a hero to the people, would also quiet their misgivings about the landgrab that was afoot. Yet the Cherokees despised him. Officials therefore had little choice but to have him arrested to stand trial for murder. Christian "undertook to order a party of militia to be raised to guard him least he might be rescued." Dunmore's agents had to pin something on him. "You may be assured," Christian warned, "that if he is cleared at Court, that he will ruin this Country." But Christian understood the delicate position he was in. Some settlers would not allow Crabtree to face the justice his acts had merited. After officials demonstrated their good faith, then if he "should get away or be rescued, it would not be so much matter." Because Crabtree was "the most hardened depraved villain I ever heard of," Christian hoped he "might be outlawed and drove out of the Country." The "lives of many in this Country depends" on it, he warned. In the summer of 1774, it would be best to be rid of him. Christian to Preston, 22 June and 9 July 1774, Christian Correspondence, 408.

100. Preston's Address to the Cherokees, 823.

101. Arthur Campbell to Preston, 16 Oct. 1774, Preston Papers, ser. 3QQ, 124.

102. White, *Middle Ground*, 354–56.

103. Christian to Preston, 22 June 1774, Christian Correspondence, 408.

104. McConnell, *A Country Between*, 276; White, *Middle Ground*, 363.

105. Christian to Preston, 22 June 1774, Christian Correspondence, 408.

106. Lord Dunmore's circular to county lieutenants, 10 June 1774, Preston Papers, ser. 3QQ, 39.

107. Robertson to Preston, 12 Aug. 1774, Preston Papers, ser. 3QQ, 74.

108. Arthur Campbell to Preston, 29 Sept. 1774, Preston Papers, ser. 3QQ, 106.

109. Abstract of a letter from His Excellency Josiah Martin, 21 July 1774, CO 5/75, 194.

110. On the pointed accusations of Pennsylvanians, see Thwaites and Kellogg, *Documentary History of Dunmore's War*, 368–95.

111. Although he had not killed forty-nine men, women, and children, it emerged that Cresap only acted once Connolly informed him that Indians were going to war. Thomas Wharton to Samuel Wharton, 5 July 1774, Wharton letter book, 50.

112. On this, see Holton, *Forced Founders*; Anderson and Cayton, *Dominion of War*, 150; Thomas Wharton to Samuel Wharton, 5 July 1774, Wharton letter book, 52–53. Dunmore would later deny that Cresap had anything to do with the whole affair, claiming that he was a Marylander. Dunmore lied, or at least failed to explain that Cresap held a Virginia commission. See Thwaites and Kellogg, *Documentary History of Dunmore's War*, 393.

113. At first, Croghan stated his allegiance to Virginia. With Connolly's arrival at Fort Pitt, Croghan disavowed any connections to Pennsylvania, promising the new commander his full support. In a letter to Dunmore, Croghan declared he would have all his property surveyed and "put on quit rent" for Virginia. He argued that he had fallen afoul of Pennsylvanians, who claimed his property as theirs. He hoped he would be protected in his holdings "till the colony of Virginia should extend their jurisdictions or His majesty should grant a new colony," namely, Vandalia. At one point, Dunmore even named Croghan senior magistrate for Virginia's new western district. Croghan to Dunmore, 9 April 1774, in "Turmoil at Pittsburgh," 144–45, 118.

114. Thomas Wharton to Samuel Wharton, 17 May 1774, Wharton letter book, 42; "Turmoil at Pittsburgh," 140; Hinderaker and Mancall, *Edge of Empire*, 158.

115. Croghan to Michael Cresap, May 1774, in "Turmoil at Pittsburgh," 153.

116. Croghan to Connolly, 3 June 1774, George Croghan Correspondence, Cadwalader Collection, ser. 4, file 33, HSP.

117. "Turmoil at Pittsburgh," 118.

118. Ibid., 127; Thomas Lane to Preston, 26 April 1774, Preston Papers, ser. 3QQ, 18.

119. "Turmoil at Pittsburgh," 136–37, 139.

120. Croghan to Cresap, May 1774; Croghan to Connolly and McKee, 4 May 1774, in "Turmoil at Pittsburgh," 153, 149.

121. Copy of a letter from John Caldwell, 29 Sept. 1774, CO 5/75, 254.

122. Dunmore to Connolly, 20 June 1774, Croghan Correspondence, file 4.

123. Ibid. By early September, Guy Johnson sensed that the war had already begun and "they apprehended it would be general." Johnson to Dartmouth, 10 Sept. 1774, CO 5/75, 228.

124. Arthur Campbell reported that people were no longer fleeing. "Most people," he informed Preston, "seem to have a private Plan of their own, for their own particular defence." Campbell to Preston, 6 Oct. 1774, Preston Papers, ser. 3QQ, 115.

125. Arthur Campbell to Preston, 9, 23, 26 Sept. 1774, Preston Papers, ser. 3QQ, 94, 102, 104.

126. Arthur Campbell to Preston, 6 Oct. 1774, Preston Papers, ser. 3QQ, 116.

127. "Turmoil at Pittsburgh," 140; Christian to _____, 7 Sept. 1774, Christian Correspondence, 408.

128. Hinderaker, *Elusive Empires*, 193.

129. Christian to Preston, 12 July 1774, Preston Papers, ser. 3QQ, 63; "Turmoil at Pittsburgh," 138.

130. "Turmoil at Pittsburgh," 131.

131. Petition of Christian, 3 Jan. 1776, Preston Family Papers, 912.
132. Christian to Preston, 12 July 1774, Preston Papers, ser. 3QQ, 63.
133. Christian to _____, 7 Sept. 1774, Christian Correspondence, 408; Wallace, *Jefferson and the Indians*, 9.
134. Christian to _____, 7 Sept. 1774, Christian Correspondence, 408.
135. Arthur Campbell to Preston, 12 and 28 Aug. 1774, Preston Papers, ser. 3QQ, 74, 85. Also see Smith to Preston, 13 Oct. 1774, Preston Papers, ser. 3QQ, 119.
136. Christian to Preston, 12 July 1774, Preston Papers, ser. 3QQ, 63; Thwaites and Kellogg, *Documentary History of Dunmore's War*, 91–93.
137. Ingles to Preston, 14 Oct. 1774, Preston Papers, ser. 3QQ, 121.
138. White, *Middle Ground*, 363.
139. Christian to _____, 15 Oct. 1774, Christian Correspondence, 409.
140. Ibid.
141. Ingles to Preston, 14 Oct. 1774, Preston Papers, ser. 3QQ, 121.
142. Christian to _____, 15 Oct. 1774, Christian Correspondence, 409.
143. Christian to Preston, 3 Nov. 1774, Christian Correspondence, 410.
144. Indians would not be allowed even to hunt on the Kentucky side of the Ohio River, and they had to allow shipping to go down the river unmolested. Thwaites and Kellogg, *Documentary History of Dunmore's War*, xxiii.
145. Petition of the members of Congress at Philadelphia to the king, 24 Dec. 1774, CO 5/75, 238.
146. Christian to Preston, 3 Nov. 1774, Christian Correspondence, 410.
147. Christian to _____, 15 Oct. 1774, Christian Correspondence, 409.
148. Christian to Preston, 3 Nov. 1774, Christian Correspondence, 410.
149. Guy Johnson to Dartmouth, 14 Dec. 1774, CO 5/76, 10–12.
150. By September, a month before Point Pleasant, Croghan had conceded that "it is beyond doubt but that matters must be terminated this fall." "Turmoil at Pittsburgh," 130.
151. Public proclamation of the Grand Ohio Company, 22 Sept. 1775; and earlier draft of the proclamation, Ohio Company Papers, vol. 2, 12, 13, Etting Collection, HSP.
152. William Corke to Preston, 27 Oct. 1774, Preston Papers, ser. 3QQ, 126.
153. Preston to Dunmore, 23 Jan. 1775, Preston Family Papers, 862.
154. Ibid.
155. Andrew Boyd to Little Carpenter, n.d. 1775; Preston to Dunmore, June 1775, Preston Papers, ser. 4QQ, 17, 18.
156. William Boyd to Preston, 11 Jan. 1775, Preston Papers, ser. 4QQ, 2.
157. Deposition of Tomlinson, n.d., Thomas Cresap Family Papers, 26, Miscellaneous Manuscripts Collections, Library of Congress, Washington, DC. On Crawford's connections to Washington, see Anderson and Cayton, *Dominion of War*, 145, 149, 150.
158. Dunmore to Dartmouth, 24 Dec. 1774, excerpted in Thwaites and Kellogg, *Documentary History of Dunmore's War*, 371–72, 376, 386, 391.
159. Christian to Preston, 3 Nov. 1774, Christian Correspondence, 410.
160. Annie Christian, sister of Patrick Henry, had "heard a flying report that there were 4 Families killed on New River." She hoped it was false. Nonetheless, wealthy Virginians were making good on the surveying work that Dunmore had sponsored by mak-

ing their claims official. Her brother William Henry "went to Wmburg with the plots of Ohio land" to register a number of claims. Nearly all, and presumably the claims of her "brother Pat," were entered. The others would be "altered" and sent "to Wburg ameadately in hopes it will do." Annie Christian to Anne Fleming, 15 Oct. 1775, Annie Christian Personal Correspondence, 393, Bullitt Family Papers, Filson Historical Society. Certainly Dunmore pronounced that in the Ohio valley "these Scenes of distress will never be renewed, than ever was before." Thwaites and Kellogg, *Documentary History of Dunmore's War*, 387.

161. Preston to Christian, 1 May 1775, Preston Papers, ser. 4QQ, 14.

162. Hinderaker, *Elusive Empires*, 194.

CHAPTER 5: REVOLUTION AND UNCERTAINTY

1. Ian Christie, "John Murray," in Jack Greene and J. R. Pole, eds., *The Blackwell Encyclopedia of the American Revolution* (Cambridge, MA, 1991), 759–60; entry for Dunmore in *Oxford Dictionary of National Biography* (Oxford, UK, 2004–6); Woody Holton, *Forced Founders: Indians, Debtors, Slaves, and the Making of the American Revolution in Virginia* (Chapel Hill, NC, 1999); Fred Anderson and Drew Cayton, *The Dominion of War: Empire and Liberty in North America, 1500–2000* (New York, 2005).

2. Robert Gross, *The Minutemen and Their World* (New York, 1976). We have tended to separate traditional rights or prerogatives from modern rights, which we associate more properly with revolution. See, for example, E. P. Thompson's decidedly premodern take on calls for a moral economy and the rioting that follows juxtaposed with the modern process of class formation and consciousness in *Customs in Common: Studies in Traditional Popular Culture* (New York, 1993) and *The Making of the English Working Class* (New York, 1966). On revolution and the assumption that revolution must necessarily involve what we would call progressive ideological content, see Arno Mayer, *The Furies: Violence and Terror in the French and Russian Revolutions* (Princeton, NJ, 2000).

3. For an interpretation of how sovereignty was reinscribed as popular will at the time of the American Revolution, see Edmund Morgan, *Inventing the People: The Rise of Popular Sovereignty in England and America* (New York, 1988). For Morgan, great thinkers or "inventors," such as James Madison, appropriated suitable ideas from the past (267, 290–91). By contrast, what seemed to be happening in the West in these years was akin to—and did not necessarily borrow from—the process that had occurred in England in the seventeenth century when sovereignty dissolved and some groups, a few with rather unorthodox ideas, claimed authority for themselves. Scholars a generation ago seemed to be arguing that this type of dynamic explained radicalism in England during the civil war/revolution. See, for example, Richard Schalatter's review of Lawrence Stone, *The Causes of the English Revolution, 1529–1642* (New York, 1972), G. E. Aylmer, ed., *The Interregnum: The Quest for Settlement, 1646–1660* (Hamden, CT, 1972); especially the essay by Quentin Skinner; and Christopher Hill, *The World Turned Upside Down: Radical Ideas During the*

English Revolution (New York, 1972), in *American Historical Review* 78 (1973), 1052–55. For an excellent study of a similar process of popular politicization in the midst of questions about sovereignty in Ireland in the 1780s and '90s, see Jim Smyth's *The Men of No Property: Irish Radicals and Popular Politics in the Late Eighteenth Century* (London, 1998).

4. George Germain to John Stuart, 6 Nov. 1776, CO 5/77, 121, Public Record Office, London.

5. Richard Butler diary, 1 Sept. 1775, Historical Society of Pennsylvania, Philadelphia (hereafter cited as HSP).

6. The best account we have of the fortunes of Native American communities during the War of Independence is Colin Calloway's insightful study, *The American Revolution in Indian Country: Crisis and Diversity in Native American Communities* (New York, 1995). For the Ohio Country, see Richard White's *The Middle Ground: Indians, Empires, and Republics in the Great Lakes Region, 1650–1815* (New York, 1991).

7. John Stuart to William Howe, 30 Aug. 1776, CO 5/94, 43–44. Also see deposition of Sabrult Shoat, 13 May 1776, William Preston Papers, Draper MSS, ser. 4QQ, 38, Historical Society of Wisconsin, Madison; Richard Butler journal, 3 Sept. 1775, HSP; John Stuart to Germain, 23 Aug. 1776, CO 5/77, 126–27; Henry Stuart to John Stuart, 25 Aug. 1776, CO 5/77, 177.

8. Officials blustered about making use of western insecurity to achieve broader aims in putting down the rebellion in the East. At one point, for instance, Gen. Thomas Gage toyed with the idea of using Connolly to raise "the People of Detroit and other settlers in the interior country who with Indians and two Companies of the 18th Regiment at the Illinois" to create a "Diversion on the Frontiers of Pennsylvania and Virginia." But nothing came of it. See Gage to Lord Dartmouth, 20 Sept. 1775, CO 5/92, 281; Dartmouth to Johnson, 24 July 1775, CO 5/76, 124.

9. Letter of 14 Nov. 1774, CO 5/92, 20.

10. Gage to John Stuart, 12 Sept. 1775, CO 5/76, 187.

11. John Stuart to Henry Stuart, 24 Oct. 1775, CO 5/76, 189.

12. Stuart to Alexander Cameron, 16 Dec. 1775, CO 5/77, 28.

13. Johnson to Germain, 26 Jan. 1776, CO 5/77, 1.

14. Cameron to John Stuart, 9 Nov. 1775, CO 5/77, 87. See also copy of a letter from Hugh Hamilton to Cameron, 4 July 1776, CO 5/94, 62; Hamilton to Frederick Haldimand, 25 April 1778, Haldimand Add. MSS, 21781, 28–29, British Library, London; "Copy of a List of Persons Well Disposed to His Majesty's Government, Living on the Frontiers of Virginia with Remarks Returned by Lieutenant Governor Hamilton from Detroit," 3 July 1777, Croghan Papers, file 8, HSP; George Morgan to Henry Laurens, 31 March 1778, George Morgan letter book, Carnegie Library, Pittsburgh.

15. Guy Carleton to Hamilton, 6 Oct. 1776, Haldimand Add. MSS, 21781, 1.

16. Germain to Haldimand, 26 March 1777, Haldimand Add. MSS, 21781, 3; Germain to John Stuart, 2 April 1777, CO 5/78, 63–64. Although Germain wanted to pursue a more aggressive policy, especially making use of Indians along frontiers, Indian raids were not formally sponsored by Britain. Instead, Indians acted as "volunteers."

On this, see Alan Taylor, *The Divided Ground: Indians, Settlers, and the Northern Borderland of the American Revolution* (New York, 2006), 86–91.

17. Haldimand to Hamilton, 26 Aug. 1778, Haldimand Add. MSS, 21781, 20–21.

18. Pat Lockhart to William Preston, 14 May 1776, Preston Family Papers, 928, Virginia Historical Society, Richmond.

19. Copy of a letter from Morgan Jones [1777], Frontier War Papers, Draper MSS, ser. 1U, 71.

20. Deposition of Shoat, 38. See also Samuel Moorehead to Edward Hand, 19 Aug. 1777; David McClure to Hand, 8 Sept. 1777; Zackwell Morgan to Hand, 18 Sept. 1777, Frontier War Papers, ser. 1U, 84, 93, 98. See also "A Letter Attached to a War Mallet and Tomahawk," 2 Feb. 1777, enclosed in a letter from Moorehead to Morgan, 21 March 1777, Morgan letter book; and Johnson to Germain, 12 March 1778, CO 5/79, 73.

21. Johnson to Germain, 8 June 1777, CO 5/78, 133.

22. William Dells's military journal kept on expedition against the Cherokee Indians, 29 Aug.–30 Sept. 1776, Arthur Campbell Papers, folder 26, Filson Historical Society, Louisville, KY. On this, see Calloway, *American Revolution in Indian Country*; A.F.C. Wallace, *Jefferson and the Indians: The Tragic Fate of the First Americans* (Cambridge, MA, 1999), 54–60.

23. George Morgan to Dorsey Pentecost, 17 Nov. 1776, Morgan letter book.

24. Gage to Dartmouth, 20 Sept. 1775, CO 5/92, 281. On the riflemen, see Charles Royster, *A Revolutionary People at War: The Continental Army and American Character, 1775–83* (Chapel Hill, NC, 1996).

25. John Stuart to Howe, CO 5/94, 44.

26. "Narrative of William Grant, Late a Serjeant in the Rebel Army, Dated 24 Nov. 1777 from on Board the Queen's Indiaman at Gravesend," CO 5/78, 183.

27. Speech of the Congress of the United States to the Wise Men representing the Delaware Nation, delivered by the Committee for the Indian Affairs, 26 May 1779, Daniel Brodhead Papers, Draper MSS, ser. 1H, 85.

28. Officials corresponded with Delaware leaders on a regular basis to remind them "how the sentiments of England were barbarous and unjust since they proposed you to murder even the Wives and Children of your Brothers of the United States." Address of M. Gerard, 29 May 1779, William Irvine Correspondence, vol. 2, file 28, HSP.

29. Speech of the Congress of the United States to the Wise Men, 86–87.

30. John Killbuck to John Gibson, 30 Jan. 1779, Brodhead Papers, ser. H; Daniel Sullivan to George Morgan, 22 March 1777, Morgan letter book.

31. Address of M. Gerard; John Page to George Morgan and John Neville, 15 April 1777, David Shepherd Papers, Draper MSS, ser. 1SS, 53–54.

32. Zeisberger to Hand, 22 Sept. 1777, Frontier War Papers, ser. 1U, 99.

33. Speech of the Congress of the United States to the Wise Men, 86–87.

34. Daniel Brodhead to chiefs of the Wyandot Nation, 8 April 1779; Brodhead to his brothers the Shawnees, 8 April 1779, Brodhead Papers, 51–55.

35. A plan for regulating trade with the Indians on the Ohio, intercepted intelligence, enclosed in a letter from William Tryon to Howe, 18 Dec. 1775, CO 5/93, 41.

36. George Washington to Brodhead, 5 March 1779, Brodhead Papers, 34–35; memorandum from General Hand, 2 June 1777, Frontier War Papers, ser. 1U, 54.

37. Moorehead to Hand, 19 June 1777, Frontier War Papers, ser. 1U, 58; George Morgan to John Hancock, 8 Nov. 1776, Morgan letter book.

38. James Chew to Hand, 21 Oct. 1777; William McKee to Hand, 31 Dec. 1777, Frontier War Papers, ser. 1U, 122, 133. On the state of forts in the West, see Hamilton to Haldimand, 1 Feb. 1778, Haldimand Add. MSS, 21781, 26; Washington to Brodhead, 5 March 1779, Brodhead Papers, 34–35.

39. Hancock to Morgan, 19 April 1776, Instructions to George Morgan, Morgan Family Papers, box 1, Historical Society of Western Pennsylvania, Pittsburgh.

40. Morgan to Hancock, 4 Jan. 1777, Morgan letter book.

41. Morgan to Patrick Henry, 1 April 1777, Morgan letter book. Morgan had good reason to champion this view. Truth be told, he was hoping to salvage some of his holdings in the Grand Ohio Company. Despite Morgan's conflict of interest—and most who had anything to do with the West were conflicted—his self-interested pleas for peace dovetailed with American aims. See George Croghan to William Trent, 13 July 1775, Ohio Company Papers, vol. 2, 6, Etting Collection, HSP; Thomas Wharton to Samuel Wharton, 5 July 1774, Thomas Wharton letter book, 1773–84, 51, Wharton Family Papers, HSP; Trent to Morgan, 23 Jan. 1779; memorial of William Trent to the Congress of the United States, 11 Sept. 1779, Ohio Company Papers, vol. 2, 33, 40; public proclamation of the Grand Ohio Company, 22 Sept. 1775; draft of the proclamation, which states the particulars but which was cut out of the final draft, Ohio Company Papers, vol. 2, 12–13.

42. Some of these, moreover, seemed in it for the money. One fellow named McCormick, for instance, was selling cattle "to the enemy at Detroit." Commissioners for Indian affairs to William Wilson, 11 Aug. 1776, Morgan letter book.

43. Attachment, n.d. 1775, in a letter from John Brown to Preston, 10 Oct. 1775, Preston Papers, ser. 4QQ, 34. On this, see Eric Hinderaker, *Elusive Empires: Constructing Colonialism in the Ohio Valley, 1673–1800* (New York, 1997).

44. John Brown to Preston, 24 Aug. 1775, Preston Papers, ser. 4QQ, 31.

45. Thomas Lewis to Preston, 18 Aug. 1775; William Madison to Preston, July 1775, Preston Papers, ser. 4QQ, 29, 30; William Peachey to Preston, 24 Jan. 1775, Preston Family Papers, 889, Virginia Historical Society; "The Petition of William Preston to the Chairman and Delegates from the Several Counties and Borroughs in the Colony of Virginia Met in Convention," 18 July 1775, Preston Family Papers, 889, Virginia Historical Society. See also the memorial of William Christian in behalf of himself and William Preston and Arthur Campbell, 3 Jan. 1776, Preston Family Papers, 912, Virginia Historical Society.

46. William Preston to_____, 30 May 1776, Frontier War Papers, ser. 1U, 18.

47. After all, as a British agent noted, "many of the Members [of the Virginia Committee] are concerned in the Lands." Henry Stuart to Edward Wilkinson, 28 June 1776, CO 5/94, 68. On Henry and his claims in the West—both personal and political—see Thomas Perkins Abernethy, *Western Lands and the American Revolution* (New York, 1937).

48. On the so-called Harrodsburg Petitions, and Clark's role in crafting them and encouraging Virginia's elite to respond, see Wallace, *Jefferson and the Indians*, 44–45. Hinderaker, in *Elusive Empires*, argues that the petitions are evidence of the ways in which "the spirit and language of the Revolution" began animating what common people were up to (195–205). Stephen Aron sees the bid for independence from Transylvania as the triumph, though short-lived, of a "homesteading" ethic. With Virginia's rulers in place, however, common settlers would again be marginalized. *How the West Was Lost: The Transformation of Kentucky from Daniel Boone to Henry Clay* (Baltimore, 1996), 66–70.

49. Stuart to Dartmouth, 21 July 1775, CO 5/76, 150.

50. See, for instance, Henry Stuart to Wilkinson, 28 June 1776, CO 5/94, 68; Preston to _____, 30 July 1776, Preston Papers, ser. 4QQ, 61.

51. See, for example, Page to Preston, 6 Aug. 1776, Preston Family Papers, 938, Virginia Historical Society; and John Stuart to Germain, 24 Nov. 1776, CO 5/78, 72–73. Also see Henry to Morgan and Neville, 12 March 1777, and Henry to David Shepherd, 12 March 1777, Morgan letter book.

52. Resolution of the Council at Williamsburg, 12 March 1777, Shepherd Papers, ser. 1SS, 43–44.

53. Henry explained that "the great variety of War in which this state is engaged, makes it impossible to spare such a number of men for this Expedition." Henry to county lieutenants, 10 March 1777, Preston Family Papers, folder 6, Filson Historical Society.

54. Minutes and Resolution of Virginia Council Concerning Letters from William Preston About Indians, 19 Feb. 1778, Preston Family Papers, 978, and Minutes of Virginia Council Outlining Col. Preston's Defense Plans, 27 March 1778, 982, Virginia Historical Society.

55. Struthers's unit achieved nothing. His captain, "though a brave Irishman, could but barely write his name." For the following two years, he turned out again. They fought no Indians and had, as Struthers recorded, "no triumphs in battle to record nor defeats to lament." John C. Dann, ed., *The Revolution Remembered: Eyewitness Accounts of the War for Independence* (Chicago, 1980), 253–54.

56. After the county lieutenant of Botetourt County, William Fleming, pleaded with leaders in Williamsburg for help in 1776, an official responded with kind words but few resources. No troops would come. Look to God, he suggested: "Heartily pray that your back Inhabitants may be protected from the merciless savages, by the Valour and Spirit of its Inhabitants." William Purdie to Fleming, 8 Aug. 1776, Frontier War Papers, ser. 1U, 32. Also see Archibald Cary to Preston, 22 July 1776; Preston to president of the Council, 2 Aug. 1776, Preston Papers, ser. 4QQ, 62, 64.

57. Bowman to Isaac Hite, 10 Jan. 1778, Hite Correspondence, Bodley Family Papers, Filson Historical Society.

58. Christian to Preston, 8 June 1776, William Christian Correspondence, Bullitt Family Papers, folder 410, Filson Historical Society.

59. Pentecost to Hand, 7 Aug. 1777, Frontier War Papers, ser. 1U, 76.

60. Todd to Preston, 17 May 1776, Preston Papers, ser. 4QQ, 41.

61. Todd to Preston, 22 June 1776, Preston Papers, ser. 4QQ, 52.
62. James McGavock to Preston, 22 July 1776, Preston Papers, ser. 4QQ, 56; Preston to Fleming, 10 May 1778, Frontier War Papers, ser. 2U, 16; Cary to Preston, 22 July 1776, Preston Papers, ser. 4QQ, 62.
63. Page to Fleming, 9 Sept. 1776, Frontier War Papers, ser. 1U, 35.
64. William Fleming to Nancy Fleming, 25 Sept. 1779, Fleming Family Papers, Filson Historical Society.
65. Morgan to the commissioners for Indian affairs, 3 June 1776, Native American History Collection, William Clements Library, University of Michigan, Ann Arbor.
66. Morgan and Neville to Henry, 1 April 1777, Morgan letter book.
67. See, for example, Morgan to Pentecost, 16 Feb. 1777, Morgan letter book.
68. Morgan to Hancock, 12 Feb. 1777, Morgan letter book.
69. Morgan to Hancock, 15 March 1777, Morgan letter book.
70. Morgan to Shepherd, 31 March 1777, Morgan letter book.
71. Morgan to Laurens, 29 Nov. 1778, Morgan letter book. See also "George Morgan's Reasons for Launching an Expedition Against Detroit," 17 July 1778, Morgan letter book.
72. For a start, the officials he answered to—the commissioners for Indian affairs— though based in Philadelphia, sided with the Virginians. Morgan believed these men were stirring the pot in the West, veering the region toward violence. He became a lone voice. On their differing views, see commissioners to the Committee of Congress for Indian Affairs, 2 Aug. 1776; commissioners to Henry, 31 Aug. 1776; commissioners' circular to frontier counties, 29 Sept. 1776, Morgan letter book.
73. Hand to Richard Henry Lee, 21 Dec. 1777, *Pennsylvania Magazine of History and Biography* 43 (1919), 280–81.
74. Chew to Hand, 23 Oct. 1777, Frontier War Papers, ser. 1U, 124.
75. Pentecost to William Harrod, 12 Nov. 1776, Pittsburgh and Northwest Virginia Papers, Draper MSS, ser. 4NN, 34–35; resolution of Virginia Council, 27 March 1778, Preston Family Papers, 982, Virginia Historical Society; resolution of Virginia Council, 12 March 1777, Shepherd Papers, ser. 1SS, 43–44. Henry's approach, though rational and in this instance just, was ill attuned to frontier sensibilities. Henry to Shepherd, 27 March 1777, Shepherd Papers, ser. 1SS, 49; Henry to commissioners for the Cherokee treaty, 3 March 1777, Preston Papers, ser. 4QQ, 80; Henry quoted in resolution of Virginia Council, 19 Feb. 1777, Preston Family Papers, 978, Virginia Historical Society.
76. Preston to Fleming, 18 July 1776, Frontier War Papers, ser. 1U, 24.
77. Zeisberger to Morgan, 21 Nov. 1776, Morgan letter book; Zeisberger to _____, 29 July 1777, Frontier War Papers, ser. 1U, 69.
78. Matthew Arbuckle to Hand, 26 July 1777, Frontier War Papers, ser. 1U, 68; William Russell to Preston, 7 July 1776, Preston Papers, ser. 4QQ, 53.
79. Preston to Fleming, 25 July 1776, Frontier War Papers, ser. 1U, 26. See also John Stuart to Howe, 22 Dec. 1776, CO 5/94, 155.
80. Arthur Campbell to Fleming, 11 Aug. 1777, Frontier War Papers, ser. 1U, 78. A chronicle of the events at Boonesborough, the epicenter of Indian attacks in 1777, records one man killed in April and three killed in July in the most notable sieges.

See John Filson, *The Discovery, Settlement, and Present State of Kentucke* (Wilmington, DE, 1784), 61–62.

81. James to _____, 22 June 1777, Frontier War Papers, ser. 1U, 59.

82. See, for example, Preston to Fleming, 18 July 1776; Pentecost to Hand, 7 Aug. 1777; and Thomas Walker to John Harris and John Montgomery, 31 Aug. 1776, Frontier War Papers, ser. 1U, 24, 76, 34.

83. Russell to Preston, 7 July 1776, Preston Papers, ser. 4QQ, 53. Also see Samuel Moorhead to Hand, 22 Sept. 1777, Frontier War Papers, ser. 1U, 101; William Russell to Preston, 24 and 25 July 1776, Preston Papers, ser. 4QQ, 59, 60.

84. Rev. Mr. Todd to Preston, 16 May 1777, Preston Papers, ser. 4QQ, 154.

85. Northumberland County Committee of Safety minutes, 25 March 1776, HSP. Up and down the frontier, as Morgan explained, the movement of men away from the frontier "occasions considerable uneasiness in the minds of Frontier Inhabitants." Morgan to Hancock, 2 March 1777, Morgan letter book.

86. Resolution of the Senate [of Virginia], 30 Oct. 1776, Pittsburgh and Northwest Virginia Papers, ser. 4NN, 32.

87. McGavock to Preston, 14 Aug. 1776, Preston Papers, ser. 4QQ, 69.

88. Petition of the fort-people of Buffaloe Creek, 13 Aug. 1777, Frontier War Papers, ser. 1U, 82.

89. Subscription of settlers of Grave Creek, 2 Jan. 1777, Pittsburgh and Northwest Virginia Papers, ser. 4NN, 45; Moorhead to Hand, 5 Aug. 1777, Frontier War Papers, ser. 1U, 75.

90. George Vallandigham to Hand, 11 April 1778, Frontier War Papers, ser. 2U, 11. See also George Woods and Thomas Smith to Hand, 23 Nov. 1777, Frontier War Papers, ser. 1U, 131.

91. Fleming to the governor of Virginia, 19 July 1778, Frontier War Papers, ser. 2U, 37. Also see John Frazier to Fleming, 17 Sept. 1777; and Campbell to Fleming, 11 Aug. 1777, Frontier War Papers, ser. 1U, 95, 78.

92. Christian to Preston, 8 June 1776, Christian Correspondence, folder 410.

93. Stephen Trigg to Preston, 14 June 1778, Preston Papers, ser. 4QQ, 176; Hand to county lieutenant of Botetourt, 12 Aug. 1777, Frontier War Papers, ser. 1U, 80.

94. On the refusal of Virginia to support a congressional campaign against Detroit, see Abernethy, *Western Lands*, 197–98, 201. Also see Clark to Henry, 29 April 1779, in *The George Rogers Clark Papers, 1771–1781: Virginia Series, Vol. III, Collections of the Illinois State Historical Library* (Springfield, IL, 1912), 172. Later entreaties for cooperation were also rebuffed. Christian argued the issue was one of who was asking. "Lord deliver us from such oppression," he declared, asserting that the people would not stand to be drafted for an expedition that he considered an "absurdity." The new commander at Fort Pitt, Lachlan McIntosh, he feared, had little grasp of the situation in the West. "It seems to me," Christian noted, "he has no Thought at all of the Shawnese, but that Detroit is his object." Henry to county lieutenant of Botetourt, 20 Nov. 1778; Christian to his brother, 22 Nov. 1778, Frontier War Papers, ser. 2U, 50, 51.

95. Resolution of U.S. Congress, 25 July 1778, Frontier War Papers, ser. 2U, 41.

96. Henry to Preston, 27 June 1778, Preston Family Papers, folder 7, Filson Historical Society.

97. On the composition of Clark's force and Dunmore's, see Reuben Gold Thwaites and

Louise Phelps Kellogg, *Documentary History of Dunmore's War* (Harrisonburg, VA, 1974), xxv.

98. Patrick Henry was asking the commander at Fort Pitt as the expedition was getting under way to spare no expense in helping Virginians for the march. He did not say that Detroit was the reason they were going, but the Mississippi, to secure trading rights. See Henry to officer commanding at Fort Pitt, 15 Jan. 1778, Patrick Henry file, Filson Historical Society. Clark claimed his motives were pure. See Clark to Mason, 19 Nov. 1779, in *Clark Papers*, 115, 116. Near the turn of the last century, James Alton James suggested that Clark was, in fact, concerned with the defense of the vulnerable. See his introduction, as well as "Secret Instructions to Clark, 2 Jan. 1788," and "Public Instructions to Clark, 2 Jan. 1778," in *Clark Papers*, lix, 34–36. It is clear that the Indians were not a threat, and British troops were not garrisoning the region. See Wallace, *Jefferson and the Indians*, 64; Jack Sosin, *The Revolutionary Frontier, 1763–83* (New York, 1967), 117.

99. In October 1778, groups of men refused to march with Clark when Henry called up the militias. See Courts-Martial Ordered, 1778, Shepherd Papers, ser. 1SS, 121–28. Clark to Mason, 19 Nov. 1779, in *Clark Papers*, 117, 118. On this sordid enterprise, and the issue of desertion, see Sosin, *Revolutionary Frontier*, 117–18; Hinderaker, *Elusive Empires*, 215; and White, *Middle Ground*, 369. Abernethy is especially hard on Clark and his motives, suggesting that the truth of what was afoot ensured that few common folk in the Pittsburgh area and in Kentucky would join Clark. See *Western Lands*, 193–204.

100. Deposition of William Gelaspey, 13 Dec. 1782; deposition of George Davidson, 24 Dec. 1782; deposition of Robert George, 28 Jan. 1783, Auditor of Public Accounts, Western Commissioner Papers, Correspondence and Vouchers, Depositions, box 671, folder 1, Library of Virginia, Richmond.

101. Hamilton to Haldimand, 14 Oct. 1778, Haldimand Add. MSS, 21781, 50. Clark admits he even threatened Indians that "if they did not want their own Women and Children massacred, they must leave off killing ours." See Clark to Mason, 19 Nov. 1779, in *Clark Papers*, 127.

102. Clark to inhabitants of Vincennes, 13 July 1778, and "Oath of Inhabitants of Vincennes, 20 July 1778," in *Clark Papers*, 52, 56. The small force was splintering further at this point, dwindling to about a hundred. Sosin, *Revolutionary Frontier*, 118.

103. Germain to Henry Clinton, 1 July 1778, CO 5/96, 13–14; Arent De Peyster to Haldimand, Haldimand Add. MSS, 21756, 3–4.

104. Hamilton diary, Haldimand Add. MSS, 24320, 3; Hamilton to Haldimand, 18 Dec. 1778, Haldimand Add. MSS, 21781, 54–57.

105. Hamilton to commander at Natchez, 13 Jan. 1779, CO 5/97, 235. Also see Hamilton to Stuart, 25 Dec. 1778, CO 5/80, 163.

106. Hamilton diary, 1–11. Hamilton's and Clark's accounts of what transpired appear eerily similar. The reason may be that Clark had no qualms about his hatred of Indians. Both he and Hamilton agreed that Clark showed Indians little mercy or treated them in a patronizing fashion. He was, after all, an Indian hater. On this, see White, *Middle Ground*, 368; and Wallace, *Jefferson and the Indians*, 65.

107. Hamilton to Haldimand, 6 July 1781, Haldimand Add. MSS, 24320, 40–41; Clark to Mason, 19 Nov. 1779, in *Clark Papers*, 142–43, 144.

108. Clark to Mason, 19 Nov. 1779, in *Clark Papers*, 144. Hamilton to Haldimand, 6 July 1781, Haldimand Add. MSS, 24320, 40–42. Clark and his officers also knew that the men would react favorably to his theatrics. See "Journal of Joseph Bowman," in *Clark Papers*, 159. On the recounting of the incident as drama—for both Clark and Hamilton—see White, *Middle Ground*.

109. Extracts from the resolves in Council, Williamsburg, 16 June 1779, CO 5/98, 136; commissioners to Henry, 31 Aug. 1776, Morgan letter book.

110. Hamilton to Haldimand, 6 July 1781, Haldimand Add. MSS, 24320, 40–41.

111. Joseph Bowman to Hite, 14 June 1779, Joseph Bowman Papers, Miscellanea Collection, Filson Historical Society; Clark to Benjamin Harrison, 10 March 1779, in *Clark Papers*, 305.

112. Butler journal, 5 Sept. 1775.

113. Hamilton to Haldimand, 6 July 1781, Haldimand Add. MSS, 24320, 43.

114. Brodhead to Joseph Reed, 22 Jan. 1781, Daniel Brodhead letter book, 37–41, HSP. Also see William Fleming to Anne Fleming, 15 Dec. 1779, William Fleming Papers, reel 432, A 5–7, Library of Virginia; declaration of Charles Campbell, 24 April 1778, CO 5/79, 164; Trigg to Fleming, 14 Jan. 1779, Fleming Papers, reel 432, G 7; John May to Samuel Beall, 30 and 16 Aug. 1779, Samuel Beall Correspondence, Beall-Booth Family Papers, folder 1, Filson Historical Society. Abernethy argues that the whole affair amounted to a landgrab. See *Western Lands*, 197–98, 200, 252–55.

115. "Instructions to Clark from the Virginia Council, 12 Dec. 1778," in *Clark Papers*, 80. Clark to Jefferson, 23 Sept. 1779, CO 5/81, 147; Brodhead to Reed, 25 Feb. 1781, Brodhead Papers, ser. 3H, 74–75.

116. See Henry to Clark, 12 Dec. 1778, Clark to Mason, 19 Nov. 1779, and Clark to Henry, 9 March 1779, in *Clark Papers*, 75, 152, 154, 304. The General Assembly passed an act creating Illinois County on December 9, 1778. It did so by pointing to the conquest of the region, in addition to charter claims, by "the successful expedition." Clarence Alvord, ed., *Cahokia Records, 1778–1790* (Springfield, IL, 1907), 9–11.

117. Brodhead to Reed, 10 March 1781, Brodhead Papers, ser. 3H, 87.

118. Deposition of John Rogers, n.d. 1781, Auditor of Public Accounts, Western Commissioner Papers, Correspondence and Vouchers, Depositions, box 671, folder 1. Also see Joseph Bowman to Hite, 14 June 1779, Bowman Papers; "Declaration of the Inhabitants of Cahokia to M. Colonel Balme, 21 Sept. 1780," in Alvord, *Cahokia Records*, 535–53.

119. See General Account of the Expenses of General Clark's Expedition to Detroit, and Board of Commissioners to the Court of Kaskaskia, 4 Dec. 1782, Auditor of Public Accounts, Western Commissioner Papers, Correspondence and Vouchers, Depositions, box 671, folders 1 and 2.

120. William Irvine to Washington, 2 Dec. 1781, William Irvine Papers, Draper MSS, ser. 1AA, 124–25.

121. Joseph Bowman to Hite, 14 June 1779, Bowman Papers; Joseph Bowman to Hite, 6 March 1780, Hite Correspondence.

122. See Clark to Shepherd, 18 March 1781, and the court-martial records of the expedition, Shepherd Papers, ser. 2SS, 7, 27–54; and John Bowman to Clark, 13 June 1779, in *Clark Papers*, 331.

123. Deposition of Angus Cameron, 20 Jan. 1783; deposition of Martin Carney, 22 Jan. 1783; deposition of Boston Denmore, 23 Jan. 1783, Auditor of Public Accounts, Western Commissioner Papers, Correspondence and Vouchers, Depositions, box 671.

124. John Shy, *A People Numerous and Armed: Reflections on the Military Struggle for American Independence* (Ann Arbor, MI, 1990), 236. A number of other historians note this change but see it in terms of class. Al Young, for instance, discerns a similar shift throughout Revolutionary America. He argues that deference was giving way to a class consciousness; see *The Shoemaker and the Tea Party: Memory and the American Revolution* (Boston, 2000). Gary Nash argues that "though they were called the 'rabble' and told they had no right to participate in politics if they were illiterate or propertyless, common people were acquiring a sense of their importance despite the manipulations of those above them." *The Unknown American Revolution: The Unruly Birth of Democracy and the Struggle to Create America* (New York, 2005), 32. On this, also see Gregory Knouff, *The Soldiers' Revolution: Pennsylvanians in Arms and the Forging of Early American Identity* (University Park, PA, 2004), 13–16.

125. On the law and its implications, see Abernethy, *Western Lands*, 202, 218–28; Aron, *How the West Was Lost*, 70–73; Hinderaker, *Elusive Empires*, 200–5; and Wallace, *Jefferson and the Indians*, 45–46. For a good discussion of the chaos unleashed by the law—and the land jobbers' role in it—see Todd to Jefferson, 18 Aug. 1779, in *Clark Papers*, 357. Clark and his men certainly made out well with the law, garnering 168,000 acres. "Grant of Land to Clark, 29 Jan. 1780," in *Clark Papers*, 393.

126. Aron, *How the West Was Lost*, 73.

127. May to Beall, 16 Aug. 1779, Beall Correspondence, folder 1.

128. May to Beall, 15 April 1780, Beall Correspondence, folder 1. Abernethy, Hinderaker, and Aron argue that the ways in which the lower sort contested the land law are significant. Abernethy, of course, sees any form of resistance as an indictment of the greedy, non-civic-minded grandees of Virginia society. See *Western Lands*, 228, 249. Hinderaker, in *Elusive Empires* (200–1), sees resistance as a product of ideas or Revolutionary ideology, what Bernard Bailyn called "the contagion of liberty" in *Ideological Origins of the American Revolution* (Cambridge, MA, 1968). Aron sees this as an issue of class, but, measured by its outcomes—that the wealthy would prevail—one that proved not especially meaningful. See *How the West Was Lost*, 77. Therefore, the two perspectives—one rooted in ideas, the other in social reality—reflect the broader debate about how to approach the study of the American Revolution.

129. Haldimand to De Peyster, 24 June 1781, Haldimand Add. MSS, 21781, 13.

130. This type of transformation is highlighted in Gordon Wood's *Radicalism of the American Revolution* (New York, 1991); and T. H. Breen's *Marketplace of Revolution: How Consumer Politics Shaped American Independence* (New York, 2005). For Wood, the critical shift is one in discourse, from a society bounded by "monarchical" ideas and assumptions to one liberated by "republican" ideals. Breen sees the shift in

terms of practices, namely, sacrifice, participation, and the construction of "trust" among common men and women who took part in boycotts.

131. Preston to _____, 14 June 1778, Frontier War Papers, ser. 2U, 25.

132. John Dodge to the commissioners, 10 Jan. 1783, Auditor of Public Accounts, Western Commissioner Papers, Correspondence and Vouchers, Depositions, box 671, folder 5.

133. Caleb Wallace to Fleming, 15 Feb. 1780; Todd to _____, 14 Nov. 1780, Frontier War Papers, ser. 2U, 74, 75.

134. Wharton to Trent, 13 Nov. 1782, Ohio Company Papers, vol. 2, 62.

135. May to Beall, 29 April 1780, Beall Correspondence, folder 1.

CHAPTER 6: REVOLUTION AND VIOLENCE

1. Minutes of Virginia Council, 27 March 1778, Preston Family Papers, 982, Virginia Historical Society, Richmond.

2. Colin Calloway, *The American Revolution in Indian Country: Crisis and Diversity in Native American Communities* (New York, 1995), 167–72.

3. William Howe to George Germain, 5 March 1778, CO 5/95, 116–17, Public Record Office, London.

4. See, for instance, Daniel Brodhead to Samuel Irwin, 2 Feb. 1781, Daniel Brodhead letter book, 50–51, Historical Society of Pennsylvania, Philadelphia (hereafter cited as HSP).

5. Minutes of Virginia Council, 19 Feb. and 27 March 1778, Preston Family Papers, 978, 982.

6. Preston and William Fleming to _____, 14 March 1778, William Preston Papers, Draper MSS, ser. 4QQ, 163, Historical Society of Wisconsin, Madison.

7. Henry Hamilton to Frederick Haldimand, 1 Feb. 1778, Haldimand Add. MSS, 21781, 26, British Library, London.

8. George Morgan to John Hancock, 15 March 1777, George Morgan letter book, Carnegie Library, Pittsburgh.

9. "George Morgan's Reasons for Launching an Expedition Against Detroit," 17 July 1778, Morgan letter book. This is known, infamously, as the Squaw Campaign. Hand led the troops from Fort Pitt, but militiamen took it upon themselves to kill the women and child. As a British officer noted, they had "struck at the wrong place" and had to discover some means—if possible—"to atone for their Error." Hamilton to Haldimand, 25 April 1778, Haldimand Add. MSS, 21781, 28–29. On this, see John Grenier, *The First Way of War: American War Making on the Frontier* (Cambridge, UK, 2005), 153–54.

10. We have two schools of thought on this transformation during the Revolution on the frontier. For those who argue that these years proved critical, violence precipitated racism or racism generated violence. To cite just two recent studies, Gregory Knouff suggests that racial objectification of Indians explains the appalling brutality of frontiersmen. "The net result of this wartime consolidation of white identity, its equation with the Revolutionary cause, and the view of various Indian nations as a singular non-

white group," he writes, "was the racist brutalization of warfare." See *The Soldiers' Revolution: Pennsylvanians in Arms and the Forging of Early American Identity* (University Park, PA, 2004), 179. John Grenier, on the other hand, argues that the military culture of genocidal warfare did not emerge during the Revolution but, in fact, animated American military cultures from the period of initial settlement. Racial views emerged later. See *First Way of War*, 11. These perspectives, of course, replicate broader debates over the origins of white-Indian animosity and the attitudes that would lead to Indian removal for whatever period historians focus on to explain these phenomena. They also parallel an older debate over slavery and race, whether racism begot slavery, or slavery begot racism. For this debate, see David Brion Davis, "Constructing Race: A Reflection," *William and Mary Quarterly*, 3rd ser., 54 (1997), 7-18.

11. John Killbuck to Brodhead, 23 Oct. 1779, Daniel Brodhead Papers, Draper MSS, ser. 1H, 121.

12. Bush to Hand, 17 May 1779, "Correspondence of General Edward Hand," *Pennsylvania Magazine of History and Biography* 33 (1909), 355.

13. Diederick Brehm to Haldimand, 5 July 1779, Haldimand Add. MSS, 21781, 65.

14. Speech of the Congress of the United States to the Wise Men representing the Delaware Nation, delivered by the Committee for the Indian Affairs, 26 May 1779, Brodhead Papers, ser. 1H, 85; Brodhead to Reed, 22 Jan. 1781, Brodhead Papers, ser. 3H, 52. Also see Brodhead to Killbuck, 23 Feb. 1779, and Killbuck to McIntosh, 15 March 1779, Brodhead Papers, ser. 1H, 30, 45.

15. Brodhead to William Irvine, 14 Dec. 1780, and Brodhead to Joseph Beelor, 4 March 1781, Brodhead Papers, ser. 3H, 16-17, 76-78. On the Delawares and war, see Fred Anderson and Andrew Cayton, *The Dominion of War: Empire and Liberty in North America, 1500–2000* (New York, 2005), 172.

16. Ephraim Douglas to Irvine, 29 Aug. 1781, William Irvine Correspondence, vol. 4, HSP.

17. Thomas Brown to Germain, 6 April 1782, CO 5/82, 277; Christian to Arthur Campbell, 22 March 1780, Arthur Campbell Papers, folder 1, Filson Historical Society, Louisville, KY; Anthony F. C. Wallace, *Jefferson and the Indians: The Tragic Fate of the First Americans* (Cambridge, MA, 1999), 54–60; Calloway, *American Revolution in Indian Country.*

18. Brodhead to David Shepherd, 5 March 1781, David Shepherd Papers, Draper MSS, ser. 2SS, 1. For large-scale Delaware attacks in 1780, see Brodhead to Shepherd, 19 Sept. 1780, Shepherd Papers, ser. 1SS, 211.

19. Henry to the governor of New Orleans, 14 Jan. 1778, CO 5/81, 141.

20. Haldimand to Arent De Peyster, 12 Feb. 1780 and 24 June 1781, Haldimand Add. MSS, 21781, 9, 13.

21. John Butler to Haldimand, 14 Dec. 1777 (two letters), Haldimand Add. MSS, 21765, 1, 4; Henry Clinton to Germain, 12 Aug. 1778, CO 5/96, 83.

22. Big Cat to Brodhead, 12 Sept. 1780, Brodhead Papers, ser. 1H, 144.

23. Big Cat to Brodhead, 13 and 4 May 1779, Brodhead Papers, ser. 2H, 1, 6-7.

24. See, for example, Haldimand to De Peyster, 19 May 1782, Haldimand Add. MSS, 21781, 14-15.

25. Brehm to Haldimand, 15 May 1779, Haldimand Add. MSS, 21759, 51; William Elliot to John Holmes, 30 May 1780, Haldimand Add. MSS, 21760, 277.

26. Butler to Mason Bolton, 8 July 1778, CO 5/96, 106–7. For a recent treatment of Butler, see Gary Nash, *The Unknown American Revolution: The Unruly Birth of Democracy and the Struggle to Create America* (New York, 2005), 251–52.

27. Butler to Bolton, 8 July 1778, CO 5/96, 106–7. Interestingly, the most disturbing passages in the manuscript copy of the letter, held in the Public Record Office in Kew, were crossed out. On the issue of exaggeration and fabrication, see Knouff, *Soldiers' Revolution*, 168–69; and Fon Boardman, *Against the Iroquois: The Sullivan Campaign of 1779 in New York State* (New York, 1978).

28. Walter Butler to Philip John Schuyler, 12 Nov. 1778, Haldimand Add. MSS, 21765, 74. For a similar account from Bedford, Pennsylvania, see Guy Johnson to Haldimand, 11 Aug. 1780, Haldimand Add. MSS, 21766, 10. The British vacillated between restraining and encouraging Indian "savagery." Commanders who ordered forays to the frontier reminded their troops "to avoid the destruction of Women and Children, and every Species of Cruelty." H. Watson Powell to Haldimand, 7 Sept. 1781, Haldimand Add. MSS, 21755, 119.

29. Extract of a letter from Archibald McDonnell to John Butler, 5 Aug. 1779, CO 5/98, 289.

30. Girty to Richard B. Lernoult, 6 Sept. 1779, Haldimand Add. MSS, 21760, 48; Bolton to Haldimand, 10 Nov. 1779, Haldimand Add. MSS, 21755, 83; Matthew Elliot to Lernoult, 11 Oct. 1779, Haldimand Add. MSS, 21760, 248–49.

31. Haldimand to De Peyster, 6 July 1780, Haldimand Add. MSS, 21781, 9–10.

32. De Peyster to Bolton, 16 May 1780, Haldimand Add. MSS, 21760, 285.

33. Haldimand to Clinton, 29 Aug. 1779, CO 5/98, 285.

34. John Butler to Haldimand, 12 Feb. and 2 April 1779, Haldimand Add. MSS, 21765, 80, 91; Grenier, *First Way of War*, 158.

35. Douglas to Irvine, 29 Aug. 1781, Irvine Correspondence, vol. 4.

36. May to Samuel Beall, 28 May 1780, Samuel Beall Correspondence, Beall-Booth Family Papers, folder 1, Filson Historical Society.

37. Ebenezer Lane to Irvine, 14 Sept. 1781, Irvine Correspondence, vol. 4. Not only were these areas affected. Butler's son, Walter Butler, along with Joseph Brant attacked settlements in Cherry Valley. Unlike the Wyoming reports, these were not exaggerated. Alexander Macomb to Hamilton, 4 Feb. 1779, in *The George Rogers Clark Papers, 1771–1781: Virginia Series, Vol. III, Collections of the Illinois Historical Library* (Springfield, IL, 1912), 107.

38. Campbell to Preston, 13 June 1780, Preston Papers, ser. 5QQ, 33.

39. May to Beall, 15 March 1780, Beall Correspondence, folder 1.

40. "Petition from Inhabitants of Boonesborough, 10 March 1780," and "Petition from Inhabitants of Bryan's Station, 13 March 1780," in *Clark Papers*, 398, 401.

41. Interestingly—and fittingly enough—Indians also knew Kentucky as "the Middle Ground." See James Filson, *The Discovery, Settlement, and Present State of Kentucke* (Wilmington, DE, 1784), 8.

42. See ibid., 70–74.

43. Killbuck to Brodhead, 7 June 1780, Brodhead Papers, ser. 1H, 134; Grenier, *First Way of War*, 158–59. Alan Taylor argues that settlers "compulsively told stories of death and destruction," explaining the terrorizing effects of rumors and news in this context. See *The Divided Ground: Indians, Settlers, and the Northern Borderland of the American Revolution* (New York, 2006), 136.

44. Killbuck to Brodhead, 7 June 1780, Brodhead Papers, ser. 1H, 134.

45. Bird to De Peyster, 1 July 1780, Haldimand Add. MSS, 21760, 316. They then faced another round of the same in 1781. See, for instance, Alexander McKee to De Peyster, 26 Sept. 1781, Haldimand Add. MSS, 21761, 172.

46. See, for instance, Bird to De Peyster, 1 July 1780, Haldimand Add. MSS, 21760, 316.

47. For a list of those held, their ages, and where they were captured, see "Returns and Lists of Prisoners held in Quebec," Haldimand Add. MSS, 21843, 1, 3, 5, 15, 40, 48, 62, 109–11.

48. Ibid., 109–10, 111.

49. Haldimand to Lernoult, 13 June 1779, Haldimand Add. MSS, 21781, 8. On his foray through the West in 1780, one commander made sure to dispatch the Mahons and another family, the McGuires, to Quebec, all of whom he regarded as "really Rebels." Bird to De Peyster, 24 July 1780, Haldimand Add. MSS, 21760, 331.

50. John Butler to Haldimand, 20 Jan. and 2 Feb. 1778, Haldimand Add. MSS, 21765, 9–10, 13.

51. John Taylor to Preston, 23 March 1780, Preston Papers, ser. 5QQ, 26.

52. Walter Daniel to the commissioners, 3 Feb. 1783, Letters to the Western Commissioners, Western Commission Papers, box 671, folder 5, Library of Virginia, Richmond.

53. William Irvine to Ann Irvine, 14 Nov. 1781, Irvine Correspondence, vol. 5, 13. Kentucky was especially hit hard. On this, see Christian to Benjamin Harrison, William Christian Correspondence, Bullitt Family Papers, folder 412, Filson Historical Society.

54. Price to John Fox, 30 May 1780, Haldimand Add. MSS, 21760, 276. Stephen Aron, in *How the West Was Lost: The Transformation of Kentucky from Daniel Boone to Henry Clay* (Baltimore, 1996), sees a similar dynamic at work, though he argues that conflict did not erupt into class warfare over the merits of the homesteading ethic because some settlers, such as Daniel Boone, began to style themselves petty speculators (73–74).

55. See, for example, Northumberland County Committee of Safety minutes, 14 Dec. 1776 and 1 Jan. 1777, HSP.

56. Peters to Irvine, 27 March 1781, Irvine Correspondence, vol. 4, 44.

57. Michael Everly to Irvine, 26 Aug. 1782, Irvine Correspondence, vol. 6, 107.

58. Brodhead to Peters, 7 Dec. 1780, Brodhead letter book, 17.

59. Brodhead to Washington, 27 March 1781, Brodhead Papers, ser. 3H, 92–93.

60. Jefferson to Preston, 21 March 1780, Preston Papers, ser. 5QQ, 24.

61. Preston to _____, March 1780, Preston Papers, ser. 5QQ, 28.

62. See, for example, John Butler to Haldimand, 15 May 1778, Haldimand Add. MSS, 21765, 30; and Governor Josiah Martin to Clinton, 20 March 1776, CO 5/93, 148–50.

63. De Peyster to Bolton, 16 May 1780, Haldimand Add. MSS, 21760, 285.

64. De Peyster to Powell, 25 April 1781, McKee to De Peyster, 26 Sept. 1781, Haldimand Add. MSS, 21761, 57, 172.

65. John C. Dann, ed., *The Revolution Remembered: Eyewitness Accounts of the War for Independence* (Chicago, 1980), 264.

66. Deposition of John Green, 4 May 1778, Frontier War Papers, Draper MSS, ser. 2U, 14.

67. O.L. [pseudonym for either David Zeisberger or John Heckewelder] to Brodhead, 29 June 1779, Brodhead Papers, ser. 1H, 104.

68. Brodhead to Washington, 27 March 1781, Brodhead Papers, ser. 3H, 92–93.

69. Hamilton to Haldimand, 25 April 1778, Haldimand Add. MSS, 21781, 28–29.

70. Dann, *Revolution Remembered*, 280–82.

71. Filson, *Discovery, Settlement*, 63–70. See also John Mack Faragher's *Daniel Boone: The Life and Legend of an American Pioneer* (New York, 1992).

72. Bird to De Peyster, 24 July 1780, Haldimand Add. MSS, 21760, 331. Aron sees disaffection as a response to settler dissatisfaction with Virginia's land policies and how they imperiled the homesteading ethic. See *How the West Was Lost*, 73.

73. Christian to Harrison, 28 Sept. 1782, Christian Correspondence, folder 412.

74. Letter from Harrodsburg, 1780, Harrodsburg, Kentucky, file, Filson Historical Society.

75. Brodhead to Washington, 27 March 1781, Brodhead Papers, ser. 3H, 92–93. Also see Christian to Harrison, 28 Sept. 1782, Christian Correspondence, folder 412.

76. Harrison to Campbell, 6 March 1783, Campbell Papers, folder 3.

77. William Moore to Irvine, 17 Dec. 1781, Irvine Correspondence, vol. 5, 21.

78. Brehm to Haldimand, 28 May 1779, Haldimand Add. MSS, 21759, 53. Fort Laurens was abandoned about the time the letter was written.

79. Brodhead to Peters, 7 Dec. 1780, Brodhead letter book, 16.

80. Brodhead to Reed, 22 Jan. 1781, Brodhead Papers, ser. 3H, 48–52.

81. Douglas to Irvine, 23 Jan. 1781, Irvine Correspondence, vol. 4, 21; proceedings of a general court-martial, Feb. 1782, Irvine Papers, vol. 5, 49–50, HSP. "At present," Brodhead lamented in 1781, "we are desolate of every liquor, except vile whiskey warm from the dirty stills." Brodhead to Ephraim Blaine, 22 Jan. 1781, Brodhead Papers, ser. 3H, 54–55.

82. Intelligence report, 10 June 1782, Haldimand Add. MSS, 21762, 59; De Peyster to Powell, 17 March 1781, Haldimand Add. MSS, 21761, 22. Anderson and Cayton, *Dominion of War*, 172; Richard White, *The Middle Ground: Indians, Empires, and Republics in the Great Lakes Region, 1650–1815* (New York, 1991), 380–86.

83. Intelligence received from Mr. Elliott, 17 April 1781, Haldimand Add. MSS, 21761, 53.

84. See, for example, Brodhead to Shepherd, 17 July 1779, Shepherd Papers, ser. 1SS, 165; Brodhead to Reed, 2 Nov. 1780, Brodhead letter book, 5.

85. Washington to Brodhead, 21 April 1779, Brodhead Papers, ser. 1H, 58–59.

86. Washington to Brodhead, 4 Jan. 1780, Brodhead Papers, ser. 1H, 122.

87. Washington to Brodhead, 4 July 1780, Brodhead Papers, ser. 1H, 139.

88. See, for example, Brodhead to Shepherd, 9 May, 20 May, 4 Sept. 1780, Shepherd Papers, ser. 1SS, 201, 203, 209.

89. Brodhead to Washington, 17 Oct. 1780, Brodhead letter book, 1–3; Thomas Madison to Preston, 9 Nov. 1780; Preston to the governor of Virginia, 20 April 1782, Preston Papers, ser. 5QQ, 86, 118.

90. Unsigned letter, 11 March 1781, Irvine Correspondence, vol. 4, 39; Brodhead to Reed, 22 Jan. 1781, Brodhead Papers, ser. 3H, 48–52.

91. Remonstrance of the Virginia troops to General Irvine, March 1782, Irvine Correspondence, vol. 5, 64.

92. Douglas to Irvine, 29 Aug. 1781, Irvine Correspondence, vol. 4, 104.

93. Brodhead to _____, 28 Oct. 1781, Brodhead Papers, ser. 3H, 151. Brodhead, in fact, had led an expedition against Indians in 1778 up the Allegheny into Seneca lands, burning a number of settlements. Cayton and Anderson argue that Americans—the government, that is—"*intended* to achieve the expansion of control and hence the imposition of order by military means on a dangerous frontier." This they see as a "shift in the character of imperialism." Of course, as they note, these aims were not achieved. Perhaps they were attempted in Iroquoia. They were not attempted by the national government in the Ohio valley, that is until well after the War of Independence. Anderson and Cayton, *Dominion of War*, 176.

94. Irvine to Washington, 2 Dec. 1781, William Irvine Papers, Draper MSS, ser. 1AA, 123.

95. Remonstrance of the Virginia troops to General Irvine, 64.

96. Petition of inhabitants of Pittsburgh, 29 May 1782; court-martial at Pittsburgh, 19 Aug. 1782, Irvine Correspondence, vol. 6, 7, 101. Also see Irvine to Ann Irvine, 29 May 1782, Irvine Correspondence, vol. 6, 2.

97. Brodhead to county lieutenants, 24 Aug. 1781, Brodhead letter book, 92.

98. Brodhead to Samuel Irwin, 2 Feb. 1781, Brodhead Papers, ser. 3H, 63. By 1780, Henry McBride and John Harden from the area around Wheeling were signing agreements with Indian bounty hunters to ransom captives since the government had failed to redeem loved ones. Articles of Agreement Made by and between Lewis (an Indian) and Henry McBride and John Harden, Brodhead Papers, ser. 1H, 137, 138.

99. Dann, *Revolution Remembered*, 255–56.

100. Thomas Irwin to Irvine, 21 Dec. 1781, Irvine Correspondence, vol. 5, 26.

101. Complaint of John McDonald, 24 July 1780, Preston Papers, ser. 5QQ, 43.

102. The ideas that animated the revolutionaries, we have learned, have any number of names. However the ideas are labeled, most agree that they were largely English, oppositional, in full flower during the seventeenth century, and had become the bedrock of British thought in the eighteenth century. The gist is this: what had been radical in the seventeenth century in England had in the British eighteenth century—though not in the Irish or American context—been tamed. One of the best studies still remains Caroline Robbins, *The Eighteenth-Century Commonwealthman* (Cambridge, MA, 1959). Although American historians have debated the content of the ideology, those who do agree that ideas mattered.

103. Brodhead to Peters, 7 Dec. 1780, Brodhead Papers, ser. 3H, 20–21.

104. Walter Butler to Clinton, 18 Feb. 1779, Haldimand Add. MSS, 21765, 83–84.

105. William Irvine to Ann Irvine, 29 Dec. 1781, Irvine Correspondence, vol. 5, 31; Brodhead to Blaine, 22 Jan. 1781, Brodhead letter book, 43.

106. Brodhead to David Zeisberger, 21 Jan. 1781, Brodhead Papers, ser. 3H, 40.

107. On this justification, see Daniel Richter, *Facing East from Indian Country: A Native History of Early America* (Cambridge, MA, 2003), 221–23.

108. For a narrative of the massacre, see ibid.; Gregory Dowd, *A Spirited Resistance* (Baltimore, 1992), 85–87; and especially Thomas Slaughter, *The Whiskey Rebellion: Frontier Epilogue to the American Revoluton* (New York, 1986), 75–78.

109. Calloway, *American Revolution in Indian Country*, 39; Notes of a Meeting Between Some of the Principal Warriors of the Six Nations and Brigadier General Maclean, 12 Dec. 1782, Haldimand Add. MSS, 21756, 93–94.

110. Moore to Irvine, 13 April 1782, Irvine Correspondence, vol. 5, 78.

111. De Peyster to Haldimand, 7 Jan. 1783, Haldimand Add. MSS, 21756, 94.

112. Irvine to _____, 9 May 1782, Irvine Correspondence, vol. 5, 104.

113. Dann, *Revolution Remembered*, 256.

114. Humble Petition of Frontier Inhabitants, 13 April 1782, Irvine Correspondence, vol. 5, 77.

115. Certificate of Irvine, June 1782, Irvine Correspondence, vol. 6, 40; James Marshal to Irvine, 29 May 1782, Irvine Correspondence, vol. 6, 8.

116. Dann, *Revolution Remembered*, 310–14; De Peyster to Haldimand, 8 April 1782; John Turney to De Peyster, 7 June 1782; William Campbell to De Peyster, 11 June 1782, Haldimand Add. MSS, 21762, 13, 66, 62. Edmond Polk put the number killed and missing at forty. See Polk to Irvine, 11 June 1782, Irvine Correspondence, vol. 6, 22.

117. John Knight, *Narrative of a Late Expedition Against the Indians* (Philadelphia, 1783), 5–10.

118. Ibid., 11–12. Knight, who witnessed the torture of Crawford, was sent to a Shawnee village to meet a similar fate. Luckily for Knight, he escaped by stealing away naked at night on a horse. Six days later, he made it to Wheeling, "an emphatic spectacle of human distress." See ibid., 20–25; and Douglas to Irvine, 26 July 1782, *Pennsylvania Magazine of History and Biography* 1 (1877), 46.

119. Extract of a letter from William Caldwell to De Peyster, 13 June 1782, Haldimand Add. MSS, 21762, 80.

120. Allan Maclean to Haldimand, 16 Dec. 1782, Haldimand Add. MSS, 21756, 88.

121. Brodhead to Joseph Reed, 2 Nov. 1780, and Brodhead to Richard Peters, 7 Dec. 1780, Brodhead letter book, 6, 17.

122. Hamilton to Haldimand, n.d. 1778, Haldimand Add. MSS, 21781, 38.

123. This refers to both the killings at Gnadenhütten and subsequent massacres of Shawnees. See Notes of a Meeting Between Some of the Principal Warriors of the Six Nations and Brigadier General Maclean, 93–94. See also Return of Prisoners of War Sent from Detroit, 16 May 1782, and Powell to Haldimand, 1 July 1782, Haldimand Add. MSS, 21762, 44, 100, on this apparent shift in Indian behavior.

124. Brown to Thomas Townshend, 12 Jan. 1783, CO 5/82, 347. On this theme, see Knouff, *Soldiers' Revolution*, 178–79, 184–85.

125. John Dodge, *An Entertaining Narrative of the Cruel and Barbarous Treatment and Extreme Sufferings of Mr. John Dodge During His Captivity Among the British, at Detroit* (Danvers, MA, 1780), 18.

126. On similar shifts in earlier times, see Jill Lepore, *The Name of War: King Philip's War and the Origins of American Identity* (New York, 1998).

127. See Haldimand to De Peyster, 12 March 1783, Haldimand Add. MSS, 21781, 17. For the Indians' emerging new world in the West, see memorial from the Mingoes, Shawnees, and Delawares, 8 June 1782, Haldimand Add. MSS, 21762, 66–67.

128. Thomas Brown to Germain, 6 April 1782, CO 5/82, 277; Substance of a Talk from the Little Turkey and the Head Men and Warriors of the Over Hill Cherokees to Lt. Col. Thomas Brown, Superintendent of Indian Affairs, 17 Nov. 1783, CO 5/82, 446.

129. Brodhead to John Heckewelder, 21 Jan. 1781, Brodhead Papers, ser. 3H, 42.

130. Douglas to Irvine, 26 July 1782, *Pennsylvania Magazine of History and Biography* 1 (1877), 45; John Butler to Robert Matthews, 5 Aug. 1782, Haldimand Add. MSS, 21765, 294; Michael Huffnagle to Irvine, 15 July 1782, Irvine Correspondence, vol. 6, 54.

131. John Butler to Matthews, 5 Aug. 1782, Haldimand Add. MSS, 21765, 294; Huffnagle to Irvine, 15 July 1782, Irvine Correspondence, vol. 6, 54.

132. John Butler to Matthews, 15 July 1782, Haldimand Add. MSS, 21765, 292.

133. Irvine to Edward Stevens, 3 Sept. 1782, Northern, Interior, and Western Counties Papers, 5, HSP.

134. Marshal to Irvine, 15 Sept. 1782, Irvine Correspondence, vol. 7, 5.

135. Alexander Breckenridge to Preston, 21 Oct. 1782, Preston Papers, ser. 5QQ, 112.

136. May to Beall, 21 Oct. 1782, Beall Correspondence, folder 2.

137. Huffnagle to Irvine, 17 July 1782, Irvine Correspondence, vol. 6, 56.

138. John Evans to Irvine, 30 June 1782, Irvine Correspondence, vol. 6, 39.

139. Charles Foreman to Irvine, 21 May 1782, Irvine Correspondence, vol. 5, 113. See also the Petition of a Number of the Inhabitants of Westmoreland County, 27 Dec. 1782, Irvine Correspondence, vol. 7, 62.

140. Humble Petition of the Inhabitants Near Mr. Alexanders Well's Mill, 2 May 1782, Irvine Correspondence, vol. 5, 98; George Vallandigham to Irvine, 6 June 1782, Irvine Correspondence, vol. 6, 16.

141. John Irwin to Irvine, 30 May 1782, Irvine Correspondence, vol. 6, 12. See also Petition of the Frontier Inhabitants of Brush Creek, 22 June 1782; Archibald Leech to Irvine, 27 June 1782; Thomas Moore to Irvine, 6 June 1782, Irvine Correspondence, vol. 6, 31, 36, 15.

142. Knight, *Narrative of a Late Expedition*, 3.

143. Petition of the Frontier Inhabitants of Brush Creek, 30.

144. Edward Cook to Irvine, 24 June 1782, Irvine Correspondence, vol. 6, 33.

145. Marshal to Irvine, 15 Oct. 1782, Irvine Correspondence, vol. 7, 29.

146. Huffnagle to Irvine, 17 July 1782, Irvine Correspondence, vol. 6, 56. People wanted someone to "lead us into the Field where our actions shall more loudly proclaim the sentiments of our hearts." Robert Beall and Thomas Moore to Irvine, 23 June 1782, Irvine Correspondence, vol. 6, 32.

147. Irvine to Stevens, 3 Sept. 1782, Northern, Interior, and Western Counties Papers, 5.

148. Clark to Irvine, 13 Nov. 1782, Irvine Correspondence, vol. 7, 42.

149. May to Samuel Beall, 21 Oct. 1782, Beall Correspondence, folder 2.

150. Benjamin Lincoln to Irvine, 24 July 1782; James Potter to Irvine, 10 Aug. 1782, Irvine Correspondence, vol. 6, 65, 92.

151. Harrison to Irvine, 21 Aug. 1782, Irvine Correspondence, vol. 6, 102.

152. Irvine to Ann Irvine, 28 Aug. 1782, Irvine Correspondence, vol. 6, 111.

153. Robert Morris to Irvine, 4 April 1782, Irvine Correspondence, vol. 5, 69.

154. The people were, they declared, "anxious" for an expedition. The official who reported the resistance, James Marshal, pleaded with Irvine to help him weaken resistance by breathing "new Life to the Expedition." Marshal to Irvine, 17 July 1782, Irvine Correspondence, vol. 6, 57.

155. William McCleery to Irvine, 30 June 1782, Irvine Correspondence, vol. 6, 38.

156. Mr. Smith to Irvine, 28 Aug. 1782, Irvine Correspondence, vol. 6, 107.

157. Marshal to Irvine, 26 Aug. 1782, Irvine Correspondence, vol. 6, 108.

158. Irvine to Ann Irvine, 12 April 1782, Irvine Correspondence, vol. 5, 76.

159. Alan Taylor sees this sentiment as signaling a critical shift not only in race and discourse but also in state policy. "The new republic served its white citizens, who expected to dispossess Indians—deemed inferior and doomed," he argues. He is right, of course. The question is when and how the state acted on behalf of the common settlers, now animated by race hatred. See *Divided Ground*, 107.

160. Irvine to Ann Irvine, 12 April 1782, Irvine Correspondence, vol. 5, 76.

161. Certificate of Irvine's support for Crawford's expedition, June 1782, Irvine Correspondence, vol. 6, 40.

162. Irvine to Ann Irvine, 12 April 1782, Irvine Correspondence, vol. 5, 76.

163. See, for instance, Joseph Bowman to Isaac Hite, 10 June 1782, Hite Correspondence, Bodley Family Papers, Filson Historical Society.

164. For an example of how "the most respectable inhabitants of the district" knew that they had to placate race-addled "*country warriors*," see Douglas to Irvine, 26 July and 4 Aug. 1782, *Pennsylvania Magazine of History and Biography* 1 (1877), 44–46, 46–48.

165. Footnote added to 1783 edition of Knight's *Narrative of a Late Expedition*, 30–38.

166. Ibid.

167. John Servier to Arthur Campbell, 16 Feb. 1782, Campbell Papers, folder 2.

168. Settlers conceded that they "still desire to be in Subjection to the Authority." But at issue was the form of that authority. See Remonstrance from the Settlers from the Head Waters of the Ten Mile and Buffaloe in Washington County to Irvine, 7 Aug. 1782, Irvine Correspondence, vol. 6, 83.

169. Humble Petition of Frontier Inhabitants to Irvine, 5 April 1782, Irvine Correspondence, vol. 5, 71.

170. Benjamin Logan to Harrison, 31 Aug. 1782, Benjamin Logan Correspondence, Bullitt Family Papers, folder 515, Filson Historical Society.

171. Ibid.; White, *Middle Ground*; Calloway, *American Revolution in Indian Country*; Aron, *How the West Was Lost*.

172. Logan to Harrison, 31 Aug. 1782, Logan Correspondence, folder 515; Grenier, *First Way of War*, 161.

173. Logan to Harrison, 31 Aug. 1782, Logan Correspondence, folder 515.

174. Boone cited as an appendix to Filson, *Discovery, Settlement*, 49–50.

175. Minutes of Piankashaw Council at Post St. Vincent's, 15 April 1784, cited as an appendix in Filson, *Discovery, Settlement*, 82.

CHAPTER 7: SOUTH AND NORTH

1. Thomas Marshall to George Rogers Clark, 27 Jan. 1783, Auditor of Public Accounts, Western Commissioner Papers, Correspondence, box 671, folder 3; and Board of Western Commissioners to Benjamin Harrison, 23 Dec. 1782 and 17 Feb. 1783, Board of Western Commissioners, Journals, box 670, 14–15, 67–68, Library of Virginia, Richmond.

2. Harrison to Arthur Campbell, 6 March 1783, Arthur Campbell Papers, folder 3, Filson Historical Society, Louisville, KY.

3. Marshall to Clark, 27 Jan. 1783, Western Commissioner Papers, box 671, folder 3.

4. Marshall to ____, 22 Dec. 1782, Frontier War Papers, Draper MSS, ser. 2U, 133, Historical Society of Wisconsin, Madison. This characterization also defines the way that many historians view the mentality of frontiersmen. Carl Bridenbaugh, for instance, has portrayed "back settlement" people as "undisciplined, emotional, courageous, aggressive, pugnacious, fiercely intolerant, and hard-drinking, with a tendency to indolence." See *Myths and Realities: Societies of the Colonial South* (New York, 1963), 133. Sean Wilentz characterizes frontier ideas emerging at the time of the American Revolution as a "country" variant of a more urbane bundle of "city" democratic ideals. The city version is cosmopolitan, and the country localist. See *The Rise of American Democracy: Jefferson to Lincoln* (New York, 2005), 61.

5. Eric Hinderaker, *Elusive Empires: Constructing Colonialism in the Ohio Valley, 1673–1800* (New York, 1997), 237.

6. *Pittsburgh Gazette*, 26 Aug. 1786.

7. Merrill Jensen, *The Articles of Confederation* (Madison, WI, 1940); Peter Onuf, *Statehood and Union: A History of the Northwest Ordinance* (Bloomington, IN, 1987).

8. John Dickinson, *By the President and Supreme Executive Council . . . a Proclamation, Dated 31 July 1783* (Philadelphia, 1783).

9. The most recent—and most astute—interpretations of the land ordinances suggest that their passage proved critical to the emergence of an American imperial vision. From their passage, the die is cast. See, for instance, Hinderaker, *Elusive Empires*; and Peter Onuf, *The Origins of the Federal Republic: Jurisdictional Controversies in the United States, 1775–1787* (Philadelphia, 1983).

10. "Journal of Col. John May, of Boston, Relative to a Journey to the Ohio Country, 1789," *Pennsylvania Magazine of History and Biography* 45 (1921), 146, 149; "Narrative of John Heckewelder's Journey to the Wabash in 1792," *Pennsylvania Magazine of History and Biography* 11 (1887), 469–70.

11. On Lewis, see "Mrs. Mary Dewee's Journal from Philadelphia to Kentucky, 1787–88," *Pennsylvania Magazine of History and Biography* 28 (1904), 196; and "Narrative of John Heckewelder's Journey to the Wabash in 1792," *Pennsylvania Magazine of History and Biography* 12 (1888), 34–35. For Christian, see Frederick Edwards to Christian, 7 May 1785, William Christian Correspondence, Bullitt Papers, folder 413, Filson Historical Society.

12. Extract from Dr. Manasseh Cutler journal, 19 Aug. 1788, 19, Tupper Family Papers, Marietta, Ohio, Collection, Ohio Historical Society, Columbus; Fred Anderson and

Andrew Cayton, *The Dominion of War: Empire and Liberty in North America, 1500–2000* (New York, 2005), 181.

13. "Narrative of John Heckewelder's Journey," vol. 11, 53; Lowell Harrison, *George Rogers Clark and the War in the West* (Lexington, KY, 1976), 107.

14. See, for example, Boone to John Phillips and John Young, 30 July 1789, Indians and Indian War Papers, Gratz Collection, case 4, box 4, Historical Society of Pennsylvania, Philadelphia (hereafter cited as HSP); and Robert Patterson travel journal, Dec. 1784, Robert Patterson Papers, Filson Historical Society.

15. Steven Aron, *How the West Was Lost: The Transformation of Kentucky from Daniel Boone to Henry Clay* (Baltimore, 1996), 75.

16. "Mrs. Mary Dewee's Journal," 197; Elizabeth Perkins, *Border Life: Experience and Memory in the Revolutionary Ohio Valley* (Chapel Hill, NC, 1998).

17. See, for instance, "Letters of Mrs. Ann Biddle Wilkinson from Kentucky, 1788–89," *Pennsylvania Magazine of History and Biography* 56 (1932), 48.

18. Henry could not order local officials to move other claimants off his land; instead, he had to ask locals how he should proceed in the face of the changing landscape of Kentucky land arrangements. Henry to Christian, 17 March 1786, Christian Correspondence, folder 414.

19. Greenup to Robert Patterson, 7 Oct. 1788, Robert Patterson Papers, Draper MSS, ser. 2MM, 55.

20. Mills to Patterson, 17 March 1791, Patterson Papers, ser. 3MM, 29.

21. John May to Samuel Beall, 27 June 1786, Samuel Beall Correspondence, Beall-Booth Family Papers, folder 5, Filson Historical Society.

22. Campbell to John Brown, 29 Dec. 1787, Campbell Papers, folder 4.

23. Josiah Harmar to Henry Knox, 14 May 1787, Josiah Harmar Papers, letter book B, 77, William Clements Library, University of Michigan, Ann Arbor.

24. Harmar to Knox, 15 June 1788, Harmar Papers, letter book C, 61.

25. Harmar to Robert Thompson, 7 Aug. 1788, and Harmar to Knox, 17 Aug. 1788, Harmar Papers, letter book D, 28–29, 34.

26. See, for example, Craig Thompson Friend, ed., *The Buzzel About Kentuck: Settling the Promised Land* (Lexington, KY, 1999).

27. R. Daniel to William Christian, 27 Oct. 1784, Christian Correspondence, folder 412. See also Samuel Beall to Walter Beall, 1 April 1789, Beall Correspondence, folder 7.

28. Joseph Scott to George Muler, 2 March 1785, Harry Innes Papers, General Correspondence, folder 2, Library of Congress, Washington, DC.

29. "Narrative of John Heckewelder's Journey," vol. 12, 179.

30. Aron, *How the West Was Lost*, 73–80; Hinderaker, *Elusive Empires*, 238.

31. William Fleming to Innes, 23 June 1784, Innes Papers, General Correspondence, folder 2.

32. For these disputes and their meanings for Kentucky's history, see Aron, *How the West Was Lost*.

33. "Journal of Col. John May," 117.

34. Ibid., 147.

35. Ibid., 153–54.

36. James Filson, *The Discovery, Settlement, and Present State of Kentucke* (Wilmington, DE, 1784), 46.

37. Extract of a letter dated 3 May 1787, Fayette County, Kentucky, Campbell Papers, folder 4.

38. D. W. Meriwether to _____, 14 Sept. 1785, David Meriwether Papers, Filson Historical Society.

39. "A Free Trade out of the Mississippi" would, he contended, offer the "only answer to domestic tranquillity, wealth, weight, and Importance." James Wilkinson to James Hutchinson, 20 June 1785, *Pennsylvania Magazine of History and Biography* 12 (1888), 56. Also see Anderson and Cayton, *Dominion of War*, 182.

40. Harmar to Knox, 14 May 1787, Harmar Papers, letter book B, 77.

41. Innes to Brown, 7 Dec. 1787, Innes Papers, General Correspondence, folder 2.

42. Harmar to Thomas Mifflin, 25 June 1785, Harmar Papers, letter book A, 75. On the confederation, see Alan Taylor, *The Divided Ground: Indians, Settlers, and the Northern Borderland of the American Revolution* (New York, 2006), especially for the ways in which the Iroquois brokered deals with the British; and, of course, Richard White, *The Middle Ground: Indians, Empires, and Republics in the Great Lakes Region, 1650–1815* (New York, 1991).

43. "Narrative of John Heckewelder's Journey," vol. 12, 37.

44. Boone to Nathaniel Rochester, 7 May 1789, Daniel Boone Papers, Filson Historical Society.

45. "Journal of Col. John May," 148–49.

46. "Notes of a Journey from Philadelphia to New Madrid," *Pennsylvania Magazine of History and Biography* 36 (1912), 212–13.

47. "Narrative of John Heckewelder's Journey," vol. 11, 470.

48. *A True and Wonderful Narrative of the Surprising Captivity and Remarkable Deliverance of Mrs. Frances Scott* (Boston, 1786), 2, 7–9.

49. Greenup to Smith and McCourt, 17 March 1783, Simon Kenton Papers, Draper MSS, ser. 6BB, 34.

50. May to Samuel Beall, n.d., but received May 1786, Beall Correspondence, folder 5. Also see May to Samuel Beall, 27 June 1786, Beall Correspondence, folder 5.

51. Anderson and Cayton, *Dominion of War*, 181.

52. David Campbell to Arthur Campbell, 27 Dec. 1784, Campbell Papers, folder 3.

53. Henry to Christian, 17 March 1786; Samuel McDowell to Henry, 18 April 1786; May to Henry, 19 April 1786; McDowell to Henry, 18 April 1786; May to Henry, 19 April 1786, Christian Correspondence, folder 414. See also Annie Christian to Elizabeth Christian, 17 Aug. 1787, Annie Christian Correspondence, Bullitt Family Papers, folder 393.

54. An interesting account of the ins and outs of the negotiations can be found in Gordon Wood, *The Americanization of Benjamin Franklin* (New York, 2003).

55. Anthony F. C. Wallace, *Jefferson and the Indians: The Tragic Fate of the First Americans* (Cambridge, MA, 1999), 66. Alan Taylor suggests that it was Indian insistence that kept the British in their posts in the West. They were not, as he illustrates, "mere pawns in an imperial game." *Divided Ground*, 116–17.

56. Harmar to Knox, 1 June 1785, Harmar Papers, letter book A, 65–66. See, for example, Ebenezer Denny journal, 13 June 1786, Denny Papers, Denny-O'Hara Family Papers, Historical Society of Western Pennsylvania, Pittsburgh.

57. "Letters of Mrs. Ann Biddle Wilkinson," 40.

58. "Journal of Col. John May," 110, 119, 160.

59. McDowell to Fleming, 11 Nov. 1785, Frontier War Papers, ser. 2U, 139.

60. "Journal of Col. John May," 163.

61. Breckinridge to Joseph Cabbel Jr., 23 July 1793, Breckinridge Family Papers, vol. 9, Library of Congress; Aron, *How the West Was Lost*, 92. See also Henry to William Christian, 25 Feb. 1786, Christian Correspondence, folder 414; Annie Christian to William Christian, Frontier War Papers, ser. 2U, 140; Van Swearingen to William Crahan, 31 May 1787, Samuel Brady and Lewis Wetzel Papers, Draper MSS, ser. 1E, 86.

62. Filson, *Discovery, Settlement*, 21, 79.

63. Isaac Hite to Abraham Hite, 26 April 1783, Isaac Hite Papers, Filson Historical Society.

64. Harmar to John Hamtramck, 14 Nov. 1786, Harmar Papers, letter book B, 5; Logan to Edmund Randolph, 17 Dec. 1786, Benjamin Logan Correspondence, Bullitt Family Papers, folder 515. In September 1786, as George Rogers Clark prepared to stage a raid, more than four hundred of his men abandoned him once more, and as an expedition the foray achieved nothing. Clark, however, did manage to draw the fire of a great number of Shawnees, allowing Lincoln to face no opposition. See Harmar to Knox, 15 Nov. 1786, Harmar Papers, letter book B, 9–10. Also see Hinderaker, *Elusive Empires*, 240–41.

65. Harmar to Hamtramck, 14 Nov. 1786, Harmar Papers, letter book B, 5.

66. "Proceedings of a General Court Martial . . . for the Trial of Colonel Hugh McGary," 21 March 1787, Alexander S. Bullitt Military Papers, Bullitt Family Papers, folder 48.

67. Harmar to member of Congress from New York, 10 Dec. 1786, Harmar Papers, letter book B, 25–26.

68. William Finney to Patterson, 3 July 1786, Patterson Papers, ser. 1MM, 141.

69. Ebenezer Denny journal, 21 Dec. 1785, Historical Society of Western Pennsylvania.

70. For Innes, the great divide looming in America was between East and West, between those who enjoyed peace and those still mired in a state of war. To drive home the point, he reckoned that from 1783 — the end of the War of Independence — and the close of 1787, Indians had killed three hundred people in or near Danville, Kentucky, taken another fifty, and stolen two thousand horses. Innes to Brown, 7 Dec. 1787, Innes Papers, General Correspondence, folder 2.

71. Innes to Brown, 4 April 1788, Innes Papers, General Correspondence, folder 3; Harrison, *George Rogers Clark and the War in the West*, 104–6.

72. Randolph to David Shepherd, 25 July 1787, David Shepherd Papers, Draper MSS, ser. 2SS, 95.

73. McDowell to Fleming, 20 Dec. 1787, Frontier War Papers, ser. 2U, 143.

74. Innes to Brown, 20 Feb. 1788, Innes Papers, General Correspondence, folder 3.

75. Saul Cornell suggests as much, arguing that westerners appeared to be "plebeian"

anti-federalists, sharing some of their sentiments yet somehow different from eastern republicans. See *The Other Founders: Anti-Federalism and the Dissenting Tradition in America, 1788–1828* (Chapel Hill, NC, 1999).

76. Harmar to Arthur St. Clair, 8 May 1789, Harmar Papers, letter book E, 84.

77. John Mills to Winthrop Sargent, 17 April 1791, Winthrop Sargent Papers, reel 3, Massachusetts Historical Society, Boston.

78. Harmar to Knox, 15 Dec. 1788, Harmar Papers, letter book E, 10–11.

79. In 1788, news spread of the Spaniards seizing property on the east side of the Mississippi River near where a fellow named Sullivan had settled. Sullivan, who had taken part in an infamous mutiny of the Pennsylvania line during the war, had written letters to a Spanish minister, declaring that "it is the universal sentiment of the inhabitants westward of the Allegheny Mountains" to seize New Orleans. According to an official who ordered his arrest, Sullivan had "a mutinous disposition" and was "an insignificant Banditti." Harmar to Hamtramck, 13 Oct. 1788, Harmar Papers, letter book D, 63; Harmar to Knox, 10 Jan. 1788, Harmar Papers, letter book B, 164–65.

80. Campbell to Knox, n.d. 1789, Campbell Papers, folder 4.

81. Governor of Virginia to Shepherd, 16 June 1787, Shepherd Papers, ser. 2SS, 89; Innes to Brown, 4 April 1788, Innes Papers, General Correspondence, folder 3. Also see John Marshall to George Nicholas, 26 April 1789, Innes Papers, General Correspondence, folder 4.

82. Undated MS on admission of western states, Alexander Scott Bullitt Papers, Bullitt Family Papers, folder 578. To be sure, some absentee landlords hoped statehood would better safeguard their claims in such a period of flux (Aron, *How the West Was Lost*, 87).

83. Harmar to Knox, 8 May 1789, and Harmar to Hamtramck, 25 Oct. 1789, Harmar Papers, letter book F, 3, 64.

84. Bullitt to the governor of Virginia, 16 May 1787, Bullitt Papers, folder 6.

85. On the land ordinances and their role in creating an "empire" based on territorial expansion in the West, see Hinderaker, *Elusive Empires*, 226–32; and Onuf, *Origins of the Federal Republic*.

86. Harmar to John Dickinson, 15 Jan. 1785, Harmar Papers, letter book A, 26; White, *Middle Ground*.

87. Wallace, *Jefferson and the Indians*, 163; Onuf, *Statehood and Union*.

88. John Cleves Symmes, *To the Respectable Public* (Trenton, 1787).

89. Harmar to Knox, 7 Sept. 1788, Harmar Papers, letter book D, 45–46. James Henry to Patterson, 13 March 1789, Patterson Papers, ser. 2MM, 93.

90. "Narrative of John Heckewelder's Journey," vol. 12, 35.

91. Ohio Company, *Articles of an Association by the Name of the Ohio Company* (Worcester, MA, 1786), 2–3.

92. S. P. Hildreth, *Biographical and Historical Memoirs of the Early Pioneer Settlers of Ohio* (Cincinnati, 1852), 104.

93. Ibid., 250.

94. Ibid., 104.

95. Court and Legal Papers, Backus-Woodbridge Papers, 1422–28, Ohio Historical Society.

96. To ensure so, they would give free land to members of the company who owned at least one share. The thinking went that "in order to begin *right*, there will be no *wrong* habits to combat, and no inveterate systems to overturn—there is no rubbish to remove, before you can lay a foundation." Manasseh Cutler, *An Explanation of the Map Which Delineates That Part of the Federal Lands* . . . (Salem, MA, 1787), 20.

97. James Mitchell Varnum, *An Oration Delivered at Marietta, July 4, 1788* (Newport, RI, 1788), 5.

98. On the egalitarianism of the early settlement, see Douglas Hurt, *The Ohio Frontier: Crucible of the Old Northwest* (Bloomington, IN, 1996), 157.

99. On New Englanders and Indians in the seventeenth century, see James Axtell, *Natives and Newcomers: The Cultural Origins of North America* (New York, 2001), 145–73.

100. Varnum, *Oration*, 5, 10, 8.

101. Harmar to Dickinson, 1 May 1785, Harmar Papers, letter book A, 54; Proclamation of the Governor of Virginia, 20 Aug. 1794, Pittsburgh and Northwest Virginia Papers, Draper MSS, ser. 5NN, 66; Thomas Gist Jr. to Patterson, 29 April 1785, Patterson Papers, ser. 1MM, 137; John Armstrong to Harmar, 13 April 1785, Harmar Papers, vol. 2, 56.

102. Kim Gruenwald argues that the North and South formed a common "western world," one defined along the lines of trade. See *River of Enterprise: The Commercial Origins of Regional Identity in the Ohio Valley, 1790–1850* (Bloomington, IN, 2002).

103. Harmar to Knox, 14 May 1787, Harmar Papers, letter book B, 80.

104. Harmar to Knox, 15 Dec. 1788 and 10 Feb. 1789, Harmar Papers, letter book E, 10–11, 45.

105. "Narrative of John Heckewelder's Journey," vol. 11, 472–74. Also see "Journal of Col. John May," 138.

106. Subscription list for Fourth of July celebration, 18 June 1788, Miscellaneous Papers, Backus-Woodbridge Collection; Benjamin Tupper typescript, 69, Marietta, Ohio, Collection.

107. Harmar to John Doughty, 28 April 1789, Harmar Papers, letter book E, 80.

108. Extract from Cutler journal, 1788, 20, 23.

109. Harmar to Knox, 13 July 1786, Harmar Papers, letter book A, 137.

110. Federal authorities in the region therefore had a stake in the company's success. Josiah Harmar was a proprietor of the Ohio Company. Rufus Putnam, a commanding figure in early Marietta, served in the army while he was chief judge of Ohio. Secretary of War Henry Knox owned stock in the Ohio Company. Andrew Cayton, *The Frontier Republic: Ideology and Politics in the Ohio Country, 1780–1825* (Kent, OH, 1986), 16–21. Cayton argues that the alignment of such characters points to the federalist origins of the Ohio Company's settlement. On Knox and his approach to Indian policy, see Taylor, *Divided Ground*, 238–39.

111. Reginald Horsman, "American Indian Policy in the Old Northwest, 1783–1812," *William and Mary Quarterly*, 3rd ser., 18 (1961), 35–53.

112. Harmar to Knox, 1 June 1785; Harmar to Mifflin, 25 June 1785, Harmar Papers, letter book A, 65–66, 75.

113. Harmar to Knox, 4 Sept. 1786 and 22 Oct. 1785, Harmar Papers, letter book A, 145, 98–99; Gary Nash, *The Unknown American Revolution: The Unruly Birth of Democracy and the Struggle to Create America* (New York, 2005), 387.

114. Harmar to Knox, 4 Aug. 1786, Harmar Papers, letter book A, 145. Also see Harmar to Knox, 14 Jan. 1790, Harmar Papers, letter book G, 7; "Narrative of John Heckewelder's Journey," vol. 12, 38–39, 42.

115. Harmar to Richard Henry Lee, 1 May 1785, Harmar Papers, letter book A, 55–56.

116. Denny to Harmar, 23 Aug. 1785, Harmar Papers, vol. 2, 110; Harmar to Knox, 22 Oct. 1785, and orders delivered to Captain John Doughty, Fort McIntosh, 3 Oct. 1785, Harmar Papers, letter book A, 98–99, 96–97. Also see Hinderaker, *Elusive Empires*, 240.

117. Harmar to John Carpenter, 26 April 1789, Harmar Papers, letter book E, 76.

118. Resolution of Settlers West of the Ohio River, 5 April 1785, Harmar Papers, vol. 2, 51. In March 1785, some settlers called for a convention "for the forming of a constitution for the governing of inhabitants." All persons, they declared, "have an undoubted right to pass into any vacant country and there to form their constitution." The federal government had no authority to "forbid" the people trying to establish a society. Advertisement and declaration signed by Jon Emerson, 12 March 1785, Harmar Papers, vol. 2, 44.

119. Armstrong to Harmar, Harmar Papers, vol. 2, 55.

120. Irvine to Harmar, 31 May 1785, Harmar Papers, vol. 2, 77.

121. Harmar to Knox, 18 March 1787, Harmar Papers, letter book B, 59. Also see Harmar to Knox, 4 Aug. 1786, Harmar Papers, letter book A, 145.

122. Richard Butler journal, 15 March 1786, Frontier War Papers, ser. 3U, 477. See also Denny journal, 1785–91, 5 Oct., 20 Dec., 21 Dec., 31 Dec. 1785 and 21 Jan. 1786, Denny Papers.

123. Resolution of Congress, 24 Aug. 1786, Harmar Papers, vol. 4, 9.

124. Harmar to Knox, 1 Aug. 1785, Harmar Papers, letter book A, 90.

125. Harmar to Knox, 7 July 1787, Harmar Papers, letter book B, 115.

126. Of course, he saw them as a "race of savages," but at issue was culture. As he marveled at ancient earthworks erected along the Muskingum, he declared them "to be the works of some civilized people," presumably the ancestors of Ohio's Indians. Harmar to Mifflin, 19 March 1787, Harmar Papers, letter book B, 61.

127. Varnum, *Oration*, 13.

128. Putnam to George Washington, 24 July 1790, in Rowena Buell, ed., *The Memoirs of Rufus Putnam* (Boston, 1903), 232–33.

129. Solomon Drowne, *An Oration, Delivered at Marietta, April 7, 1789* (Worcester, MA, 1789), 8.

130. Putnam to Fisher Ames, 1790, in Buell, *Memoirs of Putnam*, 244–45. Also see Butler journal, 5 March 1786, 467.

131. S. P. Hildreth, *Pioneer History: Being an Account of the First Examinations of the Ohio Valley* (Cincinnati, 1848), 428.

132. Tupper to Mrs. Stone, 18 Nov. 1788, Tupper Family Papers, box 2, folder 1, 6–7. On this theme, also see Minerva Nye to Mrs. Stone, 19 Sept. 1788, Tupper Family Papers, box 2, folder 1, 4–5.

133. Tupper to Mrs. Stone, 18 Nov. 1788, Tupper Family Papers, box 2, folder 1, 6–7.

134. Drowne, *Oration*, 9.

135. Harmar to St. Clair, 8 May 1789, Harmar Papers, letter book E, 83. See also Symmes to Patterson, 25 Sept. and 20 June 1789, Patterson Papers, ser. 2MM, 106, 101; petition of people of Grave Creek, 18 May 1790, Shepherd Papers, ser. 2SS, 173.

136. Shepherd to Knox, 10 May 1790, Shepherd Papers, ser. 2SS, 171–72.

137. Obediah Robins to Harmar, 28 Aug. 1785, Harmar Papers, vol. 2, 113.

138. Robins to William Ferguson, 29 Sept. 1786, Harmar Papers, vol. 4, 43. Even the French settlers heading to Gallipolis understood the nature of the world they were entering. One group, for example, implored the president for protection because of "the numerous accounts in the public papers" of atrocities. Appeal to the President of the United States, 19 May 1790, Scioto Land Company Records, Correspondence file, 1790, HSP.

139. Varnum, *Oration*, 5. Although New Englanders did not by any means view Indians the way settlers in Kentucky did, they did take what they regarded as prudent measures as tensions gripped the West in the immediate aftermath of Harmar's defeat. See, for instance, A. B. Hulbert, ed., *The Records of the Original Proceedings of the Ohio Company* (Marietta, OH, 1917), vol. 2, 58–59.

140. Knox to Shepherd, 17 July 1790, Shepherd Papers, ser. 2SS, 181–83.

141. Knox to the lieutenant of Mason County, Kentucky, 29 July 1790, Henry Knox Correspondence, Isaac Shields Papers, Filson Historical Society.

142. Levi Todd to Patterson, 11 Nov. 1790, Patterson Papers, ser. 3MM, 21.

143. Proceedings of a Court of Inquiry Held at Fort Washington, 15 Sept. 1791, Frontier War Papers, ser. 4U, 25–36.

144. On chastisement, see Cayton, *Frontier Republic*, 36, 38. This stance has also been called "modified aggression." See Nash, *Unknown American Revolution*, 382; and Reginald Horsman, *Expansion and American Indian Policy, 1783–1812* (East Lansing, MI, 1967). Alan Taylor is clear on this point. By the early 1790s, federal officials had rejected "conquest theory." They followed, as he argues, Iroquois advice and adopted a William Johnson–like diplomatic approach. *Divided Ground*, 264.

145. Hulbert, *Records*, vol. 2, 57, 59.

146. Hildreth, *Biographical and Historical Memoirs*, 104.

147. Hildreth, *Pioneer History*, 429–30.

148. Ibid.; Joseph Barker, *Recollections of the First Settlement of Ohio* (Marietta, OH, 1958), 67–68.

149. Hildreth, *Pioneer History*, 431–33.

150. Harmar to Hamtramck, 15 Jan. 1791, Harmar Papers, letter book I, 6–7. For other attacks, see Shepherd to Absalom Baird, 5 May 1792, Brady and Wetzel Papers, ser. 1E, 99.

151. Benjamin Biggs to Beverley Randolph, March 1791, Pittsburgh and Northwest Virginia Papers, ser. 5NN, 23–24.

152. Shepherd to _____, 25 Jan. 1791, Shepherd Papers, ser. 3SS, 1.
153. Capt. de Luziere to St. Clair, 20 Feb. 1791, in William Henry Smith, ed., *The St. Clair Papers* (Cincinnati, 1882), vol. 2, 199. Putnam blamed the failed Harmar expedition against the Shawnees. But he insisted, everything he and others had said notwithstanding, that the attack did not come as a total surprise. "I have Sometime ben of the opinion that the Spring would open with a general attack on the frontier," he suggested. Putnam to _____, 6 Jan. 1791, in Buell, *Memoirs of Putnam*, 248.
154. Putnam to _____, 6 Jan. 1791, in Buell, *Memoirs of Putnam*, 247.
155. Hulbert, *Records*, vol. 2, 67–71.
156. Harmar to Symmes, 21 Jan. 1791, Harmar Papers, letter book I, 10–11; "Narrative of John Heckewelder's Journey," vol. 12, 44, 48; Brown to Innes, 1 Feb. 1791, Innes Papers, General Correspondence, 1791; Innes to Knox, 7 July 1790, Innes Papers, General Correspondence, 1790.
157. Innes to Brown, 4 April 1788, Innes Papers, General Correspondence, folder 3; Shepherd to _____, 1789, Shepherd Papers, ser. 2SS, 157–58.
158. Putnam to _____, 6 Jan. 1791, in Buell, *Memoirs of Putnam*, 248.
159. Hulbert, *Records*, vol. 2, 72–73.
160. Innes to Brown, 4 April 1788, Innes Papers, General Correspondence, folder 3.
161. Innes to Bullitt, 10 May 1790, Bullitt Papers, folder 6.
162. Kim Gruenwald argues that as early as 1790 New Englanders in Ohio were troubled by the question of the Mississippi. After this time, the pleas to open up the river and deal with the British became much more shrill. See *River of Enterprise*, 16–17, 22.
163. Putnam to Washington, 28 Feb. 1791, in Jack Warren, ed., *Papers of George Washington*, Presidential Series (Charlottesville, VA, 1998), vol. 7, 470.
164. Putnam to Washington, 24 July and 20 Dec. 1790, in Mark Mastromarino, ed., *Papers of George Washington*, Presidential Series (Charlottesville, VA, 1996), vol. 6, 121–22; vol. 7, 100–1.
165. It would, westerners hoped, ensure that the accommodation between settlers and speculators would hold, allowing the trappings of a healthy social fabric to flourish. The failure to protect the West, which included opening the Mississippi, would "prevent our Inhabitants from improving in Arts and Science as it will deprive us of all foreign intercourse and we shall become mere barbarians." Innes to Brown, 7 Dec. 1787, Innes Papers, General Correspondence, folder 2.
166. Innes to Knox, 7 July 1790, Innes Papers, General Correspondence, folder 5.

CHAPTER 8: WEST AND EAST

1. Harmar to Henry Knox, 19 July 1789, Josiah Harmar Papers, letter book F, 21–22, William Clements Library, University of Michigan, Ann Arbor; proceedings of a general court-martial held at Fort Washington, 28 June 1790, Simon Kenton Papers, Draper MSS, ser. 6BB, 60–80, Historical Society of Wisconsin, Madison.
2. Harmar to Henry Lee, 27 Sept. 1789, Kenton Papers, ser. 6BB, 48.
3. Deposition of James Patton, 13 Feb. 1790; deposition of Jake Young, 5 May 1790, Kenton Papers, ser. 6BB, 55–56, 57.
4. Deposition of William Caldwell, Feb. 1790, Kenton Papers, ser. 6BB, 52.

5. Proceedings of a general court-martial held at Fort Washington, 60–67.

6. Harmar to Lee, 27 Sept. 1789, Harmar Papers, letter book F, 55.

7. Proceedings of a general court-martial held at Fort Washington, 80.

8. Harmar to John Hamtramck, 13 Jan. 1790, Harmar Papers, letter book G, 5.

9. Harmar to Lee, 3 Aug. 1790, Harmar Papers, letter book H, 21.

10. On this view of Washington, see Gordon Wood, *Revolutionary Characters: What Made the Founders Different* (New York, 2006), 29–64.

11. "Journal from Jersey to Monongahalia, Aug. 11, 1788," *Pennsylvania Magazine of History and Biography* 52 (1928), 200.

12. Some historians describe the rebels' antics as a "localist insurrection" against established authority or as evidence of a "plebeian" or "populist" impulse for violence. They therefore portray these rebels west of the mountains in the same light they understand other frontier settlers. On this, see Saul Cornell, *The Other Founders: Anti-Federalism and the Dissenting Tradition in America, 1788–1828* (Chapel Hill, NC, 1999); and Stanley Elkins and Eric McKitrick, *The Age of Federalism* (New York, 1993).

13. William Findley, *History of the Insurrection, in the Four Western Counties of Pennsylvania* (Philadelphia, 1796), 67. The Whiskey Rebellion, as it has been called, was a "frontier epilogue" to the American Revolution, a moment that tells us as much about the local concerns of people living on the frontier as it does about the nature and outcomes of the Revolution. So suggests the best treatment, by far, of this series of events, Thomas Slaughter's *Whiskey Rebellion: Frontier Epilogue to the American Revolution* (New York, 1986). Although Slaughter illustrates how westerners adopted the language and ritual of the War of Independence, he still views the frontiersmen as an emotional, troubling lot. This treatment, it should be noted, like all studies of the Whiskey Rebellion since, draws heavily on Slaughter's definitive narrative. A rejoinder to Slaughter is Terry Bouton's dissertation, which views the Whiskey Rebellion in light of other "regulator" movements that emerged in backcountry regions in the period around the War of Independence. Bouton's study is particularly strong in its emphasis on the local economy. See "Tying Up the Revolution: Money, Power, and the Regulation in Pennsylvania, 1765–1800" (Ph.D. diss., Duke University, 1996).

14. Innes to Knox, 10 March 1790, Harry Innes Papers, General Correspondence, Library of Congress, Washington, DC.

15. St. Clair to John Brown, 25 June 1791, Innes Papers, General Correspondence. Also see Richard Butler to David Shepherd, 11 June 1791, David Shepherd Papers, Draper MSS, ser. 3SS, 43. With this move, leaders in Virginia wiped their hands of the West, claiming that since Congress had earmarked money to move federal troops west, their responsibilities for defending the West had ended. They would no longer fund militias. Beverley Randolph to Shepherd, 25 March 1791, Shepherd Papers, ser. 3SS, 13.

16. Knox to Shepherd, 27 May 1791; John Neville to Shepherd, 6 May 1791, Shepherd Papers, ser. 3SS, 27, 29.

17. Circular letter to the lieutenants of the counties of Kentucky from Arthur St. Clair, 23 Aug. 1791, Arthur St. Clair Papers, Filson Historical Society, Louisville, KY.

18. Anthony F. C. Wallace, *Jefferson and the Indians: The Tragic Fate of the First Americans* (Cambridge, MA, 1999), 171. Peter Onuf argues that "the Federalists had no in-

tention of winning the war in the West." Certainly this was the case in the early 1790s. Officials hoped that the region could be pacified through, as Onuf puts it, frontier "self-help," the disbursement of public lands, and a few raids by mounted riflemen. All could be accomplished, in other words, without help from the "military establishment." See *Jefferson's Empire: The Language of American Nationhood* (Charlottesville, VA, 2000), 42. It's fair to say that the government considered this a major expedition, though it was hastily put together and poorly executed and planned. See Richard Kohn, *Eagle and Sword: The Federalists and the Creation of the Military Establishment in America, 1783–1802* (New York, 1975), 109. Yet if something beyond chastisement were envisioned or if this expedition was part of a plan on the part of the government to extend empire west, this army was a poor vehicle for doing so.

19. Winthrop Sargent diary of St. Clair expedition, 10 Oct. 1791, Winthrop Sargent Papers, reel 1, 10, Massachusetts Historical Society, Boston.

20. Samuel Newman diary, 30 June–23 Oct. 1791, Frontier War Papers, Draper MSS, ser. 4U, 102–10.

21. For the best treatment of Native American motivations and responses to Harmar and St. Clair, see Richard White's *Middle Ground: Indians, Empires, and Republics in the Great Lakes Region, 1650–1815* (New York, 1991); and Wallace, *Jefferson and the Indians*, 171–75.

22. "John Adlum on the Allegheny: Memoirs for the Year 1794," *Pennsylvania Magazine of History and Biography* 84 (1960), 317.

23. Henry Bidinger to Shepherd, 27 Oct. 1791, Shepherd Papers, ser. 3SS, 59.

24. "Narrative of John Heckewelder's Journey to the Wabash in 1792," *Pennsylvania Magazine of History and Biography* 11 (1887), 466.

25. Knox to Isaac Shelby, 24 April 1793, Isaac Shelby Papers, Henry Knox Correspondence, Filson Historical Society.

26. Wayne to Shepherd, 23 June 1792, Shepherd Papers, ser. 3SS, 127.

27. James Wilkinson to Lee, 2 April 1792, Kenton Papers, ser. 6BB, 97.

28. "Narrative of John Heckewelder's Journey to the Wabash in 1792," *Pennsylvania Magazine of History and Biography* 12 (1888), 178.

29. Hardin's letters to his wife, 20 April, 10 May, 19 May 1792, John Hardin Papers, Filson Historical Society.

30. "Narrative of John Heckewelder's Journey," vol. 12, 46. Also see Arthur Campbell to John Steele, 28 March 1792, Arthur Campbell Papers, folder 6, Filson Historical Society; George Rogers Clark to Jonathan Clark, 11 May 1792, George Rogers Clark Papers, Filson Historical Society. On Hardin's fate, see "Narrative of John Heckewelder's Journey," vol. 12, 45.

31. Indians asked that the Ohio River serve as a dividing line between their land and the whites who threatened it. They did not want to "live in too close proximity" with the types of settlers that infested the frontier. This proposal, of course, proved unworkable. "Narrative of John Heckewelder's Journey," vol. 12, 171.

32. Extract from Dr. Manasseh Cutler journal, 1788, 15–16, Tupper Family Papers, Marietta, Ohio, Collection, Ohio Historical Society, Columbus. Also see "Journal of

Griffith Evans, 1784–85," *Pennsylvania Magazine of History and Biography* 65 (1941), 226; "Journal of Col. John May, of Boston, Relative to a Journey to the Ohio Country, 1789," *Pennsylvania Magazine of History and Biography* 45 (1921), 135.

33. "Journal of Col. John May," 114–15. A resident did not find the area around Pittsburgh very charming. On this, see Ephraim Douglas to William Irvine, 11 Feb. 1784, William Irvine Correspondence, vol. 8, Historical Society of Pennsylvania, Philadelphia (hereafter cited as HSP); and Slaughter, *Whiskey Rebellion*, 68–70.

34. *Pittsburgh Gazette*, 10 Nov. 1787.

35. "Journal of Col. John May," 132.

36. Ibid., 116.

37. "Mrs. Mary Dewee's Journal from Philadelphia to Kentucky, 1787–88," *Pennsylvania Magazine of History and Biography* 28 (1904), 190.

38. Douglas to Irvine, 11 Feb. 1784, Irvine Correspondence, vol. 8.

39. Benjamin Biggs to Randolph, March 1791, Benjamin Biggs Papers, Draper MSS, ser. 5NN, 23–24.

40. See, for instance, James Marshall to Benjamin Franklin, 6 Nov. 1787, Samuel Brady and Lewis Wetzel Papers, Draper MSS, ser. 1E, 90.

41. Shepherd to Knox, 10 May 1790, Shepherd Papers, ser. 2SS, 171–72.

42. George McCully to Clement Biddle, 5 May 1792, Brady and Wetzel Papers, ser. 1E, 100. On Kentucky attacks in 1792, see Wilkinson to Innes, 29 Feb. 1792, Innes Papers, General Correspondence.

43. Baird to Mifflin, 28 June 1792, Frontier War Papers, ser. 4U, 207; "Narrative of John Heckewelder's Journey," vol. 11, 468–69; *Pennsylvania Gazette*, 4 Jan. 1792.

44. Douglas to Irvine, 11 Feb. 1784, Irvine Correspondence, vol. 8. A number, after all, had "been indian hunters" during the war. "John Adlum on the Allegheny," 292.

45. "Narrative of John Heckewelder's Journey," vol. 11, 468, 469.

46. Cornplanter to Quaker officials, Oct. 1790, Indians and Indian Wars Papers, Gratz Papers, case 4, box 4, HSP.

47. On these dynamics in western Pennsylvania, see R. Eugene Harper, *The Transformation of Western Pennsylvania, 1770–1800* (Pittsburgh, 1991), 29–40, 55–56, 69, 172; Bouton, "Tying Up the Revolution," 39, 44, 45, 289. Also see Slaughter, *Whiskey Rebellion*, 65.

48. Bouton, "Tying Up the Revolution," 288.

49. "John Adlum on the Allegheny," 287–88.

50. One landowner, for example, who claimed an island in the Ohio near Fort Pitt had to contend with a squatter named John Arney, who along with a few friends had girdled some trees, claimed the island through improvement, and sold half of it to his brother. M. Finley to Irvine, 13 May 1784, Irvine Correspondence, vol. 8, 100. The wealthier used periods of intensive Indian raids, when the movement of squatters slowed, to send out surveyors to mark out bounds for warrants. During these times, surveyors could expect to earn a half-dollar a day versus the going rate of $10 per month. Unsurprisingly, many overcame their fears. "John Adlum on the Allegheny," 287–88.

51. Bouton, "Tying Up the Revolution," 39, 44, 224, 271.

52. Slaughter argues that of all the frontier regions, "western Pennsylvania had fared worst of all during the 1780s." Most were scraping by, and "conditions were getting worse." *Whiskey Rebellion*, 57, 65.

53. Harper, *Transformation of Western Pennsylvania*, 29. Also see Thomas Duncan Smith and Andrew Henderson to His Excellency the president of the Supreme Executive Council of the Commonwealth of Pennsylvania, 5 June 1788, Northern, Interior, and Western Counties Papers, 205, HSP.

54. Harper, *Transformation of Western Pennsylvania*, 149–57.

55. Douglas to Irvine, 6 July 1783, Irvine Correspondence, vol. 8, 27.

56. "Narrative of John Heckewelder's Journey," vol. 11, 468, 469.

57. *An Address from the Inhabitants of Wyoming and Others . . . to the People at Large of the Commonwealth of Pennsylvania* (Hudson, NY, 1786).

58. Findley, *History of the Insurrection*, 27, 41. For a description of the production of whiskey, see "Journal of Col. John May," 110–11.

59. Findley, *History of the Insurrection*, 27, 41.

60. The frontier economy depended on whiskey. "All the rye made in those parts," the traveler continued, "is distilled into whisky, and wheat is often given in exchange for it." Whiskey served as currency and "like Montero's cap, in Tristram Shandy, is the *wager*—the *gift*—and in some instances the *oath* of three-fourths of the inhabitants of our western counties." *Pennsylvania Gazette*, 27 Aug. 1788. Also see Slaughter, *Whiskey Rebellion*, 71.

61. Douglas to Irvine, 11 Feb. 1784, Irvine Correspondence, vol. 8.

62. *Pittsburgh Gazette*, 14 April 1787.

63. Richard Butler journal, 16 and 18 March 1786, Frontier War Papers, ser. 3U, 478, 480.

64. *Pennsylvania Gazette*, 4 March 1789. On the "best poor man's country," see James Lemon, *The Best Poor Man's Country: A Geographical Study of Early Southeastern Pennsylvania* (Baltimore, 1972).

65. Elkins and McKitrick, *Age of Federalism*, 226.

66. Coxe to Hamilton, 19 Oct. 1792, Letters Sent by the Commissioner of the Revenue and the Revenue Office, 1792–1807, Records of the Internal Revenue Service, 58-2-1, National Archives, College Park, MD.

67. A. J. Dallas to Baird, 25 July 1794, Frontier War Papers, ser. 4U, 226.

68. A Meeting of Committees from Several Townships of the County of Fayette, 10 Sept. 1794, Whiskey Rebellion Collection, Library of Congress.

69. Hugh Henry Brackenridge, "Incidents of the Insurrection in Western Pennsylvania, 1794," in *A Hugh Henry Brackenridge Reader, 1770–1815* (Pittsburgh, 1970), 329. On Tom, see Slaughter, *Whiskey Rebellion*, 184–85.

70. *Pennsylvania Gazette*, 8 Oct. 1794.

71. Brackenridge, "Incidents of the Insurrection," 303. Brackenridge argued that the name Tom the Tinker was "assumed by the people who were active in some of the masked riots" of the period.

72. *Pennsylvania Gazette*, 6 March 1799.

73. *Pittsburgh Gazette*, 26 April 1794.

74. In June 1791, for instance, representatives from the western Pennsylvania counties of

Westmoreland, Allegheny, Washington, and Fayette met at the old fort at Redstone to form a committee, to petition Congress, and to discuss plans with other frontier regions. Findley, *History of the Insurrection*, 41–42.

75. Neville to George Clymer, 17 Nov. 1791, Oliver Wolcott Jr. Papers, folder IX.10, vol. 19, no. 11, Connecticut Historical Society, Hartford.

76. *Dunlop's American Daily Advertiser*, 1 Sept. 1792, attached in a letter from Clymer to Oliver Wolcott Jr., 28 Sept. 1792, Wolcott Papers, no. 5.

77. *Pittsburgh Gazette*, 10 Sept. 1791.

78. Neville to Clymer, 8 Sept. 1791, Wolcott Papers, no. 12.

79. Deposition of Francis Gibson, 11 Oct. 1794, William Rawle Family Papers, 1791–1796, vol. 1, 49, HSP. As one witness observed, "That *old root of bitterness*, which the adoption of the Federal Government planted in the hearts of many here, is beginning to sprout with great vigour." *Pennsylvania Gazette*, 17 Sept. 1794. On the symbolism and ritual of pole raising, see Slaughter, *Whiskey Rebellion*, 206–10.

80. William Lyon to Mifflin, 12 Sept. 1794, Wolcott Papers, no. 31.

81. Deposition of Rosewell Douty, 27 Dec. 1794, Rawle Papers, vol. 1, 89.

82. Notes on Cumberland County testimony, n.d., Rawle Papers, vol. 1, 119.

83. Deposition of James Jenkins, 12 Nov. 1794, Rawle Papers, vol. 1, 61.

84. For the McGrath account, see his deposition, 2 Dec. 1794, Rawle Papers, vol. 1, 86. Adopting the symbol of the harp may have made sense for McGrath and some of his fellow frontier insurgents if they had migrated from Ireland or were the sons of those who had. On some of the human links between the two movements, see Kerby Miller, David Doyle, et al., eds., *Irish Immigrants in the Land of Canaan: Letters and Memoirs from Colonial and Revolutionary America, 1675–1815* (New York, 2003). On the other hand, as Jim Smyth demonstrates in *The Men of No Property: Irish Radicals and Popular Politics in the Late Eighteenth Century* (London, 1998), Defenderism—the most likely rural insurgent group that would have informed the rebels' tactics given the period of time such American and Irish movements flourished—was a localized phenomenon until 1791. Given the tight time frame, it's unlikely that Irish rural insurgency groups had a direct and profound effect on the rebels in western Pennsylvania. Moreover, the English and the Welsh, and of course the Scots, had some experience with such tactics. American frontiersmen also had their own precedents, particularly the Black Boys of the 1760s, though these, it must be admitted, could have been informed by earlier Irish rural insurgency movements, such as the Whiteboys or Oakboys. So suggests Kevin Kenny in *The American Irish: A History* (New York, 2000), 38.

85. Deposition of Jenkins, 12 Nov. 1794, Rawle Papers, vol. 1, 61.

86. Deposition of Benjamin Wells, 26 May 1795, Rawle Papers, vol. 1, 110.

87. Deposition of George Rowan, 27 Sept. 1794, Rawle Papers, vol. 1, 33.

88. Deposition of Henry Lebo, 7 Jan. 1795, Rawle Papers, vol. 1, 94.

89. Jasper Yeates and William Bradford to Edmund Randolph, 5 Sept. 1794, Whiskey Rebellion Collection; Slaughter, *Whiskey Rebellion*, 206–10.

90. Deposition of Owen Aston, 30 March 1795, Rawle Papers, vol. 1, 101.

NOTES TO PAGES 228-233

91. Findley, *History of the Insurrection*, 85, 136, 119. On this theme, see Bouton, "Tying Up the Revolution."

92. *Pittsburgh Gazette*, 23 Aug. 1794.

93. *Pennsylvania Gazette*, 13 Aug. 1794; minutes of the Democratic Society in Philadelphia, 11 and 18 Sept. 1794, 145, 148, HSP.

94. Minutes of the Democratic Society in Philadelphia, 18 Sept. 1794, 165–66. Also see Bouton, "Tying Up the Revolution," 443–44.

95. Sean Wilentz sees the rebels as epitomizing "the refractory post-Revolutionary country democracy" that imperiled the voice of more urbane Democratic-Republican societies in places like New York and Philadelphia. See *The Rise of American Democracy: Jefferson to Lincoln* (New York, 2005), 62–64.

96. Deposition of Benjamin Young, 9 Dec. 1794, Rawle Papers, vol. 1, 73. On these types of responses and what he regards as appeals to "order" over "liberty," see Slaughter, *Whiskey Rebellion*, 127–42.

97. Deposition of Jenkins, 12 Nov. 1794, 61.

98. *Pennsylvania Gazette*, 7 Jan. 1795.

99. William Sutherland to Matthew Buher, 30 Oct. 1794, Rawle Papers, vol. 1, 60.

100. A *Petition and Remonstrance to the President and Congress* (Philadelphia, 1794).

101. Committee Meeting of Citizens of Washington County, 15 Feb. 1794, and Constitution of Hamilton's District of Washington County, 28 Feb. 1794, Rawle Papers, vol. 1, 15, 18; Slaughter, *Whiskey Rebellion*, 163–65.

102. Bouton, "Tying Up the Revolution," 416, 425.

103. Findley, *History of the Insurrection*, 56–57.

104. *Dunlop's American Daily Advertiser*, 1 Sept. 1792; Neville to Clymer, 15 Sept. 1791, Wolcott Papers, no. 10.

105. Deposition of Wells, 29 Jan. 1794, Wolcott Papers, no. 19.

106. Neville to Clymer, 15 Sept. 1791, Wolcott Papers, no. 10.

107. Neville to Clymer, 11 Dec. 1791, Wolcott Papers, no. 12a.

108. One official lamented that "the name of him [for] whom I profess to act—a name loved and reverenced throughout all the civilized world, has . . . been publickly treated with utmost scorn." Clymer to Wolcott, 1 Oct. 1792, Wolcott Papers, no. 2.

109. Deposition of John Mason, 22 Dec. 1794, Rawle Papers, vol. 1, 85.

110. Findley, *History of the Insurrection*, 67.

111. Dallas to Baird, 25 July 1794, Frontier War Papers, ser. 4U, 226; Abraham Kirkpatrick to George Washington, 28 July 1794, Wolcott Papers, no. 23. On Neville as landowner, see Slaughter, *Whiskey Rebellion*, 67.

112. Findley, *History of the Insurrection*, 84.

113. Ibid., 94.

114. "March on Pittsburgh, 1794," *Pennsylvania Magazine of History and Biography* 71 (1947), 61. Findley put the number at seven thousand (*History of the Insurrection*, 98).

115. Bradford to _____, 10 Aug. 1794, Whiskey Rebellion Collection.

116. Slaughter claims that insurgents saw Pittsburgh as a luxurious "Sodom," one corrupted by antirepublican vice. See *Whiskey Rebellion*, 187.

117. Findley, *History of the Insurrection*, 102.

118. Bradford to ____, 10 Aug. 1794, Whiskey Rebellion Collection; *Pennsylvania Gazette*, 13 Aug. 1794.

119. Zachary Biggs to Edward Smith, 29 May 1794; Sutherland to Buher, 30 Oct. 1794, Rawle Papers, vol. 1, 23, 60.

120. John Breckinridge to Samuel Hopkins, 15 Sept. 1794, Breckinridge Family Papers, vol. 2, Library of Congress.

121. Rough draft of a petition on the subject of the excise laws from the inhabitants of the state of Kentucky, 4 Dec. 1793, Breckinridge Family Papers, vol. 10.

122. Proclamation of the governor of Virginia, 20 Aug. 1794, Biggs Papers, ser. 5NN, 66; Kevin Barkdale, "Virginia's Border Counties During Pennsylvania's Whiskey Rebellion," *Virginia Magazine of History and Biography* 111 (2003), 5–32; *Carlisle Gazette*, 24 Sept. 1794.

123. Isaac Darneille to Winthrop Sargent, 15 Nov. 1794, Sargent Papers, vol. 3.

124. Neville to Clymer, 7 Nov. 1792, Wolcott Papers, no. 14.

125. *Pittsburgh Gazette*, 26 July 1794.

126. *Pittsburgh Gazette*, 2 Aug. 1794.

127. "The Democratic Societies of 1793 and 1794 in Kentucky, Pennsylvania, and Virginia," *William and Mary Quarterly*, 2nd ser., 2 (1922), 239–40.

128. Benjamin Biggs to Lee, 24 Nov. 1794, Biggs Papers, ser. 5NN, 79.

129. Greene to Sargent, 25 Nov. 1792, Sargent Papers, vol. 3.

130. "Address to the Inhabitants of the United States West of the Allegany and Appalachian Mountains," 13 Dec. 1793, Innes Papers, container 11, Miscellany, Folder on Democratic Society.

131. Citizens of Kentucky, *On Saturday the 24th Instant a Numerous Meeting of Respectable Citizens . . . in Lexington* (Lexington, KY, 1794).

132. Remonstrance of Citizens West of the Allegany Mountains to the President and Congress of the United States of America, n.d., Innes Papers, container 11. On how such ideas spread throughout the West in these years, see Slaughter, *Whiskey Rebellion*, 209–15.

133. Remonstrance of Citizens West of the Allegany Mountains.

134. Citizens of Kentucky, *On Saturday the 24th Instant*.

135. Remonstrance of the Citizens West of the Allegany Mountains; "Democratic Societies of 1793 and 1794," 244.

136. "Address to the Inhabitants of the United States West of the Allegany and Appalachian Mountains."

137. Bradford to Edmund Randolph, 12 Aug. 1794, Whiskey Rebellion Collection; Slaughter, *Whiskey Rebellion*, 188. Also see Bouton, "Tying Up the Revolution," 432.

138. Findley, *History of the Insurrection*, 115.

139. Ibid., 114.

140. Ibid., 124.

141. *Carlisle Gazette*, 9 July 1794.

142. Bradford to Washington, 17 Aug. 1794, Whiskey Rebellion Collection.

143. "John Adlum on the Allegheny," 472–73.

144. "Democratic Societies of 1793 and 1794," 248–49.
145. Bouton, "Tying Up the Revolution," 433.
146. Deposition of Jenkins, 12 Nov. 1794, 61.
147. Deposition of Daniel Reese, 10 Dec. 1794, Rawle Papers, vol. 1, 77.
148. *Carlisle Gazette*, 20 Aug. 1794.
149. Bouton, "Tying Up the Revolution," 433.
150. On the failure of the whiskey rebels to create a pan-western movement, see Mary K. Bonsteel Tachau, "The Whiskey Rebellion in Kentucky: A Forgotten Episode of Civil Disobedience," *Journal of the Early Republic* 2 (1982), 239–59; and Barkdale, "Virginia's Border Counties."
151. Marshall cited in Steven Boyd, ed., *The Whiskey Rebellion: Past and Present Perspectives* (Westport, CT, 1985), 97.

CHAPTER 9: AMERICAN LEVIATHAN

1. Jefferson to Innes, 23 May 1793, Harry Innes Papers, General Correspondence, Library of Congress, Washington, DC.
2. Campbell to _____, 9 March 1790, Arthur Campbell Papers, folder 5, Filson Historical Society, Louisville, KY.
3. Campbell, 2 Jan. and 17 Feb. 1792, Campbell Papers, ser. of Unaddressed Letters, 1791–92, folder 5.
4. William Findley, *History of the Insurrection, in the Four Western Counties of Pennsylvania* (Philadelphia, 1796), vii, 22. As Kim Gruenwald argues, even settlers such as Symmes, who tended to regard Indians charitably, understood in the wake of Big Bottom that Indians and whites could not live together. See *River of Enterprise: The Commercial Origins of Regional Identity in the Ohio Valley, 1790–1850* (Bloomington, IN, 2002), 23.
5. Caleb Wallace to William Fleming, 29 Jan. 1793, William Fleming Papers, miscellaneous reel 432, H11, Library of Virginia, Richmond. See also Ballard Smith to John Preston, 10 March 1793, Preston Family Papers, 1792, Virginia Historical Society, Richmond.
6. George Rogers Clark to Jonathan Clark, 11 May 1792, George Rogers Clark Papers, Filson Historical Society.
7. For a different view, one that portrays the American Revolution less as a transformative event and more as a part of a broader "colonial" pattern of subordination, see John Wood Sweet, *Bodies Politic: Negotiating Race in the American North, 1730–1830* (Baltimore, 2003); and Francis Jennings, *The Creation of America: Through Revolution to Empire* (Cambridge, UK, 2000). For the Revolution as canonization of what had already occurred, see Jon Butler, *Becoming America: The Revolution Before 1776* (Cambridge, MA, 2001).
8. From an international perspective, it appears that the United States as a nation emerged from a "revolution against the state" that exposed the powerlessness of the new state and revealed the exceptional nature of the American Revolution during a broader worldwide age of revolutionary ferment. See, for instance, C. A. Bayly, *The*

Birth of the Modern World, 1780–1914: Global Connections and Comparisons (Oxford, UK, 2004). American historians, of late, view it differently, and we have gained a much greater appreciation of the efficacy of the state in the early Republic. See, for instance, Max Edling, *A Revolution in Favor of Government: Origins of the U.S. Constitution and the Making of the American State* (New York, 2003). When it comes to the West, some of the finest recent works suggest that the state and its officials determined the shape and thrust of western policy. Such policies were based on ideology, avarice, or a deep-seated desire for empire. For the ideological imperative angle, see especially Drew McCoy, *The Elusive Republic: Political Economy in Jeffersonian America* (Chapel Hill, NC, 1980); and Peter Onuf, *Jefferson's Empire: The Language of American Nationhood* (Charlottesville, VA, 2000). Andrew Cayton and Fred Anderson argue that the push west emerged from a "democratic imperialism" fueled by a "vision of empire that had its roots in Washington's experience," and by extension the dreams of other elites. The common people—"localist" in perspective—were delighted with the state's leading role in securing the West, but otherwise were suspicious of that state. See *The Dominion of War: Empire and Liberty in North America, 1500–2000* (New York, 2005), 196–97. Also see Cayton, "'Separate Interests' and the Nation-State: The Washington Administration and the Origins of Regionalism in the Trans-Appalachian West," *Journal of American History* 79 (1992), 39–67. Eric Hinderaker similarly sees a state intent to "extend its authority into the Ohio valley" behind expansion. His people, as well, are "localist." See *Elusive Empires: Constructing Colonialism in the Ohio Valley, 1673–1800* (New York, 1997), 236, 244. Alan Taylor, in *The Divided Ground: Indians, Settlers, and the Northern Borderland of the American Revolution* (New York, 2006), expands the role of the state to include not only the federal government but states as well, in this case New York. For a rejoinder to these types of arguments, one which posits that frontiersmen "compelled" the U.S. government to act and dictated how it should act, see John Grenier, *The First Way of War: American War Making on the Frontier* (Cambridge, UK, 2005), 171.

9. For an excellent synopsis of these events—as well as their meaning for national expansion and subsequent development—see Gregory Nobles, *American Frontiers: Cultural Encounters and Continental Conquest* (New York, 1997), 99–132.

10. Thomas Hobbes, *Leviathan*, chap. 17.

11. "Diary Kept by Dr. Robert Wellford," *William and Mary Quarterly*, 1st ser., 11 (1902), 15. Thomas Slaughter's *Whiskey Rebellion: Frontier Epilogue to the American Revolution* (New York, 1986) offers the best treatment of the suppression of the "insurrection," as well as the reasons for it.

12. "Diary Kept by Dr. Robert Wellford," 7, 9, 10; Anderson and Cayton, *Dominion of War*, 200.

13. Findley, *History of the Insurrection*, 163.

14. Journal of western expedition, 1794, Jacob Ashmead Papers, 39, Historical Society of Pennsylvania, Philadelphia (hereafter cited as HSP).

15. Abstract of Provisions Issued at Pittsburgh to the Troops of the State of Pennsylvania . . . for the Year 1794, Ebenezer Denny Business Records, Denny-O'Hara Fam-

ily Papers, folder 3, Historical Society of Western Pennsylvania, Pittsburgh. On this, see "Diary Kept by Dr. Robert Wellford," 5. Also see "March on Pittsburgh, 1794," *Pennsylvania Magazine of History and Biography* 71 (1947), especially 47, 49, 50, 51.

16. "March on Pittsburgh, 1794," 52–57.
17. John Cadwalader to Thomas Mifflin, 23 July 1794, Northern, Interior, and Western Counties Papers, 225, HSP.
18. David Mead to Ebenezer Denny, 11 Aug. 1794, Denny-O'Hara Family Papers, folder 4.
19. Denny to Mifflin, 20 March 1794, Denny-O'Hara Family Papers, folder 4.
20. William Preston to John Preston, 10 Oct. 1795, Preston Family Papers, 1940.
21. Isaac Shelby to Henry Knox, 10 Jan. 1794, Isaac Shelby Miscellaneous Papers, Filson Historical Society.
22. Anderson and Cayton, *Dominion of War*, 193. On conquest versus chastisement — what he calls a policy of "moderation and coexistence" — see Taylor, *Divided Ground*. Taylor argues that moderate officials wanted to "gain control over the long and troubled frontier." Although federalist officials did not intend to conquer, conquest, in fact, carried the day (237–39). For the military policy of the Washington administration, see Richard Kohn, *Eagle and Sword: The Federalists and the Creation of the Military Establishment in America, 1783–1802* (New York, 1975), 91–127, 139–57.
23. Hatch Dent to Campbell, 17 Sept. 1794, Campbell Papers, folder 7.
24. Brown to Innes, 20 Jan. 1782, Innes Papers, General Correspondence.
25. Brown to Innes, 13 April 1792, Innes Papers, General Correspondence. Kohn calls the administration's approach after the St. Clair disaster a "dual policy of negotiation and escalation." See *Eagle and Sword*, 151.
26. Wayne to Shelby, 18 May 1793, Isaac Shelby Papers, folder 2, Filson Historical Society.
27. Wayne to Absalom Baird, 22 July 1792, Samuel Brady and Lewis Wetzel Papers, Draper MSS, ser. 1E, 101, Historical Society of Wisconsin, Madison.
28. John Adlum to Andrew Elliott, 31 Aug. 1794, Denny-O'Hara Family Papers, folder 4.
29. Cornelius Van Horn to Denny, 10 Sept. 1794; John Wilkins to Denny, 16 Sept. 1794, Denny-O'Hara Family Papers, folder 4.
30. "John Adlum on the Allegheny: Memoirs for the Year 1794," *Pennsylvania Magazine of History and Biography* 84 (1960), 304, 309, 310–11, 318.
31. James Staats Morris to Lewis Morris, 16 Dec. 1793, Native American History Collection, William Clements Library, University of Michigan, Ann Arbor.
32. Breckinridge to Samuel Hopkins, 15 Sept. 1794, Breckinridge Family Papers, vol. 11, Library of Congress.
33. "John Adlum on the Allegheny," 467; Anderson and Cayton, *Dominion of War*, 194; Grenier, *First Way of War*, 193–203; Taylor, *Divided Ground*, 287.
34. David Barrow diary, 1795, 9, 11, Filson Historical Society.
35. "A Treaty of Peace Between the United States of America and the Tribes of Indians . . . ," 3 Aug. 1795, in *United States Statutes at Large*, vol. 7 (Boston, 1846), 49; William Preston to John Preston, 10 Oct. 1795, Preston Family Papers, 1940. On the treaty, see Richard White, *The Middle Ground: Indians, Empires, and Republics in*

the *Great Lakes Region, 1650–1815* (New York, 1991), 472; Taylor, *Divided Ground*, 293–94; Andrew Cayton, "'Noble Actors' upon 'the Theatre of Honour': Power and Civility in the Treaty of Greenville," in Cayton and Fredrika Teute, eds., *Contact Points: American Frontiers from the Mohawk Valley to the Mississippi, 1750–1830* (Chapel Hill, NC, 1998), 235–69.

36. William Preston to John Preston, 10 Oct. 1795, Preston Family Papers, 1940.

37. Breckinridge to Hopkins, 15 Sept. 1794, Breckinridge Family Papers, vol. 11.

38. Brown to Shelby, 23 Nov. 1794, Shelby Papers, folder 3.

39. William Preston to John Preston, 10 Oct. 1795, Preston Family Papers, 1940.

40. Citizens of Kentucky, *On Saturday the 24th Instant a Numerous Meeting of Respectable Citizens . . . in Lexington* (Lexington, KY, 1794).

41. Stanley Elkins and Eric McKitrick, *The Age of Federalism* (New York, 1993), 406–50; Onuf, *Jefferson's Empire*, 44.

42. "Treaty of Peace," 50–51.

43. William Preston to John Preston, 10 Oct. 1795, Preston Family Papers, 1940.

44. See John Evans to Benjamin Biggs, 2 Aug. 1795, Benjamin Biggs Papers, Draper MSS, ser. 5NN, 103.

45. Orders for the Militia, Washington County, April 1795, Military and Political Documents, Backus-Woodbridge Collection, folder 2, Ohio Historical Society, Columbus.

46. The phrase "garrison government," of course, belongs to Stephen Saunders Webb. See "Army and Empire: English Garrison Government in Britain and America, 1569–1763," *William and Mary Quarterly*, 3rd ser., 34 (1977), 1–31. For what garrison government meant in America after 1795, see Anderson and Cayton, *Dominion of War*, 219. On the role of Detroit, see Brian Leigh Dunnigan, "Fortress Detroit, 1701–1826," in David Curtis Skaggs and Larry Nelson, eds., *The Sixty Years' War for the Great Lakes, 1754–1814* (East Lansing, MI, 2001), 183.

47. Thomas Swaine to Anthony Bartlett, 27 Feb. 1795, Thomas Swaine Papers, Filson Historical Society.

48. *Pennsylvania Gazette*, 22 April 1795.

49. *Pennsylvania Gazette*, 11 Jan. 1792.

50. "John Adlum on the Allegheny," 293.

51. Pickering to Baird, 6 Jan. 1796, Frontier War Papers, Draper MSS, ser. 4U, 229.

52. James Wilkinson to Innes, 4 Feb. 1795, Innes Papers, General Correspondence.

53. Brown to Innes, 15 May 1795, Innes Papers, General Correspondence.

54. Preston to John Brady, 15 Dec. 1795, Pittsburgh and Northwest Virginia Papers, Draper MSS, ser. 4NN, 126.

55. Address to the Atlantic States, 11 May 1795, Kentucky Academy Papers, Filson Historical Society.

56. Levi Morgan to Robert Brooke, 14 Nov. 1795, Brady and Wetzel Papers, ser. 1E, 110; Gruenwald, *River of Enterprise*, 25–33.

57. For the Logan story, see "John Adlum on the Allegheny," 468–72.

58. Sweet, *Bodies Politic*, 301. The discourse of civilization would animate nineteenth-century eastern understandings of Indians. These ideas would be directly derived from Scottish stadial theory. On this, as well as the doubts some easterners had about the whole civilization project, see Joseph Lucas, "Civilization or Extinction:

Citizens and Indians in the Early United States," *Journal of the Historical Society* 6 (2006), 239.

59. In the years before he became president, Thomas Jefferson composed a piece called *Notes on the State of Virginia*, in part to refute European conceits that the Old World was superior to the New. Indeed, the same questions that had interested William Robertson when he had designed his questionnaire consumed Jefferson. On his answers, see Thomas Jefferson, *Notes on the State of Virginia*, ed. David Waldstreicher (Boston, 2002), 111, 120. On the influence of Robertson, see Richard B. Sher, "*Charles V* and the Book Trade" and Bruce Lenman, "'From Savage to Scot' via the French and the Spaniards," in Stewart Brown, ed., *William Robertson and the Expansion of Empire* (Cambridge, UK, 1997), 185, 208; David Thomas Konig, "The Second Amendment: A Missing Transatlantic Context for the Historical Meaning of 'the Right of the People to Keep and Bear Arms,'" *Law and History Review* 22 (2004). For a study of Hutcheson's role in forming Jefferson's thought, see Garry Wills, *Inventing America: Jefferson's Declaration of Independence* (New York, 1978). Jefferson did not believe that all persons were inherently equal. A slave owner and the champion of the superiority of the New World, Jefferson regarded Africans as inherently inferior. See *Notes on the State of Virginia*, 175–78.

60. Jefferson, *Notes on the State of Virginia*, 121–24; Onuf, *Jefferson's Empire*, 19–27.

61. Onuf, *Jefferson's Empire*, 16; Anderson and Cayton, *Dominion of War*, 220.

62. Anthony F. C. Wallace, *Jefferson and the Indians: The Tragic Fate of the First Americans* (Cambridge, MA, 1999); Bernard Sheehan, *Seeds of Extinction: Jeffersonian Philanthropy and the American Indian* (Chapel Hill, NC, 1973).

63. On the ideological rationale for westward expansion, see McCoy, *Elusive Republic*.

64. R. Eugene Harper, *The Transformation of Western Pennsylvania, 1770–1800* (Pittsburgh, 1991), 172–73.

65. Malcolm Rohrbough, *The Land Office Business: The Settlement and Administration of American Public Lands, 1789–1837* (New York, 1968), 17–20, 26–33, 46.

66. Stephen Aron, *How the West Was Lost: The Transformation of Kentucky from Daniel Boone to Henry Clay* (Baltimore, 1996), 83–84, 95–100, 111, 129, 150–69.

67. Ibid., 140–42; Hinderaker, *Elusive Empires*, 248–52; Timothy Shannon, "'This Unpleasant Business': The Transformation of Land Speculation in the Ohio Country, 1787–1820," in Jeffrey Paul Brown and Andrew Cayton, eds., *The Pursuit of Public Power: Political Culture in Ohio, 1787–1861* (Kent, OH, 1994). Also see Alan Taylor, *William Cooper's Town: Power and Persuasion on the Frontier of the Early American Republic* (New York, 1995), 203–4, 387–88.

68. Rohrbough, *Land Office Business*, 35, 61, 92–94, 143–44; Hinderaker, *Elusive Empires*, 248–50.

69. Remonstrance for General Assembly to Explain Land Law, Nov. 1794, Breckinridge Family Papers, vol. 11.

70. "Treaty of Peace," 52.

71. Nobles, *American Frontiers*, 103; Taylor, *Divided Ground*, 280; Hinderaker, *Elusive Empires*, 267.

72. Sean Wilentz, *The Rise of American Democracy: Jefferson to Lincoln* (New York, 2005), 117.

73. See *Carlisle Gazette*, 21 May 1794.
74. Wilentz, *Rise of American Democracy*, xviii. For a look at how common men made pleas to retain land that they believed they had earned through sacrifice, see "Deposition of Thomas McClanahan, 10 Sept. 1832," *William and Mary Quarterly*, 2nd ser., 1 (1921), 209–13; John Dann, ed., *The Revolution Remembered: Eyewitness Accounts of the War for Independence* (Chicago, 1980), 309–15.
75. Linsly to Ephraim Kirby, 2 Oct. 1797, Ephraim Kirby Papers, Duke University.
76. "James Gibbons's Notes Made During a Tour, 1804, Through Some of the Western Parts of Pennsylvania and Part of the State of Ohio," 11, 30, 32–33, 39, 63, 57, 18, HSP.
77. Backus to George Thatcher, 4 June 1797, Military and Political Documents, Backus-Woodbridge Collection, box 5. Backus later sold part of his island to an Irish immigrant named Harman Blennerhassett, who would later be a key figure in the so-called Burr conspiracy. The island, on the Ohio River between Parkersburg and Belpre, still bears Blennerhassett's name.
78. Barrow diary, 1795, 8, 10, 11, 22, 23–24, 26.
79. Benjamin Smith Barton journals, n.d., Notes on Old Town section, HSP. For an excellent study of the many uses of the Cresaps and the strange ways violence and memory interact, see Robert Parkinson, "From Indian Killer to Worthy Citizen: The Revolutionary Transformation of Michael Cresap," *William and Mary Quarterly*, 3rd ser., 58 (2006), 97–122.
80. *Pittsburgh Gazette*, 24 Jan. 1795.
81. John S. Gano narrative, Frontier War Papers, Draper MSS, ser. 2U, 142.
82. Richard Slotkin, *Regeneration Through Violence: The Mythology of the American Frontier, 1600–1860* (Middletown, CT, 1973); Sweet, *Bodies Politic*, 406–7; David Waldstreicher, *In the Midst of Perpetual Fetes: The Making of American Nationalism, 1776–1820* (Chapel Hill, NC, 1997), 269–92; Nobles, *American Frontiers*, 103–6.
83. Hector St. John Crèvecoeur, *Letters from an American Farmer and Sketches of Eighteenth-Century America* (New York, 1986), 66–67, 69–70, 72–73.
84. J.G.A. Pocock, *The Discovery of Islands: Essays in British History* (Cambridge, UK, 2005), 264; Taylor, *William Cooper's Town*, 417–27.
85. Crèvecoeur, *Letters from an American Farmer*, 76–79, 82.
86. Ibid., 177–79, 79, 16, 214.
87. On similar ideas of myth, see Daniel Richter, *Facing East from Indian Country: A Native History of Early America* (Cambridge, MA, 2003); and Laurel Thatcher Ulrich, *The Age of Homespun: Objects and Stories in the Creation of an American Myth* (New York, 2001).
88. Crèvecoeur, *Letters from an American Farmer*, 225, 206.
89. "Narrative of John Heckewelder's Journey to the Wabash in 1792," *Pennsylvania Magazine of History and Biography* 12 (1888), 49–50.
90. Address to the Citizens of the Western Country, 1832, Simon Kenton Papers, Draper MSS, ser. 6BB, 110.

EPILOGUE: GEORGE ROGERS CLARK'S MONUMENT

1. Like the Quick monument, the Clark group still receives popular attention. In this instance, however, students—not protesters—have established an impressive Web site, detailing the issue of commemoration and including newspaper entries, correspondence, biographies, and pamphlets. See the site established by the Virginia Center for Digital History at www.vcdh.virginia.edu/students/projects/commemoration/cdpindex.html. It includes snippets from the *Charlottesville Daily Progress* that covered the unveiling, as well as the pamphlet handed out at the unveiling that is referred to here. Copies of the originals are held in the University of Virginia Special Collections Library.

2. This view that the Revolution was the tragic collapse of an Atlantic community premised on the idea of liberty, one that would rise again in an informal fashion in the twentieth century, was echoed by the old imperial historian Lawrence Henry Gipson in *The British Empire Before the American Revolution* (New York, 1961–70), vol. 8, 313; vol. 10, 3–37; vol. 11, vii; vol. 13, 212–14.

3. The speeches at the unveiling are in "George Rogers Clark Pamphlet," 1, 2, 3, 5, 15, University of Virginia Special Collection Library.

4. John Bodnar, *Remaking America: Public Memory, Commemoration, and Patriotism in the Twentieth Century* (Princeton, NJ, 1992), 123.

5. Ibid., 15, 135. For a broad-ranging discussion of memory, commemoration, and making sense of the distant past through the symbols of the immediate past in such a way that both speak to the contested present, see the essays in William E. Leuchtenburg, ed., *American Places: Encounters with History: A Celebration of Sheldon Meyer* (New York, 2001).

6. Lowell Harrison, *George Rogers Clark and the War in the West* (Lexington, KY, 1976), 106–10.

7. On this notion of modernity, see Paul Gilroy, *The Black Atlantic: Modernity and Double Consciousness* (Cambridge, MA, 1993), 2.

8. This is how we could make sense of "insurrections" such as Fries's Rebellion. See Paul Douglas Newman, *Fries's Rebellion: The Enduring Struggle for the American Revolution* (Philadelphia, 2004).

Acknowledgments

Although this book centers on the Ohio River valley, it is Atlantic in conception and execution, moving from England and the West of Ireland to Pennsylvania, Ohio, and Virginia. The course of working on the book reflects its scope. I have researched it in places like London, Philadelphia, and Louisville, drafted it in Galway, revised it in Athens, and finished it in Charlottesville. Fittingly, I have incurred debts in all these places and more.

Let me start with a number of people who have commented on sections of the manuscript and, in so doing, have helped me greatly. These include Brian Balogh, Michael Brown, Nicholas Canny, Jack Epstein, Walter Hawthorne, Kevin Mattson, Paul Milazzo, and Chester Pach. Tim Breen and Robert Ingram read parts of it as well. They also listened to many of my half-cocked ideas. My thanks for these things and more. I especially appreciate the efforts of Drew Cayton, Peter Onuf, and Bruce Steiner, who labored through a very rough draft from beginning to end. I thank them for telling me when I got it right, but more to the point, when I got it wrong. I am grateful for their sacrifice of time and hope the book's the better for it.

I would be remiss if I did not note those who supported me in grant applications. Thanks go to some of those above and also to Fred Anderson, Jim Axtell, Eric Hinderaker, Kerby Miller, and Tim Shannon. My two chairs at Ohio University, Steve Miner and Norm Goda, who helped me juggle the estimable demands at OU to finish this book, also deserve my thanks. Tommy Williams of the Honors Tutorial College did yeoman's work as a research assistant. Dean Ann Fidler was kind enough to offer the services of gifted students such as Williams.

I presented portions of this book—and received wonderful feedback— at a great number of venues. These include the Ohio State University, Southern Illinois University, Miami University, the College of William and Mary, Emory University, the University of Virginia, the University of Notre Dame, Northwestern University, University College Dublin, Trinity College, Dublin, and the National University of Ireland, Galway, as well as at several conferences on both sides of the ocean. Organizations also helped. My thanks to the staff of the Public Record Office, now the National Archives at Kew; the British Library; the Library of Congress; the National Archives; the Historical Society of Pennsylvania; the Massachusetts Historical Society; the Connecticut Historical Society; the Historical Society of Western Pennsylvania; the Carnegie Library; the Ohio State Archives; the Library of Virginia; the Virginia Historical Society; the special collections of Ohio University; and the Small Special Collections Library at the University of Virginia. I received grants from and am grateful to the Filson Club in Kentucky and the Clements Library at the University of Michigan, two wonderful places to work. Thanks, too, to Daniel Rolph of the HSP, who brought the Tom Quick story to my attention. An Ohio University Research Committee grant paid for a summer in London and Philadelphia. The history department and the College of Arts and Sciences underwrote two research blitzes to the East Coast.

My greatest debt, literally, is to the American Council of Learned Societies, which awarded me a Mellon Fellowship, allowing me the time to write the book up. Without the help of the ACLS, no book.

My editor, Thomas LeBien, was wonderful and tireless throughout. He's also patient to a fault and a hell of a good editor. June Kim of Hill and Wang was also extraordinarily helpful.

My family and I decided to travel to Ireland for the year with the ACLS funding. The National University of Ireland, Galway, proved to be a wonderful choice. There I worked at the Centre for the Study of Human Settlement and Historical Change (since renamed the Moore Institute for Research in the Humanities and Social Studies). A friend calls it "the Centre for the Study of Everything That Ever Happened in the World Ever." He's right. The center hosts an extraordinary range of scholars doing fascinating work on a bewildering range of topics. I was attracted to Galway because of Nicholas Canny, the director and one of the world's foremost Atlanticists. Nicholas turned out to be the most gracious and thoughtful of hosts, opening his house and lavishing me with time and attention. Martha Shaughnessy was a marvel, answering my questions with patience and good humor and helping me get my family and my books over and back across the Atlantic safely. Two great scholars in particular showed me the ropes at Galway and were more than willing to drag me out for pints. In so doing, Enda Leaney and John Kenny made the son of the diaspora feel at home. My medievalist neighbors at the center, Mark Stansbury and Ric Graff, made me regret my decision to become an early modernist. Almost.

Other people, who did not help with the writing of the book, also merit a word for their friendship and support. First, of our friends in Ireland who made our year so memorable, two couples deserve special mention: Martina and Vincent Jordan, and Pat and Noreen Brady. We count them now among our closest and dearest. We were also feted by Ray Browne, the Battersbys, Bradleys, Griffins, Heddermans, Richardsons, and Shelleys. Each of these put us up and showed us a wonderful time from the Mizen Head to the Malin Head and all points in between. Friends on this side of the ocean similarly helped us in ways that we will always appreciate. Chief among these are Stan and Paige Alost, and Paul and Kathleen Legris. Thanks, too, to the Hawthornes of Virginia for putting me up on a research trip to Richmond; to Matt O'Brien, who did the same in Pittsburgh; and to the Dorinis and Tom Healy, who let me stay with them in D.C. I owe a special debt to my in-laws, Joseph and Dympna Doran, for looking after us throughout our whirlwind travels.

This book has an unusual dedication, but it's my book, so I guess I can do as I please. It reflects the reasons why I do what I do and the reasons why I am able to do it. But it says, I hope, more than this. My father, Michael Griffin, passed away as I was completing this project. To his memory, I dedicate this book. As I do to my mother, Johanna Griffin, and my sister, Joan. I wrote this book for my sons and daughters, Michael, Liam, Maggie, and Annie Griffin. Finally, this book is for my wife, Mary Hope Griffin. It's almost too trite to thank her for herself. But I will nonetheless. I have been blessed with each and every one of these, my people.

Index